CADOGAN GUIDES

By the same authors:
"The Cadogan Guide to Italy is the most massive, literate, and helpful guide to Italy in years."
— *International Travel News*, USA

"*Italy* by Dana Facaros and Michael Pauls is an absolute gem of a travel book, humorous, informed, sympathetic, as irresistible as that land itself."
— Anthony Clare, Books of the Year, *The Sunday Times* 1988–89

Rome:
"Irreverent, unblinkered and hard-eyed, and based on a series of 15 well thought out walks, each minutely described, the book throws the city into focus with nothing spared.... But the authors write about the city with the witty intimacy of lovers who are so familiar they can afford to be honest.... Taking you into the real Rome ... they bring to life the unexpected in a way that is both scholarly and light-hearted...."
— *Sunday Telegraph*, May 1990

Other titles in the Cadogan Guides series:

AUSTRALIA
BALI
THE CARIBBEAN
GREEK ISLANDS
INDIA
IRELAND
ITALIAN ISLANDS
ITALY
NORTHEAST ITALY
NORTHWEST ITALY
MOROCCO
NEW YORK
PORTUGAL
ROME
SCOTLAND
SOUTH ITALY
SPAIN

THAILAND & BURMA
TUNISIA
TURKEY
TUSCANY & UMBRIA

Forthcoming:
BERLIN
CENTRAL AMERICA
CZECHOSLOVAKIA
ECUADOR, COLOMBIA
  & THE GALAPAGOS
GERMANY
MEXICO
MOSCOW & LENINGRAD
PRAGUE
SOUTH OF FRANCE
SOUTHERN SPAIN

Piazza San Marco

CADOGAN CITY GUIDES

VENICE

DANA FACAROS & MICHAEL PAULS

CADOGAN BOOKS
London

THE GLOBE PEQUOT PRESS
Chester, Connecticut

Cadogan Books Ltd
Mercury House, 195 Knightsbridge, London SW7 1RE

The Globe Pequot Press
138 West Main Street, Chester, Connecticut 06412, USA

Cover design by Ralph King
Cover illustration by Liz Pichon
Maps © Cadogan Books, drawn by Thames Cartographic Services Ltd
Grand Canal Map drawn by Sue Sharples
Index by Ann Hudson

Series Editors: Rachel Fielding and Paula Levey

First published in 1991

British Library Cataloguing in Publication Data

Facaros, Dana
  Venice.—(Cadogan guides).
  1. Italy. Venice—Visitors' guides.
  I. Title   II. Pauls, Michael
914.531
ISBN 0–946313–94–6

Library of Congress Cataloging-in-Publication-Data

Facaros, Dana
  Venice/Dana Facaros & Michael Pauls: illustrations by Charles Shearer.
    p.   cm.—(Cadogan guides)
  Includes index.
  ISBN 0–87106–324–7
  1. Venice (Italy)—Description and travel—1981–   —Guide-books.
  I. Pauls, Michael.   II. Title.   III. Series.
  DG672.F25   1991   CIP
  914.5'3104929–dc20   90–21697

Photoset in Ehrhardt on a Linotron 202
Printed on recycled paper and bound in Great Britain by
Redwood Press Ltd, Melksham, Wiltshire

CONTENTS

CONTENTS

LIST OF MAPS

ABOUT THE AUTHORS

After ruining three pairs of shoes, their bank accounts, and their digestive tracts in Venice, Michael Pauls and Dana Facaros came up with this, a year late and a hundred pages too long. They hope you'll enjoy it. Already the authors of eight books on Italy, they feel they have caused enough trouble there and have moved their children, computer and library to an idyllic if somewhat draughty haven, under imminent threat from a proposed electricity pilon, somewhere in France.

ACKNOWLEDGEMENTS

We would like to thank the Venetian Tourist Office, especially Cesare Battisti; Paolo Greco in the Italian Tourist Office in London; Professor Charles Giovanelli for words of wisdom and glasses of Prosecco; the *carabinieri* of Venice and the two elderly school teachers on the back of the *accelerato*. Also special thanks are due to Graham and Bella Bannister for their kindness in things Venetian and worldly; and finally to our editor Rachel Fielding for all her help and encouragement and long 'phone calls.

The publishers would like to extend their warm thanks to Charles Shearer for his illustrations and last minute contributions from the Outer Hebrides; to Sue Sharples for her pretty *palazzi* map; to Anne Evans for copy-editing and proof-reading; to Ann Hudson for her index and valuable comments.

To Teeny, the Monk, and RBI, with love.

INTRODUCTION

medieval mosaic / San Marco.

> If the Earthly Paradise where Adam dwelt with Eve
> were like Venice, Eve would have had a difficult
> time tempting him away from it with a mere fig.
>
> —*Aretino*

As God made the Garden of Eden, the Venetians made Venice. They even made the land it stands on. They were sea folk, traders and swindlers, pirates and plunderers, with an eye for the main chance. But they also made Venice—with grit, intelligence, and centuries of risk, trial and error. They made it the richest city in the world, and pretty much burned their bridges at both ends when the jig was up. Unlike most peoples in history, the Venetians knew exactly what they were about.

A lot of people say Venice is dirty, its canals smell bad, it's too full of tourists, a rip-off. People have been saying more or less the same things for 500 years, but they keep right on coming. The allure is irresistible: Venice is one of humanity's most inspiring examples of what people can do if they use their heads and try hard. The Venetians created the strange and beautiful fabric of their city. They manipulated their environment without destroying it. They developed a government that abhorred tyranny and made the majority of its citizens happy for a thousand years.

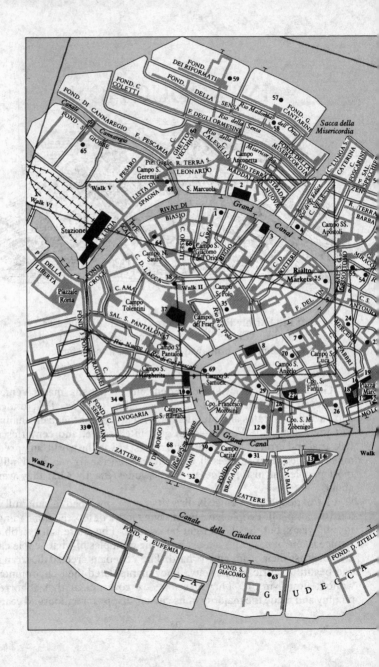

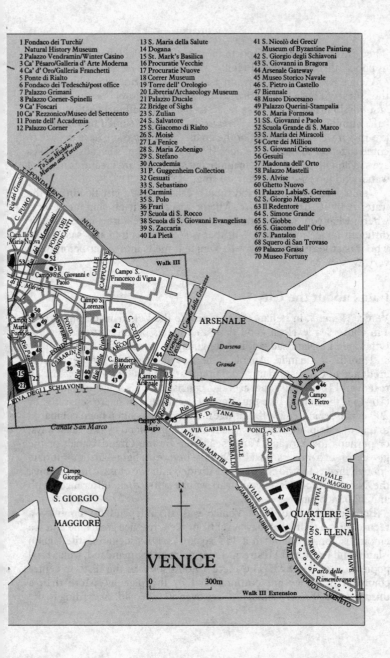

1 Fondaco dei Turchi/
  Natural History Museum
2 Palazzo Vendramin/Winter Casino
3 Ca' Pésaro/Galleria d' Arte Moderna
4 Ca' d' Oro/Galleria Franchetti
5 Ponte di Rialto
6 Fondaco dei Tedeschi/post office
7 Palazzo Grimani
8 Palazzo Corner-Spinelli
9 Ca' Foscari
10 Ca' Rezzonico/Museo del Settecento
11 Ponte dell' Accademia
12 Palazzo Corner

13 S. Maria della Salute
14 Dogana
15 St. Mark's Basilica
16 Procuratie Vecchie
17 Procuratie Nuove
18 Correr Museum
19 Torre dell' Orologio
20 Libreria/Archaeology Museum
21 Palazzo Ducale
22 Bridge of Sighs
23 S. Zulian
24 S. Salvatore
25 S. Giacomo di Rialto
26 S. Moisè
27 La Fenice
28 S. Maria Zobenigo
29 S. Stefano
30 Accademia
31 P. Guggenheim Collection
32 Gesuati
33 S. Sebastiano
34 Carmini
35 S. Polo
36 Frari
37 Scuola di S. Rocco
38 Scuola di S. Giovanni Evangelista
39 S. Zaccaria
40 La Pietà

41 S. Nicolò dei Greci/
  Museum of Byzantine Painting
42 S. Giorgio degli Schiavoni
43 S. Giovanni in Bragora
44 Arsenale Gateway
45 Museo Storico Navale
46 S. Pietro in Castello
47 Biennale
48 Museo Diocesano
49 Palazzo Querini-Stampalia
50 S. Maria Formosa
51 SS. Giovanni e Paolo
52 Scuola Grande di S. Marco
53 S. Maria dei Miracoli
54 Corte dei Million
55 S. Giovanni Crisostomo
56 Gesuiti
57 Madonna dell' Orto
58 Palazzo Mastelli
59 S. Alvise
60 Ghetto Nuovo
61 Palazzo Labia/S. Geremia
62 S. Giorgio Maggiore
63 Il Redentore
64 S. Simone Grande
65 S. Giobbe
66 S. Giacomo dell' Orio
67 S. Pantalon
68 Squero di San Trovaso
69 Palazzo Grassi
70 Museo Fortuny

They sailed uncharted waters to the court of Kublai Khan and stood up to popes' threats of eternal Hell.

Venice was built, they say, on a human scale. But which humans do they mean? Those swaggering Shakespearian fellows bursting with life and possibility at a Veronese feast, or that international aesthete in the café whining that his or her *Serenissima* has been ruined by vulgar tour groups? If we had the need, or the chance, would we still have the will to come together to build a Venice? If Venice is sad, it's because our lives are sad and ill-suited for its magnificent stage. We are creatures made of water who have forgotten how to sing.

Venice lifts your heart, and then breaks it. But a city floating in the water is by its nature elusive. Mirror images of itself shimmer everywhere; what your senses perceive dissolves and re-forms into a slightly different image just below. 'All that is solid melts into air,' said Marx, who was at least right in this. In Venice it melts into water before your very eyes.

Facts about the City

Venice (*Venezia*, in Italian, and *Veneixia* to the Venetians of long ago) is 1 m above sea level on good days and stands on the same latitude as Ottawa and Dalandzadgad, in Mongolia; it's almost due south of Oslo and north of Luanda, Angola. The raw facts of the city lend some credence to Chateaubriand's opinion that this is a '*ville contre nature*': it rests on 118 islands, the average consisting of a cake of hard clay (10–15 ft thick) iced by a hundred feet of mud. These are separated by 200 canals, reunited by 400 bridges. Its shape has often been compared to that of a dolphin, one now leashed to the mainland by two causeways; or perhaps the Yin and Yang, separated by the Grand Canal; or the gloves of two boxers shaking hands before a fight—an appropriate enough image, for the city was long divided into two cross-canal factions, the Nicolotti and Castellani, who would settle their differences with annual punch-ups.

Between 697 and 1797 Venice was an independent republic—a record for longevity that may never be broken. Its once great land and sea empire is confined now to a 457-sq-km *comune*, including the lagoon islands and Lido, and Mestre and Marghera on the mainland, with a total population of 340,873. The mere 79,000 souls in the historic centre complain that they are outnumbered by the pigeons. More than a third—some 28,000 Venetians—are over 60 years old. According to the last census, there are only 3768 children in the entire city (about the same number as the stone and painted lions), and exactly 19 fishermen, one of whom is a lady. Half the people employed in Venice are involved directly or indirectly in the tourist trade, handling an estimated three million visitors a year; a 'pendular Venetian' is one who lives in a modern apartment in Mestre but works or studies in the city and joins in the busy trail of ants who descend on Piazzale Roma each morning to bring the city back to life. Venice has the lowest per capita income of any city in the wealthy Veneto, although consumer prices are the highest in Italy, about 1% higher than Milan and 3% higher than Rome.

Few people get lost in Venice at the beginning of their stay, when they are on guard; the trouble begins when you *think* you know where you're going. Or when you stop wanting to discover the city—which is often when you really begin.

Seeing Venice

STREETS COVERED WITH WATER. PLEASE ADVISE. So Robert Benchley cabled home to his New York publisher in the 1930s. An awareness of Venice's obvious difference is only the beginning of understanding how this city is made. How would you build a city on a sheet of water? The Venetians started with a collection of tiny islands, the Realtine archipelago, including the sites of San Marco, the Rialto, and San Pietro in Castello. Over centuries, they gradually filled up the spaces in between; Quartiere Sant'Elena, on the eastern tip of the city, is one of the newest additions.

On a good map, you can see how the city is split into roughly uniform 'blocks' divided by the canals. On each of these is one or perhaps two squares (*campi*) containing the parish churches. This is the basic unit of Venice; in each *campo* you will see a well, often beautifully made from ancient architectural fragments. Collecting fresh water was crucial in this city, and here the medieval Venetians show their cleverness. They sloped the *campi* to catch all the rainwater from surrounding streets and roofs; as the water trickled in it was filtered through layers of sand before arriving in the huge cisterns beneath the wells. On your first walk around, you'll notice that neither the streets nor the canals seem to have any firm intention of leading anywhere. The canals are as much boundaries as traffic routes, and the streets are meant only to connect each part of the block with its *campo*.

The design, where facilitating movement was thought less important than establishing a sense of place and identity, gives Venice a peculiar cellular quality; it was inspired by the Greek and Arab cities of the early Middle Ages. There are many echoes of Constantinople in Venice's layout. The Grand Canal mirrors the famous Meze of the imperial capital, a great street neatly dividing the city in two; at the foot of each city is the all-important square, with a view over the water on one side—Piazza S. Marco in Venice or the Golden Square in Constantinople, containing both the religious centre (St Mark's, the Hagia Sophia) and the symbol of the state (the Doge's Palace, the Imperial Palace).

Piazza S. Marco is, by popular acclaim over the centuries, the finest square in Europe. It is so not only for the sumptuous buildings around it, but for their arrangement, the textbook example of medieval urban design. The key to it is the integration of the main buildings, St Mark's and the Palace into their surroundings, instead of leaving them isolated and open as a modern planner would do. Their intrusion into the square creates smaller, complementary spaces—the two *piazzette*—and a subtle three-dimensional composition that offers differing, equally exciting prospects from a multitude of viewpoints. Instead of infantile symmetric geometry, the composition is a carefully considered artistic whole. You can see other variations on this theme at Campo S. Maria Formosa, at S. Maria dei Miracoli, SS. Giovanni e Paolo, and around the Frari. (If you're interested, you can learn more about what's right with Venice, and wrong with your home town, in the classic *The Art of City-Building* by Camillo Sitte (1889), well known everywhere on the Continent and even in America, but never published in Britain.)

Consider also the Venetian house and what it takes to keep one standing—a solid platform of wooden piles, driven into the mud. Some of these have stood their ground for almost a thousand years. In the old merchants' palaces, the windows give a clue to the plan inside. On the ground floor, there was always one large hall running the length of the building, where business was transacted; directly above it, where the Byzantine-Gothic fenestration is at its loveliest, was another hall, the main room of the *piano nobile*, where the family lived. The most impressive façade always overlooked the water, and the main door would always be the water door, often marked by gaily painted mooring poles, or *pali*; Venetians lived in their boats the way modern city dwellers live in their cars. On top, you'll often see surviving *altane*, the sun terraces of the ladies, along with a few of the old top-heavy chimney pots, designed to limit the risk of fire, a characteristic feature that the city's Renaissance artists loved to incorporate in their paintings.

One interesting phenomenon, peculiar to Venice, is the address numbers. Venice may well have been the first city to possess such things, and the system they invented has an archaic charm. The numbering isn't by street, but by the entire *sestiere*. Each of the 'sixths' of the city has one number 1; from there the numbers wind up and down the ancient alleys in no particular pattern, terminating with a flourish as San Marco's does, near the main post office, with a huge painted sign proclaiming to all the world: *5562. THE LAST NUMBER OF THE SESTIERE SAN MARCO.* Venetians get by with a little book called the *Indicatore Anagrafico*, which matches numbers with street names. But even knowing the street name affords little comfort when a *sestiere* has several lanes of the same name, or when the names on the street signs fail to correspond with either the *Indicatore* or your map. Venetians are as accomplished at spelling as they are in the kitchen; the height of this orthographical madness comes in Campo S. Biagio, or Blasio, or Biasio—you can take a souvenir photo of three signs on one wall, with three different spellings. There aren't many stone plaques, at least compared to Rome, but if you look carefully, you'll find water-level markers from historic floods, a score of indignant memorials to Austrian bombs from World War I, and a few notices from the slapstick days of the 18th century warning you against spitting or gambling or otherwise making a spectacle of yourself.

One thing you won't see is a family coat-of-arms over a palace: the republic usually forbade such displays of vanity. There will be stone winged lions instead, several thousand of them in all, and also plenty of unexpected and random decoration: a haughty Byzantine emperor, probably stolen from Constantinople in 1204, frowning over a tiny courtyard, a duck, a griffin, a pair of 6th-century capitals, a shrine to Persephone erected by a scholarly Renaissance humanist.

Before you start navigating around Venice, you'll need to get acquainted with some specifically Venetian street talk. At first you may think you're in Spain: why 'street' and 'canal' in Venetian dialect should be *calle* and *rio* is a linguistic mystery. There is of course only one *piazza* in Venice—St Mark's, along with two *piazzette* (adjacent to it), and one *piazzale* (Roma, the car park). All the rest are properly called *campo*. A small one may be a *campiello*. Besides that, there are:

corte: a blind alley.
fondamenta: a street that runs along a canal or along the lagoon banks.
piscina (Latin for pool or reservoir): an old turning basin for boats that has been filled in to become a square.

ramo: seems to mean a street only one block long, or the extension of another street with the same name.

rio: a canal. The status of *canale* is reserved for the Grand Canal and a few others.

rio terra: a filled-in canal.

riva or *molo*: a quay.

ruga: an old word for an important street.

sacca: a basin on the city's edge; Venice being man-made, these can be rectangular, like the Sacca della Misericordia.

salizzada: a word from the old days meaning a paved street.

sotoportego: (sottoportico) an arcade or archway under a building.

And if you ever wish to pretend you are walking in the Venice of the old days, there is one clue that will help make the place come to life: the smaller streets were generally named (in Venetian dialect) after the trade or whatever other sort of enterprise went on there, and they have conserved the names up to this day. Some of the most common are:

bareteri: capmakers

beccarie: butchers

caffetier: coffee house

calderer: coppersmith

calegheri: shoemakers
   (a Latin word that survived
   only in Venice)

carbon: coal barges (on a canal)

carrozzer: carriage-maker
   (amazingly, Venice supported
   quite a few until the 17th century)

cason: police prison

cerchieri: coopers

corrazzeri: armourers

diamanter: diamond-cutters

fabbri: smiths

formagier: cheesemonger

forner: baker

frezzeria: arrow factory

fruttarol: fruiterer

luganegher: pork-butcher

malvasia: seller of malvasia wine

mandoler: almond-seller

marangon: ship's carpenter

margaritera: glass-bead-maker

mendicoli: beggars

muneghe: nuns

murer: builder

piovan: parish priest

remer: oar-maker

ridotto: gambling house

spezier: apothecary

squero: boat-yard

stagneri: tinsmiths

strazzarol: ragman

tentor: dyer

testari: silk-weavers

veriera: glazier

Travel

Arriving in Venice

By Air: Venice's Marco Polo Airport is 13 km north of the city near the lagoon, and has regularly scheduled connections from London, New York (via Milan), Paris, Vienna, Nice, Zurich, Frankfurt, Düsseldorf, Rome, Milan, Palermo and Naples. For flight information in Venice, dial 661 262. The British Airways office is at Marco Polo Airport, Tessera, tel 661 111. Alitalia is near S. Moisè at S. Marco 1757, tel 521 6111/6222; TWA have an agent, Gastaldi Tours, at Via Verdi 34, Mestre, tel 988 755.

The airport is linked with Venice by water-taxi (tel 964 084) the most expensive option (L75 000); or by *motoscafi* with S. Marco (Zecca) roughly every hour and a half, although connecting with most flights from March–Oct (L12 000 a person), and if you're catching an early flight, you can reserve a departure (tel 522 2303); or by ATVO bus with the Piazzale Roma (L5000); or cheapest of all, on the ACTV city bus No. 5, which passes by once an hour. Buses depart for the airport an hour before each flight.

Charter flights sometimes land at Treviso (30 km north). If your ticket doesn't include coach service to Venice, the cheapest way of getting into the lagoon is to buy a ticket (first) and catch the No. 6 bus into Treviso, and from there catch a bus to Venice, which runs every half hour. For charters from London, try Italy Sky Shuttle, 227 Shepherds Bush Road, London W6 7AS, tel (081) 748 1333. From New York, try CIEE, which can get you as close as Rome or Milan (tel 800 223 7402). A number of tour operators who specialize in holidays to Italy offer attractively priced 'city-breaks' to Venice. Citalia, Marco Polo House, 3–5 Lansdowne Road, Croydon, Surrey CR9 1LL, tel (081) 686 5533, probably has the widest range which are also very good value. (See 'Specialist Holidays', p. 3).

By Sea: This is the most thrilling way to approach Venice in all her majesty, although only practical if you're coming from the east. Adriatica lines (Zattere 1412, tel 520 4322) has connections every 10 days in June–September with Split (15 hours) and Dubrovnik (24 hours). There are also 34 car-ferry journeys a year—roughly every 10 days between Venice and Piraeus (2 days), Heraklion, Crete ($2^1/2$ days) and Alexandria, Egypt ($3^1/2$ days). An easier way to approach Venice in style would be to follow the path of Portia in *The Merchant of Venice*, by travelling as far as Padua to pick up the *Burchiello* (see p. 284), sailing up the Brenta Canal to Piazza S. Marco.

By Train: Of course, you can wallow in romantic splendour, Grand-Tour style, on the luxurious vintage **Venice Simplon-Orient-Express** from London to Venice via Paris, Zurich, St Anton, Innsbruck and Verona. Fares (including sharing a double cabin and all gourmet meals) start at about £850 ($1440) one-way. The Orient Express runs twice in February and every Sunday and Thursday from March to mid-November). There are several packages available for tours *en route* to Venice. For more information contact the Venice Simplon-Orient-Express Tours Ltd, Suite 200, Hudson's Place, Victoria Station, London SW1V 1JL, tel (071) 928 6000 in the UK; 30th Floor, 1155 Avenue of the Americas, New York, NY 10036, tel (212) 302 5055, in the USA.

Venice's **Stazione Santa Lucia** (the name a consolation prize to the Saint whose church had to be bulldozed for the station) is the terminus of the Orient Express and numerous other less glamorous trains from the rest of Europe and Italy. There are especially frequent connections to Padua ($1/2$ hourly), where the budget-conscious visitor may prefer to stay. All trains from Santa Lucia stop in Mestre, where you may have to change. For rail information, tel 715 555; information and tickets are also available at the CIT office at Piazza S. Marco 48/51, tel 528 5480—the information offices in the station itself are nearly always very crowded. The left-luggage office, near the tracks is L1500 per bag for each 24 hours. If you lose something on a train, tel 528 9600.

Water-taxis, *vaporetti*, and gondolas (see below) wait in front of the station to sweep you off into the city. If you've brought more luggage than you can carry, one of Venice's famous/infamous porters (distinguished by their badges) will lug it to your choice of transport, and if you pay his fare on the water-taxi, will take it and you to your hotel (official price for one or two pieces of luggage is L7700 between any two points in the historic centre)—or you can try to track down a porter once you disembark at one of the main landings or Lido.

By Car: All roads to Venice end at the monstrous municipal parking towers in **Piazzale Roma** or its cheaper annex, **Tronchetto**, nothing less than the largest car park in all Europe, which may take up the entire Lagoon before it's finished. You can leave your car here, for an arm and a leg (beginning at L18 000 a day). In the summer, at Easter and Carnival, when the causeway turns into a solid conga-line of cars waiting to park, consider the Italian Auto Club's three alternative and less expensive car parks (open to non-members): **Fusina**, with a shady, year-round campsite, located at the mouth of the Brenta Canal, south of Marghera (parking lot open summer only; *vaporetto* No. 16 to Venice); **S. Giuliano**, in Mestre, near the causeway (bus service to Venice); and **Punta Sabbioni**, in between the Lido and Jesolo (reached by ferry boat No. 17 from Tronchetto).

Specialist Holidays

A number of firms offer special holidays or help get you tickets for events:

Art in Europe (art and architecture, language and music, wine and gastronomy tours in Venice and the Veneto), Ladywell Cottage, Wildcote Lane, Ramsdan, Oxfordshire, tel (0993) 868 864

Crest Travel, Lido di Jesolo, Olivier House, 18 Marine Parade, Brighton, tel (0273) 677 777

Italviaggi (golf holidays on Venice's Lido) High Street, Gillingham, Dorset, tel (0747) 825 353

Quo Vadis (special events in Venice) 243 Euston Road, London NW1, tel (071) 388 7588

Serenissima and Heritage Travel (garden and villa tours at Ásolo, Vicenza, and Bassano del Grappa; art in Venice) 21 Dorset Square, London NW1, tel (071) 730 9841

Swan Hellenic (Venetian Lagoon and Po Delta) 77 New Oxford Street, London WC1, tel (071) 831 1515.

Customs Formalities

A passport, or a British Visitor's Card, will get you into Italy. Nationals of the UK, Ireland, USA, Canada, Australia and New Zealand do not need visas for stays of up to three months. If you plan to stay longer, to work or study, you may need a visa (see 'Living and Working in Venice', p. 332).

In accordance with Italian law, you must register with the police within three days of your arrival. If you check into a hotel or campsite this is done automatically. If you're not staying at either of these, do register at police headquarters the *Questura*, at Fondamenta S. Lorenzo, Castello, tel 520 3222 to avoid possible trouble later.

Customs can be a breeze or a storm, depending on the mood of the customs officers and how dirty, low-down and suspicious you look. Still, they can't pin nothing on you if you haven't brought along more than 150 cigarettes or 75 cigars, or not more than a litre of hard drink or three bottles of wine, a couple of cameras, a movie camera, 10 rolls of film for each, a tape-recorder, radio, phonograph, one canoe less than 5.5 m, sports equipment for personal use, and one TV (although you'll have to pay for a licence for it at Customs). Pets must be accompanied by a bilingual certificate of health from your local veterinary inspector. You can take the same items listed above home with you without hassle—except of course your British pet. US citizens may return with merchandise worth up to $400— keep your receipts. British subjects are permitted dutiable merchandise worth up to £200. To export an antique or work of art, you'll have to apply for permission at the Export Department of the Ministry of Education and pay a tax on the value of the work.

Getting Around Venice

Public transport in Venice means by water: by turgid canal cutting *vaporetti* (the all purpose water-buses) or the sleeker, faster *motoscafi* run by the ACTV (tel 528 7886). Each line has a number and is priced according to speed and distance travelled—timetables and prices are posted at each stop. There are usually lower prices for *traghetti*—a simple crossing of a body of water, be it the Grand Canal, the Giudecca Canal, or whatever, where you get off at the next stop. Note that the only canals served by public transport are the Grand Canal, the Rio Nuovo, the Canale di Cannaregio and Rio dell'Arsenale. Other stops are all on the edge of the city or on other islands, which means most of the time you'll

4

be on your own two feet—not a gruelling prospect, as Venice is so small you can walk across the whole city in an hour. If you intend to do some intense scouting that involves being on a boat at least six times in a given day, purchase a 24-hour **tourist pass** for L9000, valid for unlimited travel on all lines, or the 3-day pass for L17 000. Tickets should be purchased and validated in the machines at the landing-stages (random inspections aren't very frequent, but if you get caught without a validated ticket you'll have to pay a L15 000 fine on the spot). As many landing-stages don't always sell tickets, it's best to stock up (most *tabacchi* sell them in blocks of ten). If you plan to spend more than three or four days in Venice, the *Carta Venezia* is a good investment: it costs L8000 but is valid for three years and entitles you to pay only L500 on the *vaporetti* and L600 on the *diretti*. Get one by taking your passport and a photo-machine mugshot to ACTV central in Corte dell'Albero, on the Grand Canal by the S. Angelo stop.

Lines of interest to visitors are listed below; most run until midnight. Precise schedules are listed in the tourist office's free monthly guide, *Un Ospite di Venezia*.

Line 1 (*accelerato*, the Italian euphemism for slowpoke, L1750) runs from Tronchetto, Piazzale Roma and the Ferrovia (station), down the Grand Canal, to S. Marco and the Lido, stopping everywhere; around the clock, every 10 min, although much less frequently after 9 pm. The entire journey takes an hour.

Line 2 (*diretto*, L2500) takes the short cut from Piazzale Roma, Tronchetto, and Ferrovia through the Rio Nuovo to Rialto, Accademia, S. Marco and Lido. Every 10 min during the day, approximately once an hour at night.

Line 5 (*servizio circolare*, L1750), the circular route, runs either to the left (*sinistra*) or right (*destra*), departing every 15 min. Main points of interest are the islands of Murano and S. Michele, Fondamente Nuove, Campo della Tana (where you can take a peek inside the Arsenale), S. Zaccaria, S. Giorgio Maggiore, Redentore, Zattere, Piazzale Roma, Ferrovia, Ponte delle Guglie (Canale di Cannaregio) and Madonna dell'Orto.

Line 5 (*direttissimo*, L1750) a summer-only line from Tronchetto, Piazzale Roma, Ferrovia, Murano, S. Elena to S. Zaccaria and vice versa (every 30 min).

Line 6 (*diretto motonave*, L1750) is the large steamer from the Riva degli Schiavoni to Lido (every 20 min).

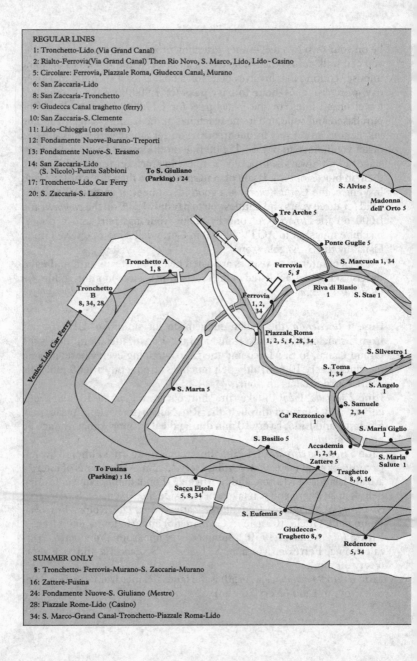

REGULAR LINES

1: Tronchetto-Lido (Via Grand Canal)

2: Rialto-Ferrovia(Via Grand Canal) Then Rio Novo, S. Marco, Lido, Lido-Casino

5: Circolare: Ferrovia, Piazzale Roma, Giudecca Canal, Murano

6: San Zaccaria-Lido

8: San Zaccaria-Tronchetto

9: Giudecca Canal traghetto (ferry)

10: San Zaccaria-S. Clemente

11: Lido-Chioggia (not shown)

12: Fondamente Nuove-Burano-Treporti

13: Fondamente Nuove-S. Erasmo

14: San Zaccaria-Lido (S. Nicolo)-Punta Sabbioni

17: Tronchetto-Lido Car Ferry

20: S. Zaccaria-S. Lazzaro

To S. Giuliano (Parking) : 24

S. Alvise 5

Madonna dell' Orto 5

Tre Arche 5

Ponte Guglie 5

Ferrovia 5, 5

S. Marcuola 1, 34

Tronchetto A 1, 8

Ferrovia 1, 2, 34

Riva di Biasio 1

S. Stae 1

Tronchetto B 8, 34, 28

Piazzale Roma 1, 2, 5, 5, 28, 34

S. Silvestro 1

S. Toma 1, 34

S. Angelo 1

S. Marta 5

S. Samuele 2, 34

Ca' Rezzonico 1

S. Maria Giglio 1

S. Basilio 5

Accademia 1, 2, 34

S. Maria Salute 1

To Fusina (Parking) : 16

Zattere 5

Traghetto 8, 9, 16

Sacca Fisola 5, 8, 34

S. Eufemia 5

Giudecca-Traghetto 8, 9

Redentore 5, 34

Venice-Lido Car Ferry

SUMMER ONLY

5: Tronchetto- Ferrovia-Murano-S. Zaccaria-Murano

16: Zattere-Fusina

24: Fondamente Nuove-S. Giuliano (Mestre)

28: Piazzale Rome-Lido (Casino)

34: S. Marco-Grand Canal-Tronchetto-Piazzale Roma-Lido

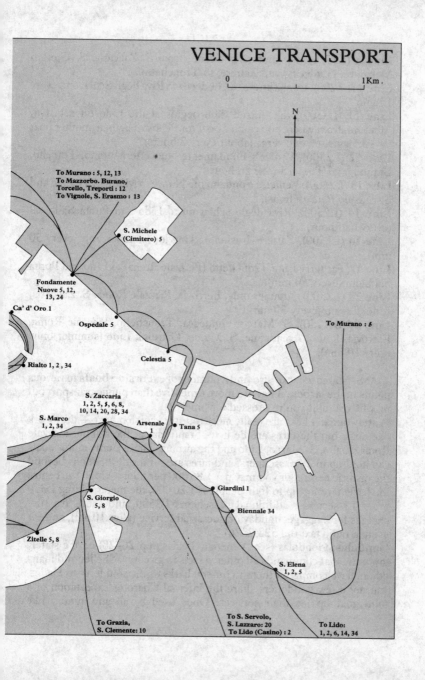

VENICE TRANSPORT

0   1 Km.

N

To Murano : 5, 12, 13,
To Mazzorbo, Burano,
Torcello, Treporti : 12
To Vignole, S. Erasmo : 13

S. Michele
(Cimitero) 5

Fondamente
Nuove 5, 12,
13, 24

Ca' d' Oro 1

Ospedale 5

To Murano : 5

Rialto 1, 2 , 34

Celestia 5

S. Zaccaria
1, 2, 5, 5, 6, 8,
10, 14, 20, 28, 34

S. Marco
1, 2, 34

Arsenale
1

Tana 5

Giardini 1

S. Giorgio
5, 8

Biennale 34

Zitelle 5, 8

S. Elena
1, 2, 5

To Grazia,
S. Clemente: 10

To S. Servolo,
S. Lazzaro: 20
To Lido (Casino) : 2

To Lido:
1, 2, 6, 14, 34

Line 8 (L1750), the motorists' friend, from S. Zaccaria, S. Giorgio Maggiore, Giudecca, and Zattere, to Tronchetto.

Line 9 (L1200), from Zattere to Giudecca to Riva degli Schiavoni, every 15 min.

Line 11 (L3500), the 'mixed' line begins at the Lido on a bus to Alberoni, from where you catch a boat for Pellestrina, then another boat for Chioggia, or vice versa (about every 2 hours).

Line 12 (L2500), Venice's Fondamente Nuove to Murano, Torcello, Burano, and Treporti (one an hour).

Line 13 (L2500), Venice's Fondamente Nuove to Murano, Vignole and S. Erasmo (one an hour).

Line 14 (L2500), Riva degli Schiavoni to Lido and Punta Sabbioni (every half hour).

Line 16 (L2500), Zattere–Fusina parking lot (summer only; every 50 min).

Line 17, car ferry from Tronchetto (Piazzale Roma) to Lido and Punta Sabbioni (every 50 min).

Line 28 (L2500), summer only, Ferrovia, Piazzale Roma, S. Zaccaria, Lido/Casino (every 30 min).

Line 34 (L1750), S. Marco, Giudecca, Tronchetto, Piazzale Roma, Ferrovia, Rialto, Accademia, S. Marco, Giardini, Lido (summer only, every 10 min).

At S. Marco you can also find a number of **excursion boats** to various points in the lagoon. They are more expensive than public transport but may be useful if you're pressed for time.

Water-taxis: These are really more tourist excursion boats—they work like taxis, but the fares are de luxe. Stands are at the station, Piazzale Roma, Rialto, S. Marco, Lido and the airport. These jaunty motor boats can hold up to 20 passengers, and fares are set for destinations beyond the historic centre, or you may pay L85 000 per hour. Within the centre the basic fare for up to four people is L20 000, the meter adding L350 every 15 seconds; additional passengers L2500, and there are surcharges for baggage, holiday or nocturnal service (after 10 pm), and for using a radio taxi (tel 523 2326).

Gondolas: Gondolas (see 'Venetian Topics', pp. 26–28) have a stately mystique that commands all other vessels to give way. Shelley and many others have compared them to funeral barks or the soul ferry to Hades, and not a few gondoliers share the infernal Charon's expectation of a solid gold tip for their services. Once used by all and sundry like carriages or taxis, they are now quite frankly for tourists who can pay the official L50 000 for a 50-minute ride (L60 000 after 8 pm), plus L25 000 for each additional half hour. Most gondolas can take six people, and, before setting out, do agree with the gondolier on where you want to go and how long you expect the journey to take, thus avoiding any unpleasantness later on.

Gondolas retired from the tourist trade are used for **gondola traghetti** services crossing the Grand Canal between its three bridges—your chance to enjoy a brief but economical gondola ride across the Canal for L300. You'll find them crossing between Fondaco dei Turchi and S. Marcuola; Pescheria and S. Sofia; Fondamenta del Vin and Riva del Carbon; S. Tomà to S. Angelo, S. Barnaba to S. Samuele. For appearance's sake you'll have to stand up for the short but precarious experience: only sissies ever sit down on *traghetti*.

Hiring a Boat: Perhaps the best way to spend a day in Venice is to bring or hire your own boat—a small motor boat or a rowing-boat—although beware of the local version of oar that requires some practice to use. You may have to be persistent even to find a boat (the Venetians are tired of rescuing tourists stranded in the Lagoon), but ask Bruno Bianchini in the Piazza S. Marco tourist office for suggestions. *Motoscafi* for hire are easier to find, especially with chauffeurs: try Cooperativa Motoscafi, S. Marco 978, tel 523 5775; Narduzzi & Solemar, S. Marco 2828, tel 528 7701, La Lagunare Motoscafi, Viale S. Marco 119/10, Mestre, tel 531 5039, or Serenissima Motoscafi, Castello 4545, tel 522 4281.

By Bus: Piazzale Roma is Venice's bus terminus. There are frequent city buses from here to Mestre, Chioggia, Marghera, and La Malcontenta; regional buses every half-hour to Padua and less frequently to other Veneto cities and Trieste. It has its own helpful tourist information office, tel 522 7404.

Car Hire: If you want to explore the mainland by car, there are hire firms with offices in Piazzale Roma, Marco Polo airport, or Mestre station: Autorent, tel 528 9494; International, tel 520 6565; Budget, tel 541 4299; Avis, tel 522 5825; Europcar, tel 523 8616; Maggiore, tel 541 5040.

Travellers with Disabilities

Thanks to the efforts of Venice's Institute for Architecture and their *Veneziapertutti* (Venice for all) campaign, the labyrinth has opened up for visitors with disabilities or limited access. The city's 411 bridges present the major obstacle in getting around, but by judicious use of the *vaporetti* a good part of the city becomes accessible, as *Veneziapertutti*'s map shows. *Motoscafi*, with their small platforms, present another challenge, especially for people in wheelchairs; *Veneziapertutti*'s map has a different colour for those areas. The *Veneziapertutti*'s booklet has a list of accessible hotels, churches, monuments, gardens, public offices, and rest rooms with facilities for the handicapped. You can write ahead to Venice's tourist office for a free copy of the booklet and map, or pick one up at the ULSS No. 16, in Piazzale Roma 3493 (*vaporetto* stop No. 1). There are plans for retractable ramps operated by magnetic cards in the future. Other sources of information are RADAR, 25 Mortimer Street, London W1M 81B, tel (071) 637 5400, which publishes an extremely useful book, *Holidays and Travel Abroad—A Guide for Disabled People*, at £3.00. In the USA, the best source book is *Access to the World: A Travel Guide for the Handicapped* by Louise Weiss ($14.95 from Facts on File, 460 Park Avenue South, New York, NY 10016).

Practical A–Z

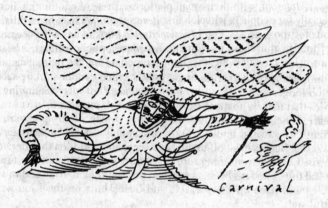

Carnival

Climate/Best Time to Go

'Obviously things have to smell of whatever they smell of, and obviously canals will reek in the summertime, but this really is too much,' complained the Burgundian Président, Charles de Brosses, back in the 18th century. But pungent canals keep Venice from getting too bijou. The various moods in Vivaldi's *Four Seasons* are a pretty accurate rendition of Venetian weather. In no other city will you be so aware of the light: on a clear, fine day no place could be more limpid and clear, no water as crystal bright as the Lagoon. The rosy dawn igniting the domes of St Mark's, the cool mist of a canal dulling the splash of an oar, the pearly twilit union of water and sky are among the city's oldest clichés.

If you seek solitude and romance with a capital R, go in November or January. Pack a warm coat, wellingtons and an umbrella and expect frequent fogs and mists. It may even snow, a rare and beautiful sight—in 1987 you could even ski-jump down the Rialto Bridge. Roughly once a century the canals and lagoons freeze up enough to skate or roast an ox. But there are also plenty of radiant diamond days, brilliant, sunny and chill; any time after October you take your chances. If there's an *acqua alta* (high water) while you're in town, don't miss the sight of Piazza S. Marco submerged in water.

As spring approaches there is Carnival, a gallant and beautiful, but so far lifeless, attempt to revive a piece of old Venice. Lent is fairly quiet, although there's an expectant undercurrent as the Venetians build up for their first major invasion of sightseers at Easter. By April the tourism industry is cranked up to full operational capacity: all the hotels, museums and galleries have reopened: the gondolas are un-mothballed, the café tables have blossomed in the Piazza, the Casino has re-located to the Lido. In June even the Italians are considering a trip to the beach.

In July and August elbow-room is at a premium. Peripheral camping grounds are packed, queues at the tourist office's room-finding service stretch longer and longer, and the police are kept busy reminding the hordes that there's no more sleeping out and no picnicking in St Mark's Square. The heat can be sweltering, the canals nastily pungent, the ancient city gasping under a flood of cameras, shorts, sunglasses and rucksacks. Scores head off to the Lido for relief; a sudden thunderstorm over the Lagoon livens things up, as do the many festivals. In autumn the city and the Venetians begin to unwind, the rains begin to fall and you can watch them pack up the parasols and beach huts on the Lido with a wistful sigh.

Average Temperatures in °C (°F):

January	February	March	April	May	June
3.8 (39)	4.1 (39)	8.2 (46)	12.6 (54)	17.1 (62)	21.2 (70)

July	August	September	October	November	December
23.6 (74)	23.3 (74)	20.4 (68)	15.1 (59)	10.5 (51)	5.0 (41)

Average Monthly Rainfall in Millimetres:

January	February	March	April	May	June
58	39	74	77	72	73

July	August	September	October	November	December
37	48	71	66	75	54

Consulates

UK: Palazzo Querini, Accademia 1051, Dorsoduro, tel 522 7202
Ireland: Largo del Nazzareno 3, Rome, tel (06) 678 2541
USA: Largo Donegani 1, Milan, tel (02) 652 841
Canada: Via Zara 30, Rome, tel (06) 844 1841

Australia: Via Alessandria 215, Rome, tel (06) 832 721
New Zealand: Via Veneto 119/a, Rome, tel (06) 851 225

Courses

You can combine a holiday in Venice with a course in Italian (though beware if you acquire a Venetian accent, your attempts to speak with non-Venetians will be an endless source of amusement). Classes are offered by the month at the Dante Alighieri Institute, by the Arsenale, tel 528 9127 between 10 and 12; Benedict School, Frezzeria 1688, tel 522 4034; Zambler, Cannaregio 3764, tel 522 4331. Europe's only school of comparative music, financed by UNESCO, holds forth between April and September with lectures, concerts, lessons and workshops, at the Fondazione Giorgio Cini, on the islet of San Giorgio Maggiore. The Università Internazionale dell'Arte, in the Palazzo Fortuny (tel 528 7542), holds courses in art restoration and stage design from October to April. Design workshops and courses in architecture are offered at the Istituto Superiore di Architettura e Design at the Palazzo Papafava, Cannaregio 3762, tel 522 4414. For more information on these, and possible scholarships, apply to the Italian Institute, 39 Belgrave Square, London SW1X 8NX, tel (071) 235 1461 or 686 Park Ave, New York, NY 10021, tel (212) 397 9300.

Crime

Venice has the lowest crime rate of any large Italian city. There's a small amount of petty crime, and bags left in the back of cars parked in Piazzale Roma are sometimes stolen. If by some unlucky chance you need to summon the police, the free emergency number is 113 (police). The *carabinieri* number is 112 (there is usually someone there who speaks English); their barracks is in Piazzale Roma, tel 523 5333. If you lose something in the city, try the Municipio, tel 520 8844; or tel 780 310 if you lost it on a *vaporetto*. To summon the fire brigade, tel 115—you'll get a look at the city's fleet of fire boats if you ride the No. 5 *vaporetto* through the Canale Scomenzera.

Electricity

The voltage in Venice is 220 ac, and outlets take two round prongs; try to pick up an adapter before you leave or at the airport as they are hard to find in the city.

13

Festivals and a Calendar of Events

Venetians, once entertained by a full calendar of state pageants, religious feast days, lotteries, itinerant jugglers, and universal singing in the streets and gondolas, nowadays get by with a lot less. The big events—Carnival, the Film Festival, the Biennale—are international and have little spontaneity outside of the controversy and disputes they inevitably engender. And after the fireworks everyone goes to bed.

Venice's renowned **Carnival**, founded back in 1094, was revived in 1979 after several decades of dormancy. It packs in the crowds, but still faces an uphill battle against the inherent Italian urge to make everything *bellissima*—at the expense of any serious carousing. This is in tame contrast to the rollicking carnival of the 18th century, ruled by the *commedia dell'arte* characters of Arlecchino (or Harlequin, a servant from Bergamo), Segnor Pantalon (a rich and pedantic old Venetian merchant, constantly being cuckolded) and Zany Corneto ('Zany' or 'Zanni' is Venetian for Gianni, a name people would call porters; it is from this madcap character that the word in English is derived). Nowadays masks are worn for the ten days before Lent, not for any high jinks but for the sake of cutting a dash and posing for photographs. In response, the art of making the masks has been revived in little workshops all over the city. The city sponsors events like celebrity performances at La Fenice, Renaissance carnival madrigals and *commedia dell'arte* performances. But if you want to have a really good time at Carnival, go to Cadiz.

Founded in 1895, the **Biennale** international art show takes place in the pavilions of the Giardini Pubblici in the summers of even-numbered years. The uneven quality of the exhibits ('Nothing more than black holes,' fumed one art critic) and the recent spate of scandal have stripped away some of its gloss. Who actually gets exhibited is decided by bureaucratic bodies in each country. Naturally there is a good deal of politicking in the larger countries, and merit is not always the prime consideration. Perhaps the most exciting thing about the Biennale are the fringe exhibits by unknowns that are shown all over Venice to coincide with the main event. In the Giardini Pubblici, the various nations' pavilions are arranged as at a World's Fair, among groves of huge, perfect linden trees. The permanant buildings, although modest, are often of some interest in themselves, such as the Netherlands', by *de Stijl* architect Gerrit Rietveld, Finland's, designed by Alvar Aalto, and Austria's, by Josef Hoffmann.

A Report on the 1990 Biennale: This year's effort seems to have generated little controversy, but not much excitement either. The larger countries, not surprisingly, put on the most tepid shows. Prize for the most brainless must unfortunately be given to Britain, nothing more than tons of rocks, shipped here at great cost and strewn about the floor. The Canadians came in a close second, with a photograph of two pairs of lips blown up to the size of a house. The most ambitious and irritating exhibit was undoubtedly the American, which consisted entirely of slogans. These, pop psychology *sententiae* dreamed up by a female artist, were carved in shining granite and displayed in five languages in banks of flashing lights—also heavily promoted on tee shirts, posters and billboards around the town.

Among the successes: Uruguay's Gonzalo Fonseca, with his concrete works evoking archaeological ruins; the *City of Precarious Symbols*, a three-dimensional room-sized composition by Venezuelan Julio Pacheco-Rivas; Gilvan Samico's Brazilian woodcuts; and especially the contribution from Down Under—paintings by Rover Thomas and Trevor Nicholls inspired both in theme and technique by the Aboriginal culture. Poland's well-known Jozef Szajna brought one of his room-sized collages of war and industrial madness, memories of the concentration camps amid landscapes of trash and rags, certainly the most unsettling exhibit; the Germans weighed in with endless stark photographs of water-tanks, mine buildings and Bessemer converters from around the world, recorded with Teutonic rigour. Local colour was often consciously inserted—as in Egypt's stylized ancient sarcophagi with television screens for heads. And even in the 90s, abstraction is still used to cover a lack of ideas: chaotically, as in the offerings of Yugoslavia or Italy, or most tidily, in those of (guess who?) the Swiss and Japanese. Above all, for those who think art is international, the Biennale is a place to see your favourite stereotypes of national characters authoritatively confirmed.

The **Venice Film Festival** unreels in the grand Palazzo del Cinema and in the Astra Cinema on the Lido. Besides the thrill of seeing your celluloid heroes in the flesh, you can get in to see some of the films, although you should arrive at the cinemas early as the tickets are sold only on the day of their showing. Venice's festival is generally ranked second after Cannes on the European circuit, and the festival's equivalent of the Oscar, the *Leone d'Oro*, is proudly flaunted by every winner's publicity machine.

15

Venice's most exciting festival, **Il Redentore**, celebrates the end of the plague of 1576. In its prayers for deliverance from the epidemic, the Senate vowed to build a church (Palladio's, on the Giudecca) and to cross over the canal on a bridge of boats to attend mass on its feast day—which the pious Venetians continue to do. Most of the excitement happens the Saturday night before, when Venetians set sail in the evening for a picnic on the water, manoeuvring for the best views of an utterly incandescent fireworks show over the Lagoon. Another holiday celebrating the end of a plague (1631) takes place with another bridge of boats over to **S. Maria della Salute**. This ceremony is notable not for its fireworks but for the chance it affords to see Longhena's unique basilica with its doors thrown open to the Grand Canal. More adrenalin flows into the **Regata Storica**, a splendid pageant of historic vessels and crews in Renaissance costumes and races by a variety of rowers down the Grand Canal—the race between gondoliers, who have special racing gondolas for the occasion, is the most intensely fought. In 1988 Venice revived its ancient marriage-to-the-sea ceremony, **La Sensa** (see 'Venetian Topics', pp. 38–40) with the mayor playing the role of the Doge in a replica of the *Bucintoro*, all of which is as corny and pretentious as it sounds, but on the same day you can watch the **Vogalonga**, or long row, from S. Marco to Burano and back to the Grand Canal. And every fourth year Venice hosts the **Regatta of the Maritime Republics**, squaring off against old rivals Pisa, Genoa and Amalfi.

1 Jan	New Year's Day on the beach, Lido
6 Jan	Regatta of the *Befana* (the kind witch who brings good kids toys on Epiphany)
10 days before Shrove Tues	Carnival
March	*Su e Zo per i Ponti* traditional, non-competitive row
25 April	Feast of St Mark, when men send their beloved a single rose; also a gondoliers' regatta and the Lion of St Mark golf championship
1 May	*Sagra della Sparesea*, asparagus festival at Cavallino
Sun after Ascension Day	*La Sensa* and *Vogalonga*
June–Sept	Biennale, even-numbered years
3 June	St Erasmus, patron saint festival
1st Sat in June	*Serenissima* Offshore Grand Prix motor-boat race

3rd week in June	Feast of S. Pietro in Volta, on Pellestrina island; SS. Giovanni e Paolo regatta for young gondoliers
1 July	Murano Regatta
3rd Sat & Sun in July	Feast of the Redentore
16 July	Feast of the Madonna del Carmine
mid-July	*Sagra del Peocio* (mussels) in Alberoni
1st Sun in Aug	Feast of the Madonna and Regatta, Pellestrina
11–12 Aug	Feast of S. Stefano, at Portosecco
16 Aug	Feast of S. Rocco
late Aug– early Sept	Venice Film Festival
Sept	Vivaldi festival and festival of contemporary music
1st Sun in Sept	*Regata Storica*
2nd Sat in Sept	Feast of S. Gerardo Sagredo at Sacca Fisola
11–14 Sept	Contest of Venetian songs and light music at the Lido Casino
3rd week in Sept	Burano Regatta
1st weekend in Oct	Venice Marathon; wine-harvest festival at S. Erasmo
Nov 10	St Martin's Day, revival of a popular fair in the streets of Venice
Nov 21	Feast of the Madonna della Salute
Dec–Jan	Opera and ballet season at La Fenice and Teatro Goldoni

Insurance

National medical coverage in the UK and Canada covers their citizens while travelling (in Britain, pick up form E111 from the local office of the Department of Health and Social Security before you leave). Nationals of other countries may want to take out travel insurance if their current policy fails to cover them while abroad. Travel agents offer policies that cover not only health, but stolen or lost baggage, and cancelled or missed flights.

Lavatories

Public ones do exist in Venice, but they are usually impossible to find without asking someone. Around Piazza S. Marco there's one in the Giardinetti Reali and in the Albergo Diurno, just on the other side of the

Ala Napoleonica (Ramo Primo a Ascensione, signposted, open 8 am–10 pm, L500 a pee; also showers, barbers, left luggage, etc.); another pay toilet is in Piazza S. Bartolomeo, and there's a free bog right in front of the Accademia. You can also find nice hygienic facilities in most museums, in the railway station and at Piazzale Roma. Otherwise, duck in a bar, as most Italians do, although in main tourist nodes you're likely to see signs saying there are no toilets, or that they're for the use of customers only (in most places, you aren't obliged to buy anything, although it's good form to do so).

Maps

No two maps of Venice ever agree, either in the actual street names and their dialect spellings, or where the back alleys actually end up. Among the first-rate maps of Venice that make a game effort to include every puny *corte* and *ramo* of every street are *Touring Club Italiano*'s large, detailed and rather expensive number (L25 000), complete with a directory of street names; the yellow *Studio FMB Bologna* 1:5000 map, with a street index on the back, which you can pick up for L6000; or for a bit more, the *Hallwag* 1:5500 map. But even the best maps aren't very much help in finding the typical Venetian address that lists only the *sestiere* and street number: for these you need a little book matching numbers to street names called the *Indicatore Anagrafico*, available in most bookshops, although even then confusion is rampant, with so many lanes in the same *sestiere* bearing the same name. If you get desperate, try to find a postman.

Medical Matters

In a medical emergency, dial 113, or more directly for an ambulance, tel 523 0000. If you have an accident or become seriously ill, go to the casualty (first aid, or *Pronto Soccorso* department of the city hospital in Campo SS. Giovanni e Paolo (tel 529 4516) or the Ospedale del Mare, 1 Lungomare d'Annunzio, Lido (tel 526 5900); if you need a doctor at night or on holidays ring 531 4481. If it's not too serious, go to a chemist—Italian pharmacists are trained to diagnose minor ills and can give you prescription drugs (although you'll pay full price for the remedy). Several *farmacie* are open all night on a rotating basis: the addresses are in the window of each, or you can ring 192 for a list, or find them in *Un Ospite di Venezia*.

18

Money

The currency is the lira, and for the newcomer all the 0s can be confusing. Although the Venetians pass up hundreds of opportunities to take advantage of the bemused tourist, a very few of them do (beware the traditional Italian method of giving change, pausing a moment before handing over the largest note, in the hope that you'll walk away and forget it). There are convenient cash or traveller's cheque exchanges in the airport and train station, and at most banks. **Banking hours** are Mon–Fri 8:30–1 and 3–4.) Head offices of major banks in Venice are all clustered in the *sestiere* of S. Marco:

Banca Commerciale Italiana: Via XXII Marzo 2188, tel 529 6811
Banca d'America e d'Italia: Via XXII Marzo 2216, tel 520 0766
Banca Nazionale del Lavoro: Bacino Orseolo 1188, tel 667 511
Banco di Napoli: Campo S. Gallo 1112 by Bacino Orseolo, tel 523 1700
Banco di Roma: Merceria dell'Orologio 191, tel 662 411
Banco San Marco: Calle Larga S. Marco 383, tel 529 3711
Credito Italiano: Campo S. Salvador, tel 957 600.

Places that exchange money outside normal banking hours include:
American Express, S. Moisè 1471, tel 520 0844, open Mon–Sat 8–8 (April–Oct)
CIT: Piazza S. Marco 4850, tel 528 5480 (Mon–Sat 8–6)
INTRAS: Piazza S. Marco at the corner of the Procuratie Nuove and the clock tower (open Mon–Sat 8:30–6)
World Vision (Thomas Cook), Calle delle Ostreghe 2457, S. Marco

Nearly every hotel of three stars or more will accept American Express, Visa, Diner's Club cards and Eurocheques. Below three stars they usually don't. Most shops and restaurants in the main tourist paths accept credit cards; others, frequented mostly by Venetians, probably don't.

Opening Hours

General opening hours for shops and offices are Mon–Sat 8 or 9–1 and from 4–7:30, although many tourist shops stay open during the siesta, and even on Sundays and holidays. Many shops (except grocers) are closed Monday morning and on 21 November for the *Festa della Salute*; markets and grocers tend to close on Wednesday afternoons. No two museums keep the same hours, so consult the text: we've tried to time the walks so you can take in most of them either before or after lunch. All churches except St Mark's take a lunch break too, generally between 12 and 4; again we've tried to note their hours in the text.

Packing

Venetians, like all Italians, love to dress up and won't venture out unless they look like they always have: elegant, abject slaves to fashion. They are also historically accustomed to seeing oddly costumed foreigners and rarely bat an eyelid at halter-tops, crotch-hugging shorts, tee shirts and ridiculous hats. Comfortable shoes are absolutely essential: the city on the water demands a great deal of walking. Outside of mid-summer, bring rain gear or an umbrella. Be warned that film and books in English cost twice as much as at home. Opera glasses or binoculars and a small torch may come in handy in gloomy churches or hotels. For picnics, pack a corkscrew and pocket knife.

Post Office

In the Renaissance, Venice's intelligence network could get news of Vasco da Gama's rounding of Cape Horn in 72 hours; nowadays a letter to Lisbon will take about three weeks. The central Venetian branch of the industrialized world's most wretched, dawdling postal tortoises is at Fondaco dei Tedeschi, by the Rialto Bridge (Mon–Sat 8:15–7). If you're having mail sent *poste restante* to Venice, have it addressed *Fermo Posta*, Fondaco dei Tedeschi 80100, give it longer than you ever imagined possible to arrive and pick it up with your passport. There are other post offices at the foot of Piazza S. Marco (Calle dell'Ascensione) and on the Zattere, although you can purchase stamps at any tobacco shop. Telegrams may be sent 24 hours a day from the central post office or by ringing 186, or 170 for international telegrams.

If it matters when your post arrives, or if you want to send a package and avoid the incredibly fussy Posta Italiana red tape, an efficent, and usually less costly alternative is Alimondo, although they're located out in Marghera (Via Portenari 5, tel 932 082), or the international courier DHL, in Mestre (Via Torino 11, tel 957 944).

Public Holidays

Shops, banks, offices and schools in Venice are also closed on official holidays: 1 January, 6 January, Easter Monday, 25 April (Liberation Day and St Mark's Feast Day), 1 May (Labour Day), 15 August (Assumption of the BVM), 1 November (All Saints' Day), 8 December (Immaculate Conception of the BVM), Christmas, and 26 December (Santo Stefano).

Religious Affairs

Venetians have always liked to go to church, some for piety's sake, and some for the music (Venetian church music was long famous throughout Europe, so much so that in the 18th century churches like La Pietà were built as concert halls), and some to flirt—many a spy's report to the Council of Ten concerns dissolute women waiting for propositions in the side chapels. The average mass was drowned in chatter until the priest raised the Host, when all dropped to their knees in silence, only to continue as rowdily as ever afterwards. Lalande, an 18th-century French astronomer, recounted perhaps the most telling anecdote on the Venetian view of religion. An English peer attended mass with a Venetian senator and failed to kneel down at the solemn moment. 'Kneel!' ordered the Venetian. 'But I don't believe in the Transubstantiation,' protested the Englishman. 'Well, neither do I, for heaven's sake,' said the Senator. 'But get down on the floor like me or get out the door!'

Nowadays Venetians are among the most pious of Italians, and whenever you want to visit a church the chances are there will be a mass going on that you ought not to interrupt. Persevere, and bring a handful of coins for the lights. On Sunday at 11:15 am, noon, 12:45 and 6:45 pm there are masses in Latin at St Mark's; at San Moisè there are readings in English at 6:15 pm on Sunday. San Giorgio Maggiore has, on Sunday at 11 am, a mass with Gregorian chant. Non-Catholic services take place at:

Anglican, St George's, Campo S. Vio 870 on Sundays at 8:30 and 11:30 pm, with a Matins service at 10:30 am.
Evangelical Waldensian and Methodist, Campo S. Maria Formosa 5170, Sunday at 11 am.
Greek Orthodox, S. Giorgio, Ponte dei Greci 3412, at 11 and 12 am on Sundays.
Lutheran Evangelical, Campo SS. Apostoli 4443.
Synagogue services, Ghetto Vecchio, tel 715 012, Saturdays.

Telephones

Venice (telephone area code 041) is fairly well supplied with telephones, along the pavements, in bars, and most other public places. Nearly all

21

take coins, although often in bars you'll need to purchase tokens (*gettoni*). Local calls rarely eat up more than L200, although once you call long distance, the telephone becomes a real hog. Don't even try it for international calls: use the metered phones in the post offices (the AAST telephones in the Salizzada del Fontego dei Tedeschi, by the Rialto Bridge, or in Piazzale Roma) or telephone from your hotel (though beware the surcharges). To reverse charges, ask to call *reversibile*. The telephone country code for UK is 0044, for the USA and Canada 001; for Australia 0061. For information (in English) on international calls or on calling with your credit card, dial 170.

Tourist Information

The main information office is in the corner of Piazza S. Marco, to the far left as you face the square (Ascensione 71c, tel 522 6356.) The branch offices at the railway station (tel 715 016) and the bus station in Piazzale Roma (tel 522 7402) offer accommodation services. There's also an office on the Marghera autostrada (tel 921 638), and on the Lido at Gran Viale 6, tel 765 721.

The main source in English for current events is *Un Ospite di Venezia*, distributed free at tourist offices. If you can read Italian, the two local newspapers are the *Gazzettino* and *Nuova Venezia*, both with listings of films etc. in Venice and the *terra firma*. Another detailed source of information is the monthly city magazine *Marco Polo*, with articles written in Italian but summarized in English.

Youth Passes

The *Comune* of Venice offers a special youth (*Carta Giovani*) pass to people between the ages of 16 and 27, which gives discounts on the city's attractions. Apply at the APT offices; take a photo and your passport.

Venetian Topics

Black Death in Venice

Whenever the 20th century leaves a bad taste in your mouth, give some consideration to the 14th. Things were bad all over Europe then, but in Italy they were so rotten that historians speak of a collective death wish in the 1340s. Calamities of every kind befell the peninsula—earthquakes, floods and some of the worst weather on record; political upheavals and disorder and wars raged everywhere (Venice was locked in its death struggle with Genoa). Bankruptcies wrecked the economy; in 1346–47 the crops were so poor that thousands of people died of starvation. Even the wine went off.

The Italians were exhausted and physically and spiritually resigned to disaster. And, as if on cue, the worst epidemic of all time, the Black Death, arrived on the scene in October 1347—brought from the Crimea on Venetian galleys (the Venetians, however, blame it on the Genoese). And as usual Venice suffered the most: as the densely populated chief port of entry from the East, the city had a dire record of 70 major epidemics in 700 years. No wonder the Venetians lived so intensely, when life itself was so precarious.

On 20 March 1348, Doge Andrea Dandolo set up a council to deal with the plague. The dead were taken on special barges to be buried at S. Erasmo on the Lido and at a new cemetery at the long lost S. Marco

Boccacalme, or simply sunk into the waters of the lagoon. Beggars were forbidden to exhibit corpses (an old custom) to raise alms. Strict immigration controls were ordered, and all travellers were ordered to spend 40 days in quarantine at Nazarethum island (its name later elided to Lazzaretto became widely used for all such islands).

All these measures were too late. At its worst the Black Death killed 600 Venetians a day; the total dead numbered an almost incredible 100,000 (about half the population). Helpless against the epidemic, most doctors in Venice either died or fled in horror. There was one exception, a health officer named Francesco da Roma, who received an annuity of 25 gold ducats as a reward for remaining in Venice during the Black Death. When asked why he stayed when everyone else fled, he replied: 'I would rather die here than live anywhere else.'

Byron Goes Swimming

Like lime (or linden) blossoms, Venice tends to relax the mind, or at least the logical centres; this is especially true in the minds of those who, like the rascally Aretino, 'live by the sweat of their ink'. Many have written their worst books about the city (the most recent culprits are Hemingway and Muriel Spark). Legions of other writers have been unable to resist the challenge of describing Venice; they strive to leave their mark on the city with the persistence of spraying tomcats. Some are mercifully content to settle for vignettes or epigrams. D.H. Lawrence, who loved the dry desert of Arizona, called Venice 'an abhorrent, green, slippery city'; for Boris Pasternak Venice was 'swelling like a biscuit soaked in tea'. In the end perhaps all descriptions meet in a soft centre, as Italo Calvino's Marco Polo commented to Kublai Khan in a lovely book called *Invisible Cities*: 'Every time I describe a city I am saying something about Venice.'

But on certain metabolisms, lime (or linden) blossoms have the opposite effect and stimulate rather than relax the brain. Doctors of literature could call it the 'Byron syndrome' and can study the symptoms from the poet's arrival in 1816, his heart full of romance as he rented a villa on the Brenta to compose the last canto of his *Childe Harolde's Pilgrimage*. Venice checks in here with a rather tepid 'fairy city of the heart.' Its canals at least afforded him the personal advantage of being able to swim anywhere (his limp made him shy); on one occasion he swam a race from the Lido to the Rialto bridge and was the only man to finish.

It wasn't long before the emotional polish of *Childe Harolde* began to crack. To Byron's surprise, romantic Venice didn't aggravate his romantic temperament, but cured him of it; the ironic detachment and mock heroics of the city's own *ottava rima* tradition made him question all his previous assumptions. He went to live in the Palazzo Mocenigo on the Grand Canal, in the company of 14 servants, a dog, a monkey, a wolf, a fox and a passionate, garlicky baker's daughter who stabbed him in the thumb with a table fork (which so angered Byron that he ordered her out, whereupon which she threw herself off the balcony into the Grand Canal). Under such circumstances, all that had been breathless passion reeked of the ridiculous, as he himself admitted:

> And the sad truth which hovers o'er my desk
> Turns what was once romantic to burlesque.

Venice and its women and its noble Armenian monks and its love of liberty galvanized Byron and set his mind free to write first *Beppo: A Venetian Story*, spoofing Venice's *cavalieri serventi* (escort/lovers—even the nuns had them), balls, and Titians and its gondolas (see below), while celebrating the freedom of its people. He wrote two bookish plays on Venetian themes, *Marino Faliero* and *The Two Foscari*, and most importantly began his satirical masterpiece, *Don Juan*.

Meanwhile too much sex was beginning to take a toll: an English acquaintance in 1818 wrote home: 'His face had become pale, bloated, and sallow, and the knuckles on his hands were lost in fat'. Byron became infatuated with the Contessa Teresa Guiccioli and left Venice to move in with her and her husband in Ravenna. But having tasted freedom in Venice, Byron began to chafe; the Contessa was 'taming' him. He bundled up the manuscript of *Don Juan* and left for Greece, only to die of fever at age 36 in its war of independence. His last moments were soothed by his faithful gondolier Tita Falsieri, who for love had followed him to Greece.

Cake Crumbs

You can usually judge a place by its cakes. Take the sensuous if somewhat Cartesian rows of tarts and éclairs in a French patisserie, or the anal-retentive, not-a-crystal-of-sugar-out-of-place perfection in Austria, or the comfortably plump pies and buns at the British baker's, or the no-holds-barred American chain doughnut shops that sell 50 varieties 24 hours a day, or the Turk's predilection for exotic delights made of roses, quinces, almonds, and pistachios with names like 'Nipples in Honey' or 'Lady's Thighs'.

And Venice? If this is your first trip, close your eyes and play psycho-geographic-pastriologist for a moment. Imagine what awaits you in the most beautiful city in the world, a centre of culture and delicate refinement, midway between the east and west, in close historical contact with the luscious Austro-Hungarian apricot and poppy-seed strudel culture and the lavish chocolate-and-cream traditions of Northern Italy and Switzerland, not to mention the honey-laden walnut confections of Greece, and the sinful masterpieces of Turkey. Just imagine it. Venetian pastries must be nothing less than an elegant, delicate synthesis of ingredients and cultures as sublime and fantastical as St Mark's.

Now open your eyes and look in the window of the typical Venetian *pasticceria* and what do you see? Spotted shoe soles called *panserotti* or *zaletti* made of yellow maize flour and laid out to dry in the sun; lengths of coarse braided rope called *kranz* with sultanas and whole almonds wedged in the cracks; miniature sarcophagi (*alleanza alla frutta*), filled with chunks of mummified candied fruit in Murano-glass colours; iron rings for mooring boats (*bussolai Buranei*); and crumbling bricks called *pan di Dogi* rejected on the building site of the Great Pyramid. Not to mention a vile assortment of dehydrated brownish balls, possibly rolled by dung beetles.

What does it all mean? Could Venice really be a very simple, and rather humble place behind its complex and variegated façades? In many ways it is. But all sugar psychology aside, these inept cakes support a great historical truth: Venetians can't cook.

Gondolas

The gondola, Venice's most enduring symbol, was first mentioned during the reign of Vitale Falier, way back in 1094. It took another five or six hundred years or so to evolve into its present form, perfectly adapted to Venice's unique environment of narrow, shallow canals that often intersect at right angles: it has a flat underside and, unlike any other vessel, an asymmetrical hull, 24 cm wider on the left than the right, so that it tends to lean on the right, creating a pivot that helps the gondolier posed on the stern manoeuvre the craft with one long oar.

A gondola measures precisely 10.87 m in length, and 1.42 m maximum width. It is built out of eight different woods—fir, cherry, mahogany, larch, walnut, oak, lime, and elm—that must be seasoned in the dockyard, or *squero*, a word believed to be derived from the Greek *eskàrion* for shipyard. It is then carefully hand-crafted, and then given the traditional ornaments: a *forcola*, or walnut oarlock, so sensuous and beautiful in shape that people buy them as works of art; the peculiar-shaped *ferro* on the prow, its six divisions said to represent Venice's *sestieri*, its double curve said to symbolize the tilde-shaped Giudecca, and the blade, said to represent in one go the Rialto Bridge and the ducal bonnet; also mandatory are two brass sea horses and the curly metal tail. The whole is painted black, still obeying sumptuary laws of 1562, which sought to limit the vast sums noble families were spending to tart up their watery carriages—note the brightly-coloured gondolas in the paintings of Carpaccio. Most of these had the now vanished *felze*, wooden shelters which protected passengers from the elements and permitted a legend-ary amount of hanky-panky behind proto-Venetian blinds, as Byron apparently knew all too well:

> And up and down the long canals they go
> And under the Rialto shoot along,
> By night and day, all paces, swift and slow,
> And round the theatres, a sable throng,
> They wait in their dusk livery of woe,
> But not to them do awful things belong,
> For sometimes they contain a deal of fun,
> Like mourning coaches when the funeral's done.
> —*Beppo*, verse 20

In the 18th century there were 14,000 gondolas; today there are less than 500, and all nearly exclusively used in the tourist trade. Every few weeks in hot weather they gather so many weeds on the bottom that they have to be cleaned. An unlucky gondola will become so warped in five years that it's only fit for ferrying passengers across the Grand Canal (*traghetto*), and when it fails there it is burned in the glass furnaces of Murano. So if 55 minutes in a gondola seems dear, figure in the expense, the mainten-ance and lifespan of the average gondola, and the brief season in which a gondolier makes his living.

Since the 14th century, each gondolier belonged to one of 16 *traghetti*, or landings, which had their own constitution and laws and clubhouse, formerly clustered along the Zattere. Much has been written on their strange cries, almost never heard today: 'Premi!' they would cry if they wanted to pass on the left, or 'Stali!' to pass on the right, and 'Sciar!' if they were about to stop. Their haunting yodels in the night in 1858 inspired Wagner, who incorporated the sound as the long horn note that begins Act Three of *Tristan and Isolde*. Nowadays, gondola music is limited to a tenor crooning Neapolitan pizza classics for organized tourist flotillas. And they were quick to quarrel, with hot-blooded insults like 'You Son of a Cow!' or 'Spy!' or 'Assassin!', or 'The Madonna of your *traghetto* is a whore not worth two candles!' or 'Your saint is a rascal who can't even make a decent miracle!'—insults that grew ever more vicious the further apart they were. For the Venetians, as Montesquieu said, were the best people in the world, and almost never came to blows. Modern gondoliers are especially genteel; most are Communists, and many are very good looking. Venetians lately have been more upset than usual over the neglect and clownishness of the Rome government. When the Prime Minister and other big shots came to Venice for a festival last year, the gondoliers to a man refused to carry them. Which proved, at least to the leader writer of *Il Gazzettino*, that 'Venetians still have backbone'.

The Guilded Society

One of the most amazing facts about Venice is that the people, completely shut out of power by the 1297 'Locking' of the *Maggior Consiglio*, never revolted in the 500 years that followed. There were occasional riots, especially by the seafarers in the Renaissance, who were universally mistreated and often cheated. But by and large, the Venetians lived much better and with more security than their mainland counterparts. When Napoleon barged in on the scene to introduce the democratic joys of the French Revolution, it was ironically the people who wept, whereas many patricians were so relieved they danced with the soldiers.

The secret of Venice's popular success was a precocious sense of social justice. Venice's merchant aristocrats, who never claimed any kind of divine right or natural superiority, knew the best way to insure their monopoly of power and their profits was to devote themselves to the public good: the only real privilege a patrician had was to serve the state. All the classes mingled together in the streets and at festivals, with no signs of deference beyond the requirements of common courtesy. There were even laws that *doubled* the punishment when a patrician committed a crime against a commoner. Europe's other aristocrats thought their Venetian cousins were bonkers.

The most important factor in maintaining social stability actually cost the patricians very little in time or money: they encouraged co-operative, independent guilds and confraternities (*scuole*), just when many European princes were trying to limit them, the way modern politicians try to bust up unions. At the fall of the Republic, there were over 300 of these corporations: six *Scuole Grandi*, or large religious and charitable confraternities (like San Rocco); large, politically influential guilds like the glass-makers and arsenal workers; the club-like *scuole* for foreigners (like San Giovanni degli Schiavoni); down to the humble fruiterers' guild, whose members had the ancient privilege of annually presenting the doge with their finest melons.

The *scuole* were the backbone of everyday life in Venice, 'republics within the Republic'. Each had its own constitution, a body of electors, a senate (*banca*) and doge (the *gastaldo*); each decided what was best for the trade or society and its members. They regulated pay, settled quarrels, controlled and maintained the standards of Venetian crafts, promoted the best craftsmen and supervised the selection of apprentices. Long before Marx's 'from each according to his abilities, to each according to his needs' Venice was paying workers at the same job a different wage, depending on whether they had a wife or children to support. Each member paid dues according to his earnings and in return had access to the guild hospital and guild school for his children, was given a pension in his old age, and knew that the *scuola* would support his wife and children if he couldn't. Many a member left the confraternity a tidy sum in his will, often to beautify the church or guild hall—today among the finest things to see in Venice. Some even loaned the Republic money in times of need.

One of the first things Napoleon did was suppress the *scuole*; to his ideal of a modern, central government, they seemed like medieval anachronisms. It was like pulling the rug out from under the people, who at one blow lost their security and their chance to control their own affairs, and it wasn't long before a third of the Venetian workforce had to turn to the modern, central government dole.

Heart of Glass

Ever since the Syrians invented glass-blowing in the 1st century, the craft has always had a certain air of magic to it, an alchemical process that transforms sand with fire and air into something hard and clear. The magical aspect was the key of Werner Herzog's 1970s' film *Heart of Glass*, in which the entire cast of non-actors played their roles while under hypnosis. The plot centred around a German glass-manufacturing family, who had forgotten the ancestral secret of making a rare ruby crystal, and it was the fatal obsession of the young son to rediscover the lost secret. There are fascinating scenes of men blowing glass before infernal kilns, while the prophet from the mountain (the only character not hypnotized) tries to dissuade the son against seeking the hidden magic.

The Romans were the first in Europe to refine this alchemy into art. Among those who took refuge from the Huns in the lagoon, there must have been a Roman glassblower or two, even though the first Venetian document to mention one dates from the 980s. The fragments of glass that survive from that period are simple and utilitarian. In the 12th century Murano invented a process of producing glass panes from blown cylinders, which brought Venetian glass its first fame, a technological breakthrough that opened up the façades and let light into the cramped, courtyard-less Venetian palaces. Perhaps the most beautiful products of this functional period are the transparent glasses and lamps, as clear as rock crystal (hence the name 'crystal'), a technique invented in the 1450s, just in time to illuminate so many Renaissance paintings.

At this stage the only way to add colour to glass was through lead enamel or *smalto*, melted over the glass or mosaic *tesserae*. But a revolution occurred on Murano in the early 15th century when Angelo Barovier (1405–60), a member of one of Venice's most venerable glass-making dynasties, began to make glass in colours. The ancient Roman technique called *murrine* was rediscovered, enabling glass-makers to create designs by laying cold pieces of different coloured glass together and firing them together in the kiln. The famous Barovier nuptial cup, with its couple bathing in a fountain, is a superb example of the new art.

After that there was no going back—beginning in the 16th century Murano became a laboratory for ever more elaborate designs and techniques: *Vetro a filigrana*, the most original technique from Murano, consisted of thread-like rods of white glass 'woven' on to the surface in free-form patterns; *vetro lattino* or milk glass, imitating Chinese porcelain; *vetro a ghiaccio*, with a rugged, ice-like surface made by suddenly dropping the temperature in the glass process; *vetro graffito*, with designs scratched on the surface with a diamond; *vetro a pettine*, or 'combed glass' or *vetro a penne* with a wavy design; or the very difficult to make *venturina* or *stellaria* glass, shot through with shiny copper crystals. Murano also learned how to make coloured glass that looked so much like semi-precious stones that in the early 1600s a law had to be passed banning the manufacture of false gemstones. You'll see examples of these revived traditional techniques on a stroll down Murano's glass canal; many factories make souvenirs you can take home without any embarrassment.

In the 19th century, when the entire industry was in decline, Murano's glass-makers stayed alive by producing tons of glass beads and geegaws for European colonialists to trade to the natives in Asia and Africa—a compromise from which their art has never really recovered. Today, collecting dust by a filigree glass bowl stands the most lurid, simpering green clown in the hemisphere; chandeliers dangling glass flowers of death glow overhead. Glossy scorpions and pyramids seem to be fashionable.

Pondering the range of kitsch belched from Murano's kilns, you begin to suspect that the whole island has been hypnotized, like Herzog's glassblowers, for the past hundred years. But alchemy, like most enchantments, is out of fashion these days, or seems forbidden, and it's really not suprising to see monsters in glass as well as in every other aspect of modern life.

The Invasion of the Body Snatchers

Long before sci-fi there were the Venetians, whose ghoulish mania for stealing the corpses of saints is one the odder perversities that criss-cross their history. Of course they had nothing to do with the origins of the cult of relics: credit for that goes mostly to Pope Gregory the Great in the 6th century, who for the glory of the Roman Catholic Church shamelessly exploited the superstitions of his age by putting the papal seal of respectability on the cult of relics, miracles and saints. Praying to, or better yet, owning a bit of a saint was like having a hot line to him or her in heaven. For centuries mouldering bones and withered cadavers (some kept 'incorrupted' with arsenic and wax) were the greatest status symbol a city could hope for, and competition for the ones deemed most influential was intense. A prime candidate for sainthood, like Catherine of Siena, would scarcely breathe her last before the relic-mongers started pulling apart her anatomy (Venice, a bit slow off the mark that time, only managed to come away with a foot).

But on the whole the Venetians were without parallel in this Hallowe'en treasure hunt; no other people went about it with so much freebooting enthusiasm or so much encouragement from the State. The reason isn't hard to seek: as a new, self-made city Venice needed relics to gain the respect of and outdo its rivals. It also needed all the ju-ju it could muster against the plague.

By 1519, the *Serenissima* had snatched 55 intact saintly bodies and hundreds of smaller relics: a veritable *cordon sanitaire* of saints, as H.V. Morton called it, including some of Heaven's biggest celebrities: SS. Lucy, Zacharias, Helen, Isidore, John the Almsgiver, Donato and the proto-martyr Stephen, the last brought from Byzantium in 1105 and carried in state on the shoulder of the Doge himself. The most celebrated and valuable haul of all, though, was the first: the theft from Alexandria in 828 of the relics of St Mark, the Apostle of the Italians, a caper plotted down to the last detail. When the Apostle was lifted from his tomb, it is said, such a sweet smell spread over Alexandria that everyone knew 'Mark was stirring' and rushed to see his tomb, but the Venetians fooled them with a substitute body. They got their prize past Egyptian customs—as depicted on the mosaics of St Mark's—by hiding it in a barrel of pickled pork.

Nabbing the remains of S. Roch (San Rocco), one of the key 'plague saints,' was another coup. Before becoming a pile of desirable relics, Roch was a young nobleman of Montpellier who gave his fortune away to the poor, then made a pilgrimage to Rome. City after city he passed through was stricken by plague. He rendered what assistance he could to the sufferers he found, until on his way back home he himself was stricken with a horrid ulcer on his thigh. He retreated to a cave so no one had to hear his groans, while his faithful dog brought him food and licked his wound. Roch recovered but was so changed by his sufferings that when he returned home, claiming to be Roch, he was arrested as a spy and thrown in prison. After languishing for five years he died. His gaolers found his cell flooded with light, and there was a note saying that he would help anyone stricken with plague who called upon his name. Some Venetians disguised as pilgrims stole his body from Montpellier in 1485, before he was even canonized.

There was even a sham heist: the robbery in 1087 of St Nicholas from Myra, in Anatolia. Word of Venice's intention to steal the relics had leaked to rival Bari, whose merchants beat the Venetians to the precious body (for Nicholas, better known in the West as Santa Claus, was the patron saint of sailors). But the Venetians proved to be very poor losers. Instead of admitting defeat, they contrived a fake body and built a church to St Nick on the Lido, for centuries pretending in the face of all fact that it sheltered the real McCoy.

Lion Fever

The Venetians were hardly the only people in the world to adopt the lion as their sign, although theirs is a winged lion with a book. This of course symbolizes St Mark, but no one really knows why. Some say Mark 'roared like a lion' when he preached, or that lion cubs open their eyes after three days, the same period as the Resurrection, or that the Christians endowed each of the four Evangelists with a key astronomical constellation. The inscription in the lion's book, *Pax tibi, Marce, Evangelista meus* are the words the angel used to greet Mark in his Venetian dream. But it's the sheer number of lions that makes Venice really stand apart: there are at least a couple of thousand in the city itself and perhaps twice as many in the lands once ruled by the Republic.

The bookish lion is first believed to have made its appearance on the standard of Doge Pietro Orseolo II, when he conquered Dalmatia in the year 1000. The oldest lion to survive dates from the 13th or early 14th century. It was embedded in the base of the campanile of S. Aponal (now removed to the Correr Museum store rooms), a disembodied owl-like creature, with staring eyes, pin curls and a kind of pie pan about his head, claws digging into a closed iron-bound book. But Venice, unlike other states, had no interest in standardizing their symbol, although there were two favoured poses: the standing lion (*en passant*), or the upper torso (*sejent erect*), usually emerging from the sea, known in Venetian dialect as the *leone in molea*, 'lion in a soft shell' (because its wings are folded back like a pair of crab pincers). Each new member of the Venetian pride had to depend on the talent or attitude of the artist, and some, especially in the provinces, are among the funniest things in Italy: Chioggia still smarts over its puny 'Cat of St Mark.'

Venetian lions reached their peak in the Middle Ages and Renaissance, when they were as proud and brave as the Venetians themselves (see the regal Foscari lion on the Ducal Palace's Porta della Carta). In the Republic's death throes, in the 17th and 18th centuries, the lions responded by becoming twisted, clumsy and grotesque, reaching an incomparable nadir in the ghastly caricature of an animal in S. Giobbe. By the end of the Republic, a general lion revulsion set in, encouraged by Napoleon, who changed the inscription in the lion's book from *Pax tibi, Marce* to 'The Rights and Dignity of Man'. 'At last, he's turned the page,' quipped a gondolier. A general lion massacre took over a thousand victims in Venice itself; many lions you see today are 19th-century reproductions. Smaller felines have generally fared better, ever since

Petrarch spent time in Venice in the company of a stuffed cat called the Laura II: there are moves afoot to declare the city officially 'the stray cat capital of the world'.

Minor Venetians

It is hard to imagine any state so paranoid about fame. Merely to be a citizen of Venice was to suffer the eternal whining insistence of the republican super-ego: 'all for one and one for all' could have been the motto of these amphibious musketeers. But while there was little positive reinforcement for good citizenship, there were plenty of deterrents to encourage Venetians to toe the line—no plaques to commemorate its Marco Polos or Vivaldis, but plenty of marble inscriptions ready for the homes of thieves, traitors and other bad eggs so their descendants would live with the ignominy for ever and ever.

And so, wandering about the city, you will learn little about Venetians who actually contributed something to the world beyond the lagoon. Venetians like John Cabot, who discovered Canada for Henry VIII (he has a plaque, at the foot of Via Garibaldi, but it was put there by the grateful Canadians), and Alvise da Mosto (d. 1488), discoverer of the Cape Verde Islands and author of the first eye-witness account of the sub-Sahara, or Gianfrancesco Straparola (d. 1557) who wrote a collection of 75 bawdy tales called *Le piacevole notti*, which contained the earliest known version of *Puss in Boots*. Then there were the founders of two of Renaissance Europe's greatest publishing houses: the great Aldus Manutius (Aldo Manuzio, 1450–1515), who established the first serious publishing house, printing for the first time over a hundred Greek classics; and Gabriele Giolito (d. 1578), who built up the most important vernacular press in Italy, publishing Ariosto, Aretino, and Castiglione. Luca Pacioli (d. 1517) was a Franciscan mathematician who worked with Leonardo da Vinci in Milan on the subject of mathematical and artistic proportions. Vincenzo Catena (1480s–1531) a wealthy merchant, was the first known amateur to dabble in painting (his masterpiece, *Judith*, is in the Palazzo Querini-Stampalia). A certain Fra Mauro, who lived in the convent on the island of San Michele, drew in the 1450s the most accurate map of the world to date (now in the Biblioteca Marciana). Giovanni Poleni invented an arithmetical machine in 1709 (now in Milan's Museum of Science and Technology), the precursor of the calculator. While most people have heard of Venice's great writer of comedies, Carlo Goldoni, few know of the charming fairy-tale dramas of his rival, Carlo Gozzi, who wrote *The Love of Three Oranges* and the original *Turandot*.

Some of the most important Venetian contributions were to music: Andrea Gabrieli (d. 1586) and his nephew, Giovanni Gabrieli (d. 1612), leading composers of the richly sonorous and harmonically complex Venetian school of music, often employing several choirs; Gioseffo Zarlino (d. 1590), *maestro di cappella* at St Mark's and the leading music theoretician of his age; Ottavio Petrucci (d. 1539), inventor of a three-stage technique for printing music with movable type, who became the first commercial publisher of music in 1501 (if you've ever wondered why all musical notations are in Italian). Then there was Lorenzo da Ponte (d. 1838), Mozart's favourite Italian librettist, who somehow ended up living in the suburbs of Philadelphia.

Women lived in oriental seclusion until the 18th century. Before then, the most celebrated were prostitutes, whose wit, education and sophistication were much sought after in the Renaissance: Venice's courtesan culture rates with those of ancient Greece and medieval Japan. In the lusty 16th-century dawn of tourism, Venice had 11,654 registered tax-paying prostitutes, dressed in red and yellow 'like tulips'; there was even a guide book, listing addresses and prices. Two were as celebrated for their poetry as for their charms: the 'new Sappho', the beautiful Gaspara Stampa (1523–54), considered one of the best and most original of Renaissance women poets, who wrote elegant verses of burning passion, and Veronica Franco (1546–91), a more worldly, narrative poet who repented in her old age and founded a home for her less fortunate sisters.

Then there were honest women like Marietta Robusti (1556–1590), Tintoretto's talented daughter, but married to a man who confined her to painting portraits of his colleagues and stifled even posthumously, for none of her works are on public display. A patrician's daughter, Elena Lucrezia Corner Piscopia, became the first woman to earn a university degree (a doctorate of philosophy, at Padua, in 1678). The next century produced Contessa-cum-courtesan Marina Querini-Benzon who inspired Venice's most famous love song, *La Biondina in gondoleta*— the model for America's beloved blonde in a convertible. She was painted by Longhi and her wit was much admired by Stendhal. She remained frisky enough to have a fling with Byron in her 60s, when she was tremendously fat owing to an inordinate love for *polenta*, which she kept tucked in her bodice for convenient nibbling whenever she felt peckish—hence her nickname *Fiumetta* or 'Little Smoke'. She was last seen dancing with the poet Ugo Foscolo around Napoleon's Liberty Tree in Piazza S. Marco.

Mordor-on-the-Lagoon

For a view of a slightly different Venice, stand on the Zattere, across the broad Giudecca Canal from Palladio's Church of the Redentore, and look towards the west. Over at the far end of the Giudecca, you'll see such classics of Venetian architecture as the old Venezia Brewery, the Women's Penitentiary and the massive brick Victorian hulk called the Mulino Stucky, a flour factory built in the 1890s by a German architect; it is abandoned now, one of the most awkward and unloved landmarks of the city. On the horizon, the steel and concrete skyline of Marghera closes the view down the canal: tall smokestacks in parfait stripes, glittering oil tanks and refinery towers, the perfect arch of a pipeline crossing high over a canal.

Shelley and Keats, one supposes, would faint in dismay. John Ruskin would alternately thunder and weep. And almost every writer since, it seems, has saved up some venom for Marghera and Mestre, malignant as Tolkien's Mordor and the blight on their city of dreams, a sleazy imposition by some itchy-palmed tycoon on the forlorn *Serenissima*. From some newspaper features, you might imagine that this little patch of dark satanic mills was magically apported here from the Ruhr valley by an evil sorcerer just to spoil our fun. Imposition, though, is not exactly the correct word, for almost all of these modern atrocities were the work of Venetians.

One of the chief conspirators was a certain Count Volpi di Misurata, a local promoter who had many chances to do favours for his home town as Mussolini's finance minister in the 1920s (the Fascists were never unpopular in Venice). Mussolini himself was against the road causeway, but the Venetians managed to get it built anyhow. The authors of the wacky planning schemes that occasionally surface, intending to bring cars into the city or to fill in half the lagoon for new development, are inevitably Venetians, and since the war Venetians have voted with their feet and shown us their new idea of how a city should look—shapeless concrete Mestre.

Mestre and Marghera are Venice too, as much as Piazza S. Marco and the Rialto. The real Venice is a hard-working port city of some 340,000 souls, with all of the common reflexes and attitudes of modern port cities. In matters of aesthetics, it is as tenacious as a bulldog about preserving the past, and pathetically lazy about improving the present. It has an extremely unusual *centro storico*, one that creates unique problems in transport and economic efficiency. Its people aren't at all interested in the 'Death in Venice' complex of jaded foreigners: they want to earn an honest living. Look at that view of Marghera again: not so awful after all, perhaps—a colourful piece of abstract art, one of the more fantastical apparitions of the enchanted lagoon. It is beginning to look rather *Venetian*. And it will look even better when they get all the pollution-control equipment installed.

No Expo

'All chance is perilous, and all change unsound,' as Spenser wrote in the Fifth Canto of *The Faerie Queene*. Still, in the face of tourism's excess and the delicate sensibilities of the 'Save Venice' angels, a brave band of idealists and entrepreneurs led by foreign minister Gianni De Michelis, himself a native Venetian, attempted to promote their own fairy city as the site of Expo 2000. The theme was to be Venice as a 'City of the Mind'. Not that Venice itself has produced a blessed lot intellectually once you've counted Paolo Sarpi, but it's amazing what Venice nurtured and inspired—what in the Renaissance was known as the 'Myth of Venice'. The Republic's uniquely successful form of government was the envy of every ruler, its religious tolerance made it the printing centre of Europe for centuries, its strange setting has always inspired writers, poets and painters. The emphasis of the Expo was to be based on the city's historic solutions to contemporary issues: in bridging east and west, religious and minority tolerance, social welfare, technology and industry, medicine (its university at Padua was long Europe's top medical school), environmental control, regional government, and to look from the past to the possibilities for the new millennium.

International hackles went up at once: the *New York Times* called the plan a 'floating Disneyland', and a British critic intoned apocalyptically that it would mean the end of Venice. At home, the 'No Expo' campaign cranked up so much sound and fury that the Italian government withdrew Venice's proposal at the last minute, right from under the noses of the judges of the International Bureau of Expositions. No one really knew how many visitors the Expo would have brought to Venice (23 million in its four-month run, said opponents, or four times the annual number of tourists, even though most of the fair would be concentrated on the mainland and in the abandoned expanses of the Arsenale), but most Venetians agreed with their mayor Antonio Casellati in that it would have been a 'biblical disaster' that would have sunk the city into its own soup of algae at the very least.

No city in the world is as old and delicate and fragile. No city has fewer children—only 4000 or so—nor such a high proportion of older people, or foreigners, determined to avoid any changes beyond restoring what's already there. No city is losing its population so quickly: because of high prices, lack of jobs or comfortless unrestored housing, emigration has bled Venice to 70,000, half of its population in 1950. These facts, and a night walk in the city, bring to mind the danger of another kind of biblical disaster: that of the desert.

Perhaps the Expo was a bad idea, and as Venice is admittedly a unique case it is very hard to imagine just what it would take to bring it back to life as a real city. Perhaps the least perilous changes evolve organically, slowly and naturally; yet even those changes are threatened if Venice's native and foreign curators refuse to let their rare butterfly out of its glass paperweight to give it a chance to live or die. To see the once dauntless 'market-place of the Morning and the Evening lands' as Goethe called it, become self-absorbed with its own arthritis and its varicose canals, and Byron's 'Revel of the earth' safely tucked into bed at 10 pm is unbearably sad. If Venice, which once stole relics from everyone else is transformed into everyone else's relic, then it might as well be devoured by the algae.

La Sensa

The name comes from Ascension Day, a movable feast that takes place 40 days after Easter. For 795 years of Venetian history, it meant much more: it was Venice's own symbolic apotheosis as the husband, lord, and master of the sea.

It was on Ascension Day in the year 1000, when Doge Pietro Orseolo II began his campaign against the Dalmatians—Venice's first foreign conquest and the source of such immense civic pride that the Doge took the title 'Duke of Dalmatia'. Whatever commemorative ceremony ensued was given a boost by Pope Alexander III in 1177, who gave the Doge a ring in gratitude for his help in securing the submission of Emperor Barbarossa: 'Let posterity remember that the sea is yours by right of conquest, subject to you as a wife to her husband,' said the Pope, and the Venetians, well pleased, decided to make sure posterity didn't forget.

What really got under the skin of Venice's many rivals was her joyously excessive arrogance, much of it concentrated in the quasi-religious rituals and glittering festivities of *La Sensa*, an astute mix of politics and religion and trade fair that followed the city's maxim: *primo di tutto Veneziani, poi Christiani* (Venetians first of all, and Christians second). It was also judged the finest party the world had to offer: no place could match its voluptuous splendour or its magnificent setting.

The day began with the procession of the Arsenale workers from the church of San Martino to the Piazzetta, where the ducal barge, the *Bucintoro* waited, a 100-foot floating centrepiece of gilded statues and flame-coloured velvet. There the *Arsenalotti* would be joined by the doge, playing his usual role as high priest, accompanied by his insignia—eight banners, six long silver trumpets and an umbrella (gifts from Alexander III)—and along with his retinue of dignitaries and musicians, he would board the *Bucintoro* and be rowed out to the Lido, accompanied by a fleet of other vessels: the gilded ships of the head of police and chief magistrates, embassy gondolas, a military parade, a procession of boats carrying the heads of the confraternities, followed by the patricians' gondolas and then the boats of the people, all lavishly decorated with carpets, garlands, banners and flowers. At the church of Sant'Elena, the doge would meet the ship of the patriarch and papal nuncio and sail to the port of San Nicolò del Lido, where the choir of St Mark's would sing as the patriarch boarded the *Bucintoro* to sail to the lighthouse, where the patriarch would bless the *Serenissima* and pour holy water into the sea (the *benedictio*), after which the doge would toss a golden wedding ring into the waves (the *Deponsatio*), declaring: 'With this, we wed thee, O Sea, in sign of our true and perpetual dominion'. This was the most exciting part of the festival, not only because horns would blast and bells would peal and everyone cheered at the top of their lungs, but because the *Bucintoro* was so flimsy and unseaworthy that there was always a chance of the doge falling in the sea and consummating the marriage—as one amused Ottoman sultan predicted he would.

Afterwards the doge would visit the chapel of San Nicolò to pay homage to the phoney relics of the patron of the sea, then preside over two banquets that the public was invited to watch: one for nobles and ambassadors and another for admirals, heads of the Arsenale and priests. After this, everyone would dress in their best finery for the opening of the *Sensa* fair in the Piazza—a market that lasted for a week, and later 15 days, where the latest silks and spices from the East would be displayed, along with the finest things the city could make, from glass and gold to works of art and sculpture—Canova's *Orpheus and Eurydice* was first shown in the *Sensa* fair of 1778. Most important was a large tyrannical doll called the 'Piavola da Franza' dressed in the latest French fashions who determined what Venetian women would wear during the next season. A crucial feature of *La Sensa*'s success was the liberty to wear masks, as during Carnival, ensuring crowds in the theatres, gambling den, and bawdy houses. And at midnight, candle-lit orchestras playing love songs floated down the Grand Canal.

A Day in 18th-century Venice

Cecilia Contarini

Their nerves unstrung by disease and the consequence of
early debaucheries, allow no natural flow of lively spirits ...
They pass their lives in one perpetual doze.
—*William Beckford*

It is already the sixth hour when Cecilia Contarini wakes to a new day in
the family palazzo on the Grand Canal; her eyelids have scarcely flut-
tered when her *cavaliere servente*, Rodrigo Sagredo is at her side. 'Good
morning, *bellissima*,' he murmurs, even though Cecilia's face is still
covered with strips of milk-soaked veal. Veal removed, Rodrigo's devotion is rewarded with a tender kiss; he had covered Cecilia's gambling
losses last night without blinking.

As Cecilia steps into a steaming bath scented with myrrh, Rodrigo
entertains her with a recital of the morning's gossip, much of it concern-
ing her own husband. Giancarlo is a senator, but one whose gambling at
the Ridotto and slumming in the sestiere's *malvasie* has more than once
attracted the attention of the Ten and their spies. None of this bothers
Cecilia as much as the news that Giancarlo's older brother had heard of
his foibles and was threatening to cut back their weekly allowance again;
'Ah, la Madonna!' she sighs. Rodrigo makes soft, sympathetic noises,
and soon has his lady smiling again.

While Cecilia lingers over her morning chocolate, flicking through the engraved visiting cards left by friends (most of them amusingly erotic, although there's one she nonchalantly slips into the pocket of her dressing gown), the tutor announces the children, who file in for morning dress inspection. In their jackets of stiff lace and gold brocade they are so irresistible (and immobile) that Cecilia gives each tot a big hug and kiss before the tutor shuffles them out again; their mother will not have to see them again until tomorrow.

That ritual over, it's time for the main business of the morning: hairdressing. Seeing that his charge is in good hands for the next six hours, Rodrigo ducks out to tend to some pressing business of his own at the convent of S. Zaccaria, where his sister, a nun, can always get him a loan. 'And which patch will La Signora choose today?' asks the hairdresser, primping the last blonde curl in place. Cecilia reflects for a moment, and remembers the note in her pocket. *'Assassina'*, she whispers: the hairdresser raises an eyebrow, and they both laugh.

It's November, 1770, in the reign of Doge Alvise Mocenigo IV. Although it's the sixth hour, Cecilia, like most patricians, is not up early. All over settecento Italy time was kept on a 24-hour basis, the day beginning at the sunset, with the ringing of the Angelus; noon and midnight varied day by day. Like every Venetian lady, noble or bourgeois, Cecilia has a cavaliere servente, *or* cicisbeo, *a kind of auxiliary husband who belonged to the same social class as she; more extravagant women had several. Rodrigo's role was to squire Cecilia about town, and to provide for her every little need from the moment she awoke until she went to bed; it was he who would escort her to a reception, ball, or theatre. No husband would be caught dead with his own wife. Like most* cicisbei *Rodrigo was even written into Cecilia's marriage contract. On the surface at least, all was accepted and respectable.*

After all, there was no such a thing as a love marriage in Venice. Husbands, who had their own oats to sow, supported cicisbeatura *to free them from tending to their wives. In most patrician families, one brother would be chosen to marry and produce heirs. The others, who remained in the family* palazzo *(and some whispered darkly, shared the family wife), followed careers in politics, the priesthood, or, very rarely now in the 1700s, in the military. Each brother would be given an allowance, augmented if he were elected to an important (and invariably expensive) office; all Venetian officials, from the princely procurators and ambassadors down, were expected to pay their own expenses. Besides these burdens, most noble families would rustle up a considerable dowry to marry off their eldest daughter, in the interests of a political alliance; extra daughters were sent off to convents. These unwilling nuns were a major source of Venetian scandal, but their convents played banker to noble families, giving them loans that were rarely repaid. When Napoleon suppressed the convents, half the nobles were forced into bankruptcy.*

The Council of Ten's spies shadowing Cecilia's wayward husband could safely be ignored. The Ten's power had so eroded at the end of the Republic that they did little more than issue stern warnings, to be studiously read and studiously ignored; the one offence that could bring real trouble was criticizing the government or suggesting reforms. Venice in its decline may have lost most of its conquests, its trading ports, its navy and its prestige, but the government was dourly determined to keep itself unchanged. Giancarlo caused concern because the malvasie, named after the Greek wine they peddled (malmsey) were notoriously used as common brothels and no place for a patrician. But they were popular nonetheless: some 20 streets are still called Calle di Malvasia. But standards were slipping everywhere.

In the 18th century Venetian women began a sexual revolution that makes the 1960s look prudish. Every traveller remarked on the beauty of the women—and the fact that it was hard to tell a noble lady from a prostitute. Venice, after all, rose from the waters like Venus, and was the perfect town for love, with its little alleys and canals. Every palace had several discreet entrances, and every gondolier, if he wanted to keep his job, was committed to complete secrecy (a really indiscreet gondolier faced drowning by his brethren). Still, the essential thing about Venetian love affairs was that no one took them very seriously; Byron's mistress, who leapt into the Grand Canal, was an exception to the rule.

If Venetian women cut loose, it was partly as a reaction to the lives of their foremothers. Ever since the founding of the city, its women had been treated like Byzantine chattels, forced to live such reclusive lives that all we know about them is that they spent half their time on their altane, or rooftop terraces, bleaching their hair. Cecilia, too, was a Venetian blonde, but with the aid of the hairdresser's dyes, that red golden colour was much easier to obtain. A lot of women had opted for wigs (in 1797 there were 850 wigmakers in Venice), but Cecilia was vain about her thick hair, which properly stacked up and curled, could hold so many fashionable fruits and flowers. The milk-soaked veal on her face was the equivalent of a modern mud pack.

The average noblewoman spent six or seven hours on her appearance every morning. Although the bulk of the hairdresser's work was on the tower of hair, he was also responsible for make-up on the face and breasts. This was never extreme in Venice, and the ideal was to look as 'natural' as possible, except for the artificial moles, or patches. The wearer used these as a code for onlookers to interpret her mood: a mole placed in a dimple meant she was feeling coquettish, if placed on the nose she was feeling rather forward. The assassina, *by the corner of the mouth, was the most daring of all.*

43

Once her toilette is over, Cecilia sends the hairdresser off with a note for her admirer, then dresses for church. It is Saturday and the orphan girls at La Pietà are performing a new mass, with the lovely Albertina, the darling of Venice, playing lead violin. Rodrigo dutifully appears with Cecilia's prayer book to escort her, and the family gondola is waiting. But they are late, and some English milords, in town for Carnival, have taken Cecilia's favourite seat. A row breaks out, made comical by the language barrier. Everyone contibutes their two cents worth, a brouhaha silenced only when the music begins.

Still laughing over the incident, Cecilia and Rodrigo leave church and call at a friend's house to don the traditional Carnival disguise: white beaked masks, or *bautte*, tricorne hats and concealing, long cloaks, or *tabarri*. By the time they reach the Piazza, it is heaving with other masqueraders, dancing bears, soothsayers, dentists, and Irish weightlifters. The cafés are overflowing. Seeing her opportunity, Cecilia quickly sets a time for Rodrigo to meet her for the theatre, then adroitly loses him in the crowd to slip down a back alley off the Mercerie. On her way, as chance would have it, she passes Giancarlo and his friends, masked as Tartars and Red Indians and singing racy songs to all passers-by. Cecilia manages to slip past them, but even if Giancarlo had somehow recognized his wife, they would have pretended not to know each other.

In the aftermath of the Great Interdict, the Church had less of a role to play in Venice than anywhere in Italy. The Senate had always maintained that its citizens were Venetians first and Christians second, and it didn't care for priests who tried to cow the Venetians into repenting for their sins—it made the state look bad. By the 18th century mass for many Venetians was just another social occasion. Throughout the service they behaved appallingly, chatting, flirting, quarrelling and playing with dogs, falling silent only for the elevation of the Host. Prostitutes hung about in the side chapels. The priest only stood a chance of being heard if he had a good voice; although Rome disapproved, many priests were castrati, *because the lagoon folk couldn't resist a soprano.*

Indeed the Venetians, of every walk of life, had an 'unbelievable infatuation' for music. Visitors wrote that there was simply no escape from singing; the narrow streets and canals offer excellent acoustics. Nearly everyone played an instrument or sang; the gondoliers were famous for singing passages from Tasso back and forth to each other across the night lagoon. Even the years would be named after the visits of celebrated singers. Orphan girls at La Pietà, Ospedaletto and the Incurabili were taught music and formed into orchestras of great renown (Vivaldi wrote most of his compositions for them). Their concerts, in ballroom churches built expressly for the purpose, were as much of a must for grand tourists as purchasing a Canaletto.

Carnival in Venice was more than the traditional ten-day celebration before Lent: it meant the licence to go about masked in total anonymity. In the 18th century the wearing of masks became legal for six months of the year to bring in more tourists and to let impoverished patricians go about the streets without shame. Carnival in Venice also meant gambling and the freedom to commit any indiscretion—to say anything to anybody, to crash parties, to do just what one pleased. Dressed like Cecilia in the bautta and tabarro (the concealing long domino cloak) it was impossible even to tell the sex of the wearer. It was extremely bad form ever to show any sign of recognizing a masked person: everyone from doge to scullery maid was simply addressed as Sior Maschera, or Mr Mask. There are many astounding things about Venice, but this may astound the most: for half the year the whole citizenry played at make-believe in wonderful costumes, incognito and single-mindedly devoted to fun, debauchery and cheating at cards.

It is getting dark as Cecilia meets Claudio, her gondolier, at the back entrance of her lover's *casino*. Claudio is such a model of discretion that he, too, wears a costume over the telltale colours of the family livery, to the confusion of the snoops and informers hanging out the windows.

Tonight is the gala opening at the Teatro San Samuele, where Cecilia has a box. Although the Inquisitors insist that women wear the *bautta* and *tabarro* to the theatre, no one takes heed. Cecilia dons a glittering satin gown that plunges to the floor at the back and barely to the level of decency in front; she drips jewels, and her hair is laced with pearls. Rodrigo arrives, looking just as elegant in white knee-breeches and stockings, a pink and green embroidered waistcoat, a coat covered with stitches of gold and a tricorn hat over his wig.

As usual, Cecilia and Rodrigo gossip with their neighbours through the entire performance, pausing only when a brawl breaks out in the pit below, as the customers, dressed in their own costumes, try to steal the show. The villain of the play is so evil that the audience pelts him with fritters and stewed pears; they shout warnings to his potential victims and insist that those he kills immediately spring back to life for a bow. Cecilia and the other ladies amuse themselves by dropping their ices and candle ends on the heads of the most obnoxious people below. At the end, one of the actresses sings a moving farewell that silences the audience and causes a veritable paroxysm of rapturous howls at the end. Cecilia begins to swoon from emotion, but Rodrigo, never at a loss, is ready with a spoonful of *triaca*, or Venetian treacle, a panacea made from a recipe of

60 ingredients that dates back to the time of Nero. As always it works a treat, and the bloom returns to her cheeks.

The night is coming alive; music and laughter drift down the Grand Canal, from the streets, from the palaces. Cecilia lets Rodrigo take his fair share of liberties in the gondola, behind the blinds of the cabin, or *felze*; at supper with friends at their *casino* he feeds her the best titbits by hand. Everyone chatters and laughs at the same time and they drink too much, all in preparation for the principal excitement of the evening at the Ridotto. Here the laughter stops, as Cecilia and Rodrigo manage to squeeze into the silent throng gathered around the *biribissi* table—the ancestor of roulette. Cecilia feels lucky and wins, once, twice, before losing once, twice, a dozen times. Rodrigo gently touches her elbow; Giancarlo is standing behind her, stoically watching. Neither he nor Rodrigo can cover her losses. 'Perhaps we could sell that old Bellini Madonna in the family chapel?' she whispers. Giancarlo smiles sadly, and kisses her hand for response: his own losses make hers look like child's play. They are close to ruin, but he's too much of a gentleman to tell her, especially when she looks so beautiful.

Cecilia pleads a headache and when Rodrigo offers to escort her home, she convinces him he should stay at the Ridotto, where their luck would be sure to change. Once in her gondola, however, she gives Claudio an address far from home, and *toujours gai*, she ends up at dawn, forgetting all discretion on the arm of the French ambassador, as they wander among the morning-after crowd at the Rialto vegetable markets, each illicit couple trying to look more debauched than the next.

Perhaps Fellini is the only one who could do justice to Venetian theatre in the 18th century. It was the rage: for a population of 130,000 there were six active theatres, and this was before the construction of La Fenice. Goldoni, who put a mirror to the Venetians and their foibles was a great success. But the audience, who enthusiastically identified with the actors (and unlike in the rest of Europe, actors were much honoured in Venice), always demanded novelty, celebrity actors or singers and scantily clad ballerinas. Tastes never rose much higher than the commedia dell'arte *buffooneries of Arlecchino and Pantalone.*

Gambling was the national vice. The patricians, no longer able to gamble their fortunes at sea, squandered them every night during Carnival at the state-run casino, or ridotto. *Open to noblemen or anyone wearing a mask, the Ridotto was packed to the brim every night. So many patricians like Giancarlo met bankruptcy there that the government closed it in 1774, reluctantly giving up hefty revenues for the state coffers. But the Venetians had gambling in their blood: immediately the* casini *(informal flats or love nests, where the patricians* could relax, as they were unable to do in their museum-palaces) brought out card tables to take the Ridotto's place, and hence our English word, 'casino'.

When the famous Giacomo Casanova was young, he would have gladly joined Cecilia in the dawn pageant of the debauched and ravished at the Rialto's Erberia. But when he was old and a secret agent for the Ten, he sent in scandalized reports. Still, he failed to impress. When the Ten sacked him, he left Venice for good, with a broken heart.

History

For you live like sea birds, with your homes dispersed,
like the Cyclades, across the face of the waters...
— *from a letter to the Venetian tribunes by Cassiodorus,*
prefect of King Theodoric; AD 523

The Invention of Venice

Long before anyone ever dreamed of gondolas or plates of liver and
onions, an Indo-European people called the **Venetii** (or Henetii, or
Enetii) occupied most of northeastern Italy. They probably came from
Illyria or Asia Minor about 1000 BC, a trading nation, who also produced
some very good wine. Rome gradually developed colonies in their territory, and the Venetii settled in comfortably as Roman provincials in the
2nd century BC.

Roman Venetia, with its wealthy cities—Aquileia, Padua, Verona and
Altinum—was one of the favoured corners of Italy. Many of the islands
of the Lagoon were already inhabited; besides fishing, salt-pans furnished the most important element of the coastal economy. Several busy
Roman roads passed through Venetia on their way across the mountains
to Illyria or Pannonia, convenient for trade—and also, as Rome decayed,
for invaders. Alaric the Goth began the troubles, sacking Aquileia in 401.

Attila the Hun repeated the performance in 452: the Scourge of God, and a figure that has passed into legend in the Venetian chronicles. His destruction of Aquileia, one of the greatest cities of the Empire, started the first flight of population into the lagoons.

Apparently, it was no picturesque flight of woebegone refugees—rather a planned migration, a refounding of cities that had no chance of survival on the mainland. The first generations brought their furniture, and later returned to the old towns to bring back stone for new buildings. Small communities grew up around the lagoons: the Aquileians settled mostly in Grado, the Altinese on Torcello and Burano. The Paduans sent a colony to the island of Rivo Alto—*Rialto*, the centre of the Venice that was to be, traditionally founded on 25 March, in the year 425.

Everyone needs salt, even during the fall of empires. And the new settlements had a near monopoly on it, enough to support them through the worst troubles. With trade disrupted, they had to fall back on their own resources to ship it and to protect the ships: right from the start, necessity led them to their first steps in their ordained vocation, as a commercial nation and a naval power. Necessity also taught them to work together. As early as 466, the 12 lagoon settlements were electing their own tribunes to coordinate common actions and policy. Already in the 500s, both the Gothic kings and the eastern emperors had to treat them with kid gloves: sovereignty over them could be pretended but not easily enforced. In the **Greek–Gothic Wars** that began in 539, so destructive for the rest of Italy, the Venetians fortuitously chose the winning side. Their fleet aided the Byzantines in taking the Gothic capital, Ravenna, and in return they received their first trading privileges in the East.

In gratitude for Venetian aid, Narses the Eunuch, Justinian's victorious general, built a church to St Theodore where St Mark's stands today. More importantly, he invited the **Lombards** over the Alps to assist in his campaigns as mercenaries. These most unpleasant of all Teutonic barbarians soon overran an impoverished and exhausted Italy, and delivered the *coup de grâce* to the surviving cities of the Venetian mainland. Another, still larger wave of refugees fled to the lagoon. In these darkest of times it was clear that any future lay here.

A Candle in a Dark Age: 568–810

Through the tinted Venice glass of the republic's later historians, this early period was a golden age. One chronicler called the Venetians 'a lowly people, who esteemed mercy and innocence, and above all religion rather than riches. They affected not to clothe themselves with ornaments, or to seek honours, but when need was they answered to the call.' The simple towns scattered across the islands were as yet only wood and thatch, interspersed with gardens, each house with its little boat 'tied to posts before their doors like horses on the mainland'.

But beneath the surface some embryonic political troubles were already taking shape. To prevent the settlements from sliding into anarchy, a Patriarch of Grado named Christopher called an assembly of citizens and convinced them of the need for a single authority. In 697, a certain Paoluccio Anafesta was elected as the **first Doge** (from *dux*, the common title of Byzantine provincial governors). But there is some doubt that such a person ever existed. More likely, the decisive events occured during the **Iconoclast struggles**, beginning in 726. Emperor Leo III's war on religious images was intensely unpopular in Italy; Pope Gregory II and his new allies, the Lombards, quickly exploited the discontent. There were revolts in Ravenna, the seat of the Byzantine exarch (viceroy). A doge, Orso Ipato, elected in 726, seems to have helped the exiled exarch retake the city.

What happened next is unclear. Some reports say there was civil war in Venice between the partisans and opponents of Byzantium. However the process evolved, Venice must have been master of its destinies after 752, when the Lombards took Ravenna and effectively ended any Byzantine pretensions to rule over northern Italy.

If the Venetians were now free, their 'Golden Age' was definitely a thing of the past. Nearly all of the early doges tried to turn the office into a family dynasty. Not many of them died in bed; one Patriarch was thrown off the top of his palace's tower. Factionalism continued unchecked in a stream of intrigues, rebellions and assassinations. And the Venetians discovered a commodity even more profitable than salt—slaves, mostly Christian Slavs destined for the flesh markets of North Africa and Spain. The new state started its career with few friends. Even without the slave-trading, Venice's wealth and the essential difference of its society were enough to earn it distrust in the narrow-minded world of feudal Europe. A 10th-century official in Pavia is recorded as wondering: '...these people neither plough nor sow, but can buy corn and wine everywhere'.

The slave trading earned the Venetians one formidable enemy, the righteous Charlemagne. Since 752, the **Franks** had been the leading power in Italy, thanks to Charlemagne's father, Pepin, who delivered the peninsula from the Lombards. They claimed dominion over all northern Italy, including the lagoons, and relations were tense until 810, when amid another factional struggle the Doge, Obelario de'Antenori, actually invited the Franks to send in their army. Charlemagne's son, another Pepin, was not long in arriving.

Facing real danger, the Venetians responded with decision. The treacherous Doge was expelled, and defences rapidly organized. The channel markers and buoys were removed, making the shallow lagoon impassable to anyone not familiar with it. Malamocco, the capital, was abandoned as indefensible (unlike the present Malamocco, this island was east of the Lido), and the new Doge, **Angelo Participazio**, concentrated the defences around the Rialto. Pepin besieged them for six months, but could not penetrate the lagoon before the summer heat and disease took their toll. In the end, the Venetians had to concede a tribute, but they had survived their greatest trial so far. A treaty was signed recognizing the sovereignty of Constantinople, the convenient legal fiction under which Venice would grow and prosper for centuries to come, but also a tie that would confirm its isolation from the rest of Italy.

Doge Participazio, the hero of the hour, presided over the reconstruction. The momentous decision was made to move the capital to the **Rialto**—Participazio's home, but also a central, defensible site. The fight against Pepin had made the Venetians a united people, and from that time they combined to build Venice.

The First City of Modern Europe: 810—1032

Very soon, Participazio erected the **first Doge's Palace** for himself. The pieces were falling into place; all that was needed was the right corpse. In retrospect, the embroidered legends can be disregarded: there can be little doubt that **the theft of St Mark from Alexandria** in 828 was a calculated and brilliant manoeuvre of Venetian policy. Of the 55 holy cadavers abstracted from around the Mediterranean by Venice (see 'Venetian Topics,' pp. 31–32), this is the one that mattered. To underscore the tradition of Mark's founding of the see at Aquileia, a legend was concocted that Mark had landed in Venice, where an angel appeared to him, saying, 'Peace to you, Mark, my Evangelist; here your body shall lie'. To medieval Italy, an Evangelist in your crypt was as good as an Apostle, maybe better. Besides giving the city a powerful protector in Heaven, Mark could intervene in more mundane affairs, allowing to counter the theological and political pretensions of both Constantinople and Rome.

The body was Venice's Declaration of Independence. The Venetians wasted no time in stitching Mark's lion symbol to their banners; their newly-adopted battle-cry, '*Viva San Marco!*' would be heard around the Mediterranean for nearly a thousand years. Finding a home for the priceless relic became the first priority, and a Basilica was dedicated four years later—significantly, Mark was to rest in the shadow of the Doge's new palace, and not in the cathedral on the distant island of Olivolo.

Despite the new foundation, Venice still conducted internal affairs with anarchic contentiousness. The Participazio family continued its near-monopoly over the dogeship, although after 887 they had to share their dominance with the Candianos. One of these, **Pietro Candiano IV** (959–76) proved catastrophic. Vain and ambitious, Pietro conducted himself more like a feudal autocrat than a republican prince of merchants. His marriage with Waldrada, sister of the Marquis of Tuscany, brought him towns on the mainland, and he soon began to treat Venice as just another part of his possessions. Coercing the Venetians to help him subdue rebellious Ferrara touched off a revolt to remember in 976: a mob stormed the Doge's Palace and set it on fire, and before long the flames engulfed the still-wooden city. When the smoke cleared there were no Candianos left standing, and very little of Venice. The Orseoli became the new dynasty, until another revolt put an end to them in 1032.

Trouble came not only from within. In the 830s Arab corsairs appeared to plague Venetian shipping from their bases in Apulia and Sicily. In 899, the rampaging Magyars overran northern Italy. Once more the Lagoon saved the city, but just to sleep better the Doge built fortifications, stretching from the castle on Olivolo to the Grand Canal. Great stretches of lagoon must have been filled for it—part of the gradual process that was converting the Rialto islands into modern Venice.

The Arabs were not the only pirates. Beginning in the late 800s, Slavic **'Narentine' pirates**, so-called for their bases around the Narenta river, would lie in wait among the maze of islands on the Dalmatian coast, posing a continuous threat to Venice's trade lifeline with Constantinople. After alternately fighting the pirates and paying them tribute, the Venetians felt strong enough to decide the issue by the year 1000. **Doge Pietro Orseolo II**'s naval expedition turned into a triumphal procession through Dalmatia, as town after town swore fealty to the Republic, and the worst strongholds of the pirates were burned. Soon the doges were affecting the title 'Duke of Dalmatia', as another showpiece of Venetian folklore was evolving—the Marriage with the Sea.

In the 9th century, drawing the line between pirates and non-pirates would have been difficult. The difference comes later, when the histories are written. Most likely Venice preyed on her neighbours as much as they preyed on her, and her pretended monopoly over Adriatic shipping kept other towns from making an honest living on the sea. Croatian pirate historians, had there been any, would have noted that Venetians were still snatching off their countrymen for sale as slaves. Towards legitimate competition, Venice reacted in much the same way. Comacchio, a rival trading town on the Po, was sacked by the Venetians in 866 and completely destroyed in 932. Further afield, Amalfi, Gaeta, Bari and more ominously Pisa and Genoa, were testing seas and markets that Venice already regarded as her own.

One summer night in 998, a small boat silently entered the lagoon. At the island of San Servolo it picked up a passenger and headed for the city, where its occupants made a moonlight tour of the quiet canals. In that boat was Otto III, the young and impetuous Emperor of the Germans, and his passenger was the Doge himself. Otto had arranged this secret visit to see the city as it was, without the stifling protocol. Already, Venice had to be seen: the greatest city of western Europe (excepting perhaps Moslem Cordoba and Seville) was an inconceivable marvel to any sleepy feudal soul. On the threshhold of medieval civilization, it was also a sign of things to come.

Crusades and a Constitution: 1032–1204

The Orseolo clan lost control of the dogeship in 1026, but their faction at home, and their alliances with the emperors kept the pot boiling for another six years. When their last feeble attempt to seize power was crushed, the Venetians resolved to find a more efficient form of government. A new Doge, **Domenico Flabanico**, oversaw a complete reform. A senate was elected, along with dogal councillors, and doges were required, not requested, to seek their advice. Finally, the system by which a doge would 'associate' a kinsman with his rule as a designated successor was forbidden, eliminating the monarchical tendency once and for all.

It was a perfect time to give the ship of state an overhaul, for the Adriatic was becoming a busy place. In northern Italy the reviving towns were asserting their independence against emperor and pope, and embarking on commercial careers of their own. In the south, the big noise was being made by the **Normans**, carving out their own empire in Apulia, Calabria and Sicily. Their ambitions towards Byzantinum crossed Venice's, and battles around the Apulian coast were waged intermittently between 1081 and 1085, with the Venetians usually winning. Most importantly, this war permitted Venice to extort even greater trading concessions out of the demoralized Greeks, who had recently lost almost all Asia Minor to the Seljuk Turks. Venice attained virtual control over all Byzantine commerce, making the ancient empire a sort of gilded dependency.

Just coincidentally (and if you believe that, we have some genuine relics of St. Nicholas we'll sell you) the **First Crusade** was preached ten years later in 1095. It was clear that a major power vacuum had appeared in the eastern Mediterranean, and the Venetians were not alone in seeing the opportunity. Pisa and Genoa made their fortunes ferrying crusaders, and both soon became important players in the region. Venice, possessing little of the crusading zeal of the murderous Franks and, rather resentful of being forced to share its new windfall, kept aloof from the conflict, fleecing the Franks where possible and grabbing economic control of Levantine cities like Sidon (1102) and Tyre (1123).

Back home, the city was beginning to look more like the Venice we know. The **Basilica of St Mark** was consecrated in 1094. The city's scattered shipyards and foundries were consolidated in one place—the **Arsenal**, for centuries the backbone of Venetian power and the biggest industrial establishment in the world. There was one notable subtraction: the island of Malamocco, Venice's first capital, obliterated by a terrific storm in 1106. Two more great fires in the same year finally convinced Venice of the necessity of building in brick and stone.

For the first time in centuries, Venice was forced to look towards the mainland. In the 1140s she obtained control of much of Istria. In the 1150s, there were the Wars of the Lombard League, in which Venice aided the northern Italian cities against **Emperor Frederick Barbarossa**. The real action, however, still lay over the sea. In 1172 Venice met a startling setback as the humiliated Greeks sought to take their revenge on their insatiable creditors; in a concerted action they imprisoned the entire Venetian trading colony in Constantinople (which numbered in the tens of thousands) and seized its property. An enraged Venice, already heavily in debt from its other ventures, raised a forced loan from its citizens and sent a large fleet eastwards under **Doge Vitale Michiel**

II. Clever Byzantine diplomacy stalled the Venetians until plague ravaged their force in the Aegean.

It was a disaster that could have done permanent damage to Venetian ambition. In its wake, the returning Doge was assailed by a mob (in what is now the lobby of the Hotel Danieli) and murdered (1172), resulting in a political crisis and another wave of constitutional adjustment. 'Reform' would not exactly be the right word, for the new measures took the relatively democratic state that had evolved since 697 and turned it into a tightly controlled oligarchy. No longer were doges to be elected by the popular assembly, but by a Great Council, the *Maggior Consiglio* entirely dominated by the richest merchants. The doge himself was forced to take an oath, the *promissione ducale*, vowing to be little more than a figurehead; and upon the death of each an inquisition was to be held to see if any new provisions were necessary to keep future doges in check. The elite club of the *Maggior Consiglio* assumed control of every aspect of government, filling each state office from among its own members. To discourage factionalism, it made all its choices through complex procedures involving selection by lot or indirect election through several layers of committees.

The first doge selected under the new rules, **Sebastiano Ziani** (1172), happened to be the richest man in Venice. He served well, and under the new system Venetian prosperity made a strong comeback. In 1177, all Europe watched as Venice orchestrated the reconciliation between Barbarossa and Pope Alexander III. The visitors would have crossed the first Rialto Bridge (1173), and seen the columns of SS. Mark and Theodore recently erected in the Piazzetta. Venice largely sat out the Third Crusade; while Coeur-de-Lion and Saladin slugged it out, the *Maggior Consiglio* freshened up their fleets and their bank balances. They might have thought they had a score to settle.

A Quarter and a Half of the Roman Empire: 1204–1310

Enrico Dandolo, who accepted the silly cap and umbrella of the dogeship in 1193, was 90 years old and blind. Legend has it he lost his sight in Constantinople, either in a street brawl or at the hands of the imperial torture-masters. If he indeed held a personal grudge, he found his opportunity for revenge with the beginning of the **Fourth Crusade**. In 1201, an embassy under Geoffroi de Villehardouin came to discuss the ferrying of crusaders in Venetian ships. The following spring, some

33,000 men were to be transported to the Holy Land, at the cost of about 1¹/₃ pounds of silver each. For a kicker Venice asked for only one half of all territories conquered.

The Venetians cleverly leaked a detail of the arrangement: instead of Palestine, the destination of the Crusade was to be Egypt, the leading Moslem sea power, and Venice's biggest trading partner. This was strategically a sound move, but bad for crusading propaganda. Next spring, as a result, only one third of the expected number of crusaders assembled in Venice. The Venetians refused to lift an anchor; they wanted the full package price, and they saw no reason to waste money feeding their guests until the agreed sum was raised. The starving crusaders passed the hat round, but came up some 34,000 silver marks short. No problem, Enrico Dandolo said: simply make a stop on the way to deliver us the rebellious city of Zara (modern Zadar, Yugoslavia) on the Dalmatian coast.

Zara was taken, amidst much bloodshed. About the same time, events in Constantinople took an interesting turn—one tyrannical usurper had been tossed out by another. The deposed tyrant's son, **Alexius IV**, cried out for vengeance. Whether or not the Venetians had planned it all along, the idea was now obvious: restore the pretender Alexius to Constantinople, and perhaps pick up a bit of booty on the side. Venice's Egyptian embarrassment was solved, while providence had supplied the thick-headed French knights to square accounts with the Byzantines.

To a medieval mind, it was a breathtaking deed: divert the crusade and attack the fabulous city, the heir of Rome. The assault was quick and merciless; Dandolo himself, disembarking under the very walls under constant fire, led the Venetians and French to the attack, and Constantinople fell for the first time in its 900-year history. Alexius was crowned, but during several months of uncertainty a Greek reaction threw him out again. Now the Westerners decided that only a complete sacking would repay their expenses. On 9 April, 1204, the allies attacked again. The Greeks, although grievously outnumbered, fought bravely for three days until the Theodosian walls were breached. The carnage was frightful, and was followed by history's all-time biggest daylight robbery. After the traditional three days' sack (during Holy Week, as chance would have it) and months of more methodical looting, 900 years' accumulation of imperial spoils was packed into the holds of Venetian galleys.

Historians, inexplicably misty-eyed over corrupt, useless Byzantium, often exaggerate the crime of Dandolo and his Allies—as if they were responsible for the triumphs of the Turks two centuries later, as if they had done anything more than liquidate a bankrupt concern. The Venetians got all the best (like the famous bronze horses of the Hippodrome), and in the division of the Empire that followed they showed their cleverness again. They let the French keep the city and most of its mainland provinces, impoverished and hard to defend (their 'Latin Empire' was a disaster, and lasted less than 60 years), contenting themselves with the islands and strong points that lay along their trade routes. Still it was a considerable prize, 'a quarter and a half' of Byzantium, as the treaty quaintly put it, and a manageable little empire that wouldn't get in the way of doing business.

Venice, now a European power in her own right, lacked experience in such matters and farmed her new colonies out to her nobles to be run as feudal possessions. Politically and religiously, it was an oppressive rule, though perhaps no worse than any of the other states of the region. Venice's spectacular success, and its stranglehold over the Eastern trade, had also earned her a new supply of enemies. Of these, the most bitter and dangerous was **Genoa**. Genoese trading concessions often existed next to those of the Venetians in the cities of the Levant, and conflict was inevitable. Fighting broke out in 1253, over Acre; Venice won, but it was only the beginning of a war that was to last 127 years.

In 1261, the Greeks recaptured Constantinople from the Franks. The new Emperor, **Michael VIII Palaeologus**, was understandably anxious to be avenged on the Venetians: he gave the Genoese the Quarter of Galata in Constantinople for a base and encouraged them to seize the Black Sea and Aegean trade. Also in 1261, and not entirely coincidentally, **Marco Polo**'s father and uncle began the first of their voyages to the distant East; if there were any new trade possibilities for getting around Constantinople, Venice's merchants meant to find them.

Altogether, the 13th century was not the best of times for Venice. Business was still booming, and goods flowed into the markets of the Rialto, as one contemporary noted, 'like water from the fountain'. The city continued to deck itself with new glories: most conspicuously the churches of San Zanipolo and the Frari. But the expense of defending its new possessions put the Republic under heavy strain. Besides the wars with Genoa, the collapse of the last crusader states in the 1290s hurt trade and forced Venice into uneasy alliances with the Moslems. At home, the lower classes felt pinched, politically as well as economically. During the course of the century the *Maggior Consiglio* gradually tightened its hold over the Republic, giving the Venetian constitution the rough form it was to keep for the next 500 years.

With the famous *Serrata* (locking) of the *Consiglio* in 1297, the Venetian elite turned itself into an hereditary caste. To be inscribed in its 'Golden Book', the only qualification was to have had an ancestor in an elected office. 'Locked' out were the overwhelming majority of Venetians, with no chance of ever taking part in public life. Locked in were not only the wealthy, but also some poor people with illustrious ancestry. This new caste enforced very strict codes of conduct for itself; as soon as he turned 25, a patrician had to pay heavy taxes and was duty bound to the state for life, liable at any time to be selected for an office that probably would cost more money than it paid. The motivation for these reforms was perhaps more fear of revolution from above than from below. All over Italy, city republics were falling under the rule of strongmen *signori*, taking over where merchant elites could not resist factionalism or restrain their apppetites. The Venetian elite were re-markably clear-sighted: if their ship of state were to avoid foundering, they must remain at the helm. And if they were to have absolute privilege, they had to accept absolute responsibility.

Not that all Venetians accepted the new order of things. The first revolt among the disenfranchised occurred in 1300 and was brutally suppressed. A more serious disruption came in 1310, the Tiepolo uprising. **Baiamonte Tiepolo**, the 'Gran Cavaliere', came from a noble family that had produced two doges. But Baiamonte's supporters were nearly all noblemen, and their attempted coup found no support among the common people, who apparently had already decided that the politi-cal monopoly of one class was preferable to a tyrant. One important innovation came about as a result of the revolt, as expressed in an old song:

> In the year one thousand three hundred and ten
> In the midst of the month for harvesting grain
> Baiamonte passed over the *ponte*
> and so was formed the Council of Ten.

The Council of Ten, originally an emergency body formed to root out Baiamonte's supporters, was to become the most powerful part of the state machinery. More of a real executive than the doge, the Ten guarded Venice's internal security, looked after foreign policy, and with its sumptuary laws and sententious taboos, still found time to look after the moral conduct of the Venetians.

Genoese Wars and the Mainland Empire: 1310–1453

Meanwhile, the struggle with Genoa proceeded fitfully. A particularly exhausting round in the 1290s had seen battles from Liguria to Constantinople before the Genoese victory at Curzola (1298) and mutual exhaustion brought peace again. Once more, though, Venice had to concern itself with problems on the mainland, where ambitious tyrants like the **Visconti** of Milan and the **Scaligeri** of Verona were posing a new threat.

The next decades were relatively quiet—**Dante** visited in 1321 and got a cold reception as an emissary from Ravenna. In 1341, the Doge's Palace was completed in the form we see today. In the 1330s, Venice checked the ambitions of Verona, and found it expedient after a victorious conclusion to keep the city of Treviso to guard its increasingly important land trade routes over the Alps to Germany: like it or not, the city that had always turned its back on the land now found itself an actor on that stage, in the midst of all the intrigues and petty wars of that era at the dawn of the Renaissance.

The Black Death hit Italy in 1347—Venice's fault, in a way, since a Venetian ship transported the disease from the Crimea where it had ravaged the Mongol Golden Horde. In Venice, as in many other cities, it carried off some three-fifths of the population. Genoa suffered too, but both sides were in shape to resume hostilities only three years later. Again the conflict was conducted on an epic scale. After victories and defeats on both sides, Genoese Admiral Paganino Doria ambushed an idle Venetian fleet at Portolungo, in the Peloponnese, capturing 56 ships in 1352.

The subsequent peace gave few advantages to Genoa, but for Venice more reverses waited in store. **Marin Falier**, the splenetic 54th Doge (1354–5), attempted with the aid of disaffected Arsenal workers to stage another coup, making himself a true prince free of the constitutional burdens. The Council of Ten got wind of the plot and before most Venetians knew what was happening their Doge was missing his head and his co-conspirators were dangling from the columns of the Doge's Palace. Dalmatia was gobbled up by the King of Hungary, and in 1363 a revolt in Crete, joined by some local Venetian barons and gave the Ten a three-year headache.

The last war with Genoa, the **War of Chioggia**, began in 1378. At first the Venetians, under admiral **Vettor Pisani**, defeated the Genoese fleet near Rome; in a repeat of 1353, though, they let the Genoese surprise them in winter quarters at Pola, in Istria. Only six ships made it back to Venice, and Pisani was tossed in the the Doge's prisons—the common fate of Venetian commanders who permitted such things to happen. But Venice was in desperate straits, undefended with a huge enemy fleet speeding towards the Lagoon. As in Pepin's time, the channel markers were pulled up and the Lagoon entrances blocked. The entire population mobilized itself just in time to receive the Genoese fleet. The Genoese believed Chioggia, on the southern edge of the Lagoon, to be the key to capturing all. With their Paduan allies they stormed it in August 1379, and Venice was under siege.

The Venetians, high and low, responded to the threat with their accustomed resolve, but they had a demand that even the Doge and the Ten could not withstand. They wanted Vettor Pisani for their leader, and no other. The old Admiral's chains had to come off, and back in command, he produced the inspired plan of blockading the blockaders. In a fierce fight on the longest night of the year, he dragged out old hulks full of rocks and sunk them in the channels, cutting off the occupying force from its fleet and from the Paduans on the mainland. The Venetians knew they could not keep it up for long. The success of their gamble depended on the chance that their other fleet, under the mercurial admiral **Carlo Zeno**, would return in time before the larger Genoese force could assert itself. At the beginning of the war, Zeno had been sent out to harass Genoese shipping. He was a year overdue, and no one even knew if his fleet still existed, or where it might be.

Providence was evidently in a poetic mood, and now the city that had lived so long by fabricating legends and miracles found its reward. On New Year's morning, the sails were sighted. It was Carlo Zeno, and Venice was saved. After a year of sweeping Genoese shipping off the seas, he had come with an enormous load of booty and a fleet in fighting trim. The counter-siege continued until June, but it ended in the total annihilation of the Genoese army and fleet. Both sides were now completely exhausted. Venice, its commerce and navy intact, would recover quickly; Genoa would soon drop from the ranks of the major powers in a maelstrom of civil war and economic decline.

One lesson learned from the war was the danger of allowing the hinterlands to be in enemy hands. The Paduans, in cutting off the city's food supply, had given Venice a greater fright than all the galleys of Genoa. In addition, economic forces now made clear the need for an assured market for Venetian goods and guaranteed access to the markets of the north. Despite the dangers, Venice held her nose and plunged headfirst into the confusing, sordid world of Italian power politics. Treviso, lost in the War of Chioggia, was retaken in 1382. After a perilous involvement in the wars of **Gian Galeazzo Visconti** of Milan, who nearly gained control of all northern Italy before his death in 1402, Venice learned about the necessity of maintaining the Italian balance of power. She also emerged with two very gratifying prizes, old enemies Padua and Verona.

Mostly by diplomacy—not surprisingly for a nation that had learned subtlety from the Byzantines themselves—Venice's new career went from success to success. By 1420, she had regained Dalmatia from the Hungarians and acquired Vicenza, Friuli and most of the Veneto, a natural frontier that perfectly suited her modest ambitions.

Some Venetians wanted more, and in 1423 a growing war party secured the election of its leader, **Francesco Foscari**, as doge. At the time, Venice was at her height, the richest city in Europe, and probably the largest, with the biggest and best fleet. Her trade—increasingly a state-run affair, too costly and complex to be managed by the old merchant adventurers—dominated the Mediterranean, and her efficiency and fair-dealing earned her the grudging respect even of competitors. Some historians see 1423 as a turning point for Venice. The old Doge, **Tommaso Mocenigo**, had made a rouser of a deathbed speech, warning the Venetians not to elect Foscari in his place and not to turn their backs on the sea for adventures on land, and his words are always recalled by those who would claim that it was with Foscari that Venice went wrong.

Doge Foscari had some problems of his own, particularly a corrupt waster of a son (see Byron's *The Two Foscari*). He tried twice to resign, was refused, then finally (1457) had to be removed by the Ten on grounds of senility. But he hardly deserves the reproaches he gets from the more superficial histories. The wars of his time were only a continuation of those that had won Venice her land empire and they were certainly unavoidable. And Venice hardly turned her back on the sea; in that direction there simply was nothing left to achieve. The wars, rather genteel after the conventions of the age, were almost continuous from 1425 until 1454. And they were colourful enough. Venice employed famous mercenary captains such as **Carmagnola**, the greatest soldier of his generation, **Gattamelata** (the 'Honey Cat' from Umbria) and **Francesco Sforza**. The first turned traitor, and ended up hanging between the Piazzetta columns; the second stayed true and got a famous equestrian statue in Padua, while Sforza played his own game and finished as Duke of Milan. In the end Venice came out ahead, gaining the metal-working towns of Bergamo and Brescia to round out her borders and her new continental economy.

As the events of the next two centuries were to demonstrate, the land empire was a sound investment despite all the trouble it took to keep it. It would pay for Venice's retirement; she in turn would rule it (unlike her colonies elsewhere) with justice and sympathy—often, when an invader seized one of the mainland towns, he would find himself up against a popular insurrection bellowing *'Viva San Marco!'*. This is part of the developing 'Myth of Venice' that commanded the world's admiration: stability, continuity and impartial justice under its unique constitution. No state in Europe planned its economic affairs more intelligently or took better care of its own people. Perhaps it was only Venice's head start that made it a society more highly evolved than any in Europe—the Venice of Foscari was already a thousand years old.

Serenissima in spite of Everything: 1453–1571

Pride, for your average imperialist, is supposed to come before a fall. And directly upon digesting her new land empire, Venice's luck began to change. Soon things turned really bad, then worse, and then worse still. The dislocations in trade should have been fatal to such a strictly mercantile city, as earlier trade shifts had been to Amalfi, and Pisa. They were not. The rabid crusade of the great powers of Europe against her should have finished her off. It didn't. Politically, the 16th century was one of the ghastliest periods in European history. For Venice, it featured a murderers' row of bitter enemies—ferocious, berserk Pope Julius II; the megalomaniac Charles V, with half of Europe in his pocket; worst of all the invincible Turk, with a million men, a thousand galleys, and nothing better to do than beat on the Venetians. So how did Venice survive? In grand style, thank you, with masques and pageants, and an artistic achievement unequalled by any city of the Renaissance save only Florence.

In Istanbul's Military Museum, you can see the sword of Attila the Hun, leader of one of the 'twelve historical Turkish empires'. No Venetian would have been surprised to hear that their esteemed founding father had been a Turk, their foe of destiny. Even without him, the Venetians had been trading with various Turkish emirates for centuries around the coasts of Anatolia. The **Ottoman Turks**, who by 1400 controlled much of Greece, the Balkans and eastern Anatolia, were more of a problem.

Their talents at warfare, combining great resources with a steady discipline and the most up-to-date technology were well known to the courts of Europe. The bad news for Venice was that they were also discovering the joys of sailing. In 1352, when the Ottomans first crossed the Dardanelles, they had to pay Catalan mercenaries to ferry them over. A hundred years later they had built a fleet of excellent galleys. The Emir then was Mehmet II, **Mehmet the Conqueror**, and in 1453, he used his new navy to help realize the old Ottoman dream of the **conquest of Constantinople**. The pitiful force that defended the metropolis to the bitter end included almost as many Venetians as Greeks.

The end of this peculiar symbiosis, of seven centuries of trade between the merchants of Venice and the decadent empire, did not at first seem irreparable. Mehmet signed a liberal commercial treaty, and Venice sent Gentile Bellini to paint the Conqueror's portrait. But the Turks were just taking a rest. In the 1460s they seized the mainland Peloponnese and made inroads in Albania and Bosnia. An exhausting war of fifteen years, from 1464 to 1479, lost Venice the important island of Euboea. No assistance was available from the rest of the Italian states; engrossed in their own petty wars, they were in fact happy to see Venice's pride taken down a peg. In 1478, the Turks staged raids deep into Friuli; the fires they set could be seen from the Campanile of St. Mark's.

After signing a humiliating peace, Venice gained a short breathing space. Mehmet died in 1481, succeeded by his scholarly son Bayezit II, who abhorred warfare. As if on cue, the princes of Italy stepped in to square off with Venice once more. In 1483, a trifling argument over salt pans with the Duke of Ferrara escalated into a war with Milan, Florence and Naples. Pope Sixtus IV put Venice under an interdict in May, which was politely disregarded. Four months later half the Doge's Palace burned down when someone left a candle burning. But by the following August, while work on the rebuilding was underway, the Italian allies sued for peace. Venice picked up the city of Rovigo and some other small territories; the Pope was incensed on hearing the news, and he died the next morning.

Another minor success came with the **acquisition of Cyprus** in 1488. This island was then a curious relic of the crusades, governed by kings of the French house of Lusignan. The Venetian **Caterina Cornaro**, had married King James back in 1468, and when the King died five years later she gained the throne. The Venetians lost no time and quickly insinuated their men into all the important positions of the kingdom. Poor Caterina found herself effectively a royal prisoner. In 1488, threatened with intrigues on all sides, Venice easily convinced the Queen to give up her crown and proclaim the annexation of Cyprus by the Republic. Caterina earned in return a toy kingdom at the pretty town of Ásolo, with plenty of entertainments to wile away boredom until the War of the League of Cambrai chased her back to Venice in 1509.

For Venice, exasperating popes and snatching up islands was child's play, but further disasters were in store. Another bogey of the *Serenissima*'s history, one wearing neither turban nor tiara, appeared in 1498: none other than an honest Portuguese captain, **Vasco da Gama**, who completed the first voyage around the horn of Africa to India. Venice's monopoly of the East was gone forever. The disaster was neither immediate nor fatal, but a steady decline in receipts was recorded over the next century. Venice responded with her accustomed energy, even proposing to the Sultan of Egypt that a canal be dug across the Suez, but there was little the Republic could do.

In 1501, Venice elected a doge of substance, the first since Foscari. **Leonardo Loredan** might have passed into history with as little notice as his predecessors. It was his fate, however, to be doge during the greatest trials Venice would ever undergo.

The **Wars of Italy** had already been going on for seven years, with the consequent intrusion of foreign powers that would put an end to both Italian liberty and the Italian Renaissance. In 1494, Duke Lodovico of Milan started the commotion by inviting the King of France, **Charles VIII**, to give him a hand against his arch-enemy, Naples. Charles could not resist and marched his army down the peninsula and took Naples with surprising ease. The Italians, who had lackadaisically watched Charles' parade, now finally became alarmed. Venice took most of the initiative in forming a defensive league against the French and Venice supplied most of the money and men for the League's army, attempting to block Charles' return to France. When the League failed to do so, at the **Battle of Fornovo** (1495), it was clear to all that plenty of Italian real estate was available to any power bold enough to snatch it.

Throughout the 1490s and 1500s, the wars continued, with another invasion by Charles' successor, Louis XII, resulting in the conquest of Milan, and the retaking of Naples by the Spanish. Venice, scheming to expand towards the south and perhaps even to the Tyrrhenian coast, could not help becoming involved. Under the Borgia pope, Alexander VI (1492–1503), Cesare Borgia had created a little empire for the family in central Italy. He lost it to his father's fiery and determined successor, **Julius II**, in 1504, and Venice took advantage of the confusion to grab Rimini and several other towns of the Romagna, the property of the Papal States. That was a mistake.

Giuliano della Rovere, the story goes, won his papal election by pretending to be meek and pliable. Once enthroned as Julius II, however, he moved ruthlessly to reassert papal control over towns that had slipped away. Julius' constant appeals to foreign princes for support kept the Wars of Italy boiling, and ultimately condemned the nation to foreign rule. In 1508, Julius decided it was time to deal with Venice—the only state strong and determined enough to keep the foreigners out. Thanks to the diplomatic situation of the time, he easily arranged an alliance with the Holy Roman Empire and Austria, France, Spain and Naples, Ferrara and Mantua. This **'League of Cambrai'** intended nothing less than the partition of the Venetian empire. Julius placed Venice under another futile interdict, but much more damaging was a tremendous explosion and fire in the Arsenal in March 1509, a grave blow to the city's preparations for defence. The next month, the League declared war and French troops invaded from Lombardy.

The Venetians had few illusions about the danger they were in, but disaster struck more quickly than anyone could have guessed. As usual, Venice depended on a mercenary army, led by *condottieri* whose careless tactics allowed the French to separate and defeat their forces utterly at the **Battle of Agnadello** on 14 May 1510. Most of the discouraged mercenary companies simply went home. Venice, without an army, had lost its entire land empire at a single blow. The League wasted little time in dividing up the spoils; only Treviso and Udine, traditionally faithful, remained under the banner of St Mark.

Some of the lost towns, hardly overjoyed at the thought of replacing Venetian rule with that of greedy foreign princes, produced spontaneous revolts. In Venice itself, the government was in fearful disarray. But just as the Pope was the author of Venice's calamity, he would soon become Venice's saviour. Julius now decided that the French were the real foes of Italy and Christianity. In a typically impulsive move, Julius betrayed his allies. He made a severe peace with the frightened Venetians, requiring their ambassadors to indulge him in a double helping of the grovelling and foot-kissing so dear to Renaissance pontiffs. Not long after, he asked them to join a new League against France. After a few years of complicated changes of alliance and fortune, conflicting ambitions cancelled out and Venice, by diplomacy and the good will of its former possessions, saw nearly all of them return to the fold by 1517.

Diplomacy and luck also helped Venice stay clear of the final stage of the Wars of Italy, the deadly struggle between Emperor Charles V and King Francis I. In 1529, when the treaties of Barcelona and Cambrai set up Spanish-Imperial control across Italy, Venice lost only Ravenna and her last few port towns in Apulia. She was fortunate to be alive—the only Italian state not under the heel of Spain or the Pope. The Turks, who had providentially been busied with eastern conquests during the Italian Wars, now returned in force. Under Sultan **Suleiman the Magnificent**, Ottoman power reached its zenith: Rhodes was taken in 1522, and the great, unsuccessful siege of Vienna took place seven years later. Naval campaigns against Venice occupied most of the 1530s. Corfu, the key to the Adriatic, withstood a tremendous siege in 1537, but for the Aegean islands and Peloponnese there was no hope.

The Turks also fostered another menace that hit Venice much closer to home. The **Uskoks**, an unsavoury band of Dalmatian Slavs, repeated the story of the Narentine pirates of the 900s. Supported by the sultans, they annoyed Venetian shipping for decades. In 1570, the Turkish Wars began anew when Sultan Selim II ('the Sot', the first of the decadent Ottomans) attacked Cyprus. For once, Venice was not alone. Four years earlier, the Turks' unsuccessful attack on Malta had betrayed their ambition of dominating the entire Mediterranean, and Spain was alarmed enough to send a fleet to the East. That year, the effort came to nought when the Spanish admiral, Gian Andrea Doria of Genoa, refused to attack or cooperate in any way with the Venetian fleet. (His father, the famous Andrea Doria, had twice pulled similar tricks on the Venetians; the shameless treachery of the Dorias and indeed of all Genoese is a recurring motif in Venetian history).

Cyprus, just off the Turkish coast, had no chance of surviving. The climax of the campaign was the siege of Famagusta, where a small force under Marcantonio Bragadin distinguished itself in a hopeless defence. For his trouble Bragadin was flayed alive by the Turkish commander. The following year, the embarrassed Spaniards sent a larger force under the more trustworthy Don John of Austria, a bastard son of Charles V. More help came from the least likely of naval powers, the Papal States, and the allied fleet sailed straight for Greece. The Turks were waiting in the Gulf of Patras, and on 7 October, 1571, lines of galleys four miles long joined what was perhaps the biggest sea battle ever fought in the Mediterranean, the **Battle of Lepanto**.

It lasted less than six hours, and at the end (despite the collapse of the allies' right wing, thanks to Venice's old friend Gian Andrea Doria) the Turkish fleet was scattered. A hundred of their galleys were sunk and a hundred and thirty captured, and some 15,000 Christian slaves were liberated. When the ships brought the news to Venice and pyramids of captured turbans and banners were piled in the Piazzetta, Venice celebrated for four days. Ironically, the victory of Lepanto changed little in the Mediterranean. Two years after, when it was clear that Spain would provide no further aid—Philip II was more concerned with the Low Countries and England—Venice felt itself compelled to sue for peace. Abandoned by her allies, Venice did not regain Cyprus or anything else—only an increase in the tribute demanded by the Sultan for the last few Venetian enclaves in the East.

Venice's century of trials was almost over. The peace with Turkey would last fifty years. The Ottomans, under an unbroken line of wretched sultans were well on their way to becoming the 'Sick Man of Europe'. Venice, her trade declining every year, realized with a merchants' perspicacity that there was nothing to be done—no prospects, no risks worth taking, no chance of earning an honest sequin by land or sea. Throughout the century, the *Nobil Homini* had been doing what any wealthy class would do under the circumstances: investing in real estate. As always, they did it with a flourish. The scores of Palladian villas across the Veneto, the last word in High Renaissance refinement, are the monuments of diminished expectations and of the Venetian businessman's supremely enjoyable retirement.

Historians of a century ago tended to interpret this great turning point differently. To the virtuous Victorians, too much art and too many parties had sapped the city's will to outfox her rivals. The evidence, to the morally minded, is not lacking. There is the little matter of 11,654 registered prostitutes (13% of the female population), for example, and the directory of them published for visitors. Venice's *cinquecento*, for all the wars and troubles, was conducted as one long festival. In no century were more palaces and churches built, or more beautiful ones. While keeping their enemies at bay, the Venetians had added the Rialto Bridge, S. Giorgio Maggiore and the great palaces of the Grand Canal, along with the paintings of Carpaccio, Giorgione, Tintoretto and Veronese.

In 1573, the Venetians received another sovereign, Henry III of France. The King entered in a procession of gilded gondolas, entertained along the way by floating tableaux, firework shows and a barge on which the glass-makers of Murano turned out crystal goblets for him on the spot. The Doge gave him an album of miniatures to peruse; the one he liked best was of the celebrated courtesan-poetess Veronica Franco, and she soon arrived to keep him company and write him a sonnet. The King met Veronese and Tintoretto, who did his portrait in pastels; he bought a diamond sceptre from a jeweller on the Rialto, who always kept a few on hand in case a king should visit his shop. There was a dinner party at the Doge's Palace. Earlier in the day the King had visited the Arsenal and seen the keel of a new galley being laid. At the end of the dinner, after 1200 different dishes and an opera (one of the first ever performed) he saw the completed galley sailing under the palace windows. Like many visitors to Venice, it is recorded that after his return Henry was never quite the same again.

A Decline to Remember: 1573–1796

In Browning's words, 'Venice spent what Venice earned'. Not only Venice, but the entire Mediterranean world was declining in the last decades of the 16th century. Trade was contracting and politics were subverted by the twin vampires of Rome and Madrid. Venice had the resources to survive, but not enough to break free from the constraints of the new era. Her policy of neutrality and her centuries of diplomatic experience kept her afloat with little difficulty, but the grandchildren of the Venetian merchants and warriors found they had to resign themselves to a very different life: they could enjoy themselves, and weren't averse to it, but beyond that opportunities were limited.

For the next two centuries, history would be largely limited to vignettes: a fire in the Doge's Palace in 1577, occasioning Tintoretto's gigantic *Paradise* and the rebuilding of the Palace itself. The first state-run banks appeared in 1587. The wars against the Uskoks continued until diplomacy induced the Austrians in 1617 to stop supporting them. Along the way a really serious issue came up, one that would reflect brilliantly the maturity and decency of the Venetian state. By 1606, the Papacy was greatly weakened by its own excesses but still a dangerous power in Italian affairs. In 1606, Pope Paul V chose to make an issue over two Venetian priests, a rapist and a child molester, indicted by the Ten. Despite centuries of practice, the popes still maintained the fiction that clerics were immune to civil justice in Venice. Although this trivial affair was part of a much larger struggle, the Pope used it as a stick to beat

Venice, and for the fourth time, the hated city was placed under interdict and its leaders excommunicated.

But Venice had a secret weapon. A scholarly Servite friar named **Paolo Sarpi**, devoted to Venice and to religious tolerance, was employed by the State to refute the papal arguments, which he did with an astuteness that attracted the attention of all Europe, Protestant and Catholic. The Ten, with their accustomed waggishness, took care of any recalcitrant priests. One who refused to say mass woke up one morning to find a gallows erected in front of his church. Another, claiming that he would act as the Holy Spirit moved him, was told that the Holy Spirit had already moved the Ten to hang all traitors. Sarpi and Venice won: the interdict was lifted in 1607, and it was the last time the popes would ever try such a thing against anyone. Rome knew how to bear grudges in those days—three times the Roman Curia sent assassins after Sarpi, though they bungled each attempt.

Venice could still wage a war when required. The Turks gave her one of 25 years that began in 1645 and ended with the loss of Crete, Venice's last important overseas possession. And after 1683, when the last attack on Vienna failed, exposing the Turk's real weakness, Venice found it in her to go back on the offensive. In 1685, **Francesco Morosini** led a brilliant expedition that regained many of the lost territories in Greece. Most of these, however, slipped away again in Venice's last war with Turkey, between 1714 and 1718.

As in the rest of Italy, the 17th century had been a disaster economically for Venice. The city had responded well to the changes of the 16th century, developing new industries in glass and textiles. Now even these were forced off the market by northern competitors, while the Dutch and English took over much of the dwindling Mediterranean trade. In its decline, both the strengths and the weaknesses of Venice's unique state revealed themselves clearly. The decomposing nobility, mincing between casino and ballroom, still kept its stranglehold over politics, and to the end prevented any reforms that would bring new blood into the government. On the other hand, the uncanny machine of the constitution continued to sputter on: stability and justice were maintained, the provinces were happy, and despite rampant corruption the state finances remained perfectly solid right up until 1797.

After the last Turkish war, Venice let her fleets and armies rot. Undefended, she depended on her diplomacy and neutrality to keep the world at bay. The rest of Europe, which had come to enjoy the city as a sort of adult fun-fair was glad to leave her alone. This gayest and most cosmopolitan of all cities became a necessary stop for northerners on the Grand Tour. Besides the opera and the casino and legendary promiscuity, they came for the sense of unreality, a vacation for the mind. For the first and only time in her long history, sensible Venice succumbed completely to the sensual promise of her sea-borne home. The passing years were named for the appearances of sopranos at the opera. The first hot-air balloon in Italy ascended in 1784 from in front of St Mark's. The Ten's ridiculous spies marked it all down, but no one gave a fig. New churches were built with garish façades glorifying not God, but minor Venetian families. Spectacle became an end in itself, and with its millennium of practice, the machinery of Venetian pomp and ceremony trundled around the calendar as brilliantly as ever. Venice was full of impoverished noblemen, still forced by law to dress in silks and keep up a good front: they somehow scraped up some pennies to rent a servant for the night if by evil chance someone were to call.

'Esto perpetua'—may it last forever—as Paolo Sarpi had said on his deathbed. But the end was closer than anyone knew. First, though, comes a last surprise echo of the old spirit: **Angelo Emo**, the last admiral of Venice on Venice's last expedition. In 1790 he chastised the Barbary pirates while everyone else, including the English, was paying them tribute. Six years later, **Napoleon**'s Army of Italy was marching into the Veneto. Before he ever reached the city, Napoleon destroyed Venice in a war of nerves, alternating threats and accusations while the Venetians fretted and trembled. Neither the miserable last doge, Ludovico Manin (who had fainted when he heard of his election in 1789), nor the Ten nor anyone else could summon up the courage to organize a defence— while ironically their people were staging revolts and conducting guerrilla warfare across the occupied Veneto against their revolutionary 'liberators'.

Some Venetians too were ready to fight. When a French frigate, chased by the Austrians, took refuge in the Lagoon, the harbour patrol opened fire and took her, giving Napoleon the pretext for a final ultimatum. The thousand-year republic ended in a shameful note of *opera bouffe*: at the last meeting of the *Maggior Consiglio*, the *Nobil Homini* were frightened out of their pantaloons by the sound of gunshots—only the farewell fusilade of a loyal Dalmatian battalion on their way home. In panic, they voted their own extinction and scuttled off to their palaces before the counting was even finished. In the empty chamber, Manin is reported to have handed his doge's cap to an attendant, saying: 'You may have this, I won't be needing it any more'.

70

Just Another Provincial Capital: 1797–

'I will have no more Inquisition, no more Senate.
I will be an Attila to the Venetian state'.

—*Napoleon*

What was it about Venice that made the little fellow so mad? Was it the brute's contempt for weakness or his basic instinct to vandalize things he did not understand—or was it simply that Napoleonic types cannot stand the idea of people who refuse to drill and salute and who insist on the right to enjoy themselves? Whatever the reason, Napoleon went after Venice and its symbols with a greater relish than he showed for any of his other conquests: contractors were paid to chop down all the evangelical lions (in Venice itself they took the money but never did the work); the horses of St Mark's were removed to Paris; the French even burned the doges' state barge, the glorious *Bucintoro*. Philistine that he was, Napoleon only visited the city once—his men looted tons of paintings and sculptures just the same, and it is frightening to think how much Napoleon himself would have fancied had he ever seen it.

For all his ideological posturing, Napoleon had few scruples about handing Venice over to Austria in the Treaty of Campoformio only five months after he had taken it. During the rest of the Napoleonic wars, Venice remained a sullen, forgotten backwater under the Austrians and later under the French again. No more carnivals and intrigues, no more masked balls, only the despair of a city from which ambitious men had wrung the last drops of pride and gaiety. When the 1815 Congress of Vienna made its decisions over post-Napoleonic Europe, Venice's rightful independence was naturally forgotten. She was to be an Austrian province, and as such she found little to do but serve as a curiosity to entertain foreigners.

To the Venetians, the English were their 'swallows', because they always came back with the season. After Napoleon, they flocked to Venice in even greater numbers—Byron swimming down the Grand Canal, Shelley neglecting his children, and later John Ruskin, climbing ladders to scrutinize Gothic arches. The visitors must often have been the best show in town, for Venice, under the leaden rule of the Austrians, could never regain anything of its accustomed gaiety. Though not particularly oppressive, neither were the Austrians very sympathetic: high taxes and dreary censors were Venice's lot, along with an administration largely manned by Germans or Slavs who often knew no Italian.

71

Business dwindled to almost nothing, as the Austrians consciously favoured the port of Trieste. But while Venice was perfecting its touristic vocation, packaging romantic melancholy for northerners, another invasion was plotted: modernity mounted its attack in 1846, when an Austro-Italian syndicate built the railroad causeway over the Lagoon to the city. Along with its independence, Venice's beloved sense of separateness was gone forever.

Gone, though not forgotten, and there was a chance for an heroic interlude, a last '*Viva San Marco!*' before the city finally surrendered to history and old age. In March 1848, when revolts convulsed Europe, Venetian patriots seized the Doge's Palace and the Arsenal, and declared the Republic reborn. Their leader, who had been stewing in the Doge's old dungeons for anti-Austrian activities, was a Jewish lawyer named **Daniele Manin**. Though ironically sharing the surname of the last, disgraceful Doge, this Manin would help redeem Venice's honour, in a brave defence that lasted long after the other revolts around Italy had been crushed. Towns and villages in the Veneto, sentimentally raised money and sent soldiers. In Venice itself, Manin organized a democratic government, and some of the old noble families sold their treasures and even their palaces to help finance the cause.

The Venetians blew a hole in the new causeway, and the Austrians were reduced to mounting a blockade and bombarding the city from the mainland. British shipping, of course, ignored the blockade, and there was a hope that Lord Palmerston's sympathetic government might intervene—Venetians later blamed the failure to do so on the British consul in Venice, a friend of the Austrians named Dawkins who wrote back to London deriding the revolutionaries as 'unprincipled adventurers'. Along with Kossuth and the Hungarians, Venice was the last to hold out in the great year of failed revolutions. Hunger, and a raging epidemic of cholera, forced Manin to surrender in August 1849.

When the Austrians returned, they did their best to behave, though with Italian unification reaching its climax, they knew their days were numbered. Still, Venice and the Veneto remained one of the last bits to join the new Italian kingdom. That came courtesy of the Prussians, when they defeated Austria in 1866.

Under Italian rule, business began to improve. A new port was begun at **Marghera**, a prelude to the industrial areas, the oil port, and the road causeway, all built between the Wars when Venice was in a mood to catch up with the modern world. In 1945, Venice was not liberated until the final German collapse. Legends have grown up about it: one has it that the British forces arrived in gondolas, as the various Allied contingents raced to get in first, to have their pick of the best hotels. The New Zealanders won: as they sped their tanks over a bridge in Mestre they passed the entire German occupation force, marching out beneath them.

After the War, the earlier improvements began to have some unforeseen consequences for the city. Venetians moved into less expensive, newer housing close to their jobs on the mainland, and Mestre and Marghera grew into huge toadstool suburbs while their industries fouled the air and water of the lagoon. The city that had 170,000 people in 1936 is now down to 79,000, and the metropolitan area of which it is the centre has developed a unique and troubling split personality: on the shore, a dull Italian anytown, rather unsympathetic towards Venice and fond of initiating referendums to secede from it (the last one failed in 1990). Over the causeway, there is the fabulous invalid herself, with international legions of planners, restorationists and bureaucrats constantly checking her pulse and X-raying her tissue. Post-War Venice has seen one little plague after another: the great flood of 1966, the scare that the city was sinking, the disgusting algae invasions of the 1980s, the Pink Floyd concert of 1989 that trashed the Piazza, and of course the indispensable tourists themselves, without whom Venice would be an empty shell. Proposals have been made to charge admission at the causeway and limit the number that come in daily.

Probably more restoration work has been done here than in any other Italian city—although the need for more is still greater than any other city's. 'Moses', the huge new sea gate that is supposed to protect against further disastrous floods, is in place—although some doubt if it will work at all. Environmental paranoia, largely justified, has reached the stage where some action may result: already two new aqueducts to the mainland have ended the need for Mestre and Marghera to take so much water out of the Lagoon, thus stabilizing it and saving Venice's foundations from sinking. Even the algae problem (in 1990) seems to be subsiding, although no one really knows why.

The Queen of the Adriatic sits well-scrubbed and pretty these days, still at the mercy of its visitors but with half a mind to try and seek some more honourable employment. The doomed Expo was supposed to have served as a catalyst for economic reconstruction, with such extravagant but potentially useful proposals as an underground to unite the city with the mainland. Other ideas are in the air: a free-trade zone, or a headquarters city for international organizations. The recent political changes in central Europe may have a surprising effect. As the region's logical window on the Mediterranean, a role that thanks to the Austrians she must now share with Trieste, there may be some new chances for trade or as a cultural meeting-place for a vast part of Europe growing every day closer together. Venice's experience should not be wasted, and in the decades to come it may be that the *Serenissima* may find some real work to do once again.

Venetian Art and Architecture

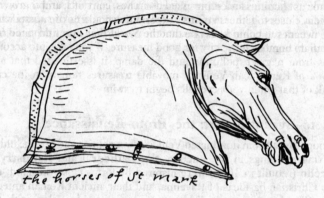

the horses of St mark

Their untrammelled genius is not overburdened with
thought, nothing about them reveals any anxiety as to the
interior life, and finally, as goes without saying, they did not
trouble themselves about historical accuracy. The truth they
sought to attain was that of colour, reflection, light, and
shade, bold foreshortening, transparency of atmosphere, and
the power of contrast.

—Pompeo Molmenti, *Venice*, 1926

If you had to pick out what sets Venetian art and architecture apart it
would have to be its sensual immediacy: it demands little from the
intellect, but everything from that tremulous bridge between the eye and
the heart. Light is its ruling deity. Giovanni Bellini and Titian pre-
Impressionistically smeared oil paints with their fingers to diffuse the
light in their canvases. Seascapes by Guardi dissolved into pure light.
Even the architects took account of the light reflecting off the water when
designing a church or palace.

After Florence, Venice was Italy's most inspired and original art city.
But as rich as it is, modern Venice offers only hints of its past glory:
Venetian art was always popular abroad, and much of the best was sold to
foreigners. The worst blow to Venice's patrimony came when Napoleon
'relocated' some 20,000 works of art to France, including so much gold

and silver that it took the French 15 days to plunder it all. Although some of the most famous pictures and statues were later returned, Venice's art and architecture continued to bleed away throughout the 19th century, as bankrupt families and suppressed churches, convents, and *scuole*, sold off their Titians. The Austrians knocked down scores of *palazzi* when their owners fell behind in taxes, and in World War I they dropped 620 incendiary bombs on the city for good measure. If you take into account losses from neglect, pollution and the damp, it is estimated that *only 4–10%* of Republican Venice's movable treasures remain in the city. Think of that when your eyeballs begin to swim.

Veneto-Byzantine Art: the 'Proto-Renaissance'

Although Byzantium dominated Venice's first politics and art, the oldest surviving buildings in the Lagoon, the **Cathedral** and **Baptistry** at **Torcello** (rebuilt in 1008) were inspired by forms closer at hand: the Early Christian basilicas of Ravenna, and their ancient Roman antecedents. The basic plan consisted of a nave and side aisles, with the triumphal arch over the chancel: Murano's **San Donato** (1125), **San Nicolò dei Mendicoli** and the Giudecca's **Sant'Eufemia** were built along these lines. But other early churches were designed in the centralized Greek-cross style, like the 11th-century **Santa Fosca**, built next to Torcello Cathedral, or the original of **Santa Maria Formosa**. The most important example, however, was the first: the **Basilica of San Marco**, built in the 830s, a copy of Constantinople's five-domed church of the Apostles—a form kept through all subsequent rebuildings.

Constantinople's other great contribution to the young city was in mosaic decoration. The dazzling mosaics of Ravenna's basilicas, begun by the last Roman emperors were finished by the new Romans of the Byzantium, who imported artists from Constantinople. These artists soon found additional work in Torcello and St Mark's. Their stiff, 'hieratic' portraiture of highly stylized, spiritual beings who live in a gold-ground paradise, with no need of shadows or perspective or other such worldly tricks, was to remain prominent in Venetian pictorial art until the 13th century. The third important artistic cross-current from Constantinople was in gold-work, namely the spectacular **Pala d'Oro** in St Mark's, ordered by Doge Ordelafo Falier in 1105, and in its final form a collaborative effort between Greek and Venetian craftsmen.

The great looting of Constantinople's treasures in 1204 did much to prolong the Byzantine influence in the Lagoon. Although most of the fabulous riches were devoted to embellishing St Mark's, marble columns, mosaic icons and carvings were incorporated into other churches as well. A new wave of Greek mosaicists emigrated to Venice to sheath St Mark's domes in gold, in images straight from the 5th century. For curiously, the loot from Constantinople sparked a retro fashion for Early Christian art (sometimes called the 'Proto-Renaissance') that lasted through the 12th and 13th centuries. The Venetians had the style down so pat that no one will ever know if some of the works date from the 6th or 13th century (St Mark's alabaster columns, for example). As Rome, the upstart, had Virgil's *Aeneid* to give the city an ancient and noble lineage, Venice (a much later upstart) has the mosaics in St Mark's to anchor it to the hallowed traditions of the Early Christian church.

But on the façade of St Mark's the Venetians took iconographic pains to show they could also claim an ancestor as illustrious as Hercules. The anonymous 13th-century sculptors of the pseudo-antique reliefs of Hercules and the basilica's side portals formed Venice's first workshop. They had hardly begun when their work was overshadowed by the far livelier, more natural figures of the **Labours of the Months** on the central portal, carved by Lombard stonemasons trained by the great Benedetto Antelami of Parma.

Venice's oldest palaces (like the **Ca' da Mosto, Ca' Farsetti**, and the **Fondaco dei Turchi**) date from the 13th century, and show a similar taste for Byzantine and Islamic designs, especially in their arches. In them you can already see the classic form of the Venetian palaces: main façade on a canal, where waterborne arrivals entered the *androne*, a long hall running through the centre of the ground floor to a less elaborate land entrance. This is where Venice's merchant princes conducted their business, with their storerooms off to the sides and their offices on the *mezzanine*. The same floor plan is repeated in the living quarters on the first floor, or *piano nobile*, where the long room is called the *portego* or *salone*, illuminated by a cluster of tall windows. In later palaces this would be the ballroom, and the family moved up to the next floor, or *secondo piano nobile*. But the basic structure remained the same throughout the centuries, leaving fashion to change only the surface decoration, and the shape and patterns of the windows and arches.

Lingering Gothic in the 14th and 15th Centuries

In many ways this was the most exciting and vigorous phase in Italian art, an age of discovery when the power of the artist was almost like that of a magician. Great imaginative leaps occurred in architecture, painting, and sculpture, especially in Tuscany—nor was it long before Tuscan masters introduced the new style to the Veneto. In Padua's Cappella degli Scrovegni (1308) **Giotto** painted all he knew about intuitive perspective, composition, and a new, more natural way to paint figures in natural settings. It was revolutionary in its day, the masterpiece of an artist who inspired the first painters of the Renaissance.

But the Venetians didn't want to know. Although Byzantine influences lingered into the 14th century, Venice by that time was ready to go Gothic in its half-oriental, flamboyant way. The once stiff Byzantine figures cautiously begin to sway in dance-like movements, like the famous *Salome* mosaic in St Mark's baptistry (1340s) and the marble statues on the basilica's rood screen, by **Jacobello and Pier Paolo dalle Masegne** (1394). The real break with the past came with the completion of the **Palazzo Ducale**, decorated with exquisite sculptural groups, capitals, and lacey Gothic tracery that had nothing to do with Byzantium. Venetian architecture in that period had more openwork than anywhere else—walls were built to define voids as well as solids: the Ca' d'Oro (1420–40s), by **Giovanni Bon** is the most effervescent example. Bon, with his son **Bartolomeo**, also designed the **Porta della Carta** (1430s), the grand entrance to the Doge's Palace and the flowery pride of Venice's late Gothic period.

The religious revivals of the 14th century saw in Venice the building of two giant brick Gothic churches to hold the crowds—**SS. Giovanni e Paolo** and the **Frari**. This being Italy, the architects were not interested in towering verticals, but in creating immense spaces; this being Venice, there was always the danger of such large structures shifting on their foundations, no matter how many piles were driven into the slime. One of the distinctive features of Venetian Gothic was the use of tie beams to add support to their aisles and arches. Another danger was weight, but Venice was able to draw upon the experience and talents of its Arsenal shipwrights: many smaller churches, like Santo Stefano and San Giacomo dell'Orio, were given lightweight wooden ship's keel roofs in the 1300s.

In painting, not only Giotto's innovations, but the more natural style of the Palazzo Ducale sculptors were ignored. The first Venetian painter to make a name for himself was **Paolo Veneziano**, who flourished in the 1330s: although still heavily Byzantine, his delight in brilliant colour was a harbinger of the Venetian school. In the 1350s, **Lorenzo Veneziano** (no relation) took another step away from Byzantium with his graceful line and soft shading to suggest three dimensions. But the strongest influence on local painters was the colourful, fairy-tale style called **International Gothic**. Two of its greatest masters, Gentile da Fabriano and Pisanello, painted frescoes (now lost) in the Palazzo Ducale at the beginning of the 15th century, but you can see the highly decorative, gilded panels by their Venetian followers (most notably **Jacobello del Fiore** and his pupil **Michele Giambono**) in the first room of the Accademia. International Gothic continued to have its adherents long into the 15th century thanks to the glowing polyptychs of **Antonio Vivarini**, father of a dynasty of painters from Murano, and his collaborator **Giovanni d'Alemagna**.

The Early Renaissance of the Quattrocento

Although the Venetians were slow to give up Gothic and join the Renaissance, the art and architecture produced in the transition period of the early 15th century was often crystalline in its freshness. Greek artists continued to arrive, taking refuge from the Turks (El Greco was to be one of these), but it was other Italians who intrigued the Venetians now—the great Florentine sculptors **Donatello** and **Verrocchio**, whose bronze equestrian statues left lessons in human form and expression, and painters like Andrea del Castagno and Paolo Uccello, who helped design mosaics in St Mark's.

The advent of Renaissance painting in Venice can be fairly concentrated on the careers of two men, father and son: Jacopo and Giovanni Bellini. **Jacopo Bellini** was a Gothic student of Gentile da Fabriano, but also collaborated with **Andrea del Castagno** in St Mark's Cappella della Madonna dei Máscoli; he painted two major cycles for the *scuole* of S. Marco and S. Giovanni Evangelista (both detroyed). But Jacopo's best surviving work is in his sketchbooks, in London and the Louvre—lovingly meticulous drawings from nature that had a major influence on his sons. **Gentile Bellini**, the elder, picked up on the meticulous in his photo-like paintings of narrative historical scenes, while **Giovanni Bellini** inherited his love for nature. Like many other painters and sculptors of his time, Giovanni was also heavily influenced by his brother-in-law, **Andrea Mantegna** of Padua, whose powerfully drawn sculptural figures exist in startling perspectives, drawn with a keen interest in antiquity. **Antonello da Messina**'s visit to Venice in the 1470s introduced Giovanni to the luminous oil-painting techniques he learned in a Flemish workshop. Lastly, **Cima da Conegliano** came to Venice from the rural Veneto and set his shimmering religious scenes against his own native hills, instructing Bellini in one of the tenets of the early Renaissance: that heaven is here on earth.

Giovanni Bellini combined all these new influences and techniques to create some of the most lyrical, sensually poetic art of the Renaissance. Throughout his long career, he never stopped experimenting, seeking new responses to nature and light and colour and atmosphere. His *Madonnas* and *Saints* are at once ideal yet human, noble and tender, warmed by the liquid sun, never striving to outdo or out-scale nature. And it is this very empathy and sense of human measure that makes Bellini's angels divine. His follower, **Vittore Carpaccio**, took this empathy with nature and actuality to a more earthly level, and painted some of the most charming narratives of all time, with enough literal detail to make his canvases important historical records (especially the *Sant' Ursula* and *San Giorgio degli Schiavoni* cycles).

The classical calm and natural nobility of Donatello's work in Padua was a formative influence on sculptors in Venice in the 1400s. **Antonio Rizzo** of Verona spent much of his career in Venice as master architect of the Ducal Palace. Two of his works, the Palace's statue of *Eve* and the Frari's Tron tomb, are Early Renaissance works in the most classic sense, harmonious and confident. **Pietro Lombardo**, his contemporary from Cremona, refined Rizzo's style in his pure Renaissance tomb of Doge Pasquale Malipiero, in SS. Giovanni e Paolo. In his exquisite little church of Santa Maria dei Miracoli and the façade of the Scuola di San Marco, Pietro Lombardo created an architectural style known as the Lombardesque, inspired by St Mark's Basilica: decorated with coloured marble sheathing, rounded arches, sculptured friezes, Corinthian capitals and coloured discs. Pietro's sons and assistants, **Tullio and Antonio Lombardo**, supplied most of Venice's best reliefs and statues from the 1480s on, their latter works inspired by antique models.

The busiest architect of the period was **Mauro Codussi** (or Coducci) a native of Bergamo, who in 1469 built the first Renaissance church in Venice, S. Michele in Isola. Like Pietro Lombardo, Codussi adapted former Venetian styles, especially Byzantine, to Renaissance forms and proportions, borrowing the plans, silhouettes, and decorative elements from older buildings. Yet he was also capable of great originality (see the staircase in the Scuola di San Giovanni Evangelista). His palaces on the Grand Canal (Palazzo Corner Spinelli and Ca' Vendramin Calergi), with their delightful synthesis of Veneto-Byzantine elements with Tuscan (double-arched windows, rusticated ground floors, etc.) became the models for many others in the next two centuries.

High Renaissance

The 16th century is often called the 'Golden Age' of Venetian Art. While the rest of Italy followed the artists in Rome in learning drawing and anatomy, the Venetians went their own way, obsessed with the dramatic qualities of light and atmosphere. The elusive, shortlived **Giorgione** of Castelfranco, a pupil of Giovanni Bellini, was the seminal figure in this new manner. In his most famous painting, the *Tempest*, the mysterious subject matter is subordinate to its tense, brooding atmosphere. Giorgione invented 'easel painting'—art that served neither Church nor State nor the vanity of a patron, but stood on its own for the pleasure of the viewer. Giorgione was also the first to paint freely, without preliminary sketches, beginning the Venetian trend away from drawing—much to the disdain of their Tuscan contemporaries.

Giorgione's brief career was linked with two fellow Bellini students and collaborators, whose works are sometimes confused with his. The first, **Sebastiano del Piombo**, left for Rome the year after Giorgione died, while the second, **Titian**, stayed in town to become a major transitional figure in Venetian art, though 95% of his works were sent abroad to a host of foreign clients, or lifted by Napoleon. Emperor Charles V held him in such respect that during a sitting he bent over to pick up one of his fallen brushes. In Titian's 90 or so years, he went from a style so imitative of Giorgione that it's virtually impossible to tell who painted some canvases, to dramatic religious compositions, full of vibrant colour and emotion (most famously, the Frari altarpiece) through a series of ripe, bar-room nudes and portraits of big shots, to his last style, epitomized in the Accademia's *Pietà*, the paint literally smeared on with his hands, and left unfinished at his death.

In spite of his achievements, Titian's artistic vision seldom rose above the obvious; with his work, true imagination and virtuosity have parted ways. Nor are his contempories especially riveting, with the exception of **Lorenzo Lotto**, who, as a potential rival was forced out of Venice by Titian's clique to spend the rest of a lonely career painting the most psychologically penetrating portraits of his generation. Another contemporary, **Palma Vecchio**, specialized in beautiful women, from courtesans to his famous *Santa Barbara* in S. Maria Formosa, in an intellectually undemanding style echoed by his prolific followers, **Bonifazio Veronese** and **Jacopo Bassano**. The latter was also influenced by the exaggerated poses and extreme lighting effects of the Mannerists (the main appeal for **El Greco** who he also influenced), although in the end Bassano and his two artist sons are best remembered for their night-time *Nativities* set in Italian barnyards.

Some 35 years younger than Titian, **Tintoretto** entered the Venetian scene of beautiful light and colour like a comet from outer space, reuniting virtuosity and imagination in his dynamic first canvases. Light and colour, or the lack of them, became the means and not the end to his feverishly visionary canvases, painted in fast furious brush strokes. The inspiration to paint was so strong in him that he would offer his services for free, or resort to tricks to get a commission, as in the case of his magnificent cycle in the Scuola di San Rocco. Unlike Giovanni Bellini, however, he was a baleful influence on his followers, who would fit Yeats' gibe, 'The best lack all conviction and the worst are full of passionate intensity'. **Palma Giovane** was only the most prolific. Fewer painters tried to follow the act of Tintoretto's elegant and urbane contemporary, **Paolo Veronese**, who arrived in Venice in the 1550s to paint lavish canvases in jewel-like colours that are the culmination of all that Venice had to teach in interior decoration and illusionism.

The most important architect, and one of the greatest sculptors in 16th-century Venice was **Jacopo Sansovino**, who adapted his training in Tuscany and Rome to create a distinctive Venetian style, richly decorated with sculpture and classical motifs that create patterns of light and shadow (especially in the Biblioteca and Loggetta). His most famous pupil, **Alessandro Vittoria**, broke away from Sansovino's graceful classicism in favour of a more emotional Mannerist style. But the lovers of antiquity were to dominate, especially in the work of the most influential architect the Veneto produced, **Palladio**. Palladio's greatest talent was in adapting classical models to modern needs: his famous villas not only fitted his client's desire to look the part of a Roman patrician in the country, but were also functional as working farm centres. His ecclesiastical buildings (S. Giorgio Maggiore, the Redentore, S. Francesco della Vigna) are concentrated in Venice—sleek, white, minimally adorned temples that stand out in the higgledy piggledy like yachts in a picturesque fishing port.

Baroque (17th Century)

As an art designed to induce temporal obedience and psychical oblivion, Baroque's effects are difficult to describe. On the whole, however, little of the most excessive brand of Baroque made it to Venice. In short, the 17th century saw more of the same Venetian palaces and and churches, only inflated into Baroque. The age does provide some exceptions to the rule that in art, less is more: **Baldassare Longhena**'s magnificent church of the Salute on the Grand Canal. Longhena, deeply indebted to both Sansovino and Palladio, was Venice's only Baroque architect of note, and his palette ranged from the massive but exuberant Ca' Pesaro to the grotesque in the Ospedaletto façade and the lugubrious in the Scalzi. Baroque frosting, most of it gone a bit rancid, is the keynote to Longhena's mediocre successors, **Alessandro Tremignon** (S. Moisè) and **Giuseppe Sardi** (S. Maria del Giglio). The best 17th-century sculptors came from elsewhere: the Genoese **Nicolò Roccatagliata**, the Flemish sculpor **Juste Le Court**, and Bernini's pupil from Rome, **Filippo Parodi**.

Meanwhile, Venetian painters, clumsily wallowing in the muddy aftermath of Tintoretto, darkened the city's churches with one diagonal, shadow-bound composition after another, reaching an hypnotic extreme in **Gian Antonio Fumiani**'s *trompe-l'oeil* ceiling for S. Pantalon. Most of the fresh inspiration was to come from outsiders, many of whom arrived in Venice as pilgrims desiring to learn more about light and the free handling of paint: the short-lived German **Johann Lys** stands out, along with two inspired, if somewhat eccentric Italians, **Francesco Maffei** of Vicenza and **Sebastiano Mazzoni**.

An 18th-Century Rococo Revival

Venice bloomed like Camille on her death bed, with a revival of talent to ease her political decline. Someone once called the 18th century the 'vegetable period' in art, but if everyone else made turnips, Venice created a charming, elegant style that became the international fashion of its day. The transition to iridescent light and graceful forms began with **Sebastiano Ricci** of Belluno, in his ceiling of San Marziale. His foil was **Giambattista Piazzetta**, who disdained colour for chiaroscuro and dramatic zigzagging compositions.

Both proved fertile inspiration for the celebrity decorator of the Rococo era, **Giambattista Tiepolo**, a virtuoso master of theatrical, buoyant ceilings, narrative, heroic frescoes set in illusionist (*quadrata*) backgrounds (as in the Palazzo Labia) and dazzling altarpieces (Sant' Alvise). He often worked with his son **Giandomenico Tiepolo**, who had no heart to continue his father's heroic style, but instead painted some highly original genre scenes (as in Ca' Rezzonico). This was also the period of the precise **Antonio Canaletto** and the more impression-istic brothers **Francesco and Gian Antonio Guardi** whose countless views of Venice were the rage among travellers on the Grand Tour; even today the majority of their works are in Britain and France. Equally popular was **Rosalba Carriera**, whose flattering Rococo pastel portraits were the rage among Europe's nobility. Another painter of the era, **Pietro Longhi**, devoted himself to genre scenes that are most interest-ing as a documentary of Venice some 200 years ago.

Meanwhile Venetian architect **Giorgio Massari** translated their Rococo sensibility into stone, especially in the lovely church/concert hall of La Pietà, while architect/sculptor **Domenico Rossi** defied gravity and reason for the Jesuits at the Gesuiti church, and in his loop-de-loop façade for S. Stae. One of the most memorable figures of the early 1700s was a furniture carver, **Andre Brustolon**, a student of Parodi, who set his imagination loose to create Italy's most densely populated furniture. The greatest sculptor to work in Venice in the late 18th century was the Neoclassical master, **Antonio Canova**, although he spent much of his career in Rome.

The 19th and 20th Centuries

Whatever artistic spirit remained at the end of the 18th century evap-orated after Napoleon. More was demolished than built in the 19th century—49 churches bit the dust, and the splendid art that adorned them was dispersed to various galleries or simply destroyed. One of the few names to drift down is that of **Gian Antonio Selva**, designer of La Fenice Opera house and the façade of S. Maurizio. Foreigners like Turner drifted in to paint the city, while John Ruskin wrote his *Stones of Venice*, which to his dismay didn't educate his readers in the glories and pitfalls of architecture as much as begin a trend for ogival arches in Manchester. But thousands were inspired to come and see the real thing, and when sea bathing became popular, the Lido was developed with its outrageous eclectic turn-of-the-century hotels. Another attraction was the great international art exhibits of the **Biennale**, inaugurated in 1895, and still one of the most prestigious in Europe (see p. 14). Holding international exhibitions has become big business in Venice today; many are excellent, and bring visitors back over and over again.

In the 20th century the local scene has been grim, though not for lack of trying. The Italian movements of the age—Futurism with its emphasis on speed, and the Metaphysical School with its emphasis on stillness—

had little response from Venice. In 1946 Renato Guttuso and Emile Vedova founded an avant-garde group, the *Fronte Nuova*, with more talk than notable results. Again the main input has come from abroad, particularly from the USA, which has always had a certain empathy for Venice. Peggy Guggenheim's Collection of contemporary art arrived in Venice like a breath of fresh air, but misplaced atavism prevented the construction of Frank Lloyd Wright's palace on the Grand Canal (although when the same authorities vetoed a hospital designed by Corbusier, even Corbusier agreed they were right).

All said and done, preservation has pretty much pre-empted creation in fragile, delicate old Venice. Saving the city and its art has become a major preoccupation of Italians and foreigners alike. The British Venice in Peril Fund, begun after the flood in 1966, is one of the most active of the 32 international organizations, and Americans and Italians have contributed buckets of money to keep the old girl afloat, most of it now spent in cooperation with the local UNESCO office, Amici dei Musei e Monumenti Veneziani. But will any new artists ever swim against the tides of municipal embalming fluid?

Artists' Directory

This includes the principal architects, painters and sculptors represented in Venice. The list is far from exhaustive, bound to exasperate partisans of some artists and do scant justice to the rest, but we've tried to include only the best and most representative works you'll find in Venice (and in the 'Day Trips').

Antonello da Messina (*c.* 1430–79), a Sicilian painter who visited Venice. Antonello was one of the first Italians to perfect the Van Eyckian oil painting techniques of Flanders; his compelling mastery of light, shadows, and the simplification of forms was a major influence on Giovanni Bellini (see the great but damaged *Pietà* in the Museo Correr).

Barbari, Jacopo De' (d. 1515), precise pupil of Alvise Vivarini whose most famous work is the bird's-eye-view plan of Venice in the Museo Correr.

Basaiti, Marco (1470–*c.*1530), student and collaborator of Alvise Vivarini (Accademia).

Bassano, Jacopo (da Ponte; 1510–92), *paterfamilias* of a clan of artists working mainly from Bassano del Grappa. Jacopo's began by painting in the monumental Central Italian style, but is better known for churning out a whole succession of religious night scenes in rustic barnyards. Son Francesco (1549–92) was his most skilled assistant and follower; the more prolific Leandro less so (*Return of Jacob*, in the Palazzo Ducale).

Bastiani, Lazzaro (*c.* 1420–1512), probably Carpaccio's master, and the painter responsible for the *Baby Carpaccios* (S. Alvise).

Bella, Gabriel (1730–99), Venice's charming naïf painter of city scenes, a valuable source of information about the 18th century despite the technical ineptitude (Palazzo Querini-Stampalia).

Bellini, Gentile (1429–1507), elder son of Jacopo, famous for his detailed depictions of Venetian ceremonies and narrative histories (*Procession of the Relic of the True Cross*, Accademia) and his portrait of *Sultan Mehmet II*, now in the National Gallery in London, painted during a sojourn in Istanbul. (Gentile was such a hit with the Sultan that the latter presented him with the head of a freshly decapitated criminal, to help him paint a scene of St John the Baptist. At this point Gentile asked to go home, and showing no hard feelings, the Sultan sent him back to Venice with a beautiful gold chain.)

Bellini, Giovanni ('Giambellino', *c.* 1431–1516), the greatest early Renaissance painter of Northern Italy, an innovator who kept experimenting even into his 80s, and greatly influenced (and was influenced by) his pupils, Giorgione and Titian. No artist before him painted with such sensitivity to light, atmosphere, colour and nature; none since have approached the almost magical tenderness that makes his paintings transcendent (masterpieces in the Accademia, S. Zaccaria, the Frari, and S. Pietro Martire, on Murano).

Bellini, Jacopo (1400–70), father of Giovanni and Gentile, father-in-law of Mantegna, all of whom were influenced by Jacopo's beautiful drawings from nature. In Venice his best works are his Madonnas, more natural and lifelike than others of his generation (Accademia).

Bon, Bartolomeo (d. 1464), prolific Venetian sculptor and architect, designer of the Porta della Carta.

Bon, Giovanni (d. 1444), late Gothic sculptor and architect of great refinement, designer of the Ca' d'Oro.

Bonifazio de'Pitati (Bonifazio Veronese; 1478–1553), the most talented follower of Palma Vecchio (Accademia).

Bordone, Paris (1500–1571), student and imitator of Titian, whose best work hangs in the Accademia.

Brustolon, Andrea (1662–1732), Rococo furniture-maker of extraordinary imagination that borders on Proto-kitsch (Ca' Rezzonico).

Calendario, Filippo (d. 1355), master architect of the Doge's Palace (this is disputed), and probably the inventor of its unique top-heavy design, he was executed for his part in the Falier conspiracy.

Canaletto, Antonio (1697–1768), master of meticulous Venetian *vedute*, or views, but stay in England to see his paintings—there is but one in the Accademia, and two in the Ca' Rezzonico.

Canova, Antonio (1757–1822), of Possagno, Europe's Neoclassical celebrity sculptor, the favourite of Napoleon and Benjamin Franklin (Museo Correr, Frari; also **Possagno**).

Carpaccio, Vittore (*c.* 1465–1525), the most charming of Venetian artists, with fairy-tale paintings full of documentary details from his life and times (major cycles at Scuola di S. Giorgio Schiavone and the Accademia; his *Two Women* in the Museo Correr is Venice's first genre painting).

Carrà, Carlo (1881–1966), started out as a Futurist but changed gears to the Metaphysical School in Ferrara with de Chirico (Peggy Guggenheim).

Carriera, Rosalba (1675–1758), a Venetian portraitist and miniaturist, was perhaps the first woman to make a good living as an artist: her soft, pastel portraits were the rage of the powdered wig set not only in Venice, but in Paris and Vienna (Accademia and Ca' Rezzonico).

Castagno, Andrea del (1423–1457), a Tuscan master of striking form and precise drawing, who visited in 1445 and left the city food for thought in St Mark's and S. Zaccaria.

Chirico, Giorgio de (1888–1978), a Greek-Italian who was one of the founding fathers of the Metaphysical School in Ferrara (1916–1918), best known for his uncanny urban landscapes dotted with classical odds and ends and mannikins (Peggy Guggenheim).

Cima da Conegliano, Giovanni Battista (1459–1518), whose luminous autumnal colours and landscapes were inspired by Bellini—as Bellini was inspired by several of his compositions (Madonna del Orto, Accademia, and Carmini; also **Conegliano, Este**).

Codussi, Mauro (*c.* 1420–1504), architect from Bergamo, who worked mainly in Venice; a genius at synthesizing traditional Venetian styles with the classical forms of the Renaissance, and the first to use Istrian stone for façades (S. Michele, S. Zaccaria, staircase at the Scuola di S. Giovanni Evangelista, Palazzo Vendramin-Calergi).

Crivelli, Carlo (*c.*1435–1495), meticulous Venetian painter enamoured of luminous, almost 3-D perspective, crystalline forms, garlands, and cucumbers; he spent most of his time in the Marches (Accademia).

De Pisis, Filippo (1896–1956), a Neo-Impressionist from Ferrara who spent a long period in Venice (Peggy Guggenheim).

Donatello (1386–1466), of Florence, was the best Italian sculptor of the *quattrocento*, if not of all time, never equalled in technique, express-iveness or imaginative content. He spent a long period in **Padua**, casting his *Gattamelata* statue and altar for the Basilica di S. Antonio (also a statue in the Frari).

Francesco di Giorgio Martini (1439–1502), Tuscan architect, sculp-tor and painter of grace and symmetry (Carmini).

Gambello, Antonio (d. 1481), is generally given credit for bringing Renaissance architecture to Venice in the form of the Arsenal Gate, though he is also responsible for the northern Gothic elements of S. Zaccaria, so who knows?

Giambono, Michele (*c.* 1420–1462), painter and mosaicist, one of the princes of Venetian retro; while everyone else moved onto the Renais-sance, Giambono was still churning out rich paintings in graceful Inter-national Gothic (Accademia, altarpieces in St Mark's).

Giorgione (Giorgio Barbarelli, *c.* 1478–1510), got his nickname 'Great George' not only for his height, but for the huge influence he had over Venetian painting. Although he barely lived past 30 and only several paintings are undisputedly by his hand, his poetic evocation of atmos-phere and haunting, psychological ambiguity was echoed not only by his followers, Titian (whom he chose to assist him in the lost Fondaco dei Tedeschi frescoes) and Sebastiano del Piombo, but by his master Gio-vanni Bellini (Accademia).

Giotto di Bondone (*c.* 1267–1337), was one of the most influential painters in Italian art, the first to break away from stylized Byzantine forms in favour of a more 'natural' and narrative style. Although most closely associated with Florence and Assisi, he painted his masterpiece in **Padua**: the Cappella degli Scrovegni.

Guardi, Francesco (1712–1793), younger brother of **Gian Antonio**, with whom he often worked, making attributions sometimes difficult. Guardi's favourite subject was Venice, but his views, unlike Canaletto's, are suffused with light and atmosphere; some canvases approach Im-pressionism (Ca' d'Oro, Accademia, Angelo Raffaele).

Guariento (14th century), a Paduan follower of Giotto, whose greatest work, a massive fresco of *Paradise* in Venice's Doge's Palace was lost in a fire—only fragments remain.

Jacobello del Fiore (*c.* 1370–1439), Venetian master of International Gothic, very fond of raised gold embossing (Accademia).

Le Court Juste (1627–1679), Flemish sculptor who spent many years in Venice; his main work is the theatrical *Plague* altarpiece in the Salute.

Leopardi, Alessandro (d. 1522) classicizing sculptor responsible for completing Verrocchio's *Colleoni* monument and casting the ornate flagstaffs in front of St Mark's.

Lombardo, Pietro (*c.* 1435–1515), founder of Venice's greatest family of sculptors and architects, strongly influenced by Donatello's work in Padua (SS. Giovanni e Paolo, S. Giobbe, S. Francesco delle Vigna, and S. Maria dei Miracoli).

Lombardo, Tullio (*c.* 1455–1532), son of Pietro, with whom he often worked; Tullio was an exquisite marble sculptor, best known for his tombs (SS. Giovanni e Paolo) and classical reliefs (Ca' d'Oro, Venice and Basilica of S. Antonio, **Padua** which also has a relief by his brother Antonio); **Antonio Lombardo** (*c.* 1458–*c.* 1516) was a major figure in the Venetian High Renaissance, though most of his surviving works are now in Leningrad's Hermitage.

Longhena, Baldassare (1598–1682), Venetian architect, a student of Scamozzi, whose best work was one of his first: the church of the Salute (also Ca' Pesaro).

Longhi, Pietro (1702–1785), there may not have been photographers in 18th-century Venice, but there was Pietro Longhi to portray society's foibles dutifully (Ca' Rezzonico, Accademia, Querini-Stampalia).

Lorenzo Veneziano (active 1356–1379), disciple of Paolo Veneziano and painter in a luxuriant, golden style presaging International Gothic (Accademia; also Duomo, **Vicenza**).

Lotto, Lorenzo (*c.* 1480–1556), a native Venetian and pupil of Giovanni Bellini, best known for intense portraits that seem to catch their sitters off-guard, capturing his own restless energy on canvas; he was run out of Venice by Titian and Aretino (Accademia; also S. Nicolò, **Treviso**).

Lys, Johann (1595–1630), a German painter of verve whose career was tragically cut short by plague (S. Nicolò da Tolentino).

Maffei, Francesco (*c.* 1600–60) a painter from Vicenza, a somewhat dissonant and unorthodox painter, inspired by Lys; the *Guardian Angel* in SS. Apostoli is his masterpiece (also Museo Civico and Oratorio di S. Nicola, **Vicenza**).

Mansueti, Giovanni (*c.* 1465–1527), underrated student of Giovanni Bellini and a talented painter of narrative histories (Accademia; Museo Civico, **Vicenza**).

Mantegna, Andrea (*c.* 1420–1506), a remarkable painter and engraver born near Padua, whose interest in antiquity, sculptural forms as hard as coral, and unusual perspectives dominated art in the Veneto until the rise of his brother-in-law Giovanni Bellini (Accademia and Ca' d'Oro; also Eremitani church, **Padua**).

Dalle Masegne, Jacobello and Pier Paolo, 14th-century Venetian brothers and sculptors, influenced by the works of Tuscan sculptor Nicolò Pisano, creater of a new realistic, classically-inspired style (S. Marco).

Massari, Giorgio (1687–1766), Venetian architect who collaborated with G. Tiepolo and Vivaldi to produce some of Venice's most delightful Baroque (La Pietà, and Gesuati).

Mazzoni, Sebastiano (1611–78), Baroque painter after Lys and Maffei who marched to a different drummer (S. Benedetto) also designed the Palazzo Moro-Lin on the Grand Canal.

Morandi, Giorgio (1890–1964), an heir of the Metaphysical school; naturally austere, his still life paintings invite a subtle meditation on form (Ca' Pesaro).

Palladio (Andrea di Pietro della Gondola, 1508–80), the Veneto's most influential architect, not only for his buildings, but for his books and drawings that re-interpreted Roman architecture to fit the needs of the day (S. Giorgio Maggiore and the Redentore, the villa of **La Malcontenta**, on the **Brenta Canal**; palaces and the Basilica, **Vicenza**).

Palma Giovane (1544–1628), the most prolific painter of his day in Venice, was the great-nephew of Palma Vecchio and a follower of Tintoretto, specializing in large but usually vapid narrative paintings (every church in Venice seems to have at least one; best works in the Oratorio dei Crociferi and Querini-Stampalia).

Palma Vecchio (Jacopo Negreti, *c.*1480–1528), a student of Giovanni Bellini who successfully adopted the new sensuous style of Giorgione, and is best known for his beautiful paintings of women—both courtesans and saints (S. Maria Formosa, Accademia; also S. Stefano, **Vicenza**).

Paolo Veneziano (*c.* 1290–1360), the leading Venetian painter of the day, whose colourful Byzantine style is reminiscent of the Pala d'Oro (Accademia; also Museo Civico, **Padua**).

Parodi, Filippo (1630–1702), sculptor who adapted his master Bernini's late, flowing style (S. Nicolò da Tolentino).

Piazzetta, Giambattista (1683–1754), Venetian Baroque painter extraordinaire, who went to dramatic extremes in his use of light and dark; was first president of the Accademia (Accademia, S. Maria delle Fave, and SS. Giovanni e Paolo).

Piero della Francesca (*c.* 1420–1492), a Tuscan painter who wrote two theoretical books on perspective, then illustrated them with a lifetime's work, reducing painting to the bare essentials: mathematics, light, and colour (Accademia, Vittorio Cini Collection).

Pisanello, (Antonio Pisano, *c.* 1415–*c.* 1455), originator of the Renaissance medal and one of the leading International Gothic painters in Italy (medals in the Ca' d'Oro).

Ponte, Antonio da (1512–97), designer of the Rialto Bridge and the new prison building.

Pordenone (Giovanni de' Sacchis; 1484–1539), always wore a sword in case he should happen upon his chief rival, Titian. Pordenone had a more monumental, Roman style combined with quick brushstrokes and a tendency towards the bizarre (S. Giovanni Elemosinario, Ca' d'Oro).

Ricci, Sebastiano (1659–1734), Mazzoni's pupil, who combined a bright-coloured palette with the scenographic monumentality of Roman Baroque (S. Marziale; also Museo Civico, **Vicenza**).

Rizzo (Bregno), **Antonio** (*c.* 1445–1499), pure Renaissance sculptor and architect from Verona, who worked in Padua and Venice (*Tron* monument, Frari, Scala dei Giganti and courtyard of the Palazzo Ducale).

Roccatagliata, Nicolò (1593–1636), sculptor of elegant early Baroque bronzes (S. Giorgio Maggiore, S. Moisè).

Rossi, Domenico (1657–1737), hyper-Baroque architect and sculptor, responsible for the apsidial altars of the Gesuiti and façade of S. Stae.

Sammicheli, Michele (1484–1559), refined Venetian Renaissance architect, though best known for his fortifications, most notably in Venice, the Forte di Sant'Andrea by the Lido (also Palazzo Grimani; fortifications in **Padua**; palaces in **Treviso**).

Sansovino, Jacopo (Jacopo Tatti, 1486–1570), sculptor and architect who took his name from his Tuscan master, sculptor Andrea Sansovino. Jacopo fled the Sack of Rome in 1527 and came to Venice, where he became the chief architect to the Procurators of St Mark's and a good friend of Titian and Aretino, who promoted his career. Sansovino used his Tuscan and Roman periods to create a new decorative Venetian High Renaissance style—the rhythmic use of columns, arches, loggias, and reliefs, with sculpture playing an integral role in the building (major works include Libreria Marciana, Zecca, dome of S. Fantin, sculptures in the Ducal Palace and St Mark's; reliefs in S. Antonio, **Padua**, also Museo Civico, **Vicenza**).

Santi, Andriolo de, Paduan sculptor whose 1336 tomb of *Duccio degli Uberti* in the **Frari** was probably the proto-type of the standard Venetian tomb: a sarcophagus topped by an arch, holding an effigy of the deceased. His son, **Giovanni de' Santi** carved the unwieldy Virgin in Madonna dell'Orto.

Sardi, Giuseppe (1620–99), a muddly Baroque architect, responsible for the façades of the Scalzi and S. Maria del Giglio.

Scamozzi, Vincenzo (1552–1616), architect from Vicenza who became Palladio's closest follower, taking his ideas to classizing extremes, as in the Procuratie Nuove (and the stage of the Teatro Olimpico, **Vicenza**). He spent most of his Venetian career finishing Sansovino's library.

Sebastiano del Piombo (1485–1547), a colleague of Giorgione, and a rich autumnal colourist. Sebastiano went to Rome and became the chief notary of the Vatican (hence his nickname, from the leaden seals that still haunt the Posta Italiana); a painter after Raphael until he made enough money to stop painting altogether (S. Giovanni Crisostomo).

Selva, Gian Antonio (1751–1819), architect of La Fenice, a precocious believer that form should follow function (also façade of S. Maurizio)

Tiepolo, Giambattista (1696–1770), Venice's greatest Baroque painter, and an excellent draughtsman, a pupil of Piazzetta, though he had little use for *chiaroscuro*. Tiepolo's subjects, many mythological, live in the delightful warm afterglow of Venice's decline. In 1762, when he was 66, the Senate, wanting to engratiate itself with the king of Spain ordered him against his will to go to paint ceilings in Madrid (Palazzo Labia, Scuola dei Carmini, and Gesuati; Villa Pisani, **Stra**; Villa Valmarana, **Vicenza**).

Tiepolo, Giandomenico (1727–1804), son of Giambattista, with whom he frescoed Villa Valmarana. Giandomenico's work is more introspective and often haunting, especially his masquerades in Ca' Rezzonico and his stations of the cross at S. Polo.

Tintoretto (Jacopo Robusti, 1518–94), was given his name 'little dyer' for his father's profession. A proud, ill-tempered workaholic, his ideal was to combine Michelangelo's drawing with the colouring of Titian, but his most amazing talent was in his visionary, unrestrained and totally original composition (Scuola di S. Rocco series; the world's largest painting, in the Palazzo Ducale; Accademia and S. Giorgio Maggiore).

Titian (Tiziano Vecellio, *c.* 1480s–1576), came from Pieve di Cadore in the Dolomites to become 16th-century Venice's most popular painter, the favourite of princes, popes, and emperors. Titian made his reputation with the monumental altarpiece in the Frari, a bold handling of form and colour which would prove a pivotal influence on Tintoretto. Although Titian spent most of his life in Venice, his international reputation saw most of his canvases scattered around the courts of Europe: Titian's fine portrait of Philip II convinced Mary Tudor that she should marry him. Besides the Frari altarpieces, Venice keeps his works in S. Salvatore, the Accademia, and the Salute; also cathedral, **Treviso**.

Tura, Cosmè (c. 1430–1495), of the Ferrara school, whose singularly craggy and weirdly tortured style is immediately recognizable and for many, an acquired taste (Museo Correr, Accademia).

Veronese (Paolo Caliari, 1528–88), the most sumptuous and ravishingly decorative painter of the High Renaissance, fond of striking illusionism, shimmering colours, and curious perspectives set in pale Palladian architectural fantasies (Accademia, Palazzo Ducale, and S. Sebastiano).

Verrocchio, Andrea del (1435–88), painter, sculptor and alchemist, a follower of Donatello and teacher of Leonardo da Vinci, Verrocchio was considered the greatest bronze sculptor of the day, and was hired by the Senate to create the dynamic equestrian statue of Colleoni in front of SS. Giovanni e Paolo.

Vittoria, Alessandro (1525–1608), Venetian sculptor, a student of Sansovino famous for his bronze statuettes and portrait busts (S. Francesco della Vigna, Frari, Ca' d'Oro).

Vivarini, 15th-century family of painters from Murano, the chief rivals of the Bellini workshop, noted for their rich, decorative style. **Antonio** (c. 1415–c. 1480), a follower of Jacobello del Fiore, collaborated with Giovanni d'Alemagna to paint lavish golden altarpieces (S. Giobbe and S. Zaccaria); brother **Bartolomeo** (1432–1499) played an influential role in Venetian art through his use of colour and rhythm (S. Maria Formosa, Frari); **Alvise** (1446–1503), son of Antonio, was influenced by Antonello da Messina (Frari, S. Giovanni in Brágora).

The Grand Canal

It may be a cliché to sail down the Grand Canal in a gondola at twilight with your own true love, but it's one of the most unforgettable clichés in which you could ever indulge. Although the gold and frescoes have long ago worn off the fantasy façades of its palaces, the *Canalazzo*, as the Venetians call it, has not entirely lost the colour of past ages. It has simply become a little more prosaic, chock-a-block with grunting *vaporetti*, tourist gondolas, private boats of every shape and size, and the eternal workaday barges, carrying lettuces, bathtubs, cartons of Coca-Cola, and sides of beef all over Venice. So that you may read along while you take your first boat (if not a gondola, take the slowpoke no. 1 *accelerato*) from the station to your hotel, we have arranged the trip from north to south, ending at Piazza S. Marco.

Great thoroughfares often seem to meet bad ends: Fifth Avenue comes to grief among junkyards and gasworks over the Harlem River; the Champs Elysées leads only to the nightmare of La Defense. The Grand Canal's shabby demise comes at its northern end, among the causeways, the docks of the Tronchetto, and the colossal parking garages of Piazzale Roma. The next sight is the **Giardino Papadopoli** [1], which despite its greenery tends to blend in with its surroundings; still visible from the Canal is the memorial to the 'inventor of modern hydraulic principles'. After that comes the **railway station**, in the style of the fancier American suburban supermarkets of the 50s. Beyond it, snack stands and African pedlars line the left bank leading towards the

Lista di Spagna. From here, no more embarassments, as the Grand Canal comes into its own.

On the right bank, opposite the station, the peculiar egg-cup church is **S. Simeone Piccolo** [2], one of the youngest of Venetian churches, completed in 1738 (see p. 216). To the right of it stands the 18th-century **Palazzo Diedo** [3], once the home of Angelo Emo, the last admiral of Venice. Next you pass under the **Ponte degli Scalzi**, built in 1934, one of only three to knot the two halves of the city together. The mouldering hulk to the left is the **Scalzi** [4] church (p. 260) built for the Reformed (or *scalzi*—shoeless) Carmelites in the 1640s. To the right, the **Rio Marin** is one of the busiest canals, a shortcut to S. Marco; after it, also on the right, you'll catch a glimpse of the long **Campo S. Simeone Profeta** (p. 216). The next canal is to the left: the **Canale di Cannaregio**. On the corner is the addition to the back of **S. Geremia** [5], built to hold the relics of S. Lucia, brought here in the 1860s when her own church was demolished for the station.

Here the Canal grows more colourful, with a number of ancient palaces, both Veneto-Byzantine and Gothic. To see the best example of the genesis of the former style, wait until two more canals pass on the right. At the second stands the monumental **Fondaco dei Turchi** [6], with its arcades of round arches, a work of the 12th–13th centuries built for the Palmieri family, and passing through many owners thereafter. In 1453, the last ambassador from Constantinople sojourned here; ironically, after 1621 the palace was occupied by his Turkish successors. It served as the headquarters for Ottoman merchants in Venice until 1838, and was tidily over-restored by the Austrians to house the city's **Natural History Museum** (p. 220). Across the little canal, Rio Fontego dei Turchi, the rugged old building with the Lion of St Mark was a public granary, the **Deposito del Megio** [7].

Opposite, the Casino keeps its winter quarters in the **Palazzo Loredan-Vendramin-Calergi** [8], one of the most impressive on this stretch of the canal. A Renaissance building with Corinthian columns, it was designed by Mauro Codussi, and completed by the Lombardos in 1509, one of the first to forsake the old Gothic style for Renaissance classicism; death in Venice came for Richard Wagner here in December 1883.

From the Casino to the Rialto Bridge

The next quarter mile or so, as far as the Rialto markets, is one of the high-rent squares on Venice's Monopoly board, lined with imposing palaces on both sides.

CANALE DI CANNAREGIO

RIO DELLA MADDALENA

Campo S. Marcuola

8 23 24

25 26

RIVA DI BIASIO

RIO S. GIACOMO

RIO DEL MEGIO

RIO TRON

6 7 9 10 11 12 14 15

16 17

Campo S. Stae

13

Campo S. Simeone Grande

RIO MARIN

Ponte degli Scalzi

Railway Station

2
3

RIO DEI TOLENTINI

To Tronchetto

RIO NUOVO

THE GRAND CANAL

RIO S. POLO

53 52

54

44

RIO FOSCARI (RIO NUOVO)

45
46
47
61
62

RIO S. BARNABA

55

56

57

RIO D. TOELETTA

RIO MALPAGA

58

RIO DEL DUCA

63

64 65

RIO S. TROVASO

Campo della Carità

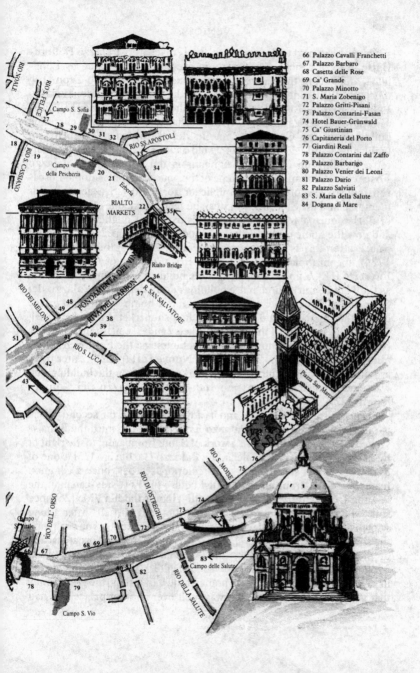

66 Palazzo Cavalli Franchetti
67 Palazzo Barbaro
68 Casetta delle Rose
69 Ca' Grande
70 Palazzo Minotto
71 S. Maria Zobenigo
72 Palazzo Gritti-Pisani
73 Palazzo Contarini-Fasan
74 Hotel Bauer-Grünwald
75 Ca' Giustinian
76 Capitaneria del Porto
77 Giardini Reali
78 Palazzo Contarini dal Zaffo
79 Palazzo Barbarigo
80 Palazzo Venier dei Leoni
81 Palazzo Dario
82 Palazzo Salviati
83 S. Maria della Salute
84 Dogana di Mare

On the right: next to the granaries, the 17th-century **Palazzo Belloni-Battaglia** [9], a sickly-sweet torte in overwrought Baroque by Longhena, architect of the Salute; the late Renaissance **Palazzo Tron** [10]; then two 15th-century Gothic palaces, the **Palazzo Duodo** [11] and **Palazzo Priuli-Bon** [12], the creamy white façade of **S. Stae** [13], on its canalside *campo* (see pp. 220–21), and next to it one of the most charming buildings on the Canal, the **Scuola dei Battiloro e Tiraoro** [14] (goldsmiths and jewellers)—not as old as it looks, but an eccentrically retro building of 1711. Its neighbour is the 17th-century **Palazzo Foscarino-Giovanelli** [15], home of the poor diplomat Antonio Foscarini, unjustly executed by the republic for treason (q.v. S. Stae, where his memorial and the State's apology can be seen); next, one of the grandest of all Baroque palaces, the **Palazzo Pésaro** [16], Longhena's last work, and now the home of the Gallery of Modern Art (see p. 222). The third palace after this is the **Palazzo Corner della Regina** [17] (rebuilt 1724), the birthplace of Caterina Cornaro, Queen of Cyprus; **Casa Favretto** [18], a fine Gothic-Byzantine building with some parts as old as the 11th century; three more buildings down comes the **Palazzo dei Brandolin** [19], another 15th-century Gothic home, and the last palace before the Fondamenta dell'Olio and the fish market. From the Canal, some of the busy life of the Rialto markets can be seen, though much is blocked out by the two ungainly market buildings: the **Fabbriche Vecchie** [20] and Sansovino's **Fabbriche Nuove** [21] (p. 224). After them are the outdoor fruit and vegetable markets, and then the building that was once Venice's treasury, the 16th-century **Palazzo dei Camerlenghi** [22].

On the left: after the Casino and its adjacent garden, the second palace is the 15th-century Gothic **Palazzo Erizzo** [23], the third the Renaissance **Palazzo Soranzo** [24], a work of Sante Lombardo; to the right of the narrow Rio della Maddalena, the **Palazzo Barbarigo** [25] is one of the last to retain some traces of its exterior frescoes, once a common feature of canal-front mansions. Just before the next side-canal on the left, the 16th-century **Palazzo Gussoni-Grimani della Vida** [26] once sported a full set of these frescoes by Tintoretto himself. After a long stretch of undistinguished palaces, mostly from the 1600s, you can't miss the spectacular **Ca d'Oro** [27], with the most fanciful and ornate façade of all Venice's Gothic palaces: this 'Golden House' completed about 1440, took its name from the heavy load of gilding that originally covered its columns and ornament. The home of the Contarinis, the great family that gave Venice eight doges, it was built over another palace that had belonged to the family of Carlo Zeno; some parts of this earlier work can still be seen. It now houses the Galleria Franchetti (pp. 248–9).

After the Ca d'Oro, a chorus of three more Gothic palaces compete for your attention: the **Palazzo Pésaro-Rava** [28], the **Palazzo Sagredo** [29], parts of which go back to the 1300s, and the 15th-century **Palazzo Foscari** [30], on the right flank of the narrow Campo S. Sofia. After these, the mood changes again with the late 16th-century **Palazzo Michiel dalle Colonne** [31], so-called for its columned portico, and the **Palazzo Michiel del Brusà** [32], an ancient palace rebuilt after a fire in 1774. With the **Ca' da Mosto** [33] on the corner of Rio di S. Giovanni Grisostomo is one of the oldest buildings on the Canal, a typical 13th-century Byzantine-Venetian building with its narrow arches, with just a hint of the peak at the top that would later grow into the full pointed arch of the Venetian Gothic. One of the great old Venetian merchant adventurers was born here in 1432: Alvise da Mosto, discoverer of the Cape Verde islands. Heading into the bend of the Canal before the Rialto Bridge, after the tiny Campiello Remer comes another 13th-century building, the much-altered **Palazzo Lion-Morosini** [34]. Just before the bridge itself, the **Fondaco dei Tedeschi** [35], austere without its once sumptuous frescoes by Giorgione and Titian was one of the largest of the foreign merchants' *khans*, home not only to the many German and Austrian traders, but those from Hungary, Bohemia and all central Europe; its less glorious fate in the present is to be Venice's main post office.

The Rialto Bridge

The earliest version of this famous bridge goes back to 1173, a simple pontoon bridge built on a string of boats. The first real bridge came in the 13th century, and it was burned during the insurrection of Baiamonte Tiepolo. Later incarnations were rickety-looking wooden structures; you can see the last of them in Carpaccio's paintings in the Accademia, with a narrow wooden drawbridge at the centre to allow the passing of sailing ships—and to cut communications when brawls between the city's rival factions got out of hand. The stone bridge, one of Venice's eternal symbols, was planned as early as 1524, but not begun until 1588. The state held a competition for the design, a prestigious commission that attracted some of the finest architects of the Renaissance—even Michelangelo submitted a proposal. Classically-minded critics since have often regretted that Palladio's design was not chosen; pictures of this survive, a truly ghastly Behemoth covered with Palladian temples and dripping with statues that would have looked as jarringly out-of-place here as a modern glass skyscraper.

Instead, the prize went to the suitably named Antonio da Ponte. The state councillors chose well, as they always did in their more grandiose undertakings: their little-known architect gave them the most Venetian of all possible bridges. Avoiding the architectural dogmas of the late Renaissance, he followed the steeply angled silhouette of the earlier bridge, covering it with slanted arcades that conceal rows of shops. The whole manages the difficult trick of harmonizing perfectly with all the buildings along the Canal, Byzantine, Gothic and Renaissance.

From the Rialto to Ca' Foscari

South of the Bridge, the Canal is lined with crowded *fondamente* on both sides.

On the left: directly after the Bridge you will see a short stretch of smaller *palazzi*, some from the 1400s or earlier and some modern reconstructions; though none are noteworthy in themselves, together they make up one of the loveliest building ensembles in Venice. Beyond these are the large **Palazzo Dolfin-Manin** [36], a work of Sansovino, and the Gothic **Palazzo Bembo** [37]. Near the end of this *fondamenta* (the Riva del Carbon) are Venice's municipal buildings, including the 12th–14th-century **Palazzo Loredan** [38] and **Palazzo Farsetti** [39]. A little further, at the next canal on the left, is the imposing Renaissance **Palazzo Grimani** [40], designed by Michele Sammicheli in the 1560s and now used as law courts. After the small canal (Rio di S. Luca), the **Palazzo Corner Contarini dai Cavalli** [41] (1445), an excellent late Gothic palace, takes its name from the horses on the coats of arms. Just before the next canal is the **Palazzo Benzon** [42], where the footloose Countess Marina Querini-Benzoni entertained Byron and legions of other notable gentlemen; to the right of the Rio Ca' Corner, the elegant building with the tri-lobed balconies is the **Palazzo Corner-Spinelli** [43], one of the definitive Venetian Renaissance palaces, designed by Codussi and modified by Michele Sammicheli.

A few forgettable palaces follow, before the huge compound of another great Venetian family. The **Palazzo Mocenigo** [44] is really four connected palaces in a row, built at various times from the 16th–18th centuries. Byron slept here, too, as did the famous mystic Giordano Bruno—who either shocked or bored his Mocenigo host so seriously with his heretical opinions that Macenigo turned him over to the Pope for burning in 1592. Next is the **Palazzo Contarini delle Figure** [45], so-called from the caryatids on the façade (every palace of this prolific family has such an appellation, so we can tell one from the other); and then there follow two more Gothic palaces, the **Palazzo Erizzo** [46] and **Palazzo Lezze** [47].

On the right: After the long Fondamenta del Vin, opposite the Palazzo Grimani are two 12th–13th century survivals, the **Palazzo Barizza** [48] and **Palazzo Businello** [49]. One street further down are two adjacent Gothic buildings both much altered and both called **Palazzo Donà** [50]; the one on the left is often referred to as 'alla Madonnetta' after the early Renaissance *Madonna* set in a shrine on its façade. After the next canal, the **Palazzo Bernardo** [51], is also 15th-century Gothic; Francesco Sforza, future Duke of Milan, lived here in the 1450s while he was still a mercenary *condottiere* working for Venice.

After the broad entrance to the Rio di S. Polo, the **Palazzo Barbarigo della Terrazza** [52] (1569) takes its name from its sumptuous roof garden; a famous collection of paintings, with most of Venice's Titians, was once kept here, but to see it now you'll have to go to the Hermitage in Leningrad—in the sad days of the 1850s the Barbarigos had to sell the collection to the Tsar. Next, the **Palazzo Pisani della Moretta** [53], a delicate Gothic confection, like so many of its fellows completely redone inside in the 18th century (and the best art here, an important Veronese, ended up in the National Gallery). As far as Ca' Foscari, two canals down, the rest is of little interest, but you can see a few Byzantine and Gothic fragments incorporated into later buildings, like the venerable stone lions in front of the **Palazzo Marcello dei Leoni** [54].

From Ca' Foscari to the Accademia Bridge

Here the Canal becomes even wider and grander; nearly all of the family names represented on this stretch can be found at least once in the list of doges.

On the right: **Ca' Foscari** [55] was built by the controversial Doge Franceso Foscari in 1437; he died here of a broken heart, not long after having been dismissed from office. One of the last great Gothic palaces, it was still thought one of the city's finest in the late Renaissance; Venice put up King Henry III of France here on his memorable visit in 1573. Next, Bartolomeo Bon's **Palazzo Giustiniani** (1452) [56], built for the family that traced its origins back to Byzantine Emperor Justinian;

palace-hopping Richard Wagner spent some time here in 1859, while he was working on *Tristan und Isolde*. Thirty years later, Robert Browning was breathing his last, next door at the massive **Ca' Rezzonico** [57]. A work of Longhena, expanded in the 1740s, it is now the **Museo del Settecento Veneziano** (see p. 198). After two more canals, the next substantial Gothic palace is the 15th-century **Palazzo Loredan** [58], later the Austrian Embassy and a nest of espionage and intrigues. To the left of the next canal, the **Palazzo Contarini degli Scrigni e Corfù** [59] are connected into one palace, half Gothic and half a 1609 work of Vincenzo Scamozzi. The wooden **Accademia Bridge**, with its single graceful arch over the Canal, has been exciting argument among Venetian and foreign aesthetes ever since it was built in 1932, replacing an iron bridge that was not much older, called the English Bridge by Venetians who saw it as an abberation of the Industrial Revolution. Behind it stands Venice's great picture gallery, the **Accademia** [60] (p. 190).

On the left: One palace before S. Samuele is the odd 13-windowed **Palazzo Moro-Lin** [61], designed by Rococo painter Sebastiano Mazzoni. Its solemn block of a neighbour, **Palazzo Grassi** [62], was built in 1748 by a wealthy family from Bologna who bought their way into the Golden Book of the nobility, and is now owned by Fiat and used for special exhibitions; it faces **Campo S. Samuele** and its church (p. 150). Just before the next canal (Rio del Duca), the **Ca' del Duca** [63] was built over an ambitious but never completed work of Bartolomeo Bon; after the canal, the 15th-century Gothic **Palazzo Falier** [64] and the **Palazzo Giustinian-Lolin** [65], another work of Longhena (1623).

From the Accademia to S. Marco

On the left: on this side of the bridge, narrow **Campo S. Vitale (S. Vidal)** opens up into the broad Campo S. Stefano; bordering it, with Venice's most enviable canal-front garden, is the **Palazzo Cavalli-Franchetti** [66], 15th-century Gothic somewhat prettified in the 1890s; across the narrow canal (Rio dell'Orso), the **Palazzo Barbaro** [67] was the home of the supremely vain family who glorified themselves on the façade of S. Maria Zobenigo (see p. 152). Among the next stretch of smaller houses, you'll be able to pick out the **Casetta delle Rose** [68]—a lovely place that was home to the sculptor Canova and later to Gabriele d'Annunzio. You'll certainly have no trouble finding the **Ca' Grande** [69], (or Palazzo Corner), one of the real monsters of the Canal, a magnificently gloomy pile that is considered one of the masterworks of Sansovino, completed in the 1560s; once the home of declining Venice's wealthiest family, it seems much better fitted for its new job—home of the State Prefecture. Next to it there's the 15th-century Gothic **Palazzo Minotto** [70]. At the narrow Campo del Traghetto, where there is a gondola ferry, you have a view up to the façade of the aforementioned **S. Maria Zobenigo** [71].

To the right of the Campo, the **Palazzo Gritti-Pisani** [72] has become the posh Gritti Palace Hotel. Five palaces down is the Gothic **Palazzo Contarini-Fasan** [73] (1475): imaginative tour guides used to tell the English this was the house of Othello's Desdemona. After the next canal (Rio di S. Moisè), comes the **Hotel Bauer-Grünwald** [74], a fine example of a 19th-century building imitating the old Venetian Gothic; next to it is the real thing, the 1474 **Ca' Giustinian** [75]. Here we are almost at Piazza S. Marco; as the canal opens up into the Basin of St Mark you will see the 15th-century port authorities, the **Capitaneria del Porto** [76] and the **Giardini Reali** [77].

On the right, the second palace after the Accademia is the **Palazzo Contarini dal Zaffo** [78], a fine work of the late 1400s decorated after the style of the Lombardos. After Campo S. Vio, the **Palazzo Barbarigo** [79] has mosaics from the 1880s (Venice still had a flourishing school of mosaicists at that time; their work, some good and some truly horrible, can be seen on churches across Italy). There's no mistaking the Canal's most peculiar landmark, the triumphantly unfinished **Palazzo Venier dei Leoni** [80]. Only the ground floor of this mid-18th-century palace was ever built (perhaps the Veniers had some setbacks at the Casino). The resulting ranch-house effect attracted an American heiress, who lived here for 30 years; her excellent taste in modern art has provided the basis for the **Peggy Guggenheim Collection** (p. 209), one of the best of Venice's many museums. The second palace after is another work influenced by the Lombardos, with a wealth of decoration in coloured marbles, the precariously leaning **Palazzo Dario** [81]. More modern mosaics can be seen on the **Palazzo Salviati** (1924) [82], built by one of the Murano glass barons.

Now your *vaporetto* has reached the end of the Canal—the grandest sight in Venice, as the ensemble of Piazza S. Marco, S. Giorgio Maggiore and the tip of the Giudecca comes into view. The last buildings on the Canal contribute to the perfect *crescendo* climax of the trip: the great domed church of **S. Maria della Salute** [83], by Longhena, and the golden ball of the 'Fortune' weathervane atop the **Dogana di Mare** [84], the old customs-house of the republic.

The Walks

Turn left at the duck... Watch out for the tiny archway on the right with the carved angel, which opens into a hidden *campo* with a Byzantine column. Follow the canal and cross the third bridge, which may lead to Moon Alley, St Moses' Pool, Behind-the-Monkey Street, or under the arches to the Court of the White Lion. Not everyone prefers to see a city by following walks laid out by some pushy travel writer, and not every city is made for it. But the maze of Venice marries necessity with delight; without a route to follow you'll miss a lot, and following the route itself is half the fun. The walks are not always easy—*nothing* about navigating in Venice is easy—but persevere; you may find yourself a child again on the best treasure hunt in the world.

Five of the walks are generally confined to the borders of the six Venetian *sestieri* (*II*, S. Marco; *III*, Castello; *IV*, Dorsoduro; *V*, S. Polo and S. Croce; and *VI*, Cannaregio). Because Venice is so compact, the walks include everything of interest, without carrying you off on many long digressions. The odd one, Walk *I*, doesn't require much walking at all; it covers only Piazza S. Marco and environs, where there is more than enough to keep you busy. Before each we have tried to estimate the time it will take—usually about four or five hours, assuming a firm and businesslike approach to sightseeing. We won't hold you to it; any of these could easily fill up an entire day. At the beginning of each, under the title, you'll find a list of the main sights, the best time or day to do it, and some chances for lunch or snacks along the way.

104

Walk I
Piazza San Marco

*St Mark's—Campanile—Libreria—Archaeology Museum—Museo
Diocesano—Clock Tower—Museo Correr—Doge's Palace*

It is ironic that of all the walks in this book, this one around Piazza S.
Marco is the longest, though it covers the least amount of ground. But
then again, few cities have so much psychologically concentrated in one
place. The quay in Piazzetta S. Marco is Venice's front door to the
Lagoon and the East, its traditional life and heart line; around the rim
stand the palaces of government and religion, the residence of the Doge,
the mint, the state library, the prisons and place of public execution, and
St Mark's Basilica, not as much a church as a compact made between
Venice and God.

There are few city squares in the world where you can easily spend an
entire day exploring, or just dawdling as the rest of world goes by dressed
in funny hats. The order of this walk may seem a bit dotty, but it is
structured around the opening times of museums. On Tuesdays the
Correr Museum is closed. To take in the secret itinerary of the Doge's
Palace (which you may find far more interesting than the effete frescoed
state rooms) reserve a place at least a day in advance with the secretary in
the Director's office on the first floor, or tel 520 4287. Tours are at 10 or
12, and tickets are L5000 (and usually after the tour, you can walk
through the state rooms on the same ticket, so be sure to do the Secret

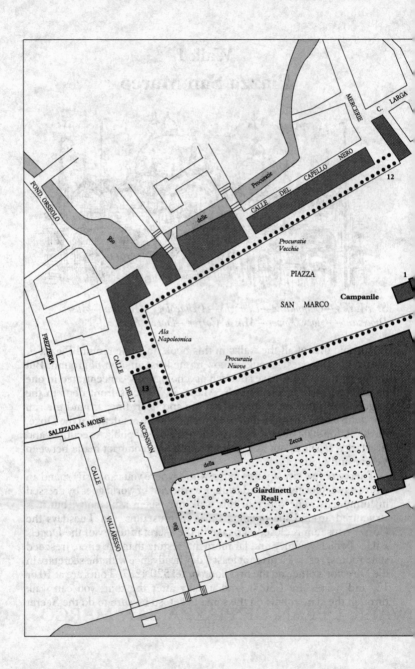

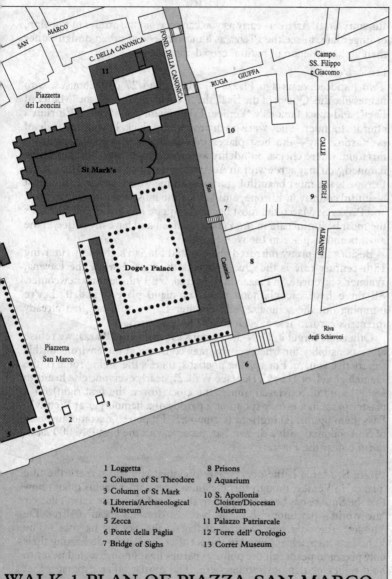

1 Loggetta
2 Column of St Theodore
3 Column of St Mark
4 Libreria/Archaeological Museum
5 Zecca
6 Ponte della Paglia
7 Bridge of Sighs

8 Prisons
9 Aquarium
10 S. Apollonia Cloister/Diocesan Museum
11 Palazzo Patriarcale
12 Torre dell' Orologio
13 Correr Museum

WALK 1 PLAN OF PIAZZA SAN MARCO

Itinerary first). Arrive as early as you can to avoid the armies of Babylon, or linger late, to see the Piazza as a masterpiece of urban design rather than a phenomenon of natural crowd control.

LUNCH/CAFÉS

Two hundred years ago Piazza S. Marco had 27 coffeehouses, with names like the 'Queen of the Sea', the 'Coach of Fortune', the 'Matter of Fact', and most famously 'Venice Triumphant', now called **Florian's** after its founder. They were open around the clock, lit with 'a dazzle of everlasting day'—the best places in Venice for a gossip, intrigue or flirtation, where checks on fidelity were very lightly kept. If expenses be damned, you may agree with an Austrian writer, who reasoned that 'since Europe is the most beautiful continent in the world, and Italy the most beautiful country in Europe, and Venice the most beautiful city in Italy, and Piazza S. Marco the most beautiful square in Venice, and Florian's the most beautiful café in the Piazza, I can sit and have my coffee in the most beautiful place in the world.'

Besides the pretty mirrored and painted Florian's, the only surviving 18th-century café is the Quadri across the Piazza, while the Lavena, Wagner's favourite, in Piazzetta S. Marco, is a 19th-century newcomer. All three have cacophonous bands or piano players, and if they're pumping out the schmaltz, add another L3000 to a tab that already threatens cardiac arrest, even for the tiniest *espresso*.

Otherwise forget it. Only the pigeons eat well in the Piazza; we refuse all responsibility for whatever you may consume in the environs of this superlative square. For visiting poobahs, there's the dining room of the Danieli Hotel, or Harry's Bar (see Walk 2); nearly everyone else heads to Calle Larga di S. Marco (under the clock tower, the first right) for a plaster pasta in a greasy spoon or a parody of a hamburger at Wendy's. Pass them up for: **Aciugheta** (Campo SS. Filippo e Giacomo, just east of S. Apollonia) with a decent bar, *pizzeria*, and the best L15 000 *menu turistico* near the Piazza.

     ☆   ☆   ☆   ☆   ☆

Piazza S. Marco is the only square dignified enough to merit the title 'piazza' in Venice, though this pickiness over names seems quaint now that the Square has been co-opted by the rest of humanity. It isn't merely 'the world's patrimony' but the 'world's drawing room' (Alfred De Musset), the only one 'worthy of having the sky for its roof'. The Venetians themselves joined in the act after the War by dedicating their only piazza to peace; all the political parties unanimously voted never to hold rallies or demonstrations here. The tourist office estimates that about half the throng milling about the Square will visit nothing else in Venice, and when their heads or cameras bob incessantly in your line of vision, as they invariably do, you might reflect that the Piazza has been swarming with Venetians and foreigners alike from the 12th century. The world's nations may debate their cease-fires in New York, but to Venice and St Mark's Square, they come, as they have for the past five hundred years, for delight.

Whatever sensations of *déjà vu* most people bring to Piazza S. Marco after seeing so many pictures never last for very long. The Venetians who walk through it day in and day out never tire of its magic, under all weathers or at any hour, whether the autumn *acque alte* have turned it into a gigantic looking glass (as they often do, as the Piazza is the lowest point in the city); or in a winter fog, when everything—the pavement, the wings of the Procuratie, the pigeons, and even the mosaics of St Mark's—dissolve into pearly grey and white *sfumato* shadows; or in the summer, when it's filled with a chattering, jaunty, fun-fair crowd from the four corners of the globe. The café orchestras grind away, swinging out old jazz tunes the way only Europeans in starched shirts and bowties can, while the huge banners flutter and the Basilica's golden mosaics catch the sun, and children bombard waddling pigeons with little bags of corn they are far too bloated to eat.

The Piazza proper is flanked by two smaller squares, the **Piazzetta dei Leoncini** to the left of the Basilica, and the **Piazzetta S. Marco** on the right, overlooking the Lagoon. What regularity these spaces may appear to possess is dispelled by a single glance at the plan: the Piazza is Italy's biggest trapezoid, 176 m long and 57 m wide before the Ala Napoleonica, expanding to 82 m in front of St Mark's.

The Square took a thousand years to evolve into this interesting shape, beginning in the 9th century, when the seat of government was moved to *Rivo alto* from Malamocco, and the seaward islet of Morso used to support a new castle for the doge and a lighthouse (site of the Campanile). The islet already had two churches, S. Theodore and S. Geminiano, built by Justinian's general, the Eunuch Narses, in the 550s in gratitude for Venice's support of Byzantium against Totila and the Goths. But most of Morso in the 9th century was planted with the vegetable gardens and orchards of S. Zaccaria convent, and when the abbess donated these to the doge in 829 (when the first chapel of St Mark's was built) the Piazza was born. It attained its current dimensions in the second half of the 12th century, thanks to the vision of the fabulously wealthy 'architect Doge' Sebastiano Ziani, who filled in the

canal that once traversed it, demolished Narses' church of S. Geminiano, and transformed what had been a crenellated wall into porticoes
for the Procurators of St Mark (now the Procuratie Vecchie). The piazza
that evolved from the Doge's foresight so pleased the Republic that later
doges were forbidden to order even the least tinkering without the
consent of the *Maggior Consiglio*.

As the only open space of any size in the city, the Piazza quickly
became the centre of Venetian social life, of religious processions and the
great Sensa fair, and of the triumphs of newly elected doges, who would
be carried around the Piazza on the shoulders of the Arsenal workers,
tossing out handfuls of gold to the people. Inter-city sports and neighbourhood rivalries filled the Piazza with crowds to watch death-defying
feats like the human towers called 'The *forze* of Hercules', or the
'Turkish tightrope' where daredevils walked down a wire stretched from
the top of the Campanile to a boat half way to S. Giorgio Maggiore, or the
ghastly Renaissance sport of binding a cat to a post to see who could butt
it to death with a shaven head. Jousts and tournaments were held here,
one attended by Petrarch, who declared Venice 'a nation of sailors,
horsemen and beauties'. The second seems surprising, for the Venetians
in the saddle were a standing joke, as they continue to be when they get
behind the wheel. But it is a fact that one of the bells in the Campanile
was named the 'Trotter', warning senators that the counsel session was
about to begin and they ought to spur their mounts to a trot, and it's
another fact that Doge Michele Steno had a stable of 400 horses dyed
saffron yellow. In later centuries, jousts were replaced with bullfights,
the last *corrida* run in 1782, in honour of the heir to the throne of Russia.
A few years later Napoleon erected a Tree of Liberty here, an event that
went down the average Venetian's throat as smoothly as the Pink Floyd
concert in 1989, when 200,000 rockers left a mess in the Piazza that took
the army three days to tidy up.

Though now bull-less, the Piazza holds exactly 13 lions, and 200
times that many pigeons, Venice's totem bird; according to a poetic
tradition, when a bird feels death approaching it flies off towards the
magical East until it drops into the sea. For one tale has it that St Mark's
pigeons are descended from a pair given by an oriental potentate to
relieve the melancholy of a *dogaressa*; another that pigeons were released
each Palm Sunday from St Mark's to re-enact Noah's release of a dove
from the ark, and as such were holy and protected from urban poachers.
The birds have returned Venice's favour with tons of droppings; ironically pigeon-coated stones better endure the air pollution wafting over

from Mestre and Marghera. Your odds of becoming a target while crossing the Piazza are 2004 to 1. Just be thankful all those winged lions stay put.

> *The head of the Piazza is crowned by* **St Mark's Basilica,** *the most irresistible church in Christendom and national shrine of the Venetian state. Squint at it, and imagine the three great banners in front as sails, the Campanile tall and straight like a mast, the ship's exotic cargo wrapped in fairy domes splashed by a roofline, where, as Ruskin wrote, 'the crests of the arches break into a marble foam, and toss themselves far into the blue sky in flashes and wreaths of sculptured spray...'; while the four bronze steeds breast the waves, like figureheads, or like sea horses themselves—the ideal temple for a sea-faring people with a marked inclination towards piracy.*

Open to visitors from 9:30–5:30, Sun and holidays 2–5:30 (strict dress code, kept by a beadle in 18th-century dress: men must wear a shirt and long trousers, women must have their shoulders covered, a minimum of décolletage, and no shorts; disabled ramp access from Piazzetta dei Leoncini). The first St Mark's was a wooden chapel hastily erected in 828 to house the Evangelist's relics just in from Alexandria. It was a decision of major importance to make his shrine the ducal chapel: not only did it declare an official move away from Venice's former (and Greek) patron saint, Theodore, but it also established the special relationship between St Mark's relics and the doge, his Vicar and *patronus et gubernator.* The official hierarchy of the Roman Catholic church had almost no say in the Basilica, where the doge served a role similar to the pope in St Peter's. For St Mark's was the core and vortex of Venetian religious-state; the glory of 'Messer San Marco' was the glory of the Republic and vice versa.

The first wooden chapel burned, along with the ducal palace, during the bloody insurrection of 976, when Doge Pietro Candiano IV was assassinated at the church door. Both the chapel and palace were immediately rebuilt in the same form, but the chapel was soon regarded as inadequate, and torn down in 1063, under Doge Domenico Contarini who sent out the order: 'make the chapel the most beautiful ever seen'. Each merchant was to bring back some embellishment, each doge was to donate large sums to its perfection. A Greek architect from Constantinople was hired to design the new church, asking in payment that the Republic erect a statue of him. But when the Senate criticized the result as a botched job, the poor architect fell from the scaffolding in dismay.

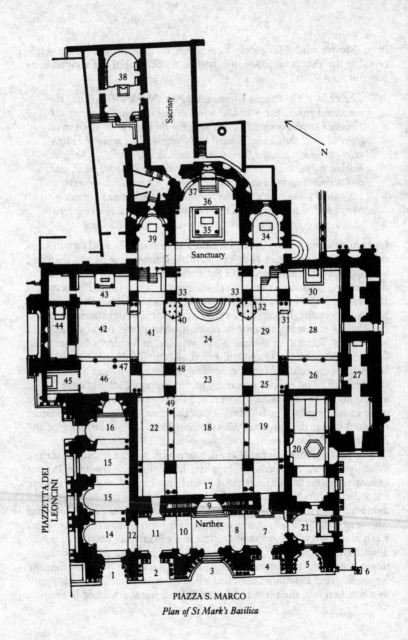

N

Sacristy

38

37
36
35
39
34

Sanctuary

43
33   33
30
40   32
44   42   41   31   28
24   29

46   47
48
45   23   25   26   27

49
16   22   18   19
20

15
17
15   9
14   12   11   10   8   7   21
Narthex

PIAZZETTA DEI LEONCINI

1   2   3   4   5   6

PIAZZA S. MARCO

Plan of St Mark's Basilica

Plan of St Mark's Basilica

Note how crooked it is! In the Middle Ages symmetry was synonymous with death. Numbers in *italics* refer to mosaics.

 1 *Translation of the Body of St Mark* (1270)
 2 *Venice Venerating the Relics of St Mark* (1718)
 3 Central door, with magnificent 13th-century carvings in arches
 4 *Venice Welcoming the Relics of St Mark* (1700s)
 5 *Removal of St Mark's Relics from Alexandria* (1700s)
 6 *Pietra del Bando*, stone from which the Signoria's decrees were read
 7 *Scenes from the Book of Genesis* (1200) and 6th-century Byzantine door of S. Clemente
 8 *Noah and the Flood* (1200s), tomb of Doge Vitale Falier (d. 1096)
 9 *Madonna and Saints* (1060s); red marble slab where Emperor Barbarossa submitted to Pope Alexander III (1177); stair up to the Loggìa and Museo Marciano
10 *Death of Noah and the Tower of Babel* (1200s)
11 *Story of Abraham* (1230s)
12 *Story of SS. Alipius and Simon, and Justice* (1200s)
14 Tomb of Doge Bartolomeo Gradenigo (d. 1342)
15 *Story of Joseph*, remade in 19th century
16 Porta dei Fiori (1200s); Manzù's bust of *Pope John XXIII*
17 *Christ with the Virgin and St Mark* (13th century, over the door)
18 *Pentecost* Dome (the earliest, 12th century)
19 On the wall: *Agony in the Garden* and *Madonna and Prophets* (13th century)
20 Baptistry, *Life of St John the Baptist* (14th century) and tomb of *Doge Andrea Dandolo*
21 Cappella Zen, by Tullio and Antonio Lombardo (1504–22)
22 On the wall: *Christ and Prophets* (13th century)
23 In arch: *Scenes of the Passion* (12th century)
24 Central Dome, the *Ascension* (12th century)
25 Tabernacle of the Madonna of the Kiss (12th century)
26 On wall: *Rediscovery of the Body of St Mark* (13th century)
27 Treasury
28 Dome of S. Leonardo; Gothic rose window (15th century)
29 In arch, *Scenes from the Life of Christ* (12th century)
30 Altar of the Sacrament; pilaster where St Mark's body was rediscovered, marked by marbles
31 Altar of St James (1462)
32 Pulpit where newly elected doge was shown to the people; entrance to the sanctuary
33 Rood screen (1394) by Jacopo di Marco Benato and Jacobello and Pier Paolo Dalle Masegne
34 Singing Gallery and Cappella di S. Lorenzo, sculptures by the Dalle Masegnes (14th century)
35 Dome, *Prophets Foretell the Religion of Christ* (12th century); Baldacchino, with Eastern alabaster columns (6th century?)
36 Pala d'Oro (10th–14th century)
37 Sacristy door, with reliefs by Sansovino (16th century)
38 Sacristy, with mosaics by Titian and Padovanino (16th century) and Church of St Theodore (15th century), once seat of the Inquisition, and now part of the sacristy: both are rarely open
39 Singing Gallery and Cappella di S. Pietro (14th century): note the Byzantine capitals
40 Two medieval pulpits stacked together
41 *Miracles of Christ* (16th century)
42 Dome, with *Life of St John the Evangelist* (12th century)
43 Cappella della Madonna di Nicopeia (miraculous 12th-century icon)
44 Cappella di S. Isidoro (14th-century mosaics and tomb of the Saint)
45 Cappella della Madonna dei Máscoli: *Life of the Virgin* by Andrea del Castagno, Michele Giambono, Jacopo Bellini
46 On wall: *Life of the Virgin* (13th century)
47 Finely carved Greek marble stoup (12th century)
48 *Virgin of the Gun* (13th century—rifle ex-voto from 1850s)
49 Il Capitello, altar topped with rare marble ciborium, with miraculous Byzantine Crucifixion panel

And so, the legend goes, the Venetians carved his likeness over the main door, leaning on his crutches, ruefully biting his fingers.

His model for St Mark's was the no longer extant Church of the Holy Apostles in Constantinople, the imperial mausoleum of Byzantium, where Constantine and the first emperors were buried (it also inspired the ruined Basilica of St John at Ephesus, and St Front in France). It is in the form of a Greek cross with cupolas over the centre crossing and over each of the arms, with a narthex wrapped around the front to the transepts (though the right narthex is now closed) and five doorways, doubled by the arches over the *loggia*. Originally these were brick (like the rest of the church) and pointed in the Gothic style, but after the conquest of Constantinople, when Venice became the ruler of its proud fraction of the Roman empire, it yearned to look the part. So the arches were rounded off, the brickwork sheathed in pillaged rare marble and stone, in the grand old Roman tradition. And could anything look more Roman than the triumphal arch of the central door, with the famous gilded horses of an ancient *quadriga* pawing the air?

The only jarring note in the Basilica's millennial collage is the gaudy Technicolour mosaics in the arches, all cocky, painterly 17th–19th-century replacements of the originals—one of which was by Paolo Uccello. Sansovino, who in 1529 became St Mark's *Proto Magister* (in charge of maintaining the church) had to remove them to reinforce the structure. The only mosaic to survive is the 13th-century lunette over the **Porta di Sant'Alipio** (the far left door) representing the *Translation of the Body of St Mark*, which not only tells the story of the relics' arrival in Venice, but features the earliest known representation of St Mark's himself (but at the time of writing under restoration until kingdom come). The bas-relief, wedged between this arch and the next, is a 3rd-century Roman one, of *Hercules and the Erymanthean Boar* (Hercules was the traditional tribal hero of the Venetii people); in the 13th century, Venetian sculptors carved an imitation *Hercules and the Hydra* to fill in the space between the righthand arches. Between the inner portals are a Byzantine figure of *St Demetrius* (left) and another Venetian imitation, of *St George* (right)—both Christian warrior saints—while the relief in the centre is of the *Annunciation*, depicting the traditional protectors of the doge: the Virgin and the Angel Gabriel.

Best of all are the three bands of **13th-century reliefs** around the central arch and its ungainly 19th-century mosaic of the *Last Judgement*. The carvings, however, are among Italy's finest, uniquely flowing, complex compositions; even the Corinthian columns that support them seem to sway in the breeze. The outermost band of reliefs shows **Venetian trades**, from shipwright to fisherman (including the finger-biting architect on the left). The middle arch is devoted to the **Labours of the Months** (February for example has nothing to do but warm himself by the fire), signs of the Zodiac, and the Virtues and Beatitudes. The order of the months is especially interesting: note that the astrological signs are a month off, as they were (correctly) in classical times, proving either that the Venetians were better scholars than astronomers, or that their obsession with imitating the Romans was perfected to an extreme. The innermost arch is dedicated to chaos, including a vineyard filled with battling beasts and the favourite medieval fancy of a lady suckling a serpent.

The **upper loggia of the façade**, with its unique horses (or rather, their copies), is crowned by statues of the saints, standing just out of reach of the late 14th and 15th century tidal froth and frills that so delighted Ruskin. Nor does any other church have so much loot embedded in its surface, picked up around the the Mediterranean like exotic stickers on an old-fashioned travelling trunk: on the right hand corner of the *loggia*, you can see an 8th-century Syrian (or Alexandrian) porphyry bust of Byzantine Emperor Justinian III Rhinotometus ('of the cut-off nose'); several aquarii with water pots on their shoulders serve as gargoyles.

But the **Piazzetta S. Marco façade** (the one most visitors used to see first) was the Republic's main trophy case, bristling with a kind of bragadoccio that in the 20th century seems almost charmingly naive: there's the **Pietra del Bando**, a stump of porphyry pinched from the Genoese in Syria in 1256, and used as a stand for the reading of proclamations, and every now and then as a pedestal for the heads of traitors until they began to smell. In 1902 it was the hero of the hour for safeguarding the Basilica when the Campanile collapsed. Near this are two free-standing **Pilasters from Acre**, decorated with rare Syrian curly carving. These were pilfered from the Genoese in 1256, and put here to get their goat, for the medieval Genoese treasured them as much as the Venetians treasured their *quadriga* of shining horses. Four porphyry **Moors**, generally thought to be 4th-century Egyptian work, huddle on the corner; according to legend, they were changed into stone for daring to break into St Mark's Treasure (the protruding part of the façade, believed to have once been part of the original ducal castle). The odds are that they're really a pair of caesars and a pair of emperors, or the *Tetrarchs*, established with Diocletian's attempt to divide the dying

Roman empire into more governable sections, the better to persecute the Christians and overtax everyone else. Below is a crude sculpture of two *putti* coming out of dragons' mouths, with the earliest known inscription in Venetian dialect: 'Man can do and must think—and must beware what may result'. This profoundly banal dictum is seconded by the legend of the 'Little Baker's Madonna' (a 13th-century mosaic of the Virgin in the upper lunette) whose pair of votive lamps are popularly said to be a reminder of the unjust execution of a young lad for murder—a true story, though the records attribute the lamps to the vow of an old sea captain lost at sea and saved by the Virgin. Among the other pretty things here are the colourful *paterae* like artists' palettes of coloured marbles and onyx, the 12th-century griffons supporting the columns of one of the arches, and the 6th-century Byzantine columns on the upper part of the façade, with capitals carved in the form of baskets overflowing with fruit.

The north, or **Piazzetta dei Leoncini façade** suffered from a band of rogue restorers in the 1860s, who decided that its sheath of polychrome marbles didn't quite look as fine as dingy grey stone—only an international campaign spared the main façade from their handiwork. Especially note the two bas-reliefs on the right: **The Twelve Apostles** symbolized by lambs, worshipping the *etoimasia*, the empty throne prepared for the Last Judgement, either a rare Byzantine work made during the Iconoclasm (7th or 8th century) or—as slippery as most of St Mark's dates—by a 13th-century school of ancient art imitators. Nearby is a charming 10th- or 12th-century relief of *Alexander the Great* transported to heaven in a car pulled by two griffons, lured by pieces of liver dangled on spears over their heads—the moral of the story, of course, being that he failed, and you can't get to Heaven on a piece of liver. Beyond the 13th-century **Porta dei Fiori** is the tomb of Daniele Manin, who last revived the Republic of Venice in 1848.

Some of the most vivid mosaics are in six shallow domes of the **narthex***, or porch.*

These, mainly Old Testament scenes, are from the 13th century, made by Greek-trained Venetian artists, who learned their lessons well. The story unfolds from the right to left, beginning with the epic of the Creation and the story of Noah (who like any Venetian has a soft spot for the lion). Note the door on the right; the bronze **Portal of San Clemente** is an 11th-century Byzantine work, a gift to Venice from Emperor Alexis Comnenos. The narthex floor's geometrical marble mosaic dates from the 11th and 12th centuries; by the main entrance, a lozenge marks the spot where Emperor Frederick Barbarossa knelt and apologized 'to St Peter and his Pope'—Alexander III in 1177. Barbarossa had tossed Alexander out of Rome and installed an antipope sympathetic to the imperial cause, but when his armies were disastrously defeated by the Lombard League, he was forced into reconciliation, stage-managed by Venetian diplomacy—one of the few gold stars Venice ever earned with the Papacy. To the right is the oldest tomb in Venice, that of the Doge who consecrated the basilica, Vitale Falier (d. 1096) 'King of kings, corrector of laws'—an epitaph that would give an 18th-century doge a heart attack. On the left behind an Islamic-inspired grille is the Tomb of the *Dogaressa Felicità Michiel* (d. 1101); her exceptional piety earned her a last resting place in the Basilica. The central door into the church retains the rare, original 11th-century mosaic of the *Virgin and Saints*.

> *Just to the right of this door, a sign invites you up a steep stone stair to the gallery, with the* **Museo Marciano** *and* **Loggia dei Cavalli***.*

Open 9:30–5; adm L2000. At the top of the stairs are a couple of rooms housing evocative fragments of the original mosaics and odds and ends, including a 16th-century double bass, which once accompanied St Mark's famous choir. The **Loggia** offers a mesmerizing pigeon-eye view of the Piazza, and lets you take in some of the rich sculptural and decorative details of the Basilica itself. The four replica horses on the façade, paid for with much fanfare by Olivetti, don't bear close examination after you've seen the originals, restored and regilded in 1979, only to be imprisoned inside—one of the saddest sights in Venice, for they were made to glint in the sun and shimmer in the light of the moon.

This, after all, is the only bronze *quadriga* (four horses that once pulled a triumphal chariot) to survive from antiquity, though no one is sure whether the Greeks or Romans cast them, or when—suggested dates range from the 3rd century BC to the 2nd AD. Constantine, no beginner in the plunder department himself, picked them up perhaps on the island of Chios or in Rome, to embellish his new capital, and the Byzantine emperors put them out to pasture in Constantinople's Hippodrome until the Venetians snatched them in 1204. Originally they stood by the Arsenal, until someone had the extraordinary idea of putting them on the terrace of the Basilica, where they soon became one of Venice's best known symbols. Napoleon took them to Paris and installed them in the Place du Carrosel, where they stayed for 18 years, until sculptor Antonio

Canova persuaded the French to return them to Venice. During World Wars I and II they were packed off to Rome for safe keeping.

The other treasures of the Museo Marciano aren't always on display: Paolo Veneziano's painted *Cover for the Pala d'Oro* (1345) and a series of early 15th-century tapestries on the *Life of Christ*, woven after designs by Nicolò di Pietro. From the **Gallery** inside the Basilica there's a wonderful view into the shadowy golden interior, and your best chance to get a close view of its mosaics.

*The **interior** of St Mark's is if anything even more lavish than the exterior. Its lofty arches, shadowy walls, dizzy catwalks and swollen domes are covered with over 4000 square yards of golden mosaics, a golden sheath that seems to breathe like a living thing when caught in the sun, gold that shimmers in ancient mystery in the evening shadows. On a high feast day, when all the candles and lamps were lit, the splendour would be overwhelming: the rich robes of the clergy, the heady fragrance of incense, the music of six orchestras of a hundred musicians each accompanying the celebrated Marciana choir, once directed by Monteverdi himself.*

*After the pagan glories of the façade and the Old Testament theme of the narthex, the mosaics here are all based on the New Testament (see plan); begun in the 11th century, they have been constantly repaired and replaced ever since, a year-round, full-time job. The peculiar catwalks over the aisles were once the women's galleries, chopped up to admit a bit of light when the side windows were covered up for more mosaics. When your neck begins to ache from gazing up into the domes, take a look at the intricate **pavement** of richly-coloured marbles and porphyry and glass, its swirling geomeric patterns subsiding into rolling waves and tidal pools.*

*The first dome, the early 12th-century **Pentecost dome** was also the first to be decorated, with mosaics representing the nations whose languages were given to the Apostles on Pentecost Sunday. Especially note the arch between this and the central dome and its exceptional 12th-century scenes of the* Crucifixion, Descent into Limbo *and* Doubting Thomas. *In the upper wall of the right aisle is another early 12th-century mosaic masterpiece,* The Agony in the Garden, *where the artist took no chances on portraying the correct posture of Christ—he kneels, falls, and falls on his face, according to the differing descriptions in the Gospels. Just below this*

*mosaic, to the right, a door leads to the **baptistry**, which with any
luck may be reopened by the time you get there.*

This was one of Ruskin's favourite places, and the Gothic **Tomb of
Doge Andrea Dandolo** (d. 1354), by Giovanni de' Santi, in front of the
door, his favourite Venetian monument. Dandolo, a man of refined
tastes and a friend of Petrarch was the last doge to be buried in the
Basilica, among the mosaics he commissioned: charming, anecdotal
scenes on the *Life of St John the Baptist*, with swivel-hipped Salome in a
red dress, dancing in triumph with the Baptist's head on a platter. Also
buried in the baptistry are, to the right, Doge Giovanni Soranzo, Dandolo's predecessor (d. 1329), and under a slab in the pavement, Jacopo
Sansovino, whose remains were brought here in 1929, to lie near the
giant font he designed. The mighty block of granite by the altar was part
of the booty picked up in Tyre in 1126, lugged into this holy place on the
chance that Christ stood on it when he fed the multitude.

A door from the baptistry leads into the **Cappella Zen**, named for the
affluent Cardinal Giambattista Zen, who like the *condottiere* Colleoni, left
the Republic his fortune on the condition that he was posthumously
recognized at St Mark's—though the Cardinal was more specific, and to
get the money the Senate ordered the Piazzetta entrance and narthex be
closed in to make him a chapel, and hired Tullio Lombardo to design it.
The doorway, decorated with a pair of 11th- or 12th-century mosaic
angels flanking a *Madonna* (a 19th-century copy), has mosaic niches with
small but expressive statues of the prophets; in the vault overhead are
mosaic *Scenes from the Life of St Mark* (13th century). Antonio Lombardo
carved the high altar's classical goddess with a child, the *Madonna of the
Shoe* in 1506.

Back in the main basilica, the central **Ascension dome** *has
concentric circles of heavenly notables around the main event, above
allegories of the Four Rivers of Paradise, spilling over, as most
Venetians probably thought, right into their own lagoon of manifest
destiny. Towards the right transept, note the 12th-century bas-relief
of the* Madonna dei Bacci *on one of the piers, a work nearly effaced
by thousands of thousands of kisses from the faithful over the
centuries. The dome, dedicated to St Leonard, is relatively austere
with its four saints, though note the lively 12th-century* Scenes
from the Life of Christ *(Entry into Jerusalem, Temptations, Last
Supper, and Washing of Feet) shimmering on the arch between the
dome and nave. On the transept's right wall mosaics, known as*

119

the Inventio *(13th century), show events that happened across the transept at the* **altar of the Sacrament**.

After the disastrous fire of 976, it was commonly believed that St Mark's body was lost in the flames. This blow to Venice's prestige was exasperated when the merchants of Bari beat the Venetians to the relics of St Nicholas of Myra (the patron of sailors). Something had to be done, and on 24 June 1094, as the new church of St Mark was being consecrated and everyone prayed for the rediscovery of Mark's relics, the good Saint was made to miraculously reappear, his arm breaking through the wall of the left pilaster (the exact spot indicated with a marble inlay and mosaic). On the nave pier, to the left, is the **altar of St James**, a lovely work in the Lombardo family style.

At the end of the right transept is the door, now locked, through which the doge would enter the basilica, topped by a giant Gothic rose window. The door with the ogival arch to its right leads into **St Mark's Treasure** *(9–5:30, L2000), housed in a room of immensely thick walls, believed to have been a 9th-century tower of the original ducal castle.*

The capture of Constantinople by the so-called Fourth Crusade, and its subsequent pillage and sack was perhaps a tragic loss of art and beauty to civilization. With equal equanimity the rough Franks smashed and melted down the treasures of the ancient Greeks and Romans as well as Byzantine; the Venetians at least had an eye for beauty as well as for the main chance. They salvaged what they could and shipped it home to the greater glory of their Messer S. Marco. Five hundred years later Napoleon and his henchmen helped themselves to most of what was left—and melted it down for 55 ingots of gold and silver.

All in all, this lends a sense of wonder to the small collection that has managed to survive. But the objects displayed are beautiful and magical in their own right: the 6th-century marble throne of St Mark carved in Alexandria, a gift from Emperor Heraclius to the Patriarch of Grado in 630, a 4th-century crystal lamp, embellished with a crab and what looks like a piranha; a Byzantine glass bucket with chase scenes; an Egyptian vase of porphyry and feldspar, perhaps as old as 3500 BC, an 11th century icon of *St Michael*, with enamel portraits and Venetian filagree, a 1st century AD onyx and agate chalice, a votive crown of Emperor Leo III, adorned with rock crystal (*c.* 900), a golden rose bush, an incense burner shaped like a five-domed Byzantine church, a turquoise bowl sent from the Shah of Persia in 1472, chalices of intricate gold embroidery studded with thumb-sized gems, a magnificently decorated dish of alabaster and enamels. Nowhere will you see a better collection of 12th-century Byzantine gold and silver.

To the right of the high altar is the large odd-shaped **ceremonial pulpit**, *where a newly bonneted doge would show himself to the people; here too is the entrance to the* **Sanctuary** *and* **Pala d'Oro** *(open 9–5:30; adm L1000).*

Straight on as you enter is the little alcove **Cappella di S. Clemente**, with sculpture by the Dalle Masegne brothers and a pretty Gothic tabernacle on the side pier to the left. Eight bronze reliefs by Sansovino line the singing gallery of the chancel. Take a close look at the four **columns** supporting the *baldacchino* over the high altar. These are the subject of another Venetian mystery: made of oriental alabaster, and sculpted with worn and murky New Testament scenes, no one is sure whether they are Byzantine works of the early 500s, or 13th-century Venetian retro art, or if, as legend has it, they were brought to Venice from Dalmatia by Doge Pietro Orseolo II in the year 1000. Under a bronze grate in front of the altar is the crypt containing the supposed relics of St Mark. Overhead, the dome is another brilliant work of the 12th century, its subject *The Religion of Christ Foretold by the Prophets*, with the typically Byzantine *Christ Pantocrator*, blessing the congregation from the apse. Under this, between the windows, are four of the oldest mosaics in the Basilica, the 11th-century *SS. Nicolas, Peter, Mark, and Hermagorus*; in the central niche is an altar with translucent alabaster columns. The left hand niche has the **sacristy door**, with bronze reliefs by Sansovino of the *Entombment* and *Resurrection*; in the frame, Sansovino included busts of himself and his best friends, Titian and the roguish Aretino.

But the highlight, of course, is the dazzling and incomparable **Pala d'Oro**, the masterpiece of generations of medieval Byzantine and Venetian goldsmiths and the most precious treasure in the Basilica. Measuring 3 m × 1 m, it consists of beautifully worked gold, set with sparkling gems: 300 sapphires, 300 emeralds, 400 garnets, 100 amethysts, 1300 pearls, not to mention handfuls of rubies and topazes to accompany 157 enamelled rondels and panels. The original altar screen was ordered from Constantinople by Doge Pietro Orseolo I in 976; and it was revised and enriched in 1105, again in Constantinople. In 1209, the

Venetians enlarged it with some of the jewels and gold they had plundered, and it was reset in its final state in 1345 by Gian Paolo Boninsegna. The miniature enamelled scenes are microscopically intricate and well crafted, but tend to get lost in the razzle-dazzle: the large figure on top is St Michael, encircled by rondels of saints and six larger panels with New Testament scenes. Below, the dominant figure is Christ Pantocrator; this and the 39 niches filled with saints are 12th-century Byzantine, while the small square panels that run along the top and sides of the lower screen, with scenes from the lives of the Evangelists, are thought to be from the original 10th-century Pala: in the one in the upper right hand corner, an angel greets St Mark from the future city of Venice.

Before leaving the sanctuary, take a look at its magnificent **rood screen** of eight columns of twilit marble, holding the silver and gold Cross (1394) by the Venetian goldsmith Marco Benato and marble statues by Jacobello and Pier Paolo Dalle Masegne, perhaps the brothers' finest works. On the left side is a second **pulpit**, built on another pulpit, made of columns of rare marbles and parapets of *verde antico*.

> *Just within the left transept, vaulted by the 12th-century* **dome of St John**, *is the busiest chapel in St Mark's, the* **Chapel of the Madonna di Nicopeia**, *festooned with hanging red lamps and candles glimmering in the permanent twilight.*

The chapel is named after the prodigious 12th-century icon of *Our Lady*, Bringer of Victory, which Byzantine emperors would carry into battle. Part of the haul of 1204, it has been venerated ever since as the Protectress of Venice. At the end of the transept is the **Cappella di S. Isidoro**, built by Doge Andrea Dandolo in 1355 to house the relics of St Isidore, stolen from Chios in 1125; and in the beautiful, pristine mosaics on the upper walls and barrel vault that tell the Saint's life story, he seems glad to go, grinning as the Venetians haul him off. Behind the altar his sarcophagus bears a 14th-century reclining effigy; by the door there's a delightful holy water stoup.

> *The next chapel in the left transept, the* **Cappella della Madonna dei Máscoli** *('of the males', for a 17th-century masculine confraternity).*

This chapel not only has confessionals in four languages, but lovely mosaics on *The Life of the Virgin* (1450s). Based on cartoons by the Tuscan Andrea del Castagno and probably Jacopo Bellini, and carried out by Michele Giambono, this chapel was one of the seeds of the

Renaissance in Venice; the scenes are set in the kind of fantasy architecture beloved by the Tuscans. A Gothic altar of 1430 embedded in a wall of rich marbles, and the figures of the Madonna and St John and St Mark are by Bartolomeo Bon. Before leaving the transept, take in the Romanesque carvings on the Greek stoup in the centre, and on the pier, a relief of the *Madonna and Child*, with perhaps the most curious and unexplained ex-voto in Italy: a rifle. And on the first pier in the left aisle, is **Il Capitello**, a tiny chapel constructed entirely of rare marble and agate to house a painted wooden *Crucifix*, believed to have once belonged to the Byzantine Emperor; abused by a blasphemer in 1290, it miracuously bled, and has been tucked in here to prevent futher mishaps.

> *In front of St Mark's, supporting three huge flags on holidays, or whenever the city feels like flying them, are Alessandro Leopardi's bronze* **flagstaff bases** *(1505), swarming with a mythological* misto del mare *of tritons and nereids. Overlooking them, and everything else in Venice, is the* Golden Archangel *of the* Annunciation *shining like a beacon atop the 99-m red brick* **Campanile**.

The lift is open, for a nearly angel-eye view, 9:30–3:30 in winter, and until 7:30 pm in high summer, other months in between (L3000). Although Venice looks strikingly canal-less from this exalted height, the secretive *Serenissima* was always very picky about who was permitted to enjoy the view, fearing that spies would peek into the Arsenal, or map the Venetians' canals through the Lagoon, easily visible at low tide. After all, when begun in 912, the tower doubled as a lighthouse, and even afterwards the function of its five bells was entirely civic. Besides the aforementioned *Trottiera*, the largest, the *Marangona*, signalled the beginning and end of the working day; the *Nona* announced noon; the *Mezza Terza* the opening of the Senate; and the small but ominous *Maleficio* rang for an execution. The elegantly classical **Loggetta** at the base, designed by Sansovino, though intended as a *Ridotto dei Nobili* (a noblemen's club) was soon given over as a guardroom to the *Arsenalotti*, 50 of whom showed up as volunteer (and apparently, totally unnecessary) policemen whenever the *Maggior Consiglio* met. In the 18th century, it became the centre of the state lottery.

The Campanile has looked the same since 1515, only what now stands is an exact replica, made after the original considerably warned everyone out of the way by opening a big crack, then genteely collapsed into a pile of dust on 14 July 1902 (the only casualty was the keeper's cat, who had run in to check its bowl). You can buy postcards of a cleverly rigged photo that looks as if it were taken as the Campanile falls; others show what the Piazza looked like without this lumbering landmark. The fact that it looked much better, no longer obscuring and outscaling St Mark's and the Ducal Palace, had no bearings at all on the decision made, the very evening of the Campanile's demise, to construct it *dov'era e com'era* ('where it was and as it was'), only this time several tons lighter, and stronger. The whole world chipped in, and the Campanile was officially reopened in 1912.

Although the *pietra della banda* diverted the cascading rubble from St Mark's, the Loggetta was completely smashed; like a jigsaw puzzle it was pieced back together, along with Sansovino's allegorical statues and reliefs; as the Loggetta was built during Venice's brief tenure over Cyprus, this includes a marble relief of *Venus* on the attic, keeping company with *Justice* (Venice's favourite persona) and *Jupiter*, a native of another Venetian possession, Crete.

Around the corner from the Campanile is **Piazzetta S. Marco**, *Venice's traditional foyer, where visitors from overseas would disembark at the Molo under the sleepless eye of the state bureaucracy.*

A few hundred years ago, one section of the Piazzetta was reserved for patricians, politicking in their trailing robes. This was known as the *Broglio* (or 'kitchen garden'), for it once grew the turnips for the nuns at S. Zaccaria. Long before modern politicans had smoked-filled rooms, the Venetians had their Broglio for making deals, and for soliciting votes whenever an election was up; a number of visitors remarked on the quaint sight of a grand patrician from one of the oldest families, bowing so low to kiss the edge of an elector's sleeve that his neck stole scraped the ground. The very Byzantine intrigues, entanglements, and machinations that went on here, some say, gave Italian, and then English the word *imbroglio*.

The Piazzetta holds one of Venice's oldest symbols: the **Two Columns**.

Take a look at these first thing in the morning, before the forests of tourists plant themselves on the steps and hide their curious medieval carvings. It's hard to tell what many of these once were, so eroded have they become from centuries of weather and bottoms, though superstitious Venetians never sit here, or walk between the columns.

The granite columns were part of the loot the Venetians picked up at Tyre in 1170. Originally there were three, but such was the difficulty in unloading them that one went overboard into the Bacino di S. Marco and still keeps the fish company there. Even thornier was the problem of getting them to stand upright, and during the reign of the 'architect Doge' Ziani the proclamation went out that whoever succeeded would be granted any *grazia onesta*. No-one could until a Lombard named Nicolo Barattieri managed the feat with wet ropes (a story suspiciously similar to the 16th-century tale of the raising of the Vatican obelisk in Rome) and asked, as his reward, permission to set up gambling tables between the two columns, thus making the area Venice's first casino. This idea was also about half a millennium ahead of its time and scandalized the government; the last thing they wanted in their municipal parlour was a gambling den. Unable to renege on the *grazia onesta*, the artful Doge decreed at the same time that all public executions should henceforth take place 'between the two red columns' (though one is really grey), and the heads of criminals be put on display there—which, as had been suspected, succeeded in driving away so many potential gamblers that Barattieri's games were soon run out of business. Most unfortunates were hanged or decapitated; on one memorable occasion in 1405, however, the Venetians woke up to find three traitors buried alive here, with only their legs sticking out of the ground.

The Venetians had a knack not only for converting their booty into self-serving symbols, but a precocious ability to create art from *objets trouvés*. The figure on one column is the obscure St Theodore with his crocodile or dragon, or fish. Venice's first patron (made redundant with the arrival of St Mark's relics, and not restored to his post until the late 13th century) was made from a Parian marble head of Mithridates of Pontus and a Roman torso, and other ancient bits, now all replaced by a copy. The second column's Lion of St Mark is actually a bronze chimera from Syria or China; the Venetians simply added wings, and slid a book under its paw.

> *On the west side of Piazzetta S. Marco is the building that Palladio thought was the most beautiful in the world since the temples of yore: Sansovino's **Libreria**, begun in 1536 and finished by Vincenzo Scamozzi in 1591.*

Made of white Istrian stone, the Libreria is the key High Renaissance building in Venice, notable not only because it recalls ancient Roman structures with its Doric and Ionian orders, frieze, and statues on the balustrade, but for the play of light and shadow in its arcades. Sansovino's training as a sculptor didn't always prepare him for some of the finer points of structure, and in 1545 the vaulted ceiling in the main hall came crashing down. The Council of Ten, never very tolerant of error, tossed Sansovino in the clink, and he was only released after Titian and his other pals pleaded for him.

To see the beautiful main hall of the original library (with its reconstructed ceiling) you'll have to ask at the Director's office at 13A, under the portico (and probably come back later). The grand stair, elaborately stuccoed by Vittoria, leads to the antechamber (with a good fresco of *Wisdom* by Titian on the ceiling) and the main hall, with medallions by Tintoretto, Veronese, and Andrea Schiavone. Despite the grand treatment, the Biblioteca Nazionale Marciana didn't have the most auspicious of starts. A farsighted official in the 14th century made a deal with Petrarch in his old age, that the Republic would take care of the poet if he would leave Venice his library. He did, in 1362, and the books were placed in some attic until a place was found for them. Another major library bequest in 1468, this time from Cardinal Bessarion (*c.* 1403–72), a native of Trebizond who did much to promote Greek scholarship and humanism in Italy, roused the Senate to found the Biblioteca Nazionale Marciana—but when it came to adding Petrarch's books, no one remembered where they were. Still, displayed in some small rooms off the main hall are treasures any library would be proud of, most beautifully the **Grimani Breviary**, illuminated in 1501 by Flemish artists (though rarely exhibited), Fra Mauro's magnificent 1459 *Map of the World* (see S. Michele, p. 275), a 14th-century illuminated Dante, codices of Homer, and Marco Polo's will.

> *At No. 17, tucked in the library portico, is the courtyard and stair up to Venice's excellent but neglected* **Archaeology Museum***; on any given day marble men and women outnumber the real ones by a hundred to one.*

Open 9–2, Sun 9–1; adm L2000. The museum was founded in 1523 when Cardinal Domenico Grimani left the state his impressive collection of Greek and Roman sculpture. The museum has recently been remodelled and gets a few points for being one of the few to be heated in the winter. A set of colossal 4th-century AD marble toes in the first room is followed by an extensive Roman coin collection, some massive pieces guaranteed to put holes in a toga pocket. The star of the Attic sculptures in Room IV is a 5th-century BC *Persephone*, called the Abbondanza

Grimani, and other strapping female statues. Among the Roman works are three fine copies of *Gallic Warriors*, presented by Attalos of Pergamon to Athens, also a violent *Leda and the Swan*, a votive relief to Cybele, and a winsome bust of a boy from the 2nd-century BC. Among the busts there's one of Pompey looking troubled, Caligula as an all-American football hero, the kind of boy you might bring home to meet your mother, though perhaps most memorable of all is the bust of the bloated Emperor Vitellus, antiquity's most legendary trencherman. Other highlights include a 2nd century sarcophagus with a naval battle, a 5th-century AD ivory casket, and a scene of the god *Mithras*, whose cult challenged Christianity in its early days, complete with his bull, dog, snake, and scorpion; a porphyry bust of the priest *Isaac* that looks quite modern, and a couple of mummies in the small Egyptian collection.

> *Next to the Libreria, facing the Molo, is another of Sansovino's creations, the* **Zecca***, or mint, a rusticated Doric building finished in 1547, replacing the 12th-century mint where the first golden ducat was produced in 1284.*

Ducats (after the 16th century, the gold coin was called the *zecchino*, hence our word for sequin, while the name ducat was used for a silver coin) were a major currency in Europe's exchanges, like the dollar is today: unlike the dollar, they were worth their weight in 24-carat gold—between 1284 and 1797 the amount of gold in the coin never varied. Over a million gold and silver coins were minted each year—three times the wealth of the entire kingdom of France. The Zecca stands out as one of the very few buildings in Venice made of solid stone; the treasure it protects these days, however, is purely literary, for it too is part of the Biblioteca Nazionale Marciana.

> *The* **Molo***, the waterfront of Piazzetta S. Marco, is solid with bobbing gondolas and excursion boats to Murano and beyond. Behind the Zecca and a row of booths offering good prices on plastic light-up gondolas is the* **Giardinetti Reali***, not much as 'royal' gardens go, but a rare patch of green (and an even rarer public WC) in the capital of stone and water. Eugene Beauharnais created it when he knocked down the Fonteghetto della Farina, or state granary, to create a view of the Lagoon from the Ala Napoleonica (see below). He also added the pretty Neoclassical pavillion called the Casino da Caffè (1807), at the time of writing undergoing restoration for its future use as a tourist information office.*

Walk down the Molo, past the Doge's Palace for the moment, to the Ponte della Paglia *(straw bridge, named for the loads of straw unloaded here for the garrisons of the Doge's Palace and prisons), invariably crowded with people all taking identical photos of the famous Istrian stone* **Bridge of Sighs** (Ponte dei Sospiri), *built in 1600 by Antonio Contino, to link the Palace with the* **Prigioni** *(1560–1614, and suitably grim, at least by Venetian standards). The legendary sighs were emitted by prisoners on their way to the State Inquisitors' office and built-in torture chamber. Across the Ponte della Paglia is the* **Riva degli Schiavoni**, *or 'Dalmatians' Quay', one of the city's favourite promenades.*

In the old days this would be lined with ships from all corners of the Mediterranean; in 1782, when it is commonly thought that Venice was about to drop dead of exhaustion, the Riva did such a thriving business (no longer in silks and spices from the Orient, perhaps, but as the major transit port for goods from the Adriatic gulf and Ionian islands) that the Riva had to be widened; the white marble strip marks its original size.

The first lane after the Prigioni, Calle degli Albanesi, is the address of the **Aquarium** *and its coy octopus (a good place to take the kids later; open daily 9 am–8 pm; adm L2000, under 10 years old L1000). Calle degli Albanesi continues back to Calle SS. Filippo e Giacomo; turn left into Ruga Giuffa and then left again just before the bridge for the* **Museo Diocesano**.

Open daily 10:30–12:30, free. S. Apollonia's Romanesque cloister—the last one remaining in Venice—has become a safe and remarkably tranquil haven for Venice's religious trappings and art orphaned by the demolition of churches. Among the more notable paintings are two by Luca *fa presto* ('quick draw') Giordano of Naples from S. Aponal, Titian's *S. Giacomo*, A. Pelligrini's *Allegory on the School of the Crucifixion*, the spooky *Transport of a Drowned Man* and a series of portraits of the *Primiceri* (head chaplains of St Mark's). Other works include a harrowing *Crucifixion* without a cross, and a wide array of reliquaries, missals, vestments, silver—and the cardinal's beret that Pope John XXIII wore as Patriarch of Venice.

From here, follow Ruga Giuffa and the Fondamenta and Calle di Canonica, which circle around the back of the 19th-century **Palazzo Patriarcale**, *adjacent to St Mark's in the Piazzetta dei Leoncini, where John XXIII, John Paul I and all the other*

*Venetian patriarchs have resided since the rational Napoleon made St Mark's a cathedral. Incorporated within is the dining hall where the doge hosted his legendary state banquets for notables and official guests; a corridor that once connected it directly to the Ducal Palace has been demolished. Also in the Piazzetta is the deconcecrated Church of **S. Basso**, now used for exhibitions. Beyond the little fountain in the centre (equipped with a special pigeon trough and bath) are the handsome pair of **porphyry lions** which take the Piazzetta's name. They were presented to the city by Doge Alvise Mocenigo III on his accession in 1722, and are endowed with some special child magnetism that proves irresistible to any crumbsnatcher who walks by. If it's on the hour, your ears will be further assaulted as two bronze giants cudgel the bell atop the magnificent **Clock Tower (Torre dell'Orologio)**.*

If the restoration is finished, you can climb past the works to the top from 9–12 and 3–6, Sun 9–12, closed Mon (L2000). *Horas non numero nisi serenas*: 'I only number happy hours', says the legend, but it doesn't always number them accurately, and gets especially muddled at the phases of the moon and signs of the zodiac. Still, it is such a fine clock, built by Mauro Codussi in 1499, with works by Paolo and Carlo Rainieri of Reggio Emilia, that other Italian cities maliciously circulated the rumour that the Venetians tore out the eyes of the Rainieri brothers to prevent them from ever building a similar one. In reality they were given a fat pension.

Like all exotic characters in Venice, the time-darkened bronze men on top of the tower are called the 'Moors', proto-Morris dancers in hairy-man dress. Their task of sounding the hours is complemented at Epiphany and during Ascension Week (La Sensa) when figures of the three Magi and an angel roll out to pay homage to the Madonna.

*The Clock Tower stands at the beginning of the **Procuratie**, the two long porticoed, arcaded buildings that face each other the length of St Mark's Square.*

The Procuratie were built as offices for the nine procurators, whose positions were elective but permanent, and whose princely status was second only to the doge. Three were responsible for the upkeep of the Basilica and six for the city on either side of the Grand Canal. The buildings are not identical; the one adjoining the Clock Tower, the **Procuratie Vecchie** was begun by Mauro Codussi in 1500 and finished by Sansovino some 30 years later. The **Procuratie Nuove** opposite were designed by Scamozzi and Longhena between 1582 and 1640. But they are close enough in appearance to continue the city's motif of looking glass reflections, which, when the Piazza is flooded, becomes surreal, and you feel as if you're inside a magic box.

Linking the Procuratie together is a similar arcaded building known as the **Ala Napoleonica**, which the French built in 1810 to replace the last incarnation of S. Geminiano (by Sansovino) out of an urge for symmetry and the crying need for a ballroom. It is a copy of the Procuratie Nuove, except for the attic, crowned by a cast of *Roman emperors*, minus a would-be title holder from Corsica.

Nowadays the city rents out the Procuratie as shops, and uses the Procuratie Nuove and Ala Napoleonica to house the city's vast historical and art collections, in the **Correr Museum**. (Open 10–4; Sun 9–12:30, closed Tues; L3000.) Founded by Teodoro Correr (d. 1830), the museum runs hot and cold like any attic, but not in any chronological order. The Neoclassicism of the Napoleonic ballroom, dining room, throne room, etc. houses works from the period, including plaster models by Canova and frescoes by Giovanni Carlo Bevilacqua. These are followed by a historical hodgepodge of state robes, ducal bonnets (a hard Phrygian cap called the *corno*) and the old-maidish nightcaps the doges wore under them, coins, battle standards, memorabilia from Lepanto, and from the career of Francesco Morosini. Among the bric-à-brac, note the pair of the 20-inch high platform shoes called *zoccoli* or *ciapine*, the Renaissance rage among Venetian ladies, because their increased height allowed them to wear more lavish gowns, even though the wearers could hardly walk (a fact apparently much appreciated by their husbands, as it kept down the risk of infidelities). Also of interest is a copy of the statue of *Marco Polo* from the temple of 500 Genies in Canton, China.

Upstairs, the picture gallery holds the best collection of Venetian paintings outside of the Accademia, including Carpaccio's *Two Venetian Ladies* (an essay in total boredom, often called *The Courtesans*, though in fact all Venetian ladies dressed that way—note their shoes) and his *Young Man in a Red Beret*, with an archtypical Venetian face. Three of the most important paintings are on the subject of the *Pietà*, one by Antonello da Messina, painted during his Venetian sojourn in the 1470s, and despite its damaged state, still offering hints of the luminosity that seduced Venetian painters. Another is by Giovanni Bellini and a third by the wiry Ferrarese painter Cosmè Tura. Another section of this floor is dedicated to the Risorgimento and Daniele Manin, who led the revolt against

Austria in 1848 (but it's often closed); another holds the minor arts—small bronzes made expressly for collectors by Tullio Lombardo and Il Riccio, lace, household items, and the outstanding *Aerial View of Venice* by Jacopo de'Barbari, engraved in 1500, and shown here with the original blocks. It is the most accurate view of the city from the period; the bad news is that this section of the museum is even more likely to be closed.

> *Across the Piazza, as you've surely noticed by now, hovers the gravity-defying* **Palazzo Ducale***, Europe's most dazzling secular building of the Middle Ages, a synthesis of the Romanesque, Gothic, and Islamic, wrapped in a diapered pattern of white Istrian stone and red Verona marble. No building of its period is as open and defenceless to the point of topsyturvydom, its massive top-heavy upper floor like a strawberry cake held up by its own frosting—a form that echoes the basic structure of the city itself, of palaces supported by millions of piles. But this fairy confection was all business, the nerve centre of the Venetian empire: the residence of the doge, seat of the senate and a score of councils, of the* Serenissima's *land and sea governments and and their bureaucracies, courts, and even the state prisons. For Ruskin it was 'the central building of the world'. The Venetians, more unassumingly, think of it as the valve of a rather large seashell.*

The original Palace was a typically walled and moated citadel, begun shortly after the city's consolidation on the Rialto in 810. It only began to assume its present shape in 1309, as the government evolved into its final form with the *Serrata del Consiglio*. In 1340 the massive hall for the *Maggior Consiglio* was begun on the seaward side—a task that took until 1419. This new building made the older sections of the Palace, facing the Piazzetta, look decrepit; but the senate had decreed that any doge who even *proposed* any changes to it faced a thousand ducat fine. Doge after doge suffered in a silent waiting game until a fire in 1419 caused severe damage, Doge Tommaso Mocenigo couldn't bear any more, and paid the fine, with which the Senate voted to build a 'more noble edifice'. Work began on 27 March, 1422 'the first act of the period properly called the "Renaissance",' groaned Ruskin. 'It was the knell of the architecture of Venice,—and of Venice herself.'

To the Venetians, however, their decline was not immediately apparent: in 1438 Doge Francesco Foscari commissioned the florid Porta della Carta in line with his pride in Venice's land expansion, and the city's greatest painters were hired to fresco the interior—all destroyed in the fires of 1574 and 1577. So much damage was done that there were serious moves to tear the remaining bits down and let Palladio start again à la classical High Renaissance. Fortunately, however, you can't teach an old doge new tricks, and it was rebuilt as it was—a rather extraordinary decision for the time. Who else in the 1570s would reconstruct a Gothic building?

The theme behind the Doge's Palace's **exterior decoration** is moral instruction and justice (and, naturally, the glory of Venice). Beautiful sculptural groups adorn the corners, most notably the *Judgement of Solomon* (c. 1410, by Jacopo della Quercia of Siena, one of the greatest early Renaissance sculptors) on the corner nearest the Porta della Carta, with a statue of the *Archangel Gabriel* overhead. On the Piazzetta corner are *Adam and Eve*, tempted by the serpent, while the *Archangel Michael* stands over with his sword to guard humanity from temptation. On the Ponte del Paglio corner is a group portraying *The Drunkeness of Noah*, an allegory on the frailty of humanity, with the *Archangel Raphael* overhead, helping to guide the tiny Tobias down the straight and narrow.

Less benign are the **two red pillars** in the *loggia* (on the Piazzetta façade), according to legend dyed by the blood of Venice's enemies, whose tortured corpses were strung out between them; one of the Palace's master builders, Filippo Calendario, was hung and quartered here for his role in the Marin Falier conspiracy. On Maundy Thursday the doge would stand between the columns to preside over a tongue-in-cheek ceremony celebrating Venice's victory over the Patriarch of Aquileia and his twelve prelates—marked by the baiting and decapitation of a bull and twelve pigs.

The rising water level over the centuries has forced the pavement to be raised the equivalent of two steps, making the **36 columns** of the ground floor colonnade seem low and squat. But these are crowned with some excellent medieval sculpture, depicting a few sacred and many profane subjects—animals, guildsmen, Turks, and Venetians, each telling a story for the benefit of the patricians strolling in the shade. One of the most beautiful is the seventh column from the basin (facing the Piazzetta), carved with a Romeo and Juliet scene of courtship, marriage, the first night, the birth of the first child, and then, after all that happiness, the child's death.

Enter the Palace through the **Porta della Carta** *(Paper Door), a florid Gothic symphony in stone by Giovanni and Bartolomeo Bon*

(1443); its name may derive from the clerks' desks that once stood near here. Originally brightly painted and gilded, it has recently undergone a thorough scouring, so that it's hard to tell that the figures of Doge Francesco Foscari and the lion are 19th-century replacements. Doge Foscari also had the Bons build him the triumphal **Arco Foscari**, *which stands at the end of the entrance passage. This was finished by Antonio Rizzo, and is decorated with bronze copies of his statues of Adam and Eve (originals now inside; the wonderfully self-assured Eve so capitivated the Duke of Mantua in the 16th century that he offered Venice the statue's weight in gold in exchange for it, a deal that the Venetians refused). Facing the arch is Rizzo's elaborately sculpted grand stairway, the* **Scala dei Giganti**, *named for the Gargantuan statues of Neptune and Mars by Sansovino (1566); among the details, see if you can find the basket of medlars, meant to symbolize cultivated, but still unripe young patricians. At the top of this stair the newly-elected doge would be crowned with a special Phrygian cap studded with gems, called the* zogia, *the 'jewel of independence' which he could only don again at Easter Mass in S. Zaccaria.*

Just within the Porta della Carta lies the delightful arcaded **Courtyard**, *or 'Cortile', designed by Antonio Rizzo after the fire of 1483; it contains two of Venice's finest well heads, and the ticket office, under the arcade to the left.*

Open April–15 Oct, 8:30–7, winter 8:30–1, and other times somewhere in between; adm L5000 (but see 'Introduction'). The visitor's entrance is by way of another grand stairway, Sansovino's **Scala d'Oro** (1580s, with gilded stuccoes by Vittoria). The **first floor**, or *primo piano nobile*, once the private apartments of the doge, is now used for frequent special exhibitions (separate admission). Even if it's open, its stripped-down unfurnished state offers few clues as to how the doge lived in this gilded cage of pomp and ritual, leading public and private councils and rites as grand as the Marriage to the Sea and as absurd as the one involving 17 women from Poveglia, who on Easter Tuesday had the right to give him a big kiss before sitting down to a ducal dinner. Senator in Senate, Citizen in City were his titles, as well as Prince of Clothes, with a wardrobe of gold and silver damask robes, and scarlet silks; and it's not surprising the most lavish room is **Sala degli Scarlatte**, or dressing room, with gilded ceiling, a chimney by Tullio and Antonio Lombardo, and a relief of the *Virgin* and *Doge Leonardo Loredan* by Pietro Lombardo. Once the doge was dressed, the rest of his procession would fall in line, including all the paraphernalia of Byzantine royalty: a naked sword, six silver trumpets, a damask umbrella, a chair, cushion, candle, and eight standards bearing the Lion of St Mark in four colours symbolizing peace, war, truce, and allegiance. Yet for all the glamour this was the only man in Venice not permitted to send or receive a private note from his wife, or any one else; nor accept any gift beyond flowers or rose water; he could not go to a café or theatre; he could not engage in any activity to raise money, but was expected to pay out of his own pocket for his robes, banquets, donations, taxes, and gifts to St Mark's. Nor could he abdicate, unless requested to so.

The office was respected, if not the man. When a doge died he was privately buried in the family tomb before the state funeral—which used a dummy corpse stuffed with straw and a wax mask, a custom originating with Doge Giovanni Mocenigo's funeral in the early 16th century, during a plague. An 'Inquisition of the Defunct Doge' was held over the dummy, to discover if the doge had kept to his *Promissione* (the oaths made before his coronation) or if his heirs owed the state any money; and it ascertained if any amendments to the *Promissione* were in order to further limit the powers of the new doge. Then the dead doge's dummy was taken to St Mark's to be hoisted in the air nine times by sailors, to the cry of 'Misericordia!', and then given a funeral service at SS. Giovanni e Paolo.

The golden stairway continues up to the *secondo piano nobile*, from where the Venetian state was governed. After the fire that destroyed its great frescoes, Veronese and Tintoretto were employed to decorate the newly remodelled chambers with mythological themes and scores of allegories and apotheosi of Venice—a smug, fleshy blonde in the eyes of these two. These paintings, most of them beaverishly over-restored into a flat, soulless paean of dead glory, are the Palace's chief interest. The first room, the **Sala delle Quattro Porte** (where ambassadors waited to be summoned before the doge) is typical, not even redeemed by the lavish ceiling stuccoes by Palladio and frescoes by Tintoretto.

Some of the best works, however, are in the next waiting room, the **Anticollegio**. On the walls are four mythological subjects by Tintoretto, designed to plant ideas of concord and harmony in the viewer: his powerful *Bacchus and Ariadne Crowned by Venus* and *Vulcan's Forge*, and less remarkable *Minerva Dismissing Mars* and *Mercury and the Graces*. Other paintings here are Veronese's *Rape of Europa*, one of his finest mythological works, and Jacopo Bassano's *Jacob Rejoins his Family*.

After digesting these paintings, visiting ambassadors would finally be admitted into the **Sala del Collegio**, or seat of Venice's inner council of 25 members, presided over by the doge. As if all the previous glitter hadn't made its point, this room is decorated with Veronese's sublimely confident and colourful ceiling, with its centrepiece of *Venice Triumphant*, and behind the throne, his equally sanguine *Doge Sebastian Venier Thanking Christ for Victory at Lepanto*.

Less attention was given to the decoration of the **Sala del Senato**, since the only ambassadors admitted here were Venetians serving abroad. But because of their reports many of the most important decisions were made in this room, by the doge and the senate, a nucleus chosen from the *Maggior Consiglio* that over the years varied from 60 to 300 members. The stale paintings are mainly by Tintoretto's school, with only a touch or two by the master.

Back through the Sala delle Quattro Porte, past Giambattista Tiepolo's *Neptune Paying Homage to Venice* (on the easel) the next stop is the **Sala del Consiglio dei Dieci**, headquarters of the dread, secret Council of Ten. The main panel of the ceiling, by Veronese, was pinched by the French and still hangs in the Louvre, but they left behind Veronese's oval *Old Man in Eastern Costume with a Young Woman*, now the star work of the room. Under this the Council of Ten (a misnomer, as the Ten were always complemented by the Doge and six councillors to make 17) deliberated and pored over the accusations deposited in the *Bocche dei Leoni*—the lions' mouths, the insidious boxes spread over the city—there's one next door in the Ten's waiting room, the **Sala della Bussola**. Although no unsigned accustions without the support of two witnesses were considered (and accusers knew they would be given the punishment of the crimes if they falsely reported) the procedure had such an evil reputation that when someone joked to Montesquieu that he was being watched by the Ten, he immediately packed his bags and left town. And woe indeed to anyone whose alibi refused to satisfy the Ten; a door in the Sala della Bussola passes through the office of the Three Heads of the Ten, in charge of investigating cases of treason—and from there bang, into the torture chamber.

From here steps descend to the old **Armoury** (Sale d'Armi), housing a fine collection of medieval and Renaissance armour, most of it showpieces that were rarely dented by halberd or sullied by guts, like the suit presented by Venice to Henry IV of France in 1603. A small stair takes you down to the small **Sala del Guariento** and the remains of Guariento's enormous fresco of the *Coronation of the Virgin* or *Paradise*

(1365–67), damaged in the 1577 fire and discovered under Tintoretto's *Paradiso* in the Sala del Maggior Consiglio. Here, too, are Rizzo's original *Adam* and *Eve*.

To the right is the magnificent **Sala del Maggior Consiglio**, originally built in 1340 and almost as large as a football field, capable of holding all 2500 patricians of the lower house of the Senate, or Great Council. Before the fire of 1577, it was beautifully decorated by Gentile da Fabriano, Giovanni Bellini, Carpaccio, and Titian, but at least one of the replacement paintings—nothing less than the biggest oil painting in the world (7 m × 22 m)—will give you pause: Tintoretto's awesome, recently-restored *Paradise*, which he painted free of charge, beginning the task at age 72. This replaced Guariento's fresco and follows the same subject, Canto XXX of Dante's *Paradiso*, listing the hierarchy of angels, saints, and Old Testament figures, and others of the heavenly vortex, 500 figures circling Chirst crowning the Virgin, the Queen of Heaven. William Blake would have appreciated it, and probably also the story of how some nosey patricians came to watch Tintoretto painting it, and commented: 'But other painters take more time and draw the figures more carefully'. To which the short tempered artist snapped: 'Because they don't have to put up with fools watching them!'

On the ceiling is the *Paradise*'s secular counterpart: Veronese's magnificent, vertiginous *Apotheosis of Venice*, its pride and confidence, even in allegory, probably very irritating to visitors, and embarassing to behold in May 1797, when Napoleon's troops were at the gate and the Council in wimpish terror voted to accept all Napoleon's demands, obliterating Venice's 1000 years of independence and its own existence. The frieze on the upper wall, by Domenico Tintoretto and assistants, portrays the first 76 doges, except for the space with a black veil that would have held the head of Marin Falier (1355) had he not been deprived of it for treason in a conspiracy to take sole power (*Hic est locus Marini Falethri decapitati pro criminibus* reads the dire inscription). The portraits of the last 44 doges, each painted by a contemporary painter, continue around the **Sala dello Scrutinio**, where the votes for office were counted. Elections for doge were Byzantine and elaborate—and frequent; the *Maggior Consiglio* preferred to chose doges who were old and wouldn't last long enough to gain a following. An easy election took only five days of lots drawn to form a committee to elect a committee to elect a committee to elect a committee to elect a doge; the longest election, Giovanni Bembo's in 1615, took 24 days.

From here the arrows point you across the **Bridge of Sighs** to the 17th-century **Palazzo delle Prigioni,** mostly used for petty offenders. The real rotters were dumped into uncomfortable *Pozzi,* or 'Wells' in the lower part of the Doge's Palace, while more illustrious offenders like Casanova were lodged in the *Piombi* or 'Leads' just under the roof (which you can visit on the Secret Itinerary). The horrible rumours of these cells, rumours encouraged by the State, made the French think they would find hundreds upon hundreds of innocent victims of the Ten rotting away inside them. With a flourish they burst in, only to have a bad case of *déjà vu.* The Bastille had only three prisoners waiting to be liberated; Venice managed to have four, but one was so fond of his cell he incessantly begged the French to let him go back. Further embarassment was averted when he died from an overdose of chocolate and rich cakes.

> *Besides the gilded state rooms created to be seen by visitors, both in the days of the Republic and now, there are the chambers where the nitty gritty business of running the state took place. In 1984 this latter section of the Palace was restored and opened to the public, but because many of the rooms are tiny, the guided tour, or* **Itinerari Segreti** *is limited to 20 people. This 'secret' tour is one of the most fascinating things to do in all Venice—it lasts an hour and a half and the only reason why more people don't know about it is because the tour commentary is in Italian. But if Italian isn't your language, read on.*

The tour begins at the top of the Scala d'Oro, but instead of turning right into the state rooms, the guide takes you left into the tiny wooden shipshape offices of the **Chancellery** on the *mezzanine,* which could easily fit aboard a fat Venetian galley—designed not only to be snug in the winter, but to make the average Venetian feel at home. The 18th-century **Hall of the Chancellery** is an elegant wooden room lined with cupboards for storing treaties, each bearing the arms of a chancellor, though Napoleon intervened before the last six cupboards could be decorated. Like most civil servants, chancellors were recruited from the *cittadini originarii*— native born Venetians, preferably at least of three generations, and rich enough not to engage in manual labour. Three chancellors managed to be elevated to the nobility (after paying the equivalent of L1,000,000,000), but as usual good service was expected and not singled out, while anything less than the best meant trouble. If a chancellor lost a document he had three days to find it or face the death penalty; one chancellor who secretly consorted with foreigners was slipped a poison cup of coffee (as was, more recently, Michele Sindona, the Vatican-related swindler).

137

Outside are the narrow stairs down which Casanova and his friend the renegade priest escaped when they broke out of the Leads. The two passed the night in an office, then calmly walked unnoticed out of the Porta della Carta in the morning, when the offices were unlocked. A gondola was waiting for them; Casanova however, stopped first for a morning coffee at Florian's Café, which according to legend, still has a copy of his bill.

Beyond the stair are the rooms of the justice department linked to the Council of Ten, especially the **Torture chamber** where the three *Signori della notte dei criminale* (judges of the night criminals) would 'put to the question' their suspects, hanging them by the wrists by the rope still dangling ominously in place. Because the victim's screams would make the civil servants next door nervous, such torture was done at twilight, and the chamber was so arranged that the light of the dying sun would fall in the victim's eyes, so that the three inquisitors would be invisible in the darkness. The two cells on either side of the rope were for the next suspects to be questioned, who, hearing the proceedings, might be encouraged to talk without all the messy rigamarole.

For psychology was one of the Republic's chief weapons even before there was a word for it, and as Venice grew old, she relied far more on her bark than her bite, encouraging police state rumours of torture and assassination and the relentless Council of Ten to make Venetians toe the line—and for the most part, it worked. The stories were so good that nearly every visitor to Venice still believes them, when in truth few states were as humane and progressive: prisoners had a legal right to a lawyer as early as the 970s; a prisoner had to be brought to trial in a month and no more; house arrest was invented for an ill prisoner in 1572; no one could be arrested without sufficient evidence; search warrants could only be issued by committee, and not by a single man; and along with Tuscany, the Republic abolished torture before anyone else, in the early 1700s.

The tour continues to the ornate **Sala dei Tre Capi**, the chamber of the three heads of the Council of Ten, who served as guardians of Venetian legality, and had to be present at all state meetings, at all appeals trials, and at every function attended by the doge, to make sure he kept to his coronation oath. As this chamber might be visited by some foreign dignitary or ambassador, it was given a lavish ceiling by Veronese, a fireplace carved by Sansovino, a luminous *Pietà* by the School of Antonello da Messina, and three paintings by Hieronymus Bosch: the peculiar *S. Libertà*, a crucified woman, a *Paradise and Inferno* and *St Jerome*, with the usual Boschian rogue's gallery of monsterettes. Another curiosity of the room is the secret passageway built into the wall; the Palace has quite a network of these, including one for busybodies that passed right behind the ducal bed; the state wouldn't even let sleeping doges lie in peace.

From here it's up to the notorious **Piombi**, or 'Leads' so named because the cells are located just under the leaded roof. In spite of their evil repute, as prisons go they are downright cosy—as good as some one-star hotel rooms, at least, with wooden walls, dry, and not too hot or cold, or crowded, with never more than two prisoners in a $7^1/_2$-ft square cell. The doors seem to be covered with at least seven different locks, but open with only one key. Casanova's cell is pointed out, where he lived comfortably enough, inviting his fellow prisoners in for the odd macaroni and cheese, and the guide offers an elaborate explanation of his escape that began through a hole in the roof. You can read more about it in his memoirs. There are wonderful views of the Piazza and Lagoon from the Leads' porthole windows.

The tour continues past a display of weapons to one of the engineering marvels of Venice: the **attic above the grand Sala del Maggior Consiglio**, where you can see exactly how the shipwrights from the Arsenale made such a vast heavy ceiling float unsupported over the room below; built in 1577, it is so well made it has yet to need any repairs. Part of the reason why is the care taken to produce the right wood. Venice's forests in the northern Veneto were planted scientifically to ensure that the trees grew tall, strong, and straight for masts or beams like these; anyone who cut one down faced the death penalty.

Next comes the palace attic, which like most attics contains both the obsolete and nostalgic—old wooden toilets, three swords (one for heads, one used in bullfights, and one that fell into a canal and was fossilized in the mud—'Nowadays' the guide remarks drily 'it would dissolve'), a collar with spikes inside, two *Bocche di Leone*, for denunciations against thieves, and the other against spies and traitors. The latter saw relatively little use, for most Venetians believed as Marin Sanudo wrote in the 1500s: 'Anyone who wishes to dissent must be mad'.

Walk II
Sestiere of San Marco

san Moise

S. Zulian—Campo S. Salvatore—S. Bartolomeo—Riva del Carbon—
S. Luca—Museo Fortuny—Campo S. Angelo—S. Stefano—
S. Samuele—Campo Francesco Morosini—S. Maria Zobenigo—
La Fenice—S. Moisè

The Sestiere of S. Marco, encompassing the big bulge west of Piazza S. Marco to the Grand Canal, manages to be both the most pedestrian and glitzy quarter of Venice: local institutions like La Fenice and Harry's Bar are here, among designer shops and swish hotels, but culture vultures will find meagre pickings—relatively, that is; any city would give its eye teeth for a few of its *palazzi* or works of art. Save this walk for an afternoon, when most of the churches are open—except Monday when Fortuny Museum is closed.

Walking Time: 3 hours

LUNCH/CAFÉS

Do Forni, Calle Specchieri 468, behind S. Zulian (AE, BA, DC). One of Venice's classics; well prepared local specialities (L55 000, more for lots of seafood).

Rosticceria San Bartolomeo, Calle della Bissa 5423, off Campo S. Bartolomeo (AE, BA, DC). Honest cooking for honest prices; *trattoria* (L18–25 000) and snack bar downstairs (L10 000).

Italy Italy, Campo S. Luca, for Italy's answer to McDonald's—one of the better national chains (L10 000).

Al Volto, Calle Cavalli (between the Grand Canal and Campo Manin); a genuine *enoteca*, with over a thousand wines and excellent snacks.

Osteria Bacareto, Calle Crosera, near Salizzada S. Samuele (AE, DC, Visa). A few outdoor tables, seafood (especially cod), lots of good wines; L30 000 (much cheaper if you eat standing up).

Rizzo Pane, Calle delle Botteghe, just off Campo S.Stefano. Best for picnic supplies.

Osteria alle Botteghe, Calle delle Botteghe; where the locals go for filling sandwiches and snacks (L3–6 000).

Paolin, Campo Francesco Morosini, for legendary pistachio ice cream.

Marchini, Ponte S. Maurizio (by the *campo* of the same name), for the best pastries and cakes in the city.

Da Raffaele, Fondamenta delle Ostreghe 2347 (just east of Campo S. Maria Zobenigo; AE, BA, DC, Visa); homemade pasta and seafood in the L50 000 range.

Harry's Bar, Calle Vallaresso 1323 (AE, BA, DC), a Venetian institution; delicious and expensive cocktails; meals (less recommended) L100 000.

La Colomba, Piscina di Frezzeria 1665 (AE, BA. DC), an intimate place, lined with paintings; great Venetian liver and onions (*fegato alla veneziana*) (L50 000, more for seafood).

☆   ☆   ☆   ☆   ☆

This walk begins under the magic clock tower of Piazza S. Marco, where it leaves the city's centre stage to enter another world: the winding lower gut of golden consumption, the **Mercerie** *(or Marzarie in Venetian dialect and on the street signs). It has five transformations, from the Merceria dell' Orologio to the Merceria 2 Aprile, strung together like brightly-lit sausages to form the shortest route from S. Marco to the Rialto Bridge.*

For a long time the *mercerie* were the only streets in Venice paved with marble blocks; they have always been lined with shops, probably offering the same kind of status economic surplus as they do now—precious silks and spices, Lacoste shirts and Opium perfume. But no one's ever accused the Venetians of offering anything but the shrewdest of bargains for their wares.

If the throngs aren't too pressing (or depressing) you can pause to pick out one of the Mercerie's *landmarks: the relief of the* **Old Woman with a mortar,** *located over the arch of Sottoportego del Nero Cappello (the first left after the clock tower).*

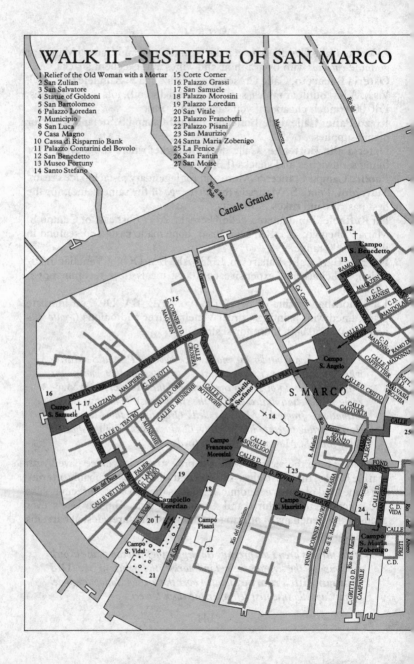

WALK II – SESTIERE OF SAN MARCO

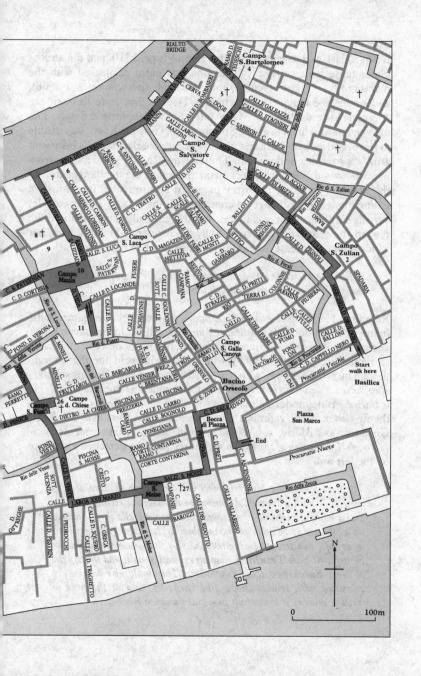

It was a dark and stormy night, the 15th of June, 1310, and the atmosphere tense with conspiracy. No one was more displeased with the *Serrata* of the *Maggior Consiglio* than the noblemen who were shut out, and under the banner of Baiamonte Tiepolo they rode through the Mercerie towards Piazza S. Marco intending to overthrow the state. The old woman who lived over the Sottoportego, Giustina Rossi, was unable to sleep, and looked out of her window only to see Baiamonte's insurgent army approaching underneath. Thinking quickly, she pried a stone from her window sill, scoring a direct hit on the skull of the standard bearer. In the rain and thunder, the army panicked and retreated in confusion, failing to meet the other rebel contingent in the Piazza. Thanks to Mrs Rossi's aim, the revolt was foiled, and the grateful Signory granted the reward she requested: the right to fly the banner of St Mark from her window on every feast day, and a promise never to raise her rent.

Follow the Mercerie crowds along to Campo S. Zulian, and its little church of **San Zulian** *(San Giuliano).*

Rebuilt in 1553 by Sansovino, S. Zulian's most remarkable feature is the figure over the door of Tommaso Rangone with all his favourite books and globes. Rangone, like many Venetians, had no modesty when it came to reminding posterity exactly who it was who paid for the church, though he is the only one who wished to be remembered for his scholarship, never a Venetian *forte* (and in fact, Rangone was from Ravenna). He is buried inside, under Palma Giovane's ceiling of *St Julian in Glory*; on the first altar on the right is a grimy Veronese: the *Pietà with SS. Rocco, Girolamo, and Marco*, a late work. Even better is Giovanni da Santacroce's *Coronation of the Virgin* with three saints, a detached altarpiece on the left wall.

The next square the Mercerie meet is Campo S. Salvatore, a busy crossroads with a memorial column to the abortive revolt of 1848, and a more memorable iron dragon, over an umbrella shop, holding up a coloured globe made of glass umbrellas. Its major buildings both wear safe, nondescript Baroque façades by the Giuseppe Sardi: the **Scuola di San Teodoro,** *now an exhibition hall, and the church of* **San Salvatore** *(San Salvador). This building's flanks are encrusted with trinket shops, like barnacles, and at the time of writing most of it is shut up in a giant wooden box.*

If you can find the entrance—an arch next to a television shop—pop inside to see its remarkable Renaissance interior, begun in 1508 by Giorgio Spavento and completed by Tullio Lombardo and Sansovino. Its unique design imaginatively fuses a long basilican nave with two aisles and a central Greek cross plan, by stringing together three Greek crosses, three domes and three transepts, and tying them together at the corners with pilasters and mini-cupolas. The clean lines and lack of decorative encrustations let the eye enjoy the interplay of space and light.

Sansovino also contributed the **Tomb of Doge Francesco Venier** (d. 1556), sculpting the fine figures of Hope and Charity at the age of 80. But Venice was known as a city of old men; the *Maggior Consiglio* even devised a special committee for patricians over 80 to keep them occupied with the state until they dropped dead. At the age of 89, Titian painted the *Annunciation* by the next altar, an unusual work that he signed with double emphasis *Titianus Fecit. 'Fecit'*. because, it is said, his patrons refused to believe that he had really painted it. The right transept contains the **Tomb of Caterina Cornaro** (d. 1510), the queen of Cyprus, at least for a little while, before the Republic convinced her of her duty as a good Venetian to cede the island to direct Venetian rule. In exchange for Cyprus Caterina got Ásolo, where luxurious ennui was first distilled into a fine art, and when she died she got a funeral fit for a queen and this better-than-middling tomb, with reliefs by Bernardo Contino.

On the high altar, Titian's *Transfiguration* is in the way of a more impressive work of art: a 14th-century silver gilt **reredos** made by Venetian goldsmiths, and after the Pala in St Mark's, their greatest masterpiece. The reredos is exposed only during Holy Week; otherwise ask the sacristan to push the button that lowers the Titian—a charming device that takes some of the glitz off the *cinquecento*'s Mr T. To the left is another painting that upstages Titian, *The Supper at the House of Emmaus* by the school of Giovanni Bellini. In front of the high altar, a glass circle set into the floor permits you to see a recently discovered merchant's tomb, with damaged frescoes by Titian's brother, Francesco Vecellio. The third chapel on the left has statues of the two major plague saints, *SS. Roch* and *Sebastian*, by Vittoria.

The adjacent monastery of S. Salvatore, now occupied by the phone company, has a cloister attributed to Sansovino, which the phone folks will let you see if you really want to. Otherwise, take the last length of the Mercerie, 2 Aprile (to the left of the church façade, under the dragon) to the main crossroads of Venice and one of its social hubs, the long and narrow and almost invariably crowded **Campo S. Bartolomeo***.*

In the middle of the Campo is a wonderfully benign bronze **statue of Carlo Goldoni**, whose comedies in Venetian dialect still make the Venetians laugh. Goldoni (1707–93) (like Hemingway, nicknamed 'Papa'), used to wander the lanes of Venice in his three-cornered hat, eavesdropping on conversations; often, he claimed, a mere turn of phrase would inspire his next play. By the smile on his jolly face he still finds his fellow citizens amusing, and if he needed fresh material, he'd find plenty every evening around seven. But perhaps 120 plays is enough for anybody.

The church of **San Bartolomeo** turns its back on the Campo, with its entrance around the corner on Salizzada Pio X. This was formerly the German church in Venice (the Fondaco dei Tedeschi, now the post office, is nearby) but few of its old parishoners would recognize it since the pedestrian rebuilding of 1723. Recently restored, it is used for the occasional exhibition; someday it may get its most famous work of art, Sebastiano del Piombo's *Organ Shutters*, back from the Accademia. Don't miss the funny face, sticking its tongue out at you from the foot of the campanile. It's a good job Ruskin didn't see this one.

Salizzada Pio X leads from here to the **Rialto Bridge** *(see 'The Grand Canal'), with views over the Grand Canal that may be more tempting than its trinket and jewellery shops. Long gone, however, is the sign 'It is Forbidden to Spit on the Swimmers'. In the snowy winter of 1987, it briefly took on a new role: Venice's only ski slope. From the bridge (without crossing it), follow the Grand Canal south on Pescheria S. Bartolomeo (soon changing its name to Riva del Ferro and then to Riva del Carbon) one of the rare walkways along Venice's 'Champs Elysés of the water god' as the French like to call it. It passes the* **Palazzo Loredan***, which, as the plaque says, was the home of Elena Lucrezia Corner Piscopia, who in 1678 became the first woman to receive a university degree (from Padua, in philosophy). The next palace, Ca' Farsetti, now serves as Venice's* **Municipio***, or City Hall.*

Just after the Municipio, *Calle Cavalli leads back to the Church of* **San Luca***, in the campiello to the right, an ungainly 19th-century reconstruction, though light and airy inside.*

146

None of the painting is worth a second glance, though there is a very damaged altarpiece by Veronese and the unmarked grave of Pietro Aretino, nicknamed by Ariosto the 'Scourge of Princes' (1492–1556).

A native of Arezzo in Tuscany (like Sansovino), Aretino ranks as the century's most lively vernacular writer, as well as the first in history to run a literary protection racket—princes and cardinals paid him *not* to write about them. Like Sansovino, he came to Venice as a refugee from Rome, after a career smearing the reputations of cardinals (for Giulio de' Medici, when he wanted to be elected pope), publishing erotic sonnets, and nearly being assassinated by a bishop. With Venice as a secure base, he began his new career of publishing brilliant letters, flattering and satirizing public figures from Emperor Charles V on down, using well-informed sources (Arentino must have had some friends in the Venetian secret service); he also had a keen eye for art, and did much to increase the reputation of his friend Titian, while annoying Michelangelo so successfully that the artist painted him in the Sistine Chapel *Last Judgement* as St Bartholomew, holding the skin of Michelangelo, whom he had 'flayed' (Titian, perhaps in response, used him as a model for Pontius Pilate). Besides getting under the skin of public figures, he wrote comedies and dialogues, mostly about brothels, poking fun at the erudition of the day. His prurient interests kept his reputation in the hands of the same kind of academics he mocked, and not only earned him an anonymous burial in this church, but lends a certain truth to the story that he died from laughing too hard at a dirty story told about his own sister.

Facing the side entrance of the church is the **Casa Magno**, *with an exceptionally fine early Gothic doorway, a masterpiece of brick work. From Campiello S. Luca, Ramo di Salizzada will take you into* **Campo Manin**, *with a statue of the fiery patriot, lawyer Daniele Manin, who led the revolt against the Austrians in 1848 (and ended up as a schoolmaster, teaching Italian in Paris). His statue looks towards his house by the little bridge on the left. The Cassa di Risparmio Bank (1964) is by Pier Luigi Nervi, Italy's most acclaimed post-war architect—and the only one to get a chance to build on a conspicuous spot in Venice.*

On this same site in 1490, Aldus Manutius (Teobaldo Pio Manuzio), a humanist teacher from Rome, founded his famous Aldine Press, with its imprint of the anchor and dolphin. Aldus's first love was Greek, and he played a major role in preserving, printing, developing a Greek type face (he also invented italics) and diffusing authorative editions of nearly every classical text to the general reading public at affordable prices. He had a unique editorial board that featured some of the greatest scholars of the Renaissance, including Pico della Mirandola and in 1508 Erasmus, who helped print his own *Adages*, a best-seller in its day. Another of Aldus' publications, Francesco Colonna's beautifully illustrated philosophical romance, *Hypnerotomachia Polifili* (or *The Dream of Polyphilus*, 1499) was an inspiration for Longhena's S. Maria della Salute.

> *From Campo Manin, Calle della Vida (under the sign for the Hotel Centauro) will take you on a short detour to the* **Palazzo Contarini del Bovolo**, *tucked in a tiny courtyard. Perhaps only one in a thousand visitors ever try to find it, though those who do are rewarded with Giovanni Candi's flamboyant external spiral stair (c. 1500), its ranks of arches curling up five storeys like an architectural ice cream parfait. The collection of medieval well-heads in the garden, thrones for a motley collection of stray pussies, is equally whimsical.*
>
> *Backtrack to Campo Manin. Of the two bridges in front of Manin's statue, take the one to the right and follow Calle S. Paternian along the wall of the Rossini Theatre, and turn right at Salizzada della Chiesa e Teatro; at no. 3998, note the Byzantine-style mosaic in a shrine of the* Madonna and Child, *smothered in necklaces. Follow the lane for Campo S. Benedetto, a boxy little square with one of Venice's more obscure churches,* **San Benedetto**, *usually open only around 5 or 6 pm and containing Baroque paintings by Sebastiano Mazzoni, Giambattista Tiepolo, and Bernardo Strozzi. More impressive than the Church, just opposite, is the façade of the 15th-century* **Palazzo Pésaro degli Orfei**, *long the home of the Spanish artist Mariano Fortuny (1871–1949), fashion designer, photographer, inventor (he designed a model for a mobile dome) and all-round Renaissance man. It is now the* **Museo Fortuny**; *Open 9–7, closed Mon; adm L5000, which nearly always includes a photography or design exhibition.*

One of the most charming things about the Palace is its unrestored condition, its rickety wooden stair and balcony in the courtyard, though if there's a popular show this fragile state will limit the access to a few people at a time. Equally unmodernized are the large rooms of Fortuny's home and studio, jammed full of paintings of nymphs, nymphs, and more nymphs. Other rooms are hung with the pleated silks to which he chiefly owes his fame today, which once tickled the backs of Sarah Bernhardt, Isadora Duncan, Eleonora Duse, and the loony Marchesa Casati.

> *Take Calle a Fianco Ca' Pesaro to the left of the Museo Fortuny; then the next left on Ramo dei Orfei, and then a right on Calle della Mandola, and you'll arrive at* **Campo Sant'Angelo**, *a large dusty square (as much as a Venetian campo can ever be large and dusty), though adorned on one side by the former Convent of S. Stefano, two Gothic palazzi, and the best view of S. Stefano's jauntily leaning tower, just to the west. As perilous as it looks, it was spared the fate of the campanile that once accompanied the long gone Church of S. Angelo, which tilted so dangerously in the 15th century that a specialist was brought in from Bologna to right it. He succeeded magnificently, making the old leaner plumb straight until the day after the scaffolding was removed and it collapsed in a pile of rubble. From Campo S. Angelo, cross over the bridge by the big pink palazzo; Calle dei Frati leads straight to the early Gothic* **Santo Stefano** *(San Stin), with its grandly florid Gothic door.*

S. Stefano has a couple of distinctions: it's the only church built directly over a canal, and more dubiously, it has had to be reconsecrated the most often—six times, because of the repeated murders that occurred within its walls. The interior, however, is most serenely Gothic, with harmoniously patterned walls and wooden ship's keel roof. On the wall by the door is the pretty equestrian **Tomb of Giacomo Surian** (d. 1493), decorated with skulls, garlands, and griffons; a bombastic bronze seal in the middle of the nave marks the grave of Doge Francesco Morosini, conqueror of the Morea.

The **sacristy** is rendered slightly claustrophobic by the large stretches of canvas on its walls, among them three late, shadowy Tintorettos: *The Washing of the Feet*, the *Last Supper*, composed at the extraordinary angle the artist favoured, and *Agony in the Garden*. Off the left aisle a door leads into the cloister, now government offices, though still containing the **Tomb of Doge Andrea Contarini** (d. 1382). Less fortunate were the hundreds of victims of the plague of 1630, buried in trenches in S. Stefano's graveyard (now Campiello Nuovo, off Calle del Pestrin facing the façade); for two hundred years it was strictly off-limits.

149

Briefly resist the natural pedestrian flow into Campo Francesco Morosini, and take Calle delle Botteghe, opposite the church façade. Then the first right, and the first left, into a lovely street called Piscina S. Samuele. Here you'll pass the most wistfully Venetian of plaques. It honours Francesco Querini, who left in 1904 'to try and explore the unknown paths of the Arctic, but who did not return victoriously . . .' Turn left into Ramo della Piscina. The next corner offers a choice of short digressions: on the right, Calle Corner o del Magazen Vecchio, leads to the charming **Corte Corner***, with a Gothic palace and Veneto-Byzantine well-head, while to the left, on Calle Crosera, you can see the curious shoe (high heel, of course) carved in the old Scuola of the Shoemakers at no. 3127.*

Continuing straight, though, Ramo di Piscina changes its name to Salizzada S. Samuele, passing a plaque for the longtime home of Veronese, where the painter died in 1588. The lane continues straight on to the Campo di S. Samuele on the Grand Canal with fine views across to the Ca' Rezzonico. On the right is the **Palazzo Grassi***, purchased by Fiat and used for some of Venice's blockbuster expositions, while in the square itself is* **San Samuele***.*

An ancient church rebuilt in 1685, S. Samuele still retains its fine old campanile; and is often called on to take some of the cultural overflow of the Grassi's shows. Of its original decoration, only some 15th-century frescoes by Paduan artists remain; little of the church recalls the reputation it had as Venice's naughtiest, recorded in a dialect doggerel:

> *Contrada piccola, grande bordel;*
> *Senza ponti, cattive campane,*
> *Omini becchi e donne putane.*
>
> (A small parish, but a big bordello
> Without bridges, with wicked bells
> Its men are cuckolds and its women whores.)

It just figures that S. Samuele was Casanova's parish church; the self-styled 'Cavalier de Seingalt' was born nearby in 1725, in Calle Malipiero (with a plaque), near the long gone Teatro di S. Samuele, where his theatrical parents once performed. As little Giacomo demonstrated a certain precocious ability, his parents destined him for the priesthood, and at S. Samuele he took minor orders, before discovering his real vocation in the bedrooms of Europe.

Circle around the right side of the Church, and take the first right at Calle Malipiero. At the end of the street, go left on Ramo Calle del Teatro and then a quick left under the Sottoportico de le Scuole will take you to Calle Fruttarol; continue straight, passing two little canals on the way to **Campo Francesco Morosini***, the south section of Campo S. Stefano. Bull baiting was the rage here until 1802, when the crush of spectators on the seats caused a tragic collapse. The bulls have been replaced by a statue of* Risorgimento *scholar Nicolò Tommaseo (1802–74), watched over by the peering eyes of several palaces:* **Palazzo Morosini** *on the east (no. 2802), home of the battling doge Francesco Morosini, and across the campo, the long classical façade of* **Palazzo Loredan** *(now the Veneto Institute of Science, Letters and Art), with its seaworthy doorknocker by Alessandro Vittoria. At the southernmost end of the campo is the deconsecrated church of* **San Vitale** *(or Vidal), with a pseudo-Palladian façade, now used for expositions.*

In its day S. Vitale was the site of an unusual ceremony, celebrating the anniversary of the execution of Doge Marin Falier; the current doge would attend mass, followed throughout by a priest bearing a phial of red liquid symbolizing the traitor's blood, a humiliating reminder of the consequences of independent action. Of the paintings, Carpaccio's *San Vitale* on a white horse with two pedestrian saints survives *in situ* over the high altar, while Sebastiano Ricci's *Immaculate Conception*, a study in blue and white draperies, is on the left. Note the ancient Roman inscription embedded in the foot of the campanile (to the left of the façade), itself a survivor of the original 11th-century church.

Opposite S. Vitale are the high iron fences of the **Palazzo Franchetti***, ornately restored in the 19th century, and one of the few palaces on the Grand Canal to have its own gardens. Behind it, tucked into own little* campo*, is the* **Palazzo Pisani***.*

The tycoons of the Pisani family suffered from the most lingering case of 'stone fever' or *mal della pietra* in Venice. You could land a Concorde in their villa at Strà, and this town palace of theirs, begun in 1614, would have reached similar proportions—or at least the Grand Canal—if the government hadn't ordered them to stop building in the mid-18th century. The Palace, now the Conservatory of Music, has two interior courtyards, linked by a *loggia*—worth popping in to see the wall of pouting Pisani busts.

From the east side of Campo Francesco Morosini (look for yellow signs per S. Marco), Calle del Spezier crosses the Rio del Santissimo (to the left you can see it passing under S. Stefano, which gives the canal its odour of sanctity). Across the bridge, just on the left, is the **Scuola degli Albanesi**, *built in 1531 as the centre of Venice's Albanian community, refugees from Ottoman imperialism who settled in this neighbourhood in the 1400s; the Lombardesque reliefs on the façade include a scene of Sultan Mehmet II studying the castle of Scutari, a property picked up by the Turks in 1479. The Albanians hired Carpaccio to paint a series on the* Life of the Virgin, *and in the 1700s, when the Albanians were too few to keep up the confraternity, it was taken over, art and all by the baker's guild; two of the paintings are now in the Ca' d'Oro and the others hidden somewhere in the Correr Museum's backrooms.*

Beyond lies Campo S. Maurizio, headquarters of Venice's antique dealers, who often turn the Square into an open-air market. The bland Church of **San Maurizio**, *rebuilt in 1806 by Gianantonio Selva is a prime candidate for Venice's most wilted wallflower, saved only by some vigorous Neoclassical reliefs on the façade. Another quirky blossom awaits just to the east: take Calle Zaguri, to the left of the façade, over a pair of bridges to* **Santa Maria Zobenigo**, *also known as S. Maria del Giglio ('of the Lily').*

Zobenigo isn't the Venetian attempt to pronounce lily, but 'Jubanico', the family who erected the Church in the 9th century. This long memory is a slap on the knuckles of the Barbaro family, who in rebuilding the Church in the 1680s had the bad taste to devote its entire façade to themselves, without even a nod to religion. The four heroic statues are of the Barbaro brothers, no-accounts as far as Venetian history is concerned. Above, allegorical figures of *Venice, Virtue, Wisdom, Honour* and *Fame* are forced to accompany the clan, while below reliefs depict maps of the towns where they gained their supposed triumphs and war trophies; you can learn quite a bit about the topography of Rome, Corfu and Padua, while Zara, Spalato and Candia are inexplicably unfinished, imposing walls with nothing inside. More pious art clutters the interior, chiefly a pair of *Evangelists* by Tintoretto behind the altar and the *Stations of the Cross* along the nave, a memory of an 18th-century competition; each artist contributed two scenes, though no one remembers who won.

152

*From here, take Calle del Piovan/Gritti (right of the façade) to
Fondamenta della Fenice: here you will see the traditional water gate
of Venice's famous theatre/opera house La Fenice. To reach it, take
the bridge to the left and circle around to the front, always taking the
right-hand path.*

Designed by Gianantonio Selva in 1792, the Operahouse was the swansong of the Republic, a last burst of fun before Napoleon. It also proved
true to its name (the 'Phoenix') rising up from the ashes of a devastating
fire in 1835 in the same design, by Selva's pupils—Neo-classical under-
statement outside, and within enough Late Empire excess to match all
comers in the *bel canto* league. It's hard to believe, but Selva was
lampooned and criticized for his precocious functionalist design of the
interior, not at all in the balanced symmetrical fashion of the day. The
Sala Apollinea, the banqueting rooms, and especially the oval, 1500 seat
auditorium with its gilded boxes are the highlights; at the time of writing
the theatre is under restoration for its 1992 bicentennial; new inexpensive seats are being added, to give casual visitors to the city more
chance to attend a performance in one of Europe's prettiest theatres.

To an Italian opera maven, La Fenice suffers comparison only with
the Teatro S. Carlo in Naples for 'genuine operatic tradition' (Milan's
La Scala is a mere upstart)—a tradition that began with two decades of
castrati, immensely popular though forbidden to don female attire 'to the
disappointment of many interested gentlemen'. But La Fenice had its
low notes as well: the premier of Verdi's *La Traviata* in 1853 was so bad
that the composer himself described it as a 'fiasco' though an improved
performance redeemed the opera the next year. But Verdi could never
stay unpopular for long, if not for his music, but for the rallying note he
sounded in the *Risorgimento*. Under the Austrians, when official public
life was denied to the Venetians, they would flock here, join in the
patriotic choruses, and do all they could to niggle their overlords behind
the cover of music. In the 20th century La Fenice rejoined the musical
vanguard with premiers of Stravinsky's *The Rake's Progress* (1951) and
Benjamin Britten's *The Turn of the Screw*.

*The square in front of the Opera house, Campo S. Fantin, is named
for the plain and crumbling 1507 Church of San Fantin by
Scarpagnino, with a perfect Renaissance dome over the sanctuary by
Sansovino. Nearby, behind an Istrian stone façade was the home of
the former Scuola della Buona Morte, a confraternity that comforted
prisoners condemned to death (Michelangelo belonged to the branch*

in Rome). The building is now occupied by the mouldering **Ateneo Veneto***, whose members might let you into see some mediocre paintings by Veronese, but then again they might not. From the bridge on Calle Verona, two streets off the* Campo*, you can see the façade of the Palazzo Contarini del Bovolo (of the spiral stair), and a plaque marking the house where Mozart stayed in 1771.*

From Campo S. Fantin take Calle del Caffetiere, behind the Campo*'s well, into Calle del Sartor delle Veste. Then a left into Calle Larga XXII Marzo, named for Daniele Manin's revolt of 1848, a wide street dotted with designer boutiques and banks. Visually closing off the east end is that spectacularly grimy, half-melted Baked Alaska of a church,* **San Moisè** *(1668).*

Open 3:30–7. Venetians who have to regularly face the façade of S. Moisè have developed a self-willed blind spot for Italy's most grotesque church, although casting their glance in the direction of the nearby Bauer-Grünwald Hotel isn't much of an improvement. Blame Alessandro Tremignon and sculptor Heinrich Meyring, but not too much: at the time of construction their grotesqueries fitted well into surroundings that included the state casino, or Ridotto (see below), where nearly all the players wore masks, and the Teatro S. Moisè, which opened in 1639 with the premier of Monteverdi's opera *Arianna* (demolished in 1876). Meyring also created the extraordinary high altar, or rock pile, of *St Moses on Mount Sinai*. But also look in the sacristy for the elegant 1633 bronze altar of the *Dead Christ and Angels*, by Niccolò and Sebastiano Roccatagliata, and over the left door for the leering skeletons on the Hallowe'en tomb of a certain *Canon Ivanovich*. And if anyone on earth still plays trivia games, you can probably stump your opponents by asking where the great Scot, financier John Law (1671–1729) ended up, after killing a man in a duel in London and fleeing to France, where he single handedly took over the national economy until his bubble burst in the Mississippi Scheme. The answer to this teaser is in the floor of S. Moisè, after spending his last years in Venice living by what he made at cards. There's an inscription on a slab near the entrance.

On the subject of cards (which appeared, and some say were invented in Venice in the early 15th century): as you continue along Salizzada S. Moisè, you'll pass the Calle del Ridotto, where no. 1332, with its grand piano nobile *windows, was once Venice's celebrated* **Ridotto***, or state-controlled gaming house, ancestor of the modern Casinò Municipale.*

Gambling seems to have been inbred in Venice, especially in its decline, when the wealthy, no longer able to stake their fortunes in shipping, had a chronic need to risk them in some other way. Cards, introduced in the 16th century, took the place of ships, and the State, seeking to take advantage of this, founded the Ridotto in 1638. Open only during the six months of Carnival (during which it was the chief attraction) it guaranteed fair play in exchange for a certain percentage of the preceedings. The State got rich, while everyone else slowly or spectacularly went bankrupt, patricians and commoners alike (the only requirement to enter was that one wore a mask); tourists like John Law made a fortune there, though others fared less well, like composer Domenico Scarlatti of Naples, who picked up a gambling habit that became the cancer of his career. In 1774 the Senate could no longer ignore the scandal and held a vote on closing the Ridotto. To encourage the members to vote according to their conscience, the vote was secret; when the votes were counted the Senate discovered to its dismay that it had voted to abolish one of its principal sources of income. But, as an observer wrote, 'Evidently, no state can keep going without the aid of vice' and over a 100 illegal *casini* ('little houses'), or social clubs, soon came to take on the meaning they have today.

> *If it's not time or your proper incarnation for a drink in Harry's Bar, down the next right (Calle Vallaresso), head up the Frezzeria on the right, Venice's scarcely noticeable red light district, and turn right on Calle del Salvador to the* **Bacino Orseolo**, *always filled with gently bobbing gondolas; the lane will take you back under the portico to Piazza S. Marco.*

Walk III
Castello

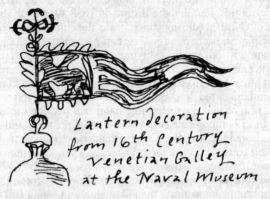

Lantern decoration from 16th century Venetian Galley at the Naval Museum

Naval History Museum—Campo Bandiera e Moro—Byzantine Art Museum—S. Zaccaria—Palazzo Querini-Stampalia—S. Maria Formosa—Campo Fava—S. Lio—SS. Giovanni e Paolo—Ospedaletto—S. Giorgio degli Schiavoni—S. Francesco della Vigna—Arsenal—S. Pietro in Castello—Giardini Pubblici

Castello, named for the long gone fortifications on the island of Olivolo, stretches from Piazza S. Marco out to the easternmost quarters of the city. One of the poorer *sestieri*, it nevertheless contains famous monuments and churches like SS. Giovanni e Paolo, the Colleoni statue, S. Zaccaria, and the magical Carpaccios in S. Giorgio Schiavoni, as well as the mighty engine that made Venice tick for so many centuries: the Arsenale. Eastern Castello is still the site of many of Venice's boatyards, littered with the rusting hulks of bygone *vaporetti* and often stinking of varnish. It is an area refreshingly void of your fellow tourists; here you'll find Venice's largest park, its most impressive display of laundry billowing overhead, and relatively few canals—ideal little neighbourhoods that could perhaps exist in many other Italian cities, made metaphysical by the total lack of traffic.

To see everything, take this walk any day from Wednesday to Saturday. On Monday, the Querini-Stampalia is closed; on Sundays and holidays the fascinating Naval History Museum by the Arsenal is closed;

if you go on Tuesday you'll have to give the Byzantine Art Museum a miss. To get into S. Zaccaria, begin at 9 am.
Walking Time: 5½ hours.

Pizzeria Pier UZ, Campo S. Maria Formosa 5245, a lively *pizzeria* in a lively piazza (L10 000).

Cip-Ciap, Calle Novo Mondo, just over the northwesternmost bridge from Campo S. Maria Formosa; one of Venice's best pizza by the slice (*a taglio*).

Da Remigio, Salizzada dei Greci 3416, typical *trattoria* patronized by a lot of locals (L30 000).

Il Golosone, Salizzada di S. Lio 5689, for a good coffee, pastry, or banana split.

Alla Nuova Speranza, Castello 145, in the Campo di Ruga; L12 000 menu, but a more hearty fare than the same amount will buy you in the tourist centre; pizzas around L6000. Outdoor tables.

Corte Sconta, Calle del Pestrin 3886, near Campo Bandiera e Moro (AE, BA, DC), Venetian seafood specialities and Venetian-Jewish desserts (L50 000).

Da Franz, Fondamenta S. Giuseppe di Castello 754, just across the canal from the church (AE); out of the way but one of Venice's top restaurants with honest to goodness good food (L40 000).

Caffè Paradiso, in the pretty yellow pavilion in the Public Gardens; sit on top for the classic view of Venice's front door.

☆   ☆   ☆   ☆   ☆

If any citizen of the Serenissima *worth his salt could come back to contemporary Venice, the first place he'd visit is the* **Naval History Museum***; for without the right stuff displayed here, there would have been no St Mark's, no doges, no Bellinis or Titians, and indeed no Venice. From St Mark's it's a ten-minute walk down the Riva degli Schiavoni—Riva di Ca' di Dio, or a ride on* vaporetto *No. 1 (Arsenale) or No. 5 (Campo della Tana).*

Open Mon–Fri 9–1, Sat 9–12, closed Sun and holidays; adm L1000 (one of the best deals in town, and as a bonus, there are explanations in English). On the **ground floor** you can learn all about Italy's one outstanding success in World War II: the 'nautical pigs' or manned torpedoes, invented by Prince Valerio Borghese. Not as kamikaze as they sound, these were operated by two divers, who would guide the weapon to its target, set the explosive and swim away. They sank 16 ships, nearly all of them British anchored in the port of Alexandria; after they had sunk

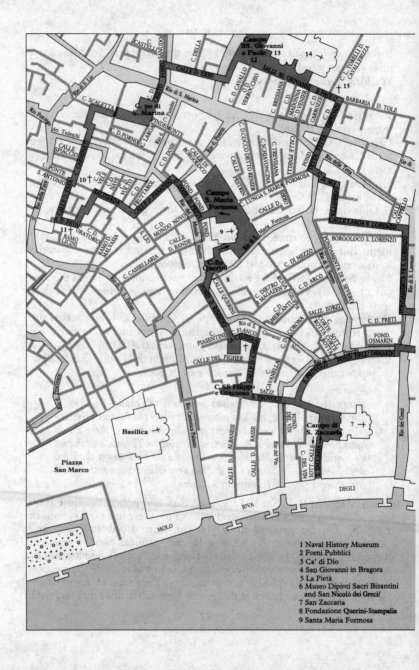

1 Naval History Museum
2 Forni Pubblici
3 Ca' di Dio
4 San Giovanni in Bragora
5 La Pietà
6 Museo Dipinti Sacri Bizantini and San Nicolò dei Greci/
7 San Zaccaria
8 Fondazione Querini-Stampalia
9 Santa Maria Formosa

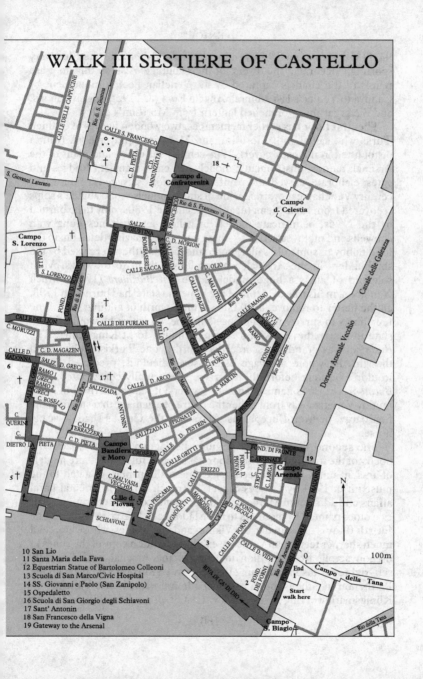

WALK III SESTIERE OF CASTELLO

CALLE DELLE CAPPUCINE

Rio di S. Giustina

CALLE S. FRANCESCO

C.D. PIETA

C.D. ANNUNZIATA

S. Giovanni Laterano

18

Campo d. Confraternità

Campo d. Celestia

Rio di S. Francesco d. Vigna

Canale delle Galeazze

Campo S. Lorenzo

SALIZ. S. GIUSTINA

CALLE ZORZI

BOMBASERI

RAMO FRANC.

CALLE S. FRANCESCO

C. D. MORION

C. ERIZZO

C.D. OLIO

CALLE SACCA

CALLE S. LORENZO

FOND. D. S. AGOSTIN

Rio di S. Agostin

CALLE MALATINA

CALLE PIRAZZI

RAMO GIUSTIN

VOLZINA

CALLE GATTE

Rio di S. Ternita

CALLE MAGNO

RAMO D.

SOTT. CALLE D'ANGELO

16

CALLE DEI FURLANI

C. MORUZZI

CALLE DEL LION

C. D. MAGAZEN

RAMO I. GRECI

SALIZ. D. GRECI

CALLE D. MADONNA

6

RAMO 2. GRECI

C. BOSELLO

C. QUERIN

DIETRO LA PIETA

5

CALLE D. PIETA

Rio della Pieta

17

SALIZZADA S. ANTONIN

CALLE D. ARCO

Rio di S. Severo

OTTON

RAMO D. GAI

C.D. MANDOLIN

C.D. PISCINI

C. D. FORNO

S. MARTIN

RAMO D. FORNO

FOND. DI CASTEL

Rio delle Gorne

Darsena Arsenale Vecchio

CALLE TERRAZZERA

C. D. PIETA

Campo Bandiera e Moro

CROSERA

SALIZZADA D. PIGNATER

CALLE D. PESTRIN

CALLE GRITTI

CALLE D. FRONTE

FOND. DI FRONTE

19

C. D. MALVASIA VECCHIA

4

C.llo d. Piovan

RAMO PESCARIA

C. D. CAGNOLETTO

CALLE ERIZZO

CALLE MOROSINA

C. D. PEGOLA

FOND. D. PIOVAN

STRETTA

C. LARGA

Campo Arsenale

SCHIAVONI

CALLE DEI FORNI

CALLE B. VIDA

C. FOND. D. PEGOLA

FOND. D. FORNI

Rio dell' Arsenale

FONDAMENTA TERESE

FOND. D. MADONNA

N

0   100m

3

RIVA DI CA' DI DIO

End

Campo della Tana

2

FOND. DEI FORNI

Start walk here

Campo S. Biagio

Rio della Tana

10 San Lio
11 Santa Maria della Fava
12 Equestrian Statue of Bartolomeo Colleoni
13 Scuola di San Marco/Civic Hospital
14 SS. Giovanni e Paolo (San Zanipolo)
15 Ospedaletto
16 Scuola di San Giorgio degli Schiavoni
17 Sant' Antonin
18 San Francesco della Vigna
19 Gateway to the Arsenal

the HMS *Valiant* on 19 December 1941 the Admiral of the Fleet very sportingly decorated the divers for their courage. Also on this floor are reliefs of the citadels captured by the Venetian fleet, a monument by Canova to Venice's last admiral, Angelo Emo (d. 1792), mighty canons, and the great three-branched lantern from Morosini's galley.

The **first floor** has earlier mementoes; two wooden figures of chained Turks who sailed with Morosini, and Morosini's prayer book (with a pistol fitted in the back cover); 17th-century sea charts and plans of the Arsenal; nautical instruments; models of Venice's ancient bridges and gates; elaborate, carved and painted decorations salvaged from a 17th-century Venetian galley; rooms full of ship's models—of Caligula's ships recovered from Lake Nemi (near Rome) in the 1930s, only to be burned by the Nazis, of intricate models of galleys and triremes hung with cobwebs and moth-eaten sails—these owe their amazing detail not to the fond hobby of some old sailor, but to the fact that they were used by the shipbuilders in the Arsenal, who preferred them to drawings. Most splendid of all is a huge model of the last *Bucintoro* (1728), which Napoleon, in his role of 'Attila of the Venetian state' had burned in 1798, all the better to remove its 60,000 sequins' worth of gilding; one of the few things to survive was the doge's throne, on which he would ride in state to marry the sea with a ring big enough to fit King Kong. The *Bucintoro* was grand but scarcely seaworthy; one Turkish sultan, who thought the whole marriage of the sea ridiculous, predicted that it wouldn't be long before the marriage was actually consumated. The *Bucintoro*'s curious name is another mystery: it may be derived in some muddy Venetian way from either the figure of a centaur that stood on the first barge, or from Bucephalus, Alexander the Great's shadow-scatty horse.

The **second floor** (models of gunboats, lagoon craft, etc.) lacks the poetry of the first, but the **third floor** has a colourful room of rare models of ancient junks and 18th-century Chinese silk panels, donated to the museum in 1964 by Jacques Sigaut, a French expert in oriental naval affairs and admirer of Marco Polo; other rooms contains charmingly naif ex-votoes painted by mariners to the Madonna dell'Arco in Naples. The **fourth floor** is dedicated to the Vikings and the Swedes, whose lions had much sharper teeth than Venice's; exhibits include a copy of the runes in dragon scroll, from the lion in front of the Arsenal, and a slightly self-righteous display claiming that it wasn't Morosini who blew up the Parthenon in Athens, but a Swedish admiral named Otto Vilhelm von Königsmark working in his employ. Last of all is a beautiful, iridescent

shell collection donated by Giuliana Coen-Camerino, alias the Venetian designer Roberta di Camerino.

*Although the gate of the Arsenal beckons from here, save it for later and head back along the Riva di Ca' di Dio, towards S. Marco. Just over the bridge, the building with the ornate frieze is the **Forni Pubblici** (1473), where the ships' biscuit for Venice's fleet and garrisons was baked to last (some Venetian hard tack, discovered in Crete, was still edible after 150 years). Just before the next bridge is the **Ca' di Dio**, a 13th-century pilgrims' hostel used by the Crusaders, and later expanded by Sansovino. This is one of the busier parts of Venice's shore, where tugboats and ferries dock and tired ACTV vaporetti rest for the night. Cross the next bridge, where the quay becomes Riva degli Schiavoni, then turn up little Calle del Forno, passing the quiet Campiello del Piovan, and taking the next left, at Calle Crosera. This leads into **Campo Bandiera e Moro**, named after three Venetian officers in the Austrian Navy who plotted a revolt in Calabria for Italian unity in 1844 and were betrayed by the English government, in whom they had confided; so noble was their effort that for 60 years this campo was dignified with the title of 'Piazza'. It is the address of the lovely Gothic Palazzo Gritti Badoer, now La Residenza Pensione, and of **S. Giovanni in Brágora** ('in the marketplace') rebuilt in 1475, with a simple, lobed brick façade.*

The equally simple interior, which retains its original ship's keel roof, contains treasures for all tastes: for relic mongers, the body of St John the Almsgiver in a glass case (though his church, S. Giovanni Elemosinario, is elsewhere), a pretty 13th-century Byzantine relief over the sacristy door, flanked by Alvise Vivarini's *Resurrected Christ* (1498) and Cima da Conegliano's *Constantine and St Helena* (currently being restored). Cima also contributed the Church's chief treasure, the high altar's *Baptism of Christ* (1494), an excellent painting restored to its original brilliant colours. In the last chapel on the left, the 15th-century *Life of St Nicholas* is a reminder of how late Byzantine influences lingered in Venetian art; also note the **baptismal font**, where in 1675 Mrs Vivaldi's red-headed son was christened Antonio.

*Take Calle del Dose ('Doge'), opposite the church, back to Riva degli Schiavoni. Turn right and cross the bridge to the white façade of **La Pietà**, stuck on only in 1906.*

Open only for concerts. though sometimes you can peek in during rehearsals. The Venetians like to call it 'Vivaldi's church,' as its predecessor was attached to a charity hospital for orphan girls (founded in 1346) where Vivaldi was chorus-master and violin teacher between 1704–38, composing some of his greatest *concerti* for star pupils. Thanks to him, the hospital's fame increased so much that the authorities had to put up the plaque you can still see on the south wall, threatening lightning bolts and excommunication upon any parent who tried to pawn their child off as an orphan. It was fashionable for visitors to attend one of La Pietà's concerts, and leave a suitably large donation towards the good work. As churches did double duty as concert halls, Giorgio Massari designed La Pietà in 1739 in an elegant oval shape, with acoustics as well as God in mind—if you do get in, note the rounded angles, the choir stalls along the back and sides, and high vaulted ceiling. The oblong vestibule served to dampen street noise, a feature that may well have been suggested by Vivaldi himself. Decorated in luscious cream and gold, with Giambattista Tiepolo's *Triumph of Faith* on top, La Pietà is just like being inside a Fabergé Easter egg.

> *Climb the steps of the bridge near La Pietà for the best view of S. Giorgio dei Greci's crazy campanile, which since its construction in 1592 has hung like a diver about to leap into Rio dei Greci. Gambling that it won't dive in quite yet, get closer by heading north along Calle della Pietà, to the right of the La Pietà, passing the warning plaque (mentioned above), and continuing straight until you reach Calle della Madonna, the neighbourhood high street. Turn left, to the canal-side entrance of the Scuola di S. Nicolò dei Greci (1678, by Longhena) and its* **Museo Dipinti Sacri Bizantini** *(Byzantine Art Museum), part of the Hellenic Centre for Byzantine and Post-Byzantine Studies.*

Open 9:30–12:30 and 2–6, Sun 9:30–12, closed Tues (L3000). The Scuola and the Orthodox church next door were the heart of a thriving Greek community that began with a handful of artists invited in to make the mosaics at Torcello and numbered 15,000 in its heyday—according to the Greeks, who now number exactly 10. ('So where'd they all go?' you might ask, and the Greeks will reply 'Some went back to Greece, some to Padua, but most fell in love with Venetians'.) The links between Greece and Venice were so close throughout history that some linguists claim much of the modern Greek language is directly derived from Venetian dialect (for example, a 'fork' in Italian is a *forchetta*, but in Venetian it's a *piroun*, similiar to the Greek *pirouni*; the utensil was introduced in Europe by the Greek wife of an early doge, though at first its use was condemned as decadent). Many Greeks, especially merchants, courtesans and artists, came to Venice in the 15th and 16th centuries when the Turks conquered Constantinople and Greece; most celebrated of these were a school of painters from Crete known in Venice as the 'Madonneri di Rialto'.

The collection, mostly from the 16th-18th centuries, points up both the glories and the limitations of late Byzantine art as artificially preserved in Venice after Byzantium had ceased to exist. Most conspicuous is its ironclad conservatism, a seeming obsession with a storied past and a total unwillingness to learn from new advances in art—the Orthodox Church, after all, never looked upon its icons as art but as objects of devotion that reflect the spirit of heaven, and one of the tenets of Orthodox faith is that fashion or style never changes up there. But their conservatism goes farther than that; in a corner of one rare and remarkable 15th-century *Nativity*, there is a girl pouring water from an amphora who could have stepped off an ancient Greek vase. Across from her, some lively *Last Judgements* serve as a reminder of how powerful and visionary this art could be even in its decay; even better is a 16th-century *Jesus and the Samaritan Girl*, set in a dreamlike landscape of purple, gold and green and a charming fairytale *Noah's Ark*. Although in some of the later icons you can see the odd western touch, none bristle with the energy of the Cretan-Venetian school's chief rebel, El Greco, who spent a few years in Italy studying Tintoretto and the Bassanos before moving to Spain.

In the 1530s, the Greeks were given permission to build an Orthodox church in Venice, and hired Sante Lombardo to design their **S. Giorgio dei Greci**, with a fine Renaissance façade and a lovely clock on its perilously listing campanile (same hours; if not open ask the custodian in the museum. Orthodox services are held Sundays at 11). Some of the finest paintings, by the 16th-century Cretan artist Michele Damaskinos, are part of the golden *iconostasis*; the older icons were brought over after the fall of Constantinople.

> Cross the Ponte dei Greci and continue along Fondamenta dell' Osmarin (rosemary) to Campo S. Provolo; a left turn here leads into the quiet Campo di S. Zaccaria, with its little garden of trees and cats, only dimly recalling two doges who were assassinated here: Pietro Tradonico (864) and Vitale Michiel II in 1172. Be on your

best behaviour; as noted on the old plaque at the entrance to the Campo, you can't gamble, argue, curse or fight here, and you had better not throw any trash under the trees either, or they just might chuck you in the Leads. To the right of S. Zaccaria is the brick patterned façade of its 13th-century predecessor, used in the winter for the lectures of an Anglo-Venetian society; left of the church, part of its 16th-century cloister has homes built into the arches. At the south end of the Campo, in Sottocalle S. Zaccaria, is a an ecletic William Morris style palazzina *with a relief of* St George. *The main attraction here, though, is one you may have seen already: the distinctive Istrian stone façade of* **San Zaccaria**—*oddly, the only church front visible from the top of St Mark's campanile.*

Open 10–12 and 4–6. The present church was begun in retro-Gothic by Antonio Gambello in 1444 and finished in the Renaissance style of Mauro Codussi in 1515, who is responsible for the façade above the level of the door, its lunettes and delicate sea shell reliefs disguising Gambello's Gothic naves. Inside Codussi converted the original plans for a rib vaulted ambulatory into an elegant ring of elliptical cupolas, lit by long narrow windows—a northern Gothic inspiration, the only one of its kind in Venice. The star attraction is Giovanni Bellini's recently restored *Madonna amd Saints* (1505) in the second chapel on the left. Large, riveting, and luminous, the perspectives of the painted columns and arch are continued into the design of the frame to create a unique sense of depth, directing the eye towards a rare visual equivalent of the music of the spheres. The saints on either side of the Madonna's throne, and the angel musicians below, are posed symmetrically, in a spiritual, self-absorbed dance; Bellini was one of the few artists capable of giving even the most common subject and composition new meaning—don't expect as much from the 17th and 18th-century artists whose canvases decorate the nave. At the end of the left aisle is the tomb and a self-portrait bust of Alessandro Vittoria (1528–1608), who also sculpted the headless figure of *S. Zaccaria* over the main door, and the two saints of the holy water stoups.

The original S. Zaccaria was founded in the 9th century to house the relics of St Zacharias, father of John the Baptist, whose body still lies in right aisle. Near this is the entrance to the **Cappella di S. Atanasio** and **Cappella di S. Tarasio** (adm L1000, and another L500 for the light machine inside); the first contains an early Tintoretto, the *Birth of St John the Baptist*, while S. Tarasio chapel, actually the chancel of the original church (with fragments of its Byzantine mosaic paving) houses three ornate *ancone* by Antonio Vivarini and Giovanni d'Alemagna, painted in the 1440s. The one in the centre, a hyper-Gothic gilt extravaganza, features carved wooden saints with expectant faces, set into the frame as if seated in theatre boxes. In the fan vault are frescoes by the Tuscan Andrea del Castagno of the same period, which, though sadly damaged, hint of how atavistic the Venetians were in the early Renaissance. A stair leads down into the murky old crypt, under whose flooded floor and pygmy vaults moulder the remains of eight doges. S. Zaccaria and its nuns enjoyed special ducal favours after the 12th century, when the abbess donated the convent garden to Doge Sebastiano Ziani; the nuns embroidered the ducal bonnets, and doge and his entourage attended a special Easter Mass here.

In the 18th century the Convent of S. Zaccaria held the more dubious honour of boasting a very fashionable salon in the convent parlour (the subject of paintings by Guardi in the Ca' Rezzonico and Pietro Longhi in the Correr Museum). Its frisky nuns were the source of many a scandal. Nearly half the sisters in those days, and most of the noble ones, had taken the veil not out of religious vocation, but because most noble families would only provide suitably enormous dowries for their eldest daughters. Girls went to convents happy to escape parental restrictions; supported by handsome incomes and pin money from home, they enjoyed a series of balls, concerts, dinner parties, games of chance (*bassetto* was especially popular) and each, of course, had her *cavaliere servente*. When the convent behaviour became too outrageous, the once fearsome Council of Ten threatened prison sentences; but when it sent its spies and agents to enforce its mandates, they were pelted with stones and turned away.

> *People with children, in the winter, will inevitably be pushed southwards, down the Sottocalle S. Zaccaria to Riva degli Schiavoni, where a modest but noisy funfair operates on the Lagoon's edge in January. The rest of the year there's nothing to see on the Riva but cafés and trinket shops—and the fierce* **Vittorio Emanuele II Monument***, a humdinger with winged lions ripping off the chains of Austrian domination, but still a favourite spot for catnaps among Venice's smaller felines.*
>
> *If this cannot distract you, leave Campo S. Zaccaria by way of Campiello S. Provolo and Salizzada S. Provolo (looking back to see*

the pretty bas-relief over its arch). This gives into Campo SS. Filippo e Giacomo; from here take Calle Rimpeto la Sacrestia (behind the kiosk) north and turn left at Calle Fianco la Chiesa (the chiesa *in question being the woebegone S. Giovanni Novo). Pass under the archway to your right and continue along little* **Fondamenta di Rimedio** *with its little iron bridges over a very narrow canal; and cross the twin bridges at its head for Campiello Querini, site of the 16th-century Palazzo Querini-Stampalia, home of the* **Fondazione Querini-Stampalia** *with its library and art gallery, founded in 1869 by Count Giovanni Querini.*

Open 10–12:30, closed Mon; adm L5000. Site of frequent and worthy special exhibits, the permanent Querini-Stampalia collection features a handful of masterpieces and bushels of the not-so-masterful, but works fascinating to anyone with a spark of curiosity about Venice in the 18th century. This was the grand age of trivialization for the aristocracy throughout Europe, but nowhere pursued so feverishly as in Venice, where the spirit of mercantile adventure that had created the mighty maritime Republic of yore had evaporated like perfume; patricians spent their days frittering away their ancestors' huge patrimonies and doing their best to look like poodles. You can see them here in the child-like paintings of Gabriel Bella and in room after room after room of Venetian *Biedermeiers* by the indefatigable Pietro Longhi.

The bright stars of the collection are scattered randomly among the sleepers, beginning with an exquisite *Coronation of the Virgin* (1372) by Donato and Caterino Veneziano. There are some not too penetrating portraits of Venetian senators by Palma Giovane, as well as his excellent unfinished marriage portraits of *Francesco Querini* and the lovely *Paola Priuli Querini*; there's a *Bacchanale* complete down to the grape-stained teeth by Nicolò Frangipane. Don't miss the room of brittle counter-Reformation hallucinations, with paintings by Pietro Liberi (1614–87: a *Man Fallen through Vice* being kicked by a midget and a whore) and Matteo dei Pitocchi (1626–1689; alarming rustic scenes full of ugly brutes and menacing skies—genre painting gone haywire). Further along you are rewarded with a pretty but damaged *tondo* of *The Virgin, Child and St John* by Lorenzo di Credi (a follower of Leonardo da Vinci), and Giovanni Bellini's *Presentation at the Temple*, an early painting inspired by his brother-in-law Mantegna that haunts with its stillness. And then a bit further along, an uncannily modern *Christ Bearing the Cross* by an anonymous follower of Pordenone, and the startling *Judith*, holding

Holofernes' head as if were a trophy, by the great amateur Vincenzo Catena.

From Campiello Querini, Calle Dietro la Chiesa winds around the back of S. Maria Formosa Church into the spacious **Campo Santa Maria Formosa***, a lively square with a market, several bars and pizzerie, and a handful of noble palaces: the* **Ca' Malpiero Trevisan** *(no. 5250, with marble discs) by Tullio's son, Sante Lombardo, the Venetian-Byzantine* **Palazzo Vitturi** *(No. 5246, with Byzantine carvings), and the 16th-century* **Palazzo Pruili***, next to the PCI (Communist Party) headquarters. And, of course, there is the white Renaissance bloom of* **Santa Maria Formosa** *itself.*

In 639, during his exile on the Rialto, Magno, Bishop of Oderzo, had a vision of the Virgin, where she appeared as a very buxom and beautiful (*formosa*) matron and ordered him to build a church wherever a little white cloud settled. It was the first Rialtine church dedicated to Mary, and when it was rebuilt in 1492 by Mauro Codussi, he maintained its original Greek cross shape. The Austrians dropped an incendiary bomb through it in 1916 (you can see a bas-relief of the *bomb* just outside the right transept door). The church has two façades, both to the greater glory of the Cappello clan, the one facing the canal a military triumph dedicated to Vincenzo Cappello (d. 1541), with never a religious symbol in view, and the one facing the *campo*, honouring even more Cappellos (and the Virgin Mary) built in 1604. Over a door in S. Maria's Baroque campanile leers the most hideous face in Venice, a grotesque mask added in 1688: '... in that head is embodied the type of the evil spirit to which Venice was abandoned', wrote Ruskin, who didn't share Venice's sense of the absurd.

If the head is the ugliest, many consider that of Palma Vecchio's *Santa Barbara* (1524) in the Chapel of the Bombardiers (in the right transept) the most beautiful in the city, the perfectly ripe Venetian Renaissance beauty—modelled on Palma's own daughter. George Eliot saw her as 'an almost unique presentation of a hero-woman', and indeed, in her life, Barbara was so heroically stubborn that her own father had her locked in a tower, and then martyred. She became the patroness of artillerymen and bombardiers (perhaps what attracted the Austrians) when her father was struck dead by lightning on his way home. The other major painting inside is Bartolomeo Vivarini's 1473 triptych of the *Madonna della Misericordia* in the first chapel on the right, the parishoners under the Virgin's protective mantle having earned their place there by paying for the painting. To the right of the main door you can take in the shrine to Pius X, the Venetian patriarch who became the last pope to be canonized, while on the left is an icon of the *Virgin*, carried on the admiral's flagship during the Battle of Lepanto. The last work of art is Codussi's grey and cream interior itself, a complex variation on the Brunelleschian Renaissance archetype, with chapels divided by double open arches.

From Campo S. Maria Formosa, walk briefly north (the direction towards which the ugly face is scowling) along the Fondamentas dei Preti and del Dose. Take the 'Bridge of Paradise' to the left over the canal to Calle del Paradiso, spanned by a 15th-century Gothic archway, bearing a relief of the Madonna *sheltering the arch's donor under her mantle. At the end of the lane turn right to Salizzada S. Lio, a busy thoroughfare; and then left the second lane (Calle di Caffetier), which leads straight into the flank of* **Santa Maria della Fava**.

St Mary of the Fava Bean is the more popular name for S. Maria della Consolazione; in the old days a pastry shop in the neighbourhood was renowned for its *fave dolci*, the sweets eaten on All Souls' Day. Built in the 18th century, it was decorated by some of the most popular artists of the period: Giambattista Tiepolo (*Education of the Virgin*), first altar on the right; the second chapel on the left holds Piazzetta's *tenebroso* masterpiece, *The Virgin Appearing to St Philip Neri* (1727), an intense, zig-zagging composition of reds and browns. This church is also dedicated to that Saint, the 16th-century Roman who helped invent modern sacred music; like Philip's Chiesa Nuova in Rome, it has a big organ and good acoustics. The statues along the nave are from the chisel of Torretto, perhaps best known as the Master of Canova.

From here, Calle della Fava will take you straight to the neigh-bourhood's other little church, **San Lio***; if it's open, a rare occur-rence, stop in to see the chapel to the right of the altar, with some fine sculptural work by Pietro and Tullio Lombardo, including a relief of the* Pietà*; on the restored ceiling is Giandomenico Tiepolo's* Apotheosis of St Leo.*

Take Calle Carminati (to the left of the façade) north of S. Lio to the intersection with Calle Scaletta, where a right turn (in front of the mattress shop) will bring you to Campo di S. Marina, with its two palazzi. Take Calle del Cristo, at the opposite end of the Campo. Cross the bridge, and turn right at the next (an iron bridge) for Calle delle Erbe, leading to Fondamenta Dandolo; just to the left from here is the grand **Campo di SS. Giovanni e Paolo**, *home to three of Venice's most celebrated landmarks, beginning with the* **Equestrian Statue of Bartolomeo Colleoni**.

Few statues have had such a rocky history. Colleoni, the Bergamask *condottiere* (1400–76), was one of the celebrity military commanders of his day, and one who well served Venice's claims on the mainland—both by leading the Republic's mercenary army and by *not* taking up other offers to fight against Venice—Venice ensured his loyalty by making him incredibly wealthy. And when Colleoni died, it was discovered that in gratitude for the Republic's goodness towards him, he would leave it the princely sum of 100,000 ducats on the condition that it erect an equestrian monument to him '*super platea S. Marco*'. After all, Colleoni's predessescor, the *condottiere* 'Honey Cat' Gattamelata, had got a fine one by Donatello in Padua (paid for by the Republic), and Colleoni wanted one, too, right where everyone could see it. Greedy for the money, but gagging at the thought of erecting a statue in the sacred Piazza S. Marco to anybody on this planet, much less a mercenary warlord, the Senate came up with the wily solution of erecting the statue in the *campo* of the Scuola S. Marco.

But the cheat ended there. In return for his ducats, Venice gave Colleoni one of the greatest equestrian statues of all time. Andrea Verrocchio, sculptor, alchemist and the master of Leonardo da Vinci and Botticelli, won the competition to make the monument in 1479, and was on the point of casting the horse when he heard a rumour that the Venetians doubted his ability to make the rider and were looking for another artist. Furious, Verrocchio broke the cast and went back to Florence. The Venetians, equally angry, banned him from Venice, and by the time the two parties were reconciled, and Verrocchio went back to work, he only had time to make the casts for the horse and rider before his death. The Republic then entrusted Alessandro Leopardi, he of the famous flagpoles in the Piazza, to cast Verrocchio's figures and the plinth beneath them, and the monument was unveiled, at last, in 1496.

In comparison the powerful dynamics of Verrocchio's Colleoni, Donatello's Gattamelata looks like the pussy cat of his nickname; in fact, it's hard to avoid noting Colleoni's striking resemblance to Klaus Kinski (though Verrocchio never laid eyes on the real *condottiere*). And it is fitting, for if Werner Herzog ever wanted to make a film about a Renaissance *condottiere*, Colleoni would fill the bill. Born into a war-like aristocratic family, and always proud of his emblem of *coglioni* ('testicles'—a play on his name) he began his mercenary career at the age of 19, in Naples, and first worked for Venice under Gattamelata in 1431. After a period of wavering between Milan and Venice, he decided to stick to the latter, but only when Milanese ambitions for north Italian domination were laid to rest (1454) was Colleoni appointed commander-in-chief of the Venetian forces. The lack of subsequent wars, large salary and enforced idleness made this an amazingly cushy job (as far as anyone knows, he only had to fight one battle in his last twenty years); to kill time, he ran his castle at Malpaga as a mixed court of artists and army pals, even entertaining the King of Denmark. Yet along with ducats, he left Venice a warning: never to give any other military commander as much power as it had given him.

On Colleoni's left is the delightful trompe l'oeil *façade of the former* **Scuola di San Marco**, *founded in 1260 and one of the six* Scuole Grandi.

Now the Civic Hospital. This is one of those unique buildings of distilled Venetian fantasy, an asymetrical, sumptuously decorated Renaissance confection replacing the original guild hall that burned in 1485. Pietro Lombardo designed its replacement, with help from his sons and Antonio Buora; in 1495 Mauro Codussi was summoned to design its upper level of six curved crowns, a rolling motif that echoes not only Tullio and Antonio Lombardos' charming shallow relief arches with lions on the ground floor, but also the domes of the other St Mark's and the city's arched bridges. The façade is vertically divided in two; the loftier, left-hand section once held the Scuola's Great Hall, drastically rearranged by the Austrians. Just within the door is the Lower Hall, and in the morning you can usually visit Scamozzi's 17th-century **San Lazzaro dei Mendicanti**, incorporated into the hospital as its funerary chapel, with a *St Ursula* by Tintoretto and a *Crucifixion* by Veronese. Better still, ask to see the medical library, formerly the Scuola's chapter room, with the most ornate coffered ceiling in Venice (16th-century). Though still a working hospital, you can usually just wander in and look around (closed from 1–3 pm 'for repose').

Next to the Scuola di S. Marco, and looming over the campo *and most of the* sestiero *of Castello is the huge Gothic church of* **Santi Giovanni e Paolo**, *better known in Venice as* **San Zanipolo**, *after St Mark's the most important church on the right bank.*

170

Open 7–12:30 and 3:30–7:30. Every now and then, Venice left its splendid isolation to join the Italian mainstream. One such occasion came during the great 13th-century religious revival begun by SS. Francis and Dominic, whose minor orders sought to bring the faith directly to the people by preaching and works of charity. Rather than dwell in self-absorbed monastaries, the Franciscans and Dominicans built jumbo utilitarian churches in the cities to bring their message to the biggest possible congregations. Every Italian city, Venice included, has one impressive example from each order; the Franciscans built Venice's Frari church, and this one is the Dominicans'. Their first church on this site, erected in 1246, was on land donated by Doge Giacomo Tiepolo (whose tomb is just to the left of the door), but it soon proved too small, and in 1333 work began on the present cavernous basilica. The design is simple, vast, and functional, its decoration, outside and in, concentrated in the lovely apse. The unfinished façade, next to the festive Scuola di S. Marco, would be invisible but for a handsome doorway attributed to Bartolomeo Bon, with marble columns from Torcello and a pair of Byzantine reliefs; a third one, of *Daniel in the lions' den*, stands off by itself in the right corner of the wall.

S. Zanipolo's steep and prodigious space, hemmed together by tie beams, braced by ten massive Istrian stone columns, and lit by a beautiful crescent of Gothic windows in the choir, was put to good use as a pantheon of doges; all their funerals were held here after the 1430, and some 25 of them went no further, but lie here in splendid Gothic and Renaissance tombs. The west wall belongs to the Mocenigo family [1], who gave the church three dead doges, the first interred in the celebrated, classical **Tomb of Doge Pietro Mocenigo** (to the left of the door) by Pietro Lombardo, assisted by his sons Tullio and Antonio (1476–81). Recently scrubbed, it is as beautiful as it is haughty, the culmination of Venice's Renaissance style, a stage for statues representing the *Three Ages of Man* and other assorted warriors, standing over a pair of reliefs of the *Labours of Hercules*. Religion is regulated to a relief at the top, but it too is suitably heroic: a triumphant *Resurrection*. An inscription proudly remarks that the tomb was paid for by the Doge's enemies (not willingly, mind you). Over and around the portal is the huge *Tomb of Doge Alvise Mocenigo I and Wife* (1577), while on the right is Tullio Lombardo's classically inspired *Tomb of Doge Giovanni Mocenigo* (d. 1485), with a fine relief of *St Mark Baptizing Annianus*.

The first item on the right wall, in the shadow of Pietro Mocenigo's mighty tomb, is a 13th century Byzantine sarcophagus, all that remains of the tomb of Doge Ranier Zeno (d. 1268). Note the flying angels supporting the *Throne of Christ*: a conventional Byzantine symbol, and a remarkable example of artistic continuity—in Augustus' day the same angels in the same poses were holding the civic crown of the caesars over public buildings.

After the first altar in the right aisle, is the **Monument to Marcantonio Bragadin** [2], the commander of Famagusta (Cyprus) in 1570, who withstood a Turkish siege for nearly a year when, outnumbered 10 to 1, he was forced to surrender. Honourable terms were negotiated, for the Venetians had defended themselves bravely, and Bragadin and his fellow commanders went to the Turkish camp to deliver the keys of the city, with exchanges of every courtesy. But the siege, which had lasted far longer than expected, had turned the Turkish commander, Lala Mustafa, into a pathological sadist; after welcoming the Venetians and their allies, he suddenly turned on them, ordering all 350 to be hacked to pieces. Even worse awaited Bragadin: first relieved of his nose and ears, he endured two weeks of agonizing torture before the pasha ordered him to be stripped naked, tied to the public scaffold, and flayed alive. Brigadin bore even this in silence until he expired. His skin was then stuffed with straw and brought as a trophy to the Sultan in Constantinople. Nine years later (if you care to believe this typically Venetian posthumous happy ending) it was stolen by a Venetian prisoner of war and returned to Venice. Bragadin's memorial was set up here in 1596, with a faded grisaille fresco depicting his martyrdom, and a bust, by a student of Vittoria, atop the urn that holds his neatly folded skin—its presence confirmed by a recent investigation sponsored by a descendant.

The adjacent chapel contains Giovanni Bellini's fine polyptych of *St Vincent Ferrer*, a fire-eating preacher who helped incite Spain's religious persecutions, here portrayed by the gentlest of painters. *Vincent Ferrer* is accompagnied by a charming *St Christopher* and rather uncomfortable *St Sebastian*, while under the polyptych is an effigy of the Blessed Tommaso Caraffini, confessor of St Catherine of Siena. In the floor of the nave, near the next chapel, is the niello-work **Tomb of Ludovico Diedo** [3] (1460s), a bizarre relief with a dragon contemplating an orrery. The next chapel, the Addolarata, was lavishly Baroqued in the 17th century, while the next, the **Chapel of the Madonna della Pace** [4] (currently under restoration), is named for a miraculous Byzantine icon brought to Venice in 1349, but the flamboyant 1708 tombs of the Valier doges, Bertucci (d. 1658) and Silvestro (d. 1700) steal the show. Giambattista Piazzetta painted the ceiling of the next chapel, the **Chapel of St Dominic** [5],

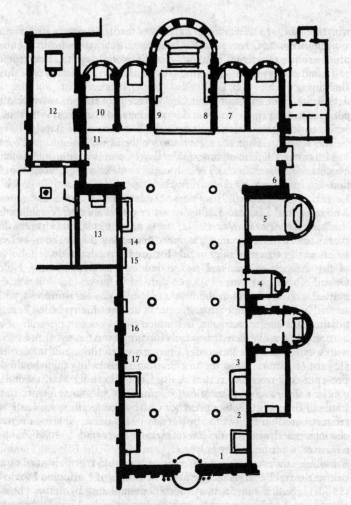

SANTI GIOVANNI E PAOLO (ZANIPOLO)

1 Tombs of the Mocenigo Family
2 Monument to Marcantonio Bragadin
3 Tomb of Lodovico Diedo
4 Chapel of the Madonna della Pace
5 Chapel of St Dominic
6 Tomb of Nicola Orsini
7 Cappella della Maddalena

8 Tombs of Doges Michele Morosini and Leonardo Loredan
9 Tombs of Doges Andrea Vendramin and Marco Corner
10 Tomb of Doge Giovanni Dolfin
11 Tomb of Doge Antonio Venier
12 Chapel of the Rosary

13 Sacristy
14 Tomb of Palma Giovane
15 Tomb of Doge Pasquale Malipiero
16 Tomb of Doge Tommaso Mocenigo
17 Tomb of Doge Nicolò Marcello

with the *Glory of St Dominic* (1727), where the hero-saint is sucked up in a luminous vortex, accompanied by a small floating orchestra. The six bronze reliefs on scenes from the *Life of St Dominic*, are the masterpieces of Bolognese sculptor Giuseppe Mazza (1720). Next comes a shrine containing the foot of St Catherine of Siena, black and tiny, and resplendent in its golden Gothic reliquary. Catherine's skill in convincing the popes to return to Rome from Avignon earned her the gratitude of an entire nation; along with St Francis she is co-patron of Italy.

The stained glass in the right transept, the finest in Venice, was made in Murano in 1473, from cartoons by Bartolomeo Vivarini and Girolamo Mocetto (one wonders why Murano didn't make more). Here, too, are first-rate paintings by Alvise Vivarini (*Christ Bearing the Cross*, 1474), Cima da Conegliano and/or Giovanni Martini da Udine's *Coronation of the Virgin*, and Lorenzo Lotto's newly restored and richly coloured *St Antonine Distributing Alms* (1542), to beggars whose faces reveal their anxious need. The usually tight-fisted Signoria paid for the two monuments in this transept, in gratitude for service rendered during the War of the League of Cambrai: the gilded equestrian **Tomb of Nicola Orsini, Prince of Nola** [6], who earned it for his brave defence of Padua, and over the door, the *Tomb of Dionigi Naldo di Brisighella*, with a second-rate statue by Lorenzo Bregno of the *condottiere* who led Venice's infantry and died in action in 1510.

In the first of five transept chapels (starting from the right), are several works by Alessandro Vittoria: a *Crucifixion* and the grand tomb of Sir Edward (*Odoardo*) Windsor, an Elizabethan Catholic exile who died in Venice in 1574. The next chapel, the **Cappella della Maddalena** [7], contains the *Tomb of Admiral Vettor Pisani*, the saviour of Venice in the Battle of Chioggia (1380), during which he was mortally wounded; it was reconstructed on the 600th anniversery of his death. Sharing the same chapel is the *Tomb of Marco Giustiniani della Bragora* (d. 1346), held up by a quartet of primitive heads.

Double lancet windows with Gothic tracery light the polygonal **chancel**: on the right wall is the splendid **Tomb of Doge Michele Morosini** [8] (d. 1382), a marriage of Gothic design and Byzantine mosaics possible only in Venice, with carvings attributed to the dalle Masegne, and the more lavish **Tomb of Doge Leonardo Loredan** [8] (d. 1520), decorated with bronze reliefs by Danese Cattaneo. On the left wall, the **Tomb of Doge Andrea Vendramin** [9] is a fine work by Tullio and Antonio Lombardo (1478) that nevertheless earned a quart of poison ink from the pen of Ruskin, the king of cranks. He caused the Venetians some alarm by ordering a ladder to clamber all over the tomb and prove that, just as he suspected, the sculpture was a sham because the sculptors hadn't bothered to finished off the parts no one would ever see, a sign of 'an extreme of intellectual and moral degradation'. To fit it in, the earlier **Tomb of Doge Marco Corner** [9] (d. 1368), took a few chops, but still preserves its fine statues by Nino Pisano of Pisa, especially his graceful central figure of the Virgin.

The chapel to the left of the high altar has some mediocre paintings by Leandro Bassano, while the next contains two sarcophagi suspended on the walls: the first is of Jacopo Cavalli (d. 1384) with an effigy by Pier Paolo Dalle Masegne and a large fresco background; the other contains the mortal remains of **Doge Giovanni Dolfin** [10] (d. 1361). In the left transept, the Dalle Masegne brothers were also responsible for the pink and white **Tomb of Doge Antonio Venier** [11] (d. 1400) and his wife and daughter, an effort that became the model for Venice's lingering transition from Gothic to the full bloom of the Lombardesque Renaissance. A door in the left transept leads to the **Chapel of the Rosary** [12], built to celebrate the victory at Lepanto, which took place on the feast day of the Madonna of the Rosary. Burned in 1867, with all of its art and fine paintings by Giovanni Bellini and Titian, temporarily lodged there, it underwent a half-century of restoration, and re-opened in 1959 with a ceiling by Veronese transplanted from the demolished church of the Umiltà.

Another string of monuments lines the left aisle, though the first work is a fragment of *Three Saints* from a polyptych by Bartolomeo Vivarini. Over the **Sacristy door** [13] is the **Tomb of Palma Giovane** [14], with busts of Titian, Palma Vecchio, and himself (just beyond the 18th-century organ). Pietro Lombardo, nearly as prolific as Palma Giovane, contributed the next work: the 1462 **Tomb of Doge Pasquale Malipiero** [15], one of the first and purest Renaissance works in Venice. The next batch of tombs includes an equestrian model for *condottiere* Pompeo Giustiniani, the **Tomb of Doge Tommaso Mocenigo** [16] (d. 1423), by Pietro di Nicolo Lamberti and Giovanni di Martino, and Pietro Lombardo's **Tomb of Doge Nicolò Marcello** [17] (d. 1474). The last altar on the left has a theatrical *St Jerome* by Vittoria (1576).

*Walk around the flank of S. Zanipolo; the small building near the apse is the **Ex-Scuola of St Ursula**, now a permanently closed chapel, containing the tombs of Giovanni and Gentile Bellini. Continue along Salizzada SS. Giovanni e Paolo to the little church* *of the* **Ospedaletto**, *blanketed by an overwrought Baroque façade designed by Longhena.*

The cumulative effect of all its strong men, lions, and giants hovers somewhere between a circus poster and low calorie nightmare—a fair reflection of the low ebb of everyday life in the declining 1670s. Also known as S. Maria dei Derelitti ('of the waifs', or 'orphans'), it belonged to a hospital and school for orphans founded in 1527; like La Pietà, its female students became internationally famous for their music (its elegant concert chamber, frescoed in the 18th century, may be seen on request). Longhena also redesigned the interior (entered by a side door of the hospital) decorated with some fairly vertiginous ceiling frescoes, including a *trompe l'oeil* organ zooming out over the altar. There is a sampling of 18th-century Venetian paintings, including a dramatic early Giambattista Tiepolo, *Abraham's Sacrifice of Isaac*, a small vignette over the fourth arch on the right. All the little scenes over the arches are good, though hard to see; some of the others on the right side are also sometimes attributed to Tiepolo.

> *Follow Calle del Ospedaletto (facing the church), which on crossing a bridge changes its name to Calle Tetta; turn left at the end of the street, over the iron bridge into Calle della Madonnetta, and then left again on Calle Larga di S. Lorenzo. At the end of the street stands the plain brick façade of* **San Lorenzo**, *originally founded in the 6th century and later the last resting place of Marco Polo. The great traveller's sarcophagus was misplaced in its 16th century restoration. The Church was damaged in World War I, deconsecrated, used as storage space, and every now and then hosts an exhibition (at writing closed for extensive restorations).*
>
> *Continue down Fondamenta di S. Lorenzo to the next bridge, and cross it for Calle del Lion. Just over the next bridge is the* **Scuola di San Giorgio degli Schiavoni**, *the little Dalmatian confraternity—little bigger than Dr Who's police box, but thanks to Vittore Carpaccio, a Tardis ready to transport you to a world of storybook delight.*

Open 9:30–12:30 and 3:30–6:30, Sun and holidays 9:30–12, closed Mon (L3000). In their long history abroad, the Venetians won more minds than hearts, but they did build up an affectionate relationship with the Dalmatians. This is in spite of a chequered history dating back to the 9th century, when Venice's merchants were harassed by Dalmation pirates. The Venetians retaliated by capturing the Dalmatians and selling them as slaves, and colonizing Dalmatian ports. For centuries Venice fought the Hungarians, the Turks, and the Dalmatians themselves over the region. Off and on it went, but by the 15th century Venice's Dalmatian community had enough interests to protect to found a *scuola*, and enough sense to hire Carpaccio to decorate it with a series on their patron saints, George, Tryphon, and Jerome.

The relationship lasted down to the very end. Dalmatian troops served as the Republic's tiny standing army, and in 1797 they were ordered home to comply with Napoleon's ultimatum. As they departed, they inadvertently played a last bitter joke on the terrified Doge and Great Council, who were holding their last session in the Palazzo Ducale to vote on the democratic government Napoleon demanded. All of a sudden shots rang out across the Riva degli Schiavoni. Scared out of their wits, the patricians broke off the debate, hurled their cowardly ballots in the box and fled in disguise—only later discovering that the shots they had heard had been fired by the Dalamatians as a farewell salute to Venice. Enough Dalmatians remained behind to look after the *scuola*, and like the Greeks at San Nicolò dei Greci, they still own it.

Carpaccio's cycle, painted between 1502 and 1508 was originally intended for the hall upstairs. Removed to the ground floor in 1551, they have had the rare fortune to stay there ever since, cosy, warm, glowing with colour, and filled with the exact, literal detail that any good storyteller uses to bring his tale to life—the bits of undigested maidens by the dragon in the painting of *St George*, just to the left of the door, or the monster brought to heel in *The Triumph of St George*. Next, *St George Baptises the Pagan King and Queen*, followed by an altar of the *Virgin and Child* by Carpaccio's son Benedetto. Then Vittore again, with the legend of the obscure Dalmatian Saint Tryphon, *St Tryphon Exorcising Emperor Gordianus' Daughter*, whose demon is a pouty little basilisk, followed by *The Agony in the Garden* and *The Calling of St Matthew* (which takes place in the Ghetto) and *St Jerome Leading his Lion into a Monastery*, a creature who wouldn't harm a fly but causes much comical consternation among the monks (though not to an incongruous band of Turks). *The Funeral of St Jerome* is followed by perhaps the best loved painting in the city: *St Augustine in His Study*, showing the good saint thoughtfully gazing out of the window, watched by his little white dog—the story follows a passage in St Augustine, who describes how he was writing a letter to St Jerome, not knowing he had died, when a heavenly light streamed down and a voice warned him it was too late. Although none of the subjects have anything to do with Venice, they are as infused with the city as if Carpaccio soaked them with a Venetian tea bag. Upstairs, the panelled hall is decorated with nutty 17th-century paintings by Andrea Vicentino, edged with members of the confraternity posing as if for a modern class picture.

> *From S. Giorgio, you can dip down Fondamenta dei Furlani (named for the Venetians' favourite Friulian dance) to see if the gormless 17th-century Church of* **San Antonin** *is open (serious restorations are underway). It contains a* Deposition *by Carpaccio's master Lazzaro Bastiani. Some six hundred years ago you would have probably been molested by a pig; in honour of St Anthony Abbot, the monks used to keep a herd of free ranging swine with bells around their necks who so visually, orally, and olfactorally made such a nuisance of themselves that the Senate ordered them to be penned up in 1409.*
>
> *Retrace your steps to the Scuola di S. Giorgio and turn west (left) over the bridge; turn right up Fondamenta S. Giorgio degli Schiavoni to its end, crossing the canal again for Corte Nuova, site of a quaint, homemade chapel with a painted ceiling and shrines to the war dead at the entrance to Calle Zorzi; follow this to Salizzada S. Giustina and turn right, then left at Ramo Ponte di S. Francesco for* **San Francesco della Vigna**, *a slice of the Renaissance lost in a remote and tired square, with the rusty skeletons of gasworks for company.*

Open 7–11:45 and 4:45–7. According to hoary, self-serving tradition, the first church on this site commemorated the spot where the living St Mark the Evangelist came closest to Venice; while sailing from Aquileia to Egypt, he fell asleep, and as his boat sailed past he had his famous 'Pax tibi...' dream. Named for the vines planted on this site in 1253 when it was donated to the Franciscans, the present church was begun in 1534 to a design by Sansovino, its foundation stone laid by Sansovino's friend, Doge Andrea Gritti. In 1572 it was given a temple façade by Palladio in bright Istrian stone, which seems a bit sad and extravagant without the flickering play of water and light that brings its whiteness to life elsewhere. Still, it was much copied for centuries, especially in and around Venice.

Sansovino's interior was reshaped according to designs by Fra Francesco Zorzi, a keen student of Renaissance philosophy, proportions, and geometry, into a spacious Latin cross with five chapels along its single nave—a dry, academic design more Tuscan than Venetian. The art is much better than the building itself: by the door bronze statues of *SS. Francis* and *John the Baptist* by Vittoria and a triptych by Alvise Vivarini. The third chapel on the right sports a pair of tombs of *Contarini* doges, the fourth chapel, belonging to the Badoer family, has a recently restored *Resurrection* attributed to Veronese, but better still is Antonio da Negroponte's 1450 shimmering *Madonna and Child Enthroned* in the right transept, a golden-robed *Virgin* in a merry spring bower full of roses and orange trees: one of Venice's hidden gems from the early Renaissance, when artists were still content to imitate nature rather than improve on it.

Doge Gritti is buried in the chancel, but there is more art in the marble-clad **Giustiniani chapel** to the left of the altar, a survivor from the original church. Designed by the Lombardos, its row of prophets are by Pietro and helpers, while the four *Evangelists* and altar are by Tullio and Sante. On the left side of the nave, perhaps the best work is Gerolamo da Santacroce's *Martyrdom of St Laurence* under the pulpit, a busy scene with a colourful assemblage and fantasy architecture.

Veronese's *Sacra Conversazione* (1562) is in the 5th chapel on the left; the third, with a bright frescoed ceiling lit by an oculus, is decorated with a quirky combination of *chiaroscuro* by Giambattista Tiepolo and sculpted garlands; while the second has a fine altarpiece by Alessandro Vittoria, including statues of *SS. Sebastian, Roch and Anthony Abbot*. A door in the left transept leads out into the simple but lovely 15th-century **cloisters**, full of flowers and lined with tombs. Near the entrance, a chapel contains a *Madonna and Child* by Giovanni Bellini and assistants. Bring L100 for the lights—a great bargain, for one of Venice's sweetest Madonnas; for background there's a pretty Italian hill town and a Dolomite or two. The main cloister leads into another, larger one, now used as a garden nursery; it has what might be Venice's only vineyard.

The south flank of the Church is skirted by a ghostly campo, *with a campanile, a Gritti palace (1525), long the residence of the Papal Nuncio, the Oratory of the Holy Stigmata, and a lofty 19th-century Neoclassical portico that failed to liven the mix. Leave the* campo *the way you came in, over the bridge and down Ramo Ponte S. Francesco; make a left turn at the end of the street, and then a quick right into Salizzada d. Gatte (the 'Paved Street of Female Cats', though the* gate *were actually Venetian for* 'legate', *or Apostolic Nuncio). But nowadays the feline conotations better fit the bill: this is a quiet and convivial neighbourhood, where much of the action seems to evolve around women stalking reluctant pussies with paper plates of leftover spaghetti, pleading 'mici, mici, mici'. Nearly every shop, no matter how incongruous, sells tins of cat food, and in some of the smaller alleys you can see little improvised kitty shelters and litter boxes (obviously a problem for the Venetian cat). Not without reason has it recently been proposed to proclaim Venice the 'World Capital of Stray Cats'.*

Continue straight, through Campo delle Gatte. A left turn at Calle del Mandolin will bring you to the charming **Campiello Due Pozzi**, *and through this, take Calle Magno, and then the first right at* **Sottoportico d'Angelo**, *(a tiny archway, easy to miss) named for the statue of the* angel *on the arch, flanked by the only* hedgehogs *in Venice. The walls of the Arsenal loom ahead, across the Gorne ('of the rain gutter'); follow them south along the Rio delle Gorne to* **San Martino** *(c. 1540) yet another church designed by Sansovino; the most impressive thing about its heavily decorated Greek cross interior is the false octagonal cupola, painted with 17th-century trompe l'oeil architectural perspectives, a style the Italians called* quadratura. *From S. Martino (left of the façade), Calle. Arsenale leads into Campo dell'Arsenale, where there is a choice of two cafés to sit at as you contemplate the twin-towered* **Gateway to the Arsenal**.

Unless you take the No. 5 *vaporetto* through its vast, derelict boatyards along the Rio dell'Arsenale, the gate is all the Italian military allows you to see of what the Senate called 'the heart of the Venetian state'. This first of all arsenals, was founded in 1104, and is believed to have derived its name from the Venetian pronunciation of the Arabic *darsina' a*, or artisans' shop. The entrance before you is the oldest, through which galleys would return after their voyages. In later centuries the Arsenal was enlarged to occupy 80 acres, surrounded by a forbidding two mile-long wall. Within this protected naval base, Venice's fleet was built, maintained and refitted for each voyage; all its provisions and equipment were stored here, as was its artillery, in an area nicknamed 'the Iron Garden'.

The Arsenal holds a unique place in the prehistory of the Industrial Revolution. Though Henry Ford sometimes get credit for inventing the assembly line, the Venetians were using the same methods 500 years earlier to produce not only more and better ships than anyone else, but fat galleys and long tapered galleasses (the bane of the Turks at Lepanto) that were as identical as Model Ts. As a result, all Venetian ships used uniform spare parts, which were available at any Venetian port; all ships could quickly be adapted to either war or trade ('trade war' in the Middle Ages being more than mere metaphor); all ships could be boarded by any Venetian crew, who would immediately 'know the ropes', so to speak. According to the last speech of Doge Mocenigo in 1423, the Arsenal employed 16,000 men, by far the most ever employed in one place before the 19th century. During the most intensive fighting with the Turks it cranked out a ship a day; on special occasions, to impress visitors like Henry III, King of France, the *arsenalati* produced a beautiful galley between the *antipasto* and dessert courses of a state feast. Dante visited this great complex twice, and as Blake would later do with his 'Dark Satanic Mills', relegated it to the *Inferno*, where its cauldrons of boiled pitch come in handy to poach crooks who sell public offices.

The **Great Gateway of the Arsenal**, touted as Venice's first Renaissance structure, was built by Antonio Gambello in 1460 (better late than never, the Venetians say) who assembled his work out of older bits—four Greek columns, Byzantine capitals, entablature and floral reliefs. After the Battle of Lepanto, two new statues were added; and in 1682, the present terrace was introduced in front to replace a drawbridge. This over the years became an honoured retirement home for old Greek lions: the two on the right, one bald and skinny with a silly toothless grin, and the other aged into an innocent Easter lamb, are originally from the Lion Terrace on the holy island of Delos, brought to Venice after the rescue of Corfu in 1718. The larger two on either side of the entrance were brought back from Greece by Francesco Morosini after his troops blew the top off the Parthenon: the one to the right, a dead ringer for the Cowardly Lion of Oz, may once have stood on the sacred road to Eleusis, while the other, sitting upright with an expression like the decayed Errol Flynn in *The Sun Also Rises*, was the famous Lion of Piraeus; if you look very closely at (or better, run your fingers over) his haunches, you can make out the runes scratched in 1040 by a member of the Byzantine Emperor's Varangian Guard led by Harald Hardrada, future king of Norway. The most ridiculous lion of all, however, is the bellicose Venetian feline over the gateway, jealously guarding a closed book (so as not to reveal the pacific '*Pax tibi Marce*' phrase), whose parents must have been a winged poodle and a wart hog.

Behind the impressive gateway there is only a small pavilion, decorated with a Sansovino *Madonna* and a cannon from the 1700s. You can usually walk in for a view through the glass of the long-deserted shipyards—what you see, extensive as it is, is only about a tenth of the Arsenal's total area; the ripest space in Venice for something new, though perhaps not in the lifetimes of the fragile spirits who run the city today.

Cross the wooden bridge here and walk back along the fondamenta *towards the Lagoon, where it opens up to form a little campo for the 18th-century naval church of* **San Biagio**. *If you have the stamina (see map of Walk III extension, p. 186), cross the bridge, turn left up broad and busy* **Via Giuseppe Garibaldi**, *a wide canal before the Napoleonic government filled it in. Near the beginning of the street, note the plaque set up on the right, marking the home of Giovanni and Sebastiano Caboto.*

The Cabots were natives of Genoa who remained long enough in the city to become Venetian merchants and citizens, before moving to the Venetian community at Bristol. In 1496 John and Sebastian sailed off in the service of King Henry VII and claimed Nova Scotia and Newfoundland for the crown (though on landing they planted not the Union Jack, but the Lion of St Mark). Their explorations inspired England to seek the fabled Northwest passage to the Orient, and led to the settlement of Canada.

Continuing down Via Garibaldi, take the sixth left (Calle del Forno, a narrow street next to a fruit stand) to the **Fondamenta della Tana**, *overlooking the high wall of the great rope factory (or* Tana), *1070 ft long. On the left rises the startling white concrete bulk of the Venice's new sports arena, providing a strong argument for not allowing any more new building in the city; the houses behind you, along the Fondamenta, are a survival of perhaps the world's first public housing, built by the state from medieval times on for workers in the Arsenale.*

Walk down to the Fondamenta's east end; this used to be a market, as you can see from the ancient stone plaque setting minimum sizes for fish on sale. Turn right on Calle Loredan and left on Fondamenta S. Gioacchino, a part of Via Garibaldi that still has its canal; the market moved here sometime long ago, and in the morning this area is a convivial jumble of ragged awnings, and fruit crates, red-nosed market ladies and furtive tomcats, the most old-fashioned and least touristy corner of all Venice.

Follow Fondamenta S. Gioacchino east over a bridge. Turn left at the next bridge, down Calle S. Gioacchino; this leads into the charming little canal called **Rio Riello***; once over the bridge (to your left), walk under the porticos of the Fondamenta to Campiello Figaretto and the adjacent Campo di Ruga. A turn left on Salizzada Stretta, the broad street (despite its name) at the end of the* campo, *and then a right on Calle Larga di Castello brings you to the remote island of Olivolo, named for its olive shape and surrounded by colourful boatyards. Excavations on Olivolo have revealed the foundations of a late Roman-early Venetian settlement; its long-gone castle lent its name to the entire* sestiere, *and later to the* **Basilica San Pietro di Castello***. This was Venice's cathedral from the 11th century until 1807, when the rationally-minded Napoleon made the ducal chapel of S. Marco the seat of Venice's patriarch.*

Open summer 8–12 and 4–7, winter 8–12 and 3–6. The lonely, distant site of Venice's Cathedral is no small comment on the Republic's hostile attitude towards the Papacy and power of the Church. In practice the Venetians were (and still are) more church-going than the Romans, but when it came to popes trying to assert any degree of temporal authority, the Venetians firmly drew the line. Their patriarch, a position assumed in 1451 from the ancient see of Aquileia, Grado, and Udine, with the same status as a cardinal, was appointed by the Venetian Senate instead of the Pope; and whenever a church problem was discussed by the Senate it was always noted at the head of the official minutes: '*Cazzadi i papalisti*' ('the supporters of the pope have been removed').

Tradition has it that in 944 a mass wedding of brides from all over the city was being held at S. Pietro when a band of Dalmatian freebooters swooped down and carried off both girls and dowries. The young men from the parish of S. Maria Formosa set off in pursuit and saved the day, catching the pirates before they got far beyond the Lagoon. This evolved into a major Venetian holiday known as the Feast of the Marys that lasted until the fall of the Republic, celebrated with a wedding of two couples from each *sestiere* at S. Pietro; eight days of parties and processions followed, and ended at Candlemas with the doge's visit to S. Maria Formosa, where he was ceremoniously presented with a straw hat and a glass of wine—in 944, Doge Pietro Candiano III had hesitated to make the journey for fear of rain and thirst.

Retired from its cathedral status and from hosting mass weddings, S. Pietro is as relaxed as any pensioner could be, nursed by a pretty if tipsy campanile in white Istrian stone built by Mauro Codussi; neighbourhood ladies pull up their lawn chairs and knit in its shadow. The first church on this site was last replaced in 1550 by a white and spacious pseudo-Palladian design, recently restored by a Los Angeles committee. In the right aisle there's a marble throne with an eight-shaped back, two Stars of David and an inscription from the Koran, part of a 13th-century Muslim tomb stone. The old belief that this was St Peter's throne from Antioch (note the old inscription above it) probably grew up when some shrewd prankster sold it to an ignorant crusader. The sanctuary was built to an elegant design by Longhena, to enshrine relics of S. Lorenzo Giustiniani—Venice's first patriarch (d. 1456) and the one consecrated body the Venetians didn't have to steal. Most essentially for the Venetians, he had some influence in Heaven during plagues, as can be seen in the painting on the right wall; it was his intercession in 1630 that earned him the fancy altar, ordered by the Senate, even though he wasn't canonized until 1690. Most compelling of all is the little **Cappella Lando** in the left aisle, with a 5th-century Roman mosaic fragment of a vase of flowers, a marble *pluteus* serving as an altar, stylized Byzantine-Veneto capitals on the columns, and a bust of *S. Lorenzo Giustiniani*, whose long face, sunken cheeks, tight lips and lines of care betray him as a true son of Venice.

> *From Campo S. Pietro, walk south down Calle dietro il Campanile (you'll find it, as the name implies, behind the campanile), and then left, along the Fondamenta Quintavalle. A right turn on Calle Quintavalle takes you over the Canale S. Pietro, a lazy broad channel full of boatyards. Continue straight, down the Fondamenta S. Anna, and turn left in Campiello Corner, leading straight into Calle G.B. Tiepolo, lined with plain 19th-century houses, to the Rio Tierrà di S. Giuseppe. A bridge to the right crosses over to the church* **San Giuseppe di Castello**.

One of Venice's most obscure churches, it was rebuilt in the 16th century and given a simple, classical façade. Within, the most prepossessing monument is the left aisle's **Tomb of Doge Marino Grimani** (d. 1605), designed by Scamozzi with figures and good reliefs (a *Nativity* with angel musicians) sculpted by Gerolamo Campagna. Its altar was dedicated in honour of the victory of Lepanto and has a relief of the battle. The battle order as shown isn't quite right— the Turks had their ships in a crescent as shown, but the Christians attacked in a straight line, with the five big galleasses in the centre leading the charge (in the relief the god Neptune seems to be cheering them on). In the sanctuary, a Grimani who served as a procurator is remembered with a monument and bust by Vittoria.

*Round the corner of Campo S. Giuseppe and you're in the **Giardini Pubblici**.*

This green oasis in the city of stone and water was planted by Eugene Beauharnais in the name of Napoleon at the expense of four churches and two monasteries, which no one mourned too deeply. Though the garbage bins could be emptied a bit more often, the Public Gardens are respectable enough, and a cool place to lounge away a hot afternoon. As one of Venice's few open spaces, they have become a repository for forgotten and bizarre memorials—a crabbed bit of concrete and rusty steel mesh labelled: 'From the Veneto to her *partigiani*'—among others. If you come in an even-numbered year you can explore the offerings in the national pavilions of the **Biennale** (see p. 14) mostly built in the 1920s; in odd-numbered years they're locked up). And as the sun sinks behind the city and melts the waters of the Lagoon into the sky, have a soul-satisfying *aperativo* on the upper terraces of the Paradiso Caffè, enjoying one of the greatest views in the world.

*You can plod even further east, if the allure of visiting Venice at its remotest is irresistible; these are on the island of **Sant'Elena**, just over the bridge. The lack of little canals winding in and out and the recent date of most of its buildings make it seem like an Italian Anywhere miraculously delivered of the national plague of automobilitis. Long an open meadow in front of a church and convent, S. Elena was a fashionable 19th-century retreat for Sunday picnics and promenades until the Austrians began to expand it for a military parade ground, and blocks of flats took over all of the meadow, excepting the crescent of the **Parco delle Rimembranze**. At the very eastern end of the island is the Church of **Sant' Elena**, hemmed in by the walls of a sports field and a naval college.*

Venice picked up the body of Constantine's saintly mother Helen in the great 13th-century haul of Eastern booty. As one of the chief saints of the Eastern church, Helen's relics merited their own church, on what was formerly an isolated island; the present Gothic version was built in 1435 by Olivetan monks. Although one of Venice's chief religious shrines, Napoleon deconsecrated it in 1807; the Austrians added insult to injury by using it as a foundry. In 1928 it was restored and reconsecrated, and though often closed, you can see its finest work of art right in front: Antonio Rizzo's monumental *Doorway Dedicated to Comandante Vittore Cappello, Kneeling Before St Helen* (1470s), celebrated for the natural realism in the Comandante's expression. In contrast to the doorway, the rest of S. Elena's façade is severe but handsome, its narrow elevation relieved by the chapels on the right and the cloister on the left. The paintings that once adorned the interior are mostly in the Accademia and other museums.

> *To get back to the centre or Lido from here, catch a No. 1 or 2 water-bus at the S. Elena landing.*

1 Basilica San Pietro di Castello
2 San Giuseppe di Castello
3 Biennale
4 Sant'Elena

N

WALK III
CASTELLO - EXTENSION

0   200m

Walk IV
Dorsoduro

Santa Maria della Salute

Accademia—Ca' Rezzonico—Campo S. Margherita—Campo dei Carmini—S. Nicolò—S. Sebastiano—S. Trovaso—Gesuati—Zattere—Salute—Peggy Guggenheim and Vittorio Cini Collections

Dorsoduro 'the hard-back' stands on tougher clay than the rest of Venice, perhaps the added smidgeon of security that encouraged the Venetians to entrust some of their most elaborate palaces and finest art to this neighbourhood. Its eastern 'hook', tipped by the Dogana di Mare, is the city's most exclusive area, where the palaces, many bought up by the insatiable Milanese, are in very good nick; others contain small galleries and art supply shops. The Zattere, running the width of Dorsoduro along the Giudecca Canal, is a favourite promenade, with a large selection of watering holes and even a touch of rare Venetian nightlife. Towards the western end of this promenade, towards the quays of the Stazione Marittima, Dorsoduro is so down at the heel that in parts it's more than a little spooky. The northern reaches, around Campo S. Margherita, has a mix of students and just plain folks, of corner bars and shops selling plastic buckets and potatoes instead of glass harlequins and carnival masks.

As the major art walk, much of your time will be spent indoors, so you may want to save it for a rainy day. It is best done on a Wednesday, Thursday, or Saturday—perhaps best of all Saturday, when you can plan

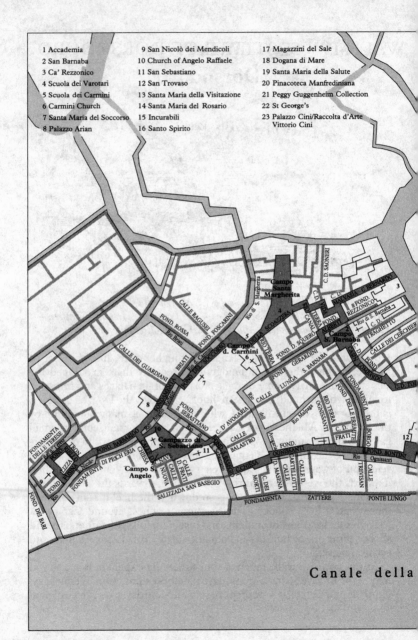

1 Accademia
2 San Barnaba
3 Ca' Rezzonico
4 Scuola dei Varotari
5 Scuola dei Carmini
6 Carmini Church
7 Santa Maria del Soccorso
8 Palazzo Arian

9 San Nicolò dei Mendicoli
10 Church of Angelo Raffaele
11 San Sebastiano
12 San Trovaso
13 Santa Maria della Visitazione
14 Santa Maria del Rosario
15 Incurabili
16 Santo Spirito

17 Magazzini del Sale
18 Dogana di Mare
19 Santa Maria della Salute
20 Pinacoteca Manfrediniana
21 Peggy Guggenheim Collection
22 St George's
23 Palazzo Cini/Raccolta d'Arte
   Vittorio Cini

Canale della

WALK IV - SESTIERE OF DORSODURO

0   200m

N

Canale Grande

S. MARCO

Campo Francesco Morosini

FOND. DOGANA ALLA SALUTE

Campo d. Salute

18

Canale

Start walk here

Campo d. Carità

Grande

End

CALLE ROTA

CALLE GAMBARA

C. CORFU

CALLE

FOND. BOLLANI

RIO TERRA CARITÀ

C. D.

PISTOR

C. LARGA

NANI

C. D. CRISTO

FOND. SANG.

CALLE TOLETTA

RIO TERRA FOSCARINI

DORSODURO

FOND.

C. D.

FRATI

13

14

Campo S. Agnese

FONDAMENTA ZATTERE

AI GESUATI

FONDAMENTA ZATTERE ALLO SPIRITO SANTO

AV. POMPEA

C. F. VENIER

PISCINA VENIER

PISCINA

PISCINA DI MEZZO

SAGNESE

1

23

22

Campo S. Vio

21

C.S.

FOND. VENIER

RIO S. VIO

C. S. GIOVANNI

BRAGADIN

CALLE CAPUZZI

FONDAMENTA

CALLE S. DOMENICO

SQUERO

C. D.

D. CHIESA

FOND ZORZI BRAGADIN

C. FORNO

NAVARO

C. D.

15

RAMO DIETRO INCURABILI

RIO TERRA S. VIO

C. D. ZUCCHERO

16

CAMPIELLO BASTION

FOND. SORANZA DETTA FORNACE

FOND. DI CA BALA

FONDAMENTA VENIER

LANZA

C. E. SOTT. MONASTERO

CALLE D. MONASTERO

MOLIN

C.E. SOTT.

C. SOTT.

ALBERA

CALLE D. SALUTE

CALLE D. MORTI

CALLE DEGLI INCURABILI

C. D. CREA

FONDAMENTE

17

19

20

Campo S. Vio I. C. I.

ZATTERE

Rio della Salute

FOND. SALUTE

AL SALONI

AL SALONI

Giudecca

a late dinner around a free evening visit to the Peggy Guggenheim Collection. On Fridays, Ca' Rezzonico is closed; on Tuesdays Peggy Guggenheim is, on Mondays it's the turn of the Accademia and Cini; on Sunday the Scuola dei Carmini. During the busy seasons, get to the Accademia when it opens at 9, or resign yourself to long waits to see some of the paintings.

Walking Time: 4 hours (*not* including the Accademia).

LUNCH/CAFÉS

S. Trovaso, Fondamenta Priuli, just west of the Accademia; a restaurant and *pizzeria*, a bit better than the Venetian odds (L20 000).

No Name Caffè, Calle C. Corfu 1491, between the Accademia and Campo S. Barnaba; a tranquil place to sit, with classical music and few tourists.

Vio, Rio Terrà Toletta, for a high-calorie recharge of cakes after the Accademia.

Locanda Montin, Fondamenta di Borgo (somewhat hard to find: take Sottoportico d. Eremite from Sacca/Calle della Toletta); a long standing oasis of good food that has always attracted an arty crowd. Best to reserve (tel 522 7151); L40–50 000.

Caffè Causin, in Campo S. Margherita; open since 1928 for coffee and ice cream and more.

Pizzeria-Trattoria Alloggi, Campo S. Margherita, outdoor tables and a pretty good and filling Venetian menu for L29 000; much less for pizza.

La Furatola Bruno e Sandro, Calle Lunga 2869, facing Calle dell'Indorador, a little trattoria on a long glum lane; no glamour, no first courses only, no credit cards, but fresh fish (L30–35 000).

Al Profeta, Calle Lunga (Visa) a *trattoria-pizzeria* that tries a bit harder than most. Few tourists; L25 000 for a full meal, L8000 for pizza.

Osteria da Toni, Fondamenta S. Biagio 1642, a neighbourhood place with simple food and tables out along the canal (L22 000).

Trattoria Paolo/S. Basilio, on the Giudecca Canal, next to the S. Basilio *vaporetto* stop; everyday Venetian fare but nice for lingering on a sunny afternoon (L20–25 000).

Nico, Zattere ai Gesuati, another contender for the best Venetian ice cream.

Bar di Gino, corner Piscina Venier and Piscina del Forner (east of the Accademia), a lively neighbourhood bar, a good place to meet the locals.

☆   ☆   ☆   ☆   ☆

Start this tour while you're fresh with the Big One, the **Gallerie dell'Accademia**, *containing the world's greatest collection of*

Venetian painting; an enchanted realm you could introduce to a Martian as a blueprint for a world composed not of atoms, but of colour and light. It's easy to find, next to the Grand Canal's wooden Accademia Bridge and its own vaporetto *stop.*

Open Tues–Sat 9–2 and Sun 9–1; adm L4000. Venice's art academy was founded just as the Republic's inspiration was petering out, in 1750, with Giambattista Piazzetta as its first director. In 1807, Napoleon, art's biggest 'centralizer' decreed that the Accademia's collection (at least those paintings he didn't steal, combined with works from the churches and monasteries he suppressed), be moved to the large religious complex he expropriated for the purpose. This included **S. Maria della Carità**, a church rebuilt in 1451 by Bartolomeo Bon, the adjacent convent designed by Palladio, the **Convento dei Canonici Lateranensi**, and the **Scuola Grande della Carità**, the oldest of the 'great' confraternities, founded in 1260 and housed in a building dating from 1343.

The collection is arranged chronologically, beginning in the former refectory of the Scuola (**Room I**) under a magnificent 14th-century wooden ceiling, recently restored to reveal ranks of cherubic faces, smiling down from their blue firmament on the altarpieces of Venice's first painters. On the entrance wall, Jacobello del Fiore's golden *Justice and Two Angels* is a lovely expression of the Republic's favourite virtue. The other subjects in the room are all religious, and most of them depict the *Coronation of the Virgin*, a theme straight from the twilight of chivalry and the Crusades. Although Paolo Veneziano's early 1300s *Coronation of the Virgin*, magnificent in its almost Islamic patterns, is not far removed from its Byzantine icon antecedents, you can begin to sense a change a few decades later in Lorenzo Veneziano's great *Annunciation* polyptych, in the more relaxed, almost dance-like poses of its figures, and in the worldly interest in things gorgeous, golden, and blond. Michele di Matteo's early 15th-century *Polyptych of St Helen and the Cross* has the most intriguing *predella* story (the finding of the Cross), while Jacopo Alberegno's 1390s *Scenes from the Apocalypse* has the most fascinating iconography; in Scene XX, the skeletons look as if they're reading dirty jokes to each other. The first real smile in Venetian art appears in Nicolò di Pietro's 1394 *Madonna, Child, and Donor*, when Venice had recovered from the Black Death, the Marin Falier conspiracy, and the War of Chioggia. On the left wall is one last *Coronation of the Virgin*, a mid-15th century International Gothic piece by Michele Giambono, set in a lush, optimistically crowded scene of Paradise.

Giambono sets the stage for the stupendous changes in **Room II**, changes so remarkable that it's easy to understand how the painters of the Renaissance seemed like magicians in the 15th century. All the works here are large altarpieces: the most sublime, Giovanni Bellini's *Sacred Conversation* is also called the *Pala di S. Giobbe*, for the church where it was orginally hung. Its architectural setting repeats the interior of S. Giobbe; on the left *St Francis* invites the viewer to contemplate the scene, accompanied by the timeless music of the angels at the Madonna's feet. Carpaccio strikes radically different moods in two paintings: a sweet *Presentation of Jesus at the Temple* and a *Crucifixion and Apotheosis of 10,000 Martyrs on Mt Ararat*, full of languid youths suffering a variety of martyrdoms at the hands of Turks in fancy dress. Marco Basaiti's *Christ Calling the Sons of Zebedee* (1510) is brilliantly coloured, with a watery fantasy background, while Cima da Conegliano's *Madonna of the Orange Tree* has a softer light, a more subtle atmosphere.

The highlights of **Room III** are Cima's *Pietà* and Bartolomeo Montagna's beautifully coloured *Madonna and Saints*. But these are mere prelimaries to **Rooms IV** and **V**, which prove, like gifts, that the best things come in small packages. Room IV has some of Giovanni Bellini's loveliest, melancholy and tender brown-eyed *Madonnas*, with the Child on the table before them, a composition that his patrons never tired of, and one that he managed to constantly vary; outstanding are the *Madonna and Child between St Catherine and the Magdalen*, wonderfully lit with its dark background, and the *Madonna with the Blessing Child*, perhaps the sweetest and saddest of them all. Other works include Jacopo Bellini's *Madonna and Child*, which looks like an icon next to his son's paintings; Hans Memling's *Portrait of a Youth*, Cosmè Tura's typically wiry and lumpy *Madonna and Child*; and Andrea Mantegna's *St George*, set amid antique pillars and garlands of fruit. The only Tuscan in the room is Piero della Francesca's youthful study in perspective, *St Jerome and Devotee*, brown, dry, and austere company for the Venetians; yet the expression on St Jerome's face couldn't be better (he looks at the donor, as much as to say 'It's all very well to pay Piero to put you here, but it won't get you any points in the Bank of Grace!').

Room V contains the most famous painting in the Accademia, Giorgione's *The Tempest*, unfortunately hard to see behind a plate of reflective glass. One of the few paintings all art historians ascribe to 'Big George', it was innovative for the importance given to atmosphere over detail. The inexplicable relationship between the soldier and mother in the foreground, the whole air of ambiguity and mystery are revolutionary in the fact that they were painted without preliminary drawings, and that they exist only for the sake of the pleasure they give. This is one of the first (and best) 'easel paintings', serving neither Church nor State nor a patron's vanity. Giorgione's other painting in the room, *Col tempo* ('with time'), has a more obvious message with its slightly sinister old woman and her all-too-true warning. Yet both pictures are uncanny; it is said that Giorgone invented easel painting to delight the bored patricians of Venice's decline, but the two paintings here would seem to reflect rather than lighten their restless ennui.

Also in Room V are Giovanni Bellini's five mysterious *Allegories*, and three more of his *Madonnas*, including the softly coloured *Madonna degli Alberetti*. In his *Pietà*, the same Bellini *Madonna* is poignantly alone in an empty brown landscape.

In **Rooms VI–IX** the lushly-coloured Venetian High Renaissance makes its first appearance, with fine works by Palma Vecchio (*Holy Family with Saints*) and his pupil, Bonifazio Veronese (*Dives and Lazarus*), and Paris Bordone (his masterpiece, *The Fisherman Presenting St Mark's Ring to Doge Bartolomeo Gradenigo*, based on the legend of a fisherman given the ring by the Saint, as an amulet to guard the city from a hurricane brewed by Satan himself). Psychologically light years away is Lorenzo Lotto's *Gentleman in his Study*, a remarkably candid portrait of a pale and anaemic fellow caught off-guard with his book, his lizard, and what appear to be torn petals of some 16th-century *fleurs du mal*.

The Venetian High Renaissance reaches a climax in **Room X**, not only in art but in size, in Veronese's masterpiece, *Christ in the House of Levi* (1573), painted for the refectory of SS. Giovanni e Paolo. The setting, in a Palladian *loggia* with a ghostly white imaginary background, almost a stage drop, is in violent contrast to the rollicking life and lush colour of the very Venetian feast in the foreground. With its Turks, cat, big Veronese hounds, midgets, Germans, and artist's self-portrait (in the front, next to the pillar on the left) it could be a scene from a Renaissance Fellini film. Instead, the original title was *The Last Supper*, and as such it fell foul of the Inquisition, which took umbrage at the animals, dwarfs, drunkards, buffoons, and especially the Germans, the evil spirits of the Reformation. Veronese was cross-examined, and in the end was ordered to make pious changes at his own expense; the artist, in true Venetian style, saved himself the time and expense by simply changing the title.

Other Veroneses in the room include a *Crucifixion*, where, in a typically Venetian manner, the clothes and pageantry tend to overwhelm the main event which is shunted off into the left-hand corner involving only a handful of figures, while prancing horsemen and ladies go about their business; and an *Annunciation*, Veronese style, in another Palladian setting, the Virgin gorgeously dressed for the occasion. His *Battle of Lepanto*, painted shortly after the event, has the Virgin and saints deciding the outcome in the clouds, just as the gods in Homer watched over the battle of Troy.

In the same room Tintoretto checks in with his first major painting, *St Mark Freeing the Slave* (1548). Inspired by Michelangelo's handling of form and composition, Tintoretto would often make small wax models of his figures and arrange them in a box, experimenting with the most dramatic lighting and poses. In this painting depicting St Mark's miraculous delivery of a slave who visited his shrine, St Mark doesn't walk into the scene, but nosedives in a dramatic loop-de-loop from the top of the canvas. Even more compelling is his *Translation of the Body of St Mark*, one of strangest paintings in Venice. The subject is the 'pious theft' from Alexandria, complete with an obligatory, nonplussed camel, but who are those pale figures on the left, fleeing in a row into a row of doorways, and who are those people sprawled on the ground? The eye is drawn past them all to a boiling orange and black sky. The two other Tintorettos in the room are slightly more traditional, *St Mark Rescuing the Saracen* in a dark and stormy whirlpool, and *St Mark's Dream* painted with son Domenico (the famous 'Pax Tibi, etc.' scene, with a dark, wet, embryonic Venice in the background).

The last great painting in Room X, *La Pietà*, was Titian's last, which he was working on in his 90s (probably for his own tomb) when felled by the plague. Dark and impressionistic and more moving than ten other Titians put together, it was left uncompleted at his death and, as the inscription states, finished by Palma Giovane.

Room XI has more by Tintoretto: his *Madonna dei Camerlenghi* ('of the Treasurers'), populated by prosperous looking Venetians, bringing the Virgin a sack of money; Old Testament scenes of *The Creation of Animals* (some of these not in any known book of zoology), *Adam and Eve* and *Cain and Abel*. *Il Ricco Epulone*, by Bonifazio de Pitati, is imbued with Veneto melancholy, none of which is present in the curved *trompe l'oeil* ceiling panels by Giambattista Tiepolo, all that survived the 1915 bomb that fell on the church of the Scalzi.

In the long corridor of **Room XII**, the colours take on the sombre tones of the murky 17th century, with landscapes by the likes of Giuseppe Zais and Marco Ricci. **Room XIII**, if it's open, is devoted to portraits by Tintoretto; **Room XIV** has more from the 17th century, most of it from foreigners living in Venice, and **Room XVI** features mythological scenes gone sour after a couple of centuries of respectability, beginning with Sebastiano Ricci's *Diana and Actaeon*, a joyless subject to begin with, here frozen, sickly, and bored—even the nymphs are homely. Giambattista Tiepolo's *Rape of Europa* is slightly more endearing, with its nonchalant bull and urinating cherub. The star of **Room XVIa** is Piazzetta's weird *Fortune Teller* (1740), the most memorable work to come from the brush of the first director of the Accademia.

Room XVII contains more paintings from the 18th century, a time when Venice proved one of the few bright spots in Italian art. But as technically brilliant and innovative as the great painters of the day were, it isn't hard to sense a loss of the old Venetian spirit; the buildings that featured in the backgrounds of Veronese and Tintoretto are now under scaffolding, or crumbling in these paintings; the bold confidence of the past has dwindled into views, interiors, genre scenes, and an obsession with the picturesque. There are works by the brothers Guardi (*Fire at S. Marcuolo*), a Canaletto with nuns, portraits by Rosalba Carriera, whose soft pastels flattered her sitters, though her best piece is a *Self-portrait*, painted in her old age, with ivy woven in her grey hair. Longhi contributes his genre scenes, one called *L'Indovino*, with a fortune teller speaking through a tube.

From **Room XVIII** (with Neoclassical architectural scenes) is the entrance to the upper level of the 15th-century Church of the Carità (**Room XXIII**), which is usually closed, but if it's your lucky day, you can take in some first-rate early Renaissance works by Gentile Bellini (including his earliest signed work, the 1445 *Portrait of the Blessed Lorenzo Giustiniani* (which may have been a processional banner—hence its weathered state) and four triptychs from the workshop of his brother Giovanni. Their Vivarini rivals get their say here, especially Bartolomeo (*Polyptych of the Nativity and Saints*) and his nephew Alvise (*Santa Chiara*). There are also paintings by Lazzaro Bastiani and Carlo Crivelli, a painter of exquisitely drawn *Madonnas* who left little behind in his native Venice. **Room XIX**, however, is always open, with more Renaissance art from Marco Basaiti (a beardless *Dead Christ*, with *putti*) and Marco Marziale (very decorative *Dinner at the House of Emmaus*).

Room XX is given over to a series of large paintings from the Scuola di S. Giovanni Evangelista, depicting the *Miracles of the True Cross*, all fascinating for their meticulously accurate depiction of late 15th-century Venice, detail that tends to overwhelm the miracles themselves. You have to look hard to find the main event in Carpaccio's bustling view of *The Patriarch of Grado Curing the Lunatic*, set by the old wooden Rialto drawbridge, in a forest of chimney pots and an exotic crowd of Venetians, foreigners and festive gondolas. The event in Gentile Bellini's famous dry, almost photographic view of Piazza S. Marco in the *Procession of the Relic of the Cross* (with St Mark's original mosaics on the façade) is the man kneeling to implore the relic to cure his son's fractured skull. Gentile's other painting here, *The Recovery of the Relic from the Canal of San Lorenzo* chronicles a mischance that occurred during the Relic's annual rounds; it fell in the canal, but floated to the surface to be recovered by the Grand Guardian of the Scuola, while Caterina Cornaro, ex-Queen of Cyprus, looks on from the extreme left, and Gentile Bellini himself joins the group in the right foreground (the fourth from the left). In Giovanni Mansueti's *Healing of a Sick Child* there's an inside view of a Venetian palace, while his *Miracle of the Relic in Campo San Lio* shows just what happens to members of the confraternity who dare to disparage the Relic—it refuses to enter the church for their funerals—and worst of all, everyone in the neighbourhood knows it.

Room XXI is entirely devoted to Vittore Carpaccio's delightful *Legend of St Ursula* series, painted in 1490–96 for the ex-Scuola di S. Orsola and recently restored (by the justly named Ottorino Nonfarmale 'Do no evil') to its original fairytale colours. The story behind the paintings is the grand and absurd tale of Ursula, daughter of King Maurus of Brittany, a tale of so long ago and far away that Carpaccio had considerable scope in interpreting the events; he went about it with his typical verve for the narrative and the literal, though naturally most of the details are from the Venice of his day In the first scene, *The Arrival of the English Ambassadors*, the ambassadors are asking the hand of Ursula for Hereus (Erero), son of the English King Conon; its very Venetian background contains a centrally planned octagonal Renaissance temple—a conceit further popularized by Perugino and his pupil Raphael. To the right we see Princess Ursula dictating the conditions of marriage to her father; marry she will, but on the condition that she is allowed three years to make a pilgrimage to Rome, and that Hereus convert to Christianity—news that her father and old nurse seem none too thrilled to hear. Then *The Return of the English Ambassadors*, who present the conditions to King Conon, a formal scene rounded out with a triumphal arch and a little monkey on the steps.

Good egg that he is, Hereus accepts Ursula's conditions, and even offers to accompany her to Rome. In the next painting, even more story-bookish than the others, he meets Ursula and together they depart for Rome in a 15th-century Venetian galley. But then comes *The Dream of Ursula*, in which the Princess has a dream of an angel foretelling her martyrdom—Carpaccio has the Saint tucked in her little bed, slippers tidily arranged underneath, her crown at the foot of the bed, while the angel, like any mortal, comes in the door. Despite the dream warning, Ursula, Hereus, and some fellow travellers—11,000 virgins—continue to the Eternal City in the next painting: *The Pilgrims Meet Pope Ciriaco before the Walls of Rome*. There are almost as many bishops as virgins. and their crocodile hats make a surreal pattern. Together with the Pope the pilgrims travel to Cologne (*Arrival at Cologne*), badly timing their arrival during a siege by the Huns, who send the 11,000 to their reward in the *Martyrdom of Pilgrims and Funeral of Ursula*.

Last of all, **Room XXIV**, the former *albergo* of the Scuola della Carità, preserves its original panelling and 15th-century ceiling with the four *evangelists*, and a Titian, which he painted for this very room—the *Presentation of the Virgin* (1538) a charming scene set before Titian's native Cadore in the Dolomites, with the child Mary walking alone up the great flight of steps to the temple, while her relatives stand anxiously below. Also painted for this room is a lovely triptych by Antonio Vivarini and Giovanni d'Alemagna, and a portrait of Cardinal Bessarion, the famous Greek scholar whose collection formed the nucleus of the Biblioteca Nazionale Marciana.

> *Leaving the Accademia, turn left at the exit and continue straight down Calle Gambara and Calle Corfu; cross the bridge at the next canal, and keep straight ahead on Calle della Toletta (no, not Toilet Lane, but Little Plank Lane, named after a long gone wooden gangway). Follow the lane as it curves right and changes its name to Sacca della Toletta, and continue straight, along a short canal and over a bridge, to* **Campo S. Barnaba**.

The small Church of **San Barnaba** (open mornings only) can claim an intimate Veronese (*The Holy Family*) and a *trompe l'oeil* ceiling painting by Constantino Cedini, but is best known in the city's annals for its *Barnabotti*, impoverished patricians who flocked to the cheap housing in the parish. The hotter bloods among them were always ready to stir things up against the government, and kept the Council of Ten's spies on their toes; others, resigned to their lot, made do on the meagre stipend supplied by the state (on the condition that they didn't marry and make any little *Barnabotti*). Some found employment at the Ridotto as bankers etc.—jobs that the Senate decreed could only be held by Barnabotti. Others begged in the crimson silken robes that, as patricians, they were required to wear, and not a few travellers remarked on the elegance of Venice's paupers. Creating a class of hungry drones was probably not the intention of the law that forbade patricians from working in crafts or trades, but it was their discontent that worked as a slow cancer in the state, and in the end caused many to hail Napoleon as their liberator.

A canal borders the northern side of the campo, *the Rio S. Barnaba. Follow it westwards (away from the church), passing the picturesque greengrocer's barge; the next bridge is the* **Ponte dei Pugni** *('of fists'), where before the days of parapets, the rival Nicolotti and Castellani (see p. 202) would meet in the middle to punch it out, the losers tumbling into the insalubrious waters of the canal. There are several bridges named Ponte dei Pugni, but this is the only one with marble footprints set in the pavement, marking the places where the contestants stood.*

Once across the Ponte dei Pugni, turn right along Fondamenta Alberti, then left on Calle delle Botteghe, and right on Calle del Fabro; at the end is the Grand Canal and then entrance to the Museo del Settecento Veneziano (see p. 102), contained in the vastness of the **Ca' Rezzonico**.

Open 10–4, Sun 9–12:30, closed Friday (L3000). This is the house where Robert Browning died in 1889 while visiting his son Penn, but if his ghost wanders these salons devoted to 18th-century Venice, it is a discreet phantom, one remembered only with a plaque visible from the Ca' Rezzonico *vaporetto* stop: 'Open my heart and you will see/'Graved inside of it 'Italy'; a couplet for which the poet is generally held responsible.

It could be that Browning's shade doesn't feel comfortable among all the stuff that the city has stowed here since purchasing the Palace in 1934, arranging it so that the average sumptious Venetian of the *settecento* would feel at home (and rearranging it so that it's hard to predict which rooms will be open at any time). One of the most charming objects stands on Giorgio Massari's Grand Stair leading up to the *piano nobile*—a droll *putto* dressed in a Russian hat and coat, by Juste Le Court. At the top is the lavish ballroom, with a ceiling by Giambattista Crosto and a mind-boggling collection of Rococo furniture by Andrea Brustolon of Belluno (1662–1732), whose chisel knew no bounds, either in craftsmanship or taste. The ceiling of the second room (on the right) was frescoed by Giambattista Tiepolo, celebrating an event of consummate social importance to the *nouveau riche* Rezzonicos: the 1758 marriage of Ludovico Rezzonico to a Savorgnan bride (of such exalted status that she is driven by Apollo and Cupid in the chariot of the Sun). In the middle of the floor is the upper half of an old gondola, with window slats that close for complete privacy. One room is devoted to Rosalba Carriera's pastel portraits of chocolate box nobles; the library, with a display of books published in Venice, has ceiling frescoes by Francesco Maffei.

The second floor offers more paintings, including two views by Canaletto (1697–1768) among the only ones left in Venice; scenes by Francesco Guardi (including the Ridotto and the famous salon held by the pretty nuns of S. Zaccaria), and 34 of Pietro Longhi's most endearing scenes of *settecento* Venice, populated by dwarfs, masked merrymakers, friars, invalids, lap dogs, plates of doughnuts (Carnival *fritelle*), charlatans, alchemists, the 'giant Magrat', washerwomen, tailors, hairdressers, and the famous rhinoceros which visited Venice in 1779 (which seems to have lacked a horn, but made a prodigious amount of rhino poo). Giambattista Piazzetta contributes a major piece of Venetian kitsch (*The Death of Darius*), and there's a candy-coloured *Interior of St Peter's* by Giampolo Panini. The 18th-century interiors nearly all have authentic furnishings—the bedroom, boudoir, and the Green Drawing Room, with laquered Venetian chinoiserie. The last set of rooms on the second floor are the most delightful, with frescoes by Giandomenico Tiepolo taken from the Tiepolo family home, Villa Zianigo, by Mestre. Painted in 1791, they are perhaps the last carefree hurrah before Venice's dotage, but show no forebodings: in *The New World* the audience dresses up to see scenes from America; Commedia dell'Arte figures, acrobats, centaurs, and satyrs sport on the walls as if tomorrow will never come.

The third floor is rumoured to have a reconstructed 18th-century pharmacy, puppet theatre, and more, but hasn't been open for years.

Leaving Ca' Rezzonico, retrace your steps to Calle delle Botteghe. Take a few steps back down this street, and take the first right, at Calle Scaleter, a tiny alley with a worn away street sign. Continue on to the next left, at Calle di Mezzo di Vida, and right at Rio Terrà Canal, which leads obliquely (to your left) into long, wing-shaped **Campo Santa Margherita***, the busy marketplace of Dorsoduro, lined with houses from the 14th and 15th centuries. Although St Margaret's Church has been closed since Napoleon, its rows of weird masks and dragons have been transplanted to an old house and an amputated campanile, on the north side of the* campo*; the Church itself has been abandoned since its last tenant, a cinema, moved out. The isolated building near the centre is the* **Scuola dei Varotari***,*

> or 'Tanners' Guild', with a relief of the Madonna della Miser-
> icordia protecting the tanners, so worn it could be anyone under her
> mantle. This must have always been one of Venice's more piquant
> corners: the tanners have since been replaced by a fishmonger.
>
> The long curved end of Campo S. Margherita, behind the Tan-
> ners' Guild, funnels into Calle della Scuola and Campo dei Car-
> mini, site of the **Scuola dei Carmini** and the **Carmini Church**.
> The Scuola, another one of the six designated Grande, is open 9–12
> and 3–6, closed Sun; adm L3000 (sometimes open for concerts).

Built on a design by Longhena in the 1660s (especially the façade facing
the Rio Terrà) it has a beautiful split stair and a ground floor entirely
decorated with 18th-century *chiaroscuri*. In the 1740s, Giambattista
Tiepolo was paid 400 *zecchini* to paint the upstairs hall ceiling; he made it
one of his best and brightest works, nine paintings centred on the *Virgin
in Gloria*. The symbolism is somewhat obscure. In the centrepiece, the
Virgin is presenting a scapular to St Simeon Stock. Who, or when, or
why this occurred is beyond the reach of our meagre scholarship. The
other eight scenes feature female allegories and angels. Some of these
are handing out scapulars; one miraculously catches a pious workman
who has just fallen off the scaffolding of a church. You'll probably notice
that most of these angels and allegories are showing off a good bit of leg,
just to 'increase the faith'; they're some of the swellest gams on display in
any Italian church, and a strong argument for those who maintain that
the major purpose behind late Baroque ceiling painting was to get divine
skirts to fly up. Beneath this unforgettable ceiling, there's only timid and
undistinguished 18th-century painting, filling large expanses of the main
hall and adjacent rooms.

For a second helping of dessert, wander into the Carmini Church,
across the lane (open 7–12 and 4:30–7:10), with a basilican interior from
the 14th century, its nave decorated with gilded Aztec cigar-store
Indians, which on closer inspection prove to be painted wooden figures
of kings and warriors carved in the 17th and 18th centuries, strangely
illuminated by the fluorescent tapers before them. The sculptural decoration, also of gilded wood, is of the same period as are the paintings,
forming a frieze on the history of the Carmelite order. None of it is grade
A art, but the total effect has a monumental if quirky charm.

The Carmini does have one major painting: Cima da Conegliano's
Nativity on the second altar on the right, set in a fine landscape bathed by

golden Veneto light. In the chapel to the right of the high altar is a bronze plaque with a relief of *The Deposition*, a rare work by the Sienese sculptor-architect, Francesco di Giorgio Martini, with a portrait on the right of Duke Federigo of Montefeltro and his famous broken nose; the women in the scene resemble the Furies in a Greek tragedy. The second altar on the left has Lorenzo Lotto's *St Nicholas of Bari*, with an eerie landscape beneath the saints. Near the door, under a vast canvas by Padovanino, is a bench carved with pagan grotesques. As you leave the Carmini, take a brief stroll down Calle della Pazienza to see its Gothic side door (across from the Scuola), decorated with a collage of Byzantine odds and ends.

> *From Campo dei Carmini, head west along the Fondamenta del Soccorso (don't cross the canal yet). At No. 2590, the small church of* **Santa Maria del Soccorso***, you can pay your respects to the celebrated courtesan-poetess Veronica Franco, who in 1519 retired here to found her asylum for less fortunate prostitutes. Though not as talented a poet as the courtesan Gaspara Stampa of the previous generation, her* Terze Rime *earned her a place among Renaissance poets still in print. Next door at No. 2596 is a truly awful 17th-century palazzo, its grotesque faces leering at all passers-by. The exotic inscription over the door is in the elegant script of Armenia, declaring the presence of the Armenian Mechitarist monks who have occupied this building since 1850.*
>
> *Cross the bridge here and turn left, continuing west along a* fondamenta *of various names, heading ever deeper into the rattiest, most unprettified corner of Venice, long a neighbourhood of fishermen, dock workers, and sailors, and also one old palace, the Gothic* **Palazzo Arian***, with a lovely six light window on the Fondamenta Briati, facing the intersection of Rio di S. Sebastiano. Turn right at a wide lane called Riello (no street sign, but on the corner is the little shop of a mad man who sells mad pictures), and then left at the Rio S. Teresa; this leads directly to* **San Nicolò dei Mendicoli** *('of the beggars'), one of Venice's most ancient churches.*

Open 7–12 and 4–7. S. Nicolò was founded in the 7th century, even before the Venetians staged their phony theft of Santa Claus' relics from Myra. Rebuilt again and again, and lastly restored in 1977 by the 'Venice in Peril' Fund, it has a Renaissance porch full of old architectural fragments, a detached Veneto-Byzantine campanile, and a sweet golden honey interior, embellished with wood sculptures, paintings by Alvise Del Friso, and on the ceiling, a *tondo* of *St Nick in Glory*, framed with a perspective border by Francesco Montemezzano. The gilded wooden statue of the *saint* on the altar is attributed to a follower of Bartolomeo Bon. Inside the main portal is a lovingly detailed model of the Church's appearance centuries ago, apparently made from sheets of styrofoam insulation.

In a way this little church was the St Mark's of this side of the Grand Canal. The inhabitants of these *sestieri* were known as the 'Nicolotti', and in this church they elected their 'Doge di Nicolotti' who would lead them in all their races, regattas, games and general punch-ups and other donnybrooks against the other half of the population, called the 'Castellani' after their headquarters in Castello.

> *Walk around S. Nicolò and retrace your steps up the long canal, here called Rio S. Nicolò. The second bridge on your right crosses over to the Church of the* **Angelo Raffaele**. *This particular corner of Venice is an uncanny place; crumbling and empty; it seems haunted in the still afternoons when no one is around. On one side of the bridge, over an outlandish shrine of the Virgin, an indignant plaque, half-effaced, records some past, unexplained desecration and the trouble someone took to restore it. On the other, the sprawling hulk of the Angel Raphael's Church looms forlornly over the* fondamenta, *with a façade sprouting a five years' shadow of stubbly weeds, along with a thriving fig tree on the cornice.* Raphael *appears in a 16th-century relief over the portal, accompanied by his dog.*

Built in 1618, the sole reason for entering this gloomy church is to take a look at the **organ parapet**, painted with a visionary, impressionistic scene of **Tobias and the Angel** (1753) by Gian Antonio Guardi, where material forms are dissolved into quick, free brushstrokes. In the derelict *campi* behind Angelo Raffaelo, there is a pretty Istrian stone well-head, one of the few with a story: the well below was dug with funds left in the will of local resident Marco Arian, who died of the plague of 1348, convinced that it was caused by contaminated water.

> *Campo Angelo Raffaele gives onto Campazzo S. Sebastiano (where the well is situated); from here you can see the back of 'Veronese's church',* **San Sebastiano***, built to thank the Saint for delivering the city from the plague of 1464.*

Open 10–12 and 3–6, Sun 12–1 and 3–6; lights L300 per section of church (essential for seeing the works). This was the parish church of Veronese, who lived around the corner. Thanks to its prior, also from Verona, he was given the chance to decorate it, which he did over two periods, from 1555–1560 and in the 1570s, managing to create a thematically unified interior—and, this being Veronese—one that blurs the bounds of art and reality. Among his visual tricks are the frescoed *loggia*, partially made from real stone and wood, and the *archer*, above one side of the nuns' choir, shooting Sebastian—on the other side of the nave.

The ceiling, which Veronese painted after his first work in the sacristy (see below), depicts the story of Esther in three panels: *The Repudiation of Vashti, Esther Crowned by Ahasuerus* and *The Triumph of the Mordecai*. The unusual Old Testament theme was used for its symbolic reference to the Virgin Mary. Vashti was the repudiated queen of Persia (Eve), Esther a Jewish girl chosen as the new queen (Mary), who helped to free her cousin Mordecai and his followers (redeeming mankind). Veronese's jewel-like colours lend a glittering sumptuousness to his monumental architectural perspectives and illusionism; note how he paints the central figures of each panel at an angle to get maximum sideways illumination (most notably the Mordecai, where the spectator's angle of vision is from under the horses' hooves). This ceiling, with the surrounding decorations added by his brother Benedetto, met with great success and brought Veronese his second commission, the wall frescoes in the upper choir with the *Martyrdoms of St Sebastian*. One of Diocletian's centurions turned Christian, Sebastian survived his first martyrdom of arrows, only to rebuke the emperor and be martyred again, this time with blows (at the time of writing the choir is still awaiting restoration).

Veronese designed the organ and painted its luminous panels; he also painted the altarpiece on the high altar, of the *Virgin and Child in Glory with Saints*, and the remarkable scenes flanking it in the choir, of *SS. Mark and Marcellinus Led to Martyrdom and Comforted by Sebastian* on the left and the *Martyrdom of St Sebastian* on the right. These are quintessential Veronese, full of action, stormy skies and big dogs, all done in magnificent costumes, set before a monumental, imaginary Rome. In the chapel to the left of the high altar, decorated in 1512 with blue and yellow majolica tiles from Urbino, are the tombs of Veronese (Paolo Caliari, d. 1588, with a bust) and his brother Benedetto (d. 1598).

There are even more Veroneses: a *Crucifixion* with the three Marys at the foot of the Cross, on the third altar on the right, set in an enormous monument designed by Sansovino for the Bishop of Cyprus. The second chapel on the left, the *Baptism of Christ* is mostly by Veronese's workshop, while the third altar on the left, the *Virgin and St Catherine and Friar* is believed to be one of his first works in Venice, as are the ceiling panels in the sacristy (door below the organ). Among the wall paintings here are works by Palma il Vecchio, Bonifazio de' Pitati (the 'other' Veronese) and Tintoretto (*Punishment of Snakes*.) A few other artists managed to get their brushes in as well: the 83-year old Titian, who used big brushstrokes to paint the altarpiece of *St Nicolas* (first on the right), and near it, Paris Bordone's dark and strange *Jonah and the Whale*.

> *Cross the bridge in front of the Church and turn right, following the* fondamenta *S. Basegio down to the next bridge. Instead of crossing it, turn left on narrow Calle della Chiesa and continue* sempre diritto—*straight on, as the Venetians say, along the Rio Ognissanti, passing a gondola yard and one of the few absolutely uninteresting churches in Venice, the* **Ognissanti***. Continue along the canal to Campo S. Trovaso, and the church of* **San Trovaso***, with its two façades, either of which seem more fitting for a public market or 19th-century factory. On 25 April 1990, this church began to collapse; they aren't sure yet how serious the damage is, and it will be closed indefinitely.*

S. Trovaso was SS. Gervasio e Protasio before the Venetians got hold of them and merged them into a single divine unit. The church held a special place in the city as neutral ground between the Nicolotti and Castellani factions, where they would come together to meet, marry, baptize, and bury (each side using its own door). Originally founded in the 10th century, former S. Trovasos on this site have burnt down twice and caved in once already; this, the fourth version, is true to its factory façades, and is dark and fairly functional within. If it reopens, look in the Cappella della Grazie, just to the right of the (south) door, to see a lovely bas-relief of *angels* on the altar by the unknown Renaissance 'Master of San Trovaso'; in the chapel exactly opposite is Michele Giambono's *San Crisogono*, a charming work reminiscent of Carpaccio's St George. Tintoretto painted some of his last works for the Church, nearly all completed by his son Domenico: a *Last Supper* in the left transept, and by the high altar, the *Adoration of the Magi* and *Expulsion from the Temple*.

In Campo S. Trovaso, no. 1083 has reliefs embedded in the wall, a grotesque face and a blacksmith scene over the door, with Cupid bringing arrows to the forge. An even older Byzantine bas-relief is embedded in the side of the 15th-century Palazzo Nani, just across the bridge from the Campo. Cross this bridge, and turn right down the Fondamenta Nani ('of the dwarfs') for the best view of the **Squero di S. Trovaso***, or gondola boat yard, its row of beached gondolas made irresistibly picturesque by its old wooden balcony covered with geraniums.*

Turn left where the Fondamenta meets its end, at the **Zattere***. This long quay, facing the Canale della Giudecca, is named after the large wooden rafts that once lined the waterfront, used for unloading timber, salt, building materials, etc. The rafts have been replaced with café and* pizzeria *platforms built out onto the water, fine places to linger and watch the* vaporetti*, buzzing like dragonflies between the freighters and tankers ploughing their way to Marghera. The first church you'll pass along the Zattere is that of the Gesuati, also known as* **Santa Maria della Visitazione** *(and sometimes even 'San Gerolamo dei Gesuati').*

This 'original' Gesuati was deconsecrated long ago, and now serves as part of an art and craft school for orphans. The entrance is through the school, just right of the façade, and usually you can just walk in and have a look around. The confusion about the name is considerable. The order of the Gesuati, founded in the 14th century, built this church and monastery in 1524. Upon their dissolution in 1668, the Dominicans snatched up the property and later built another church, the other 'Gesuati' just down the Zattere.

Mauro Codussi was at least partially responsible for the façade, a plain but distinguished Renaissance construction; Note the *Bocca del Leone* on the right of the façade, this one designated to receive gripes about hygiene and to taletell on people tossing rubbish in the canals, though most of these now go to the daily papers. Inside is a genuine surprise, a wooden ceiling painted by Umbrian or Tuscan artists of the 1500s. The central medallion, a *Visitation*, shows the gentle colours of Umbrian *cinquecento* art; surrounding it are panels with excellent portraits of prophets and saints. These works are almost unique in Venice; almost all of the other central Italian art in Venice is also on this walk, in the Palazzo Cini. After a few days of Tintoretto and Titian, a comparison with painting more in touch with the sources of the Renaissance will prove enlightening.

A few paces down the Zattere stands the other Gesuati, with a façade that echoes Palladio's Redentore across the water. Its real name is **Santa Maria del Rosario**.

Built between 1726–43 by Giorgio Massari, the interior is also an 18th-century compliment to Palladio, scenographic in its illumination and the plasticity of its walls. Giambattista Tiepolo frescoed the ceiling with the *Life of St Dominic*, the stern Saint being hauled up by angels to his heavenly reward amid suitably soaring perspectives; Tiepolo also painted the first altar on the right, the *Virgin in Glory* with three female saints, well-lit in front with a rather haughty Virgin in the background. The other paintings, including a Tintoretto *Crucifixion* and Piazzetta's *Three Saints*, and even the altar for all of its kilos of lapis lazuli, are sombre fare compared to the large *Madonna and Child* dolls in a little chapel on the left, dressed on feast days in dazzling jewels and costumes (including, it is rumoured, a pair of proper lace knickers for the *Bambino*).

Alongside the Gesuati is the pretty Rio Terrà Antonio Foscarini, which cuts through to the Ponte dell'Accademia, and is named after that unfortunate patrician who lost his head. It is one of the few calli *in Venice planted with plane trees; just past the Gesuati, on the right, is the 12th-century church of* **Sant'Agnese**, *rebuilt and with little to see inside.*

Continue along the Zattere, past the house that Ruskin rented in Venice (now an hotel), and over the Rio di S. Vio and another little canal; the large classical building adorned with two stone heads is the **Incurabili**, *one of Venice's four main hospitals, designed by Antonio da Ponte.*

Most Italian hospitals for 'incurables' were built for victims of syphilis, a gift from the New World along with tobacco and potatoes (it first appeared in Naples in 1494). This hospital, however, took on a sunnier aspect when a girls' orphanage was added in the late 16th century, which became, like La Pietà, an important conservatory, famous for its choir. Sansovino added an oval church for its concerts, but it was demolished by the Austrians in 1831; today the Incurabili is used as a childrens' home.

Further up the Zattere is the Renaissance façade of **Santo Spirito**, *which may tempt you to enter if you're a fan of Giovanni Buoncon-siglio, to see his painting of the* Redeemer and Saints. *Across the next bridge is the massive* **Magazzini del Sale**, *or salt warehouses, where the Republic stored the most precious commodity of its Lagoon.*

Not so many years ago, salt was a state monopoly in Italy and sold only in tobacco shops, and the old salt signs they sometimes preserve are the last reminders of what was once a very, very serious economic and political issue. If the saying was true, that 'the Venetians believe deeply in St Mark, quite a lot in God, and very little or not at all in the Pope, the latter sentiment had a very salty tang to it, founded on rivalries with the salt-panning papal town of Comacchio, near the Po delta in the Romagna. In 932 the Venetians put an end to the competition by attacking and sacking Comacchio and deporting all its inhabitants, founding a salt monopoly in the region that endured into the 15th century, and even afterwards brought the state a constant and considerable income—in the 16th century, 100,000 ducats out of the total 1,150,000 the state earned. (Oddly enough, ancient Rome too financed its early conquests by a local salt monopoly in Ostia). Most of the salt came from pans near Chioggia, though the Venetians imported it from as far away as the Balearic islands to control the price. Every grain of the 44,000 tons of salt that could fit in these warehouses was governed by the Salt Office, which issued licences to the exporters stating both the price and purchaser. Today the heirs of Venice's great sea captains—members of the local rowing club—use part of the warehouse as a boatyard.

> *The Zattere ends sharply at the point of Dorsoduro's promontory and its landmark, the* **Dogana di Mare** *and its bright golden ball, supported by two* Atlases, *and topped with a circus acrobat figure of* Fortune, *who serves as a weathervane with her pointer and rudder; a charming conceit, though it's hard not to notice that all three figures are sectioned like the cuts of meat in a butcher's diagram. Beginning in 1414, all goods brought into Venice by sea were unloaded here and assessed for customs duty, but the main reason for visiting now is to take in the view, a most untaxing proposition that includes Piazza S. Marco, the entire Riva degli Schiavoni, the Giudecca and Isola S. Maggiore. Then turn the sharp corner at the Dogana, and there, set at the entrance of the Grand Canal, with a perfect sense of theatrical timing and spacing (in the City of Water, the two begin to merge) is that magical white pavilion erected in honour of St Mary of Health,* **The Salute**.

Open 8–12 and 3–5. As Alfred Hitchcock always said, the worse the villain, the better the film, and the plague of 1630–31 was the most heinious since the Black Death of 1348, taking some 95,000 people to early graves. In October of 1630 the Senate vowed Mary a church if she would intervene and spare the city. Mary delivered, and the Senate did too, choosing in a competition the design of the 26-year old Baldassare Longhena, who would just live to see his life's masterpiece completed in 1682.

The ideal of a centralized domed temple was a favourite of the Renaissance, but Longhena was the first architect since the early Middle Ages to centralize his temple in the form of an octagon surrounded by an ambulatory. This unique shape is made obvious from the exterior, marked by the smaller Palladian-style façades of the chapels and the wonderful scrolls, jelly rolls big enough for Gargantua's breakfast, or tightly spun party streamers ready to shoot off across all Venice; without their festive touch the exterior of the Salute would be almost severe. Unfortunately, the main door, framed by a triumphal arch, is only open on the Salute's Feast Day, November 21, when a pontoon bridge is laid across the Grand Canal for the grand procession, and a fine sight it is, especially as you can see into the interior of the church as Longhena intended, the eye drawn in through a series of receding arches.

Stand in the centre of the octagon, and this same play of arches make the seven chapels and high altar seem even deeper than they really are (the inscription here: *Unde Origo, Inde Salus*—'From the origins comes Salvation' refers to the official date of Venice's founding, 25 March 425, which coincides with the Feast Day of Mary). One of the many debts Longhena owed the Renaissance tradition and his more immediate mentor Palladio was the white and grey colour scheme of the interior, though Longhena is far more manipulative, using the grey not to outline the structure, but as an optical device. The sanctuary, reached by steps, is almost separate from the main body, and owes much to Palladio's Redentore. A great arch, supported by four ancient Roman columns from Pola, spans the **high altar**, with its large remarkable sculptural group of *The Queen of Heaven Expelling the Plague*, designed by Longhena and sculpted by Juste Le Court (1670). Venice kneels as a suppliant before the Virgin in the clouds, whose look of disdain is enough to send the horrid old hag of plague on her way, while St Mark and St Lorenzo Giustiniani look on. In the centre is a 13th-century Byzantine *Madonna and Child*, picked up by the light fingered Francesco Morosini in Crete. This piece of Baroque theatre is made more effective by the shadowy rectangular choir behind the altar, visually united to the rest of the composition by its tier of yet three more arches.

In this church Longhena provided 17th-century Italy a stimulating if insubstantial alternative to the Baroque masters of Rome, and its influence was felt throughout the peninsula, though, surprisingly, the octagon never caught on. The art in the chapels fails to match the confection that surrounds them (the three on the right are by the over-talented Neapolitan Luca 'fa Presto' Giordano, and the third altar on the left is by Titian) but there are some treasures in the **sacristy**, to the left of the high altar (adm L1000), where the authorities brought Titian's paintings from the suppressed church of S. Spirito: over the altar, an early work, *St Mark Enthroned between SS. Rocco and Sebastiano and SS. Cosma and Damian* (the surgeon saints), this a votive for the liberation of a previous plague, and on the ceiling three recently restored canvases of violent Old Testament scenes in violent perspective: *Cain and Abel*, *David and Goliath* and *Abraham and Isaac*, all from the 1540s. Titian also painted the eight *tondi* of the *Doctors of the Church*. Next to the altar is Padovanino's *Madonna with Angels* and a model of the Salute; the *Marriage at Cana* is a 1561 work by Tintoretto.

The Salute is one of Venice's marvels, built under genuinely pious auspices. Yet less than a hundred years after its completion, a notice appeared near the entrance: 'In honour of God and His Holy Nature, please do not spit on the floor!' And if the celebrant of mass were good-looking, another note would be attached, expressing the hope that the parishoners would limit their contributions in the collection baskets to money (and not love letters!).

> *The patterned pavement in the* campo *in front of the Salute is great for playing follow-the-lines-tag; or, if you're lucky, you might get in to see Venice's most elusive museum, the* **Pinacoteca Manfrediniana**, *located in Longhena's Seminario Patriarcale, to the left of the Salute. Inside are works by Veronese, the Lombardos, Filippino Lippi and most of the other Venetian favourites, but the museum has been closed for years.*
>
> *Leave the Campo della Salute by the bridge closest the Grand Canal, next to the tunnel flanking the deconsecrated Gothic Church of* **San Gregorio** *(a restoration centre). Continue straight on down Calle S. Gregorio, opposite the church façade, to pocket-sized Campo Barbaro, noting the majestic wistaria climbing in the garden behind Ca' Dario. Almost next to it, just over the bridge, is the wacky coloured glass and twisted metal gate of the* **Peggy Guggenheim Collection**. *After the Accademia this is the most visited museum in Venice, and deservedly so; it's the freshest breath of air in Doge City.*

Open April (or in March, depending on Easter)–Oct, 11–6, closed Tues; adm L5000, students L3000; free (and usually crowded!) Sat evenings from 6–9 pm. The museum is in one of the odd-balls on the Grand Canal, the ranch-style Palazzo Venier dei Leoni, better known as the Palazzo Non Finito (begun in 1749 and never finished past the first floor). In the 1910s it was stage for the antics of the Marchesa Casati of Milan, glittering queen of decadence and folly, the Futurists' Gioconda, who held parties here with an artificial lilac jungle populated by apes, ocelots, Afghan hounds, and torch-bearing naked slaves painted with gold (who later died) until 1919 when she packed up to become the mistress of Gabriele D'Annunzio. Thirty years later the Palazzo Non Finito was purchased by another arty lady, American copper heiress Peggy Guggenheim (1898–1979) who had an irresistible smile and an irrepressible love for modern art, even marrying into it (her second husband was Max Ernst). She filled it with her treasures, and when she died, left it to the Solomon R. Guggenheim Foundation in New York to run as a museum in Venice.

The setting on the Grand Canal, the back garden (where Peggy and several of her dogs are buried) and the homey atmosphere add much to the quirky charm of the collection, which includes representative examples from the major movements of this century and a whole room of Jackson Pollocks (including his great 1942 *Moon Woman*). From husband Max Ernst there's the *Robing of the Bride* (an off-beat tribute to Peggy?); other works include Picasso's 1937 *La Baignade*, with the mysterious face on the horizon watching the two Cubist girls on the beach; Brancusi's *Bird in Space*; de Chirico's *Nostalgia del Poeta*; Dali's hysterical *Birth of Liquid Desires*; Kandinsky's *Landscape with Church*; five box constructions by Joseph Cornell; and much more by Arp, Rothko, Motherwell, Magritte, Tanguay, Severini, Moore, Malevich, Chagall, Braque, Balla, Mondrian, de Kooning, Giacometti and others. The bedroom has a mobile and bedstead by Alexander Calder, and bright paintings by Peggy's daughter Pegeen, who inherited some of her mother's *joie de vivre*. It must have been this same spirit of fun that led Mrs Guggenheim to help erect something besides a palace outside on the Grand Canal, sported by Mariano Marini's joyously obscene equestrian statue, the *Angel of the Citadel*.

Leave Peggy Guggenheim by way of Calle S. Cristoforo (right), Fondamenta Venier, and Calle della Chiesa. This is the address of Venice's Anglican church **St George**; *inside is the tombstone of the* *consul Joseph Smith (1682–1770), recently moved here from the Lido. Smith lived in Venice for 70 years, and was the foremost collector of his day. An early patron of Canaletto, he acted as an agent between the painter and the English 'Grand Tourists' who snapped up his works, leaving Venice itself only three canvases. Smith's personal collection and library were among the most fabulous of the day, and greatly enriched the royal collections when King George III purchased them in 1770.*

Next to St George's is Campo S. Vio; cross the bridge here for the Palazzo Cini (no. 864), the residence of Count Vittorio Cini (1884–1977), who, like Peggy Guggenheim, was an art collector, though his tastes were more Tuscan than modern. Since 1984 his **Raccolta d'Arte Vittorio Cini***, part of his Fondazione Cini on S. Giorgio Maggiore, has been open to the public. Open summer only, Tues–Sun 2–7.*

There are some beautiful works here, by the very first, and often anonymous wizards of the Renaissance: a splendid *Maestà* of the early 14th century, by the Master of Badia a Isola, a *Crucifixion* by Bernardo Daddi, and a *Madonna Enthroned* by the Master of the Horne Triptych. Rooms III and IV are devoted to the 15th century, with a *Judgement of Paris* by Botticelli and his workshop; a lovely, luminous *Madonna, Child, and Two Angels*, by Piero di Cosimo; *Madonnas* by Filippo Lippi and attributed to Piero della Francesca; and a double portrait by Pontormo. Ivories, china, manuscripts, books, and a 14th-century Tuscan marriage chest round out the collection.

The bridge on Campo S. Vio leads to Piscina Forner, Calle Rota and back to the Accademia, its water-bus landings and bridge over the Grand Canal.

Walk V
San Polo and Santa Croce

Stazione—S. Nicola da Tolentino—Scuola di S. Giovanni Evangelista—
S. Giacomo dell'Orio—Natural History Museum—S. Stae—
Museum of Modern Art—S. Cassiano—Rialto Markets—
Campo S. Polo—Frari—Scuola di S. Rocca—S. Pantalon

Although it takes in two *sestieri*, S. Polo and S. Croce, this walk through
western Venice is fairly untaxing in the culture department until you get
to the cavern of the Frari and Tintoretto's Scuola di S. Rocco. The walk
first crosses S. Croce, the unluckiest neighbourhood in Venice; not only
is it missing its church, but much of it has been turned into the likes of
Piazzale Roma, freight yards, the prison, and other ordinary bits that all
beauties, even 'a sea Cybele, fresh from Ocean' needs to get by in this
world. But any city would be proud of S. Croce's pretty little centre,
Campo S. Giacomo dell'Orio, or its collection of intriguing minor
churches.

S. Polo has fared much better. Its Rialto markets are still busy, even if
the wares have changed somewhat since the Middle Ages; its church of
the Frari, one of Venice's big three, is still run by the Franciscans, and its
Scuola di S. Rocco is one of the great sights in Italy, guaranteed to make
your eyes swim—which is why we put it near the end.

Plan this walk to reach the Scuola di S. Rocco by 5 pm in the summer;
as it's only open mornings in the winter, you'll have to either run this

maze like a rat to get there in time, or have the navigational skills to do this walk backwards, or just come back some other time. Other opening hours that might influence your plans are those of Scuola S. Giovanni Evangelista, open Mon–Fri mornings (ring ahead, see below). The Natural History museum is closed Mondays and afternoons, and Goldoni's House is closed Sundays and afternoons.

Walking Time: 4 hours.

LUNCH/CAFÉS

All'Anfora, Lista dei Bari, just east of S. Simone Profeta; homey café/restaurant/*pizzeria*, with some of the nicest, bargain-priced food near the station (L16 000).

Alle Oche, a popular place behind S. Giacomo dell'Orio in Campiello di Piovan, with outdoor tables overlooking a canal; 50 kinds of pizza, around L7 000, full meals L20–30 000.

Antica Bessetta, Calle Savio 1395 (from Campiello di Piovan, behind S. Giacomo dell'Orio, across the canal), beautifully prepared Venetian specialities, worth the L50 000 bill.

Trattoria al Ponte, Calle Larga 1665a (near S. Giacomo dell'Orio and bridge over Rio Fontego dei Turchi) popular and cheap, with outdoor tables (L20 000).

Trattoria Mater Domini, Calle Tiossi 2097, just north of S. Maria Mater Domini (AE, DC, Visa) with a garden and a good L15 000 menu with spaghetti *al pesto* and a wide variety of fried fish.

La Regina Cornaro, Calle della Regina 2330, near S. Cassiano (AE, BA); more experimental than most Venetian restaurants, the wine list superb (L50 000 *menu degustazione*, more *à la carte*).

Alle Poste Vecie, Pescheria 1608 (AE, DC, Visa) some of Venice's best seafood, right by the Rialto fish market (L50 000).

Do Mori, Calle Do Mori (in Rialto, north of Ruga Vecchia S. Giovanni); one of the liveliest places in Venice to duck into the shade for a glass and a snack (but no chairs, and closed during lunch).

Alla Madonna, Calle della Madonna (off Fondamenta del Vin, by the Rialto Bridge); genuine and reasonably priced home-cooking, but get there early (L25 000).

Osteria da Fiore, Calle di Scaleter 2202, north of Campo S. Polo, (AE, Visa, DC) intimate, with good traditional Venetian cooking and great wines; L45 000.

San Tomà, Campo S. Tomà, pretty tables under the pergola, delicious pizzas (L10 000).

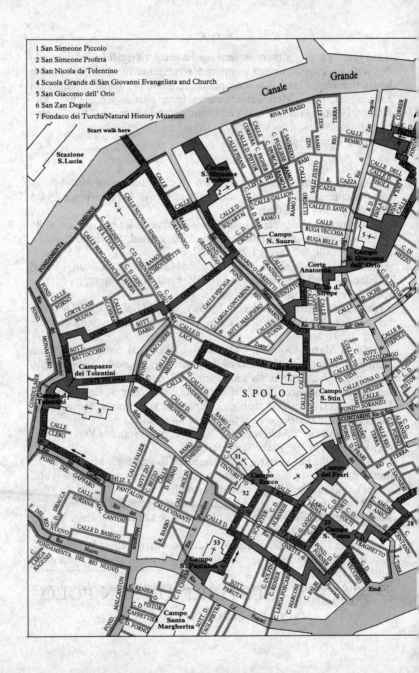

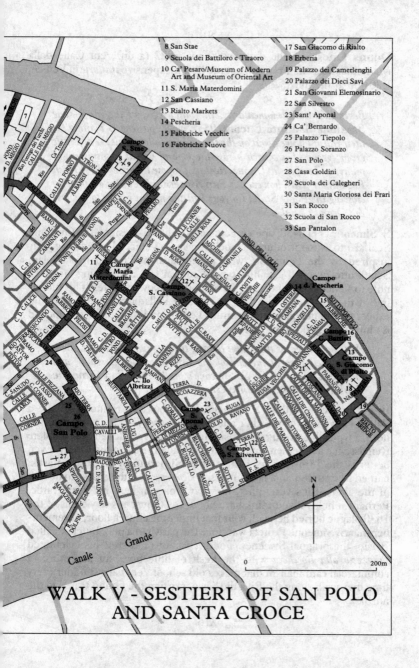

8 San Stae
9 Scuola dei Battiloro e Tiraoro
10 Ca' Pesaro/Museum of Modern Art and Museum of Oriental Art
11 S. Maria Materdomini
12 San Cassiano
13 Rialto Markets
14 Pescheria
15 Fabbriche Vecchie
16 Fabbriche Nuove
17 San Giacomo di Rialto
18 Erberia
19 Palazzo dei Camerlenghi
20 Palazzo dei Dieci Savi
21 San Giovanni Elemosinario
22 San Silvestro
23 Sant' Aponal
24 Ca' Bernardo
25 Palazzo Tiepolo
26 Palazzo Soranzo
27 San Polo
28 Casa Goldini
29 Scuola dei Calegheri
30 Santa Maria Gloriosa dei Frari
31 San Rocco
32 Scuola di San Rocco
33 San Pantalon

WALK V - SESTIERI OF SAN POLO AND SANTA CROCE

Donna Onesta, Calle della Madonna 3922 (a different Calle della Madonna, near the Frari) one of the best inexpensive *trattorie* in Venice; L20 000 at the most.

☆   ☆   ☆   ☆   ☆

> *Begin this walk, momentarily, in Cannaregio, at the ranch-style* **Stazione di Santa Lucia** *(1955), where passengers waiting for their trains lounge about on the steps and wonder about the odd little green eggcup of a church across the Grand Canal, reminiscent of many a Temple to Divine Reason proposed during the French Revolution. This, however, is* **San Simeone Piccolo**; *get there by crossing the Ponte Scalzi (to your left) the newest bridge to traverse the Grand Canal.*

S. Simeone (1718–38; open for concerts only) was designed by Giovanni Scalfarotto, who introduced Neoclassicism to Venice. Though originally inspired by the Pantheon, with its classical porch and round plan, Scalfarotto perched a Salute-type dome on top, a charming fare-well note to Venetian architecture. As Rudolf Wittkower wrote: 'This blending of the Pantheon with Byzantium and Palladio is what one would expect to find in eighteenth-century Venice, and that it really happened is almost too good to be true'.

> *Walk back towards the Scalzi Bridge, turning right at Calle Lunga; make a left turn at the end of the street, at Calle Bergami, and continue straight on for S. Simeone's big brother,* **San Simeone Profeta**, *or* **San Simeone Grande**.

Bright and cosy within, S. Simeone's famous contributors include a Palma Giovane over the altar and a *Last Supper* by Tintoretto near the door, a typically startling composition, with the Apostles all the complete Renaissance gentlemen, and the table set at an angle to the viewer. Even better is the 14th-century **Effigy of S. Simeone** by an obscure artist named Marco Romano, laid out in full *rigor mortis* in the chapel to the left of the altar; if it's very quiet, they say, you can hear his death rattle. Perhaps it helps if you think hard about the thousands of victims of the 1630 plague buried beneath your feet under the church floor, or remember that S. Simeone Profeta was once the parish of a pork butcher called Biasio, the original Sweeney Todd. Biasio would stuff his celebrated *squazzeto alla Boechera* with the flesh of little boys, an adventure in commercial cannibalism that makes old school Venetians shudder every time they walk along the Riva di Biasio, skirting the Grand Canal to the north.

216

*From Campo S. Simeone Profeta, follow the Fondamenta Rio
Marin (to the left along the canal, as you leave the Church); cross the
next bridge right, then straight ahead down Corte Canal, veering
slightly right for Campo della Lana, a blank, broad thoroughfare of
modern buildings. This takes you to the Fondamenta dei Tolentini,
where a left turn will reveal the striking Corinthian porch of* **San
Nicola da Tolentino**, *looming like a Roman ruin over the canal.*

Open 8–12 and 4:30–7. Commonly called the Tolentini, this church was
designed by Andrea Tirali (1716) and inspired by Palladio's Villa Malcontenta. Under the porch, you can see a cannonball embedded in the
façade, a souvenir left by the Austrians in the siege of 1849. The equally
Palladian interior, by Vincenzo Scamozzi (1591) is partly disguised by
the Rococo stuccoes added by a 17th-century pastry chef-cum-artist,
perhaps to compensate for lopping off the dome. The Tolentini wit-
nessed a number of Venetian dramas, the most glorious when Francesco
Morosini, after the 1685 battle for the Morea, dedicated to the church
the banner he had captured from a Turkish general with its three
dangling horsetails; the most inglorious occurred in February 1789,
when the unloved Doge Paolo Renier was secretly buried here in the
middle of night so as not to interrupt Carnival with a tedious state
funeral.

The Tolentini's prize artwork is *St Jerome Visited by an Angel* by
Johann Lys (1628) to the left of the sanctuary. Lys, from Northern
Germany, was very young and soon to die in the plague of 1630, but he
holds a special place in Venetian art as the primary exponent of the free
brushstrokes and disintegration of form, the link between the late styles
of Titian and Tintoretto and the Guardi brothers. The left wall of the
sanctuary itself is occupied by the rollicking proto-Rococo **Monument
to Patriarch Francesco Morosini** (d. 1678), by Genoese sculptor
Filippo Parodi, a tomb that doubles as a remarkable piece of theatre with
its voluminous draperies. In the right aisle you'll find two good works by
Bonifazio de Pitati, the lesser known of Venice's 'Veroneses' (i.e. he was
born in Verona): the *Banquet in the House of Herod* and *Decapitation of the
Baptist*. The facile, unstoppable Palma Giovane painted all the chapels
on the left. S. Nicola's adjacent convent is now home of the University
Institute of Architecture.

*Spare a moment for a brief diversion south along Fondamenta dei
Tolentini (to the right of the Church) to* **Fondamenta Minotto**
for a look at an exceptionally lovely canal, and above it some of

Venice's most remarkable chimney pots. Then circle around the left side of the church, by way of Campazzo dei Tolentini and Corte dei Amai; cross the bridge and turn right on Ramo Cimesin, a rare Venetian lane between walled gardens. At the first crossroads turn left, on Calle Dietro l'Archivo, another of these bothersome streets you're not allowed to gamble, argue or 'make scandals' on (as noted on the old plaque at the end). Then take a right turn on Calle del Campazzo and another right on Calle di Laca. Follow it through various name changes to Campiello Scuola, site of the **Scuola Grande di San Giovanni Evangelista,** *one of the six 'grand' confraternities of Venice, founded in 1261.*

The route passes right through the Scuola's little Renaissance **court-yard**, one of the prettiest in Venice, to which a number of artists contributed over the years. It has a lovely marble portal and screen delicately carved by Pietro Lombardo in 1481, with floral designs and a fierce eagle, along with a doorway by Mauro Codussi and a 16th-century bas-relief of the hooded confraternity members praying all in a row.

Supposed to be open if you ring Mon–Fri, 9:30–12:30, but it's best to ring ahead 522 4134. And it's worth the trouble just to see the **double ramp stairway** *by Mauro Codussi, a bravura Renaissance work, cascading in sophisticated rhythms past domes and barrel vaults. Most of the best paintings commissioned by the Scuola, by Carpaccio and Gentile Bellini, have been shuttled over to the Accademia—these are the scenes celebrating the miracles of a piece of the True Cross, the Confraternity's most prodigious relic, still behind the grille in the oratory on the first floor. It used to go for an annual outing through Venice, and dull indeed was the year that it didn't drive out a demon at the very least.*

Across the courtyard, the Church of **S. Giovanni Evangelista** (open 3–6 pm) is no place to look for art (there is a mild Tintoretto *Crucifixion* to the right of the altar), but a great place if you're in need of a kitten. The parishioners run a sort of cultural exchange programme involving tourists and Venetian strays. They can package the perfect souvenir of Venice for you to take home, complete with all necessary shots and papers, enough to satisfy the authorities of most countries (but not the UK). The Church is also the local headquarters of the cult of Kaiser Karl, a rather shadowy international effort to transform the last of the Austrian emperors into a saint (he was dethroned in 1918, but the House of

Habsburg has proved as hard to kill off as that of Transylvania). Instructions on praying for his cause are posted near the entrance. S. Giovanni also has a famous 1760 organ, often used for concerts.

> *From the courtyard, turn left on Calle dell'Olio, crossing a bridge, and another bridge to the right to Campiello di Cristo and Calle di Cristo. At Campiello della Strope turn right, and then left into Corte Anatomia, under a tiny unmarked archway. Then cross the bridge to the right for Campo S. Giacomo dell'Orio. The church of* **San Giacomo dell'Orio** *(perhaps* 'of the laurel', *from* 'alloro'*), is not the most prepossessing Venetian church from the outside, but well worth a look within. Open 7:30–12 and 5–8:30.*

Founded in the 9th century, the church and its campanile were rebuilt in 1225 to house a pair of columns, one a massive and rare piece of *verde antico* (in the right transept) that the Venetians plundered from Byzantium. Crowned by a magnificent, nearly seaworthy 14th-century ship's keel roof—built to limit the church's weight on the swampy ground—it is another Old Curiosity Shop of Venetian memories, beginning with a quatrefoil stoup of Greek marble and, in the right transept, a wall of the original church, embedded with sculptural bits from Venice's sedimentary past. A sombre *Madonna* by Lorenzo Lotto presides over the high altar, with Lorenzo Veneziano's crucifix and two marble crosses in the Lombardo style, and Lombardesque red and green geometrical patterns continued around the sanctuary. On the pier to the left of the altar, there's a rare image of the *Virgin Annunciate*, one hand raised in friendly greeting, the other holding a spindle; still to the left of the altar, are two large black and white 13th-century frescoes of *Daniel*, perhaps, and *David*.

Although the gate of the **old sacristy** on the far left is usually locked, you can look through the bars to see its numerous Palma Giovanes and Buonconsiglio's *Three Plague Saints*. The left transept has a Veronese on the altar, where you'll find the light switch to illuminate its saints and rain of *putti* bearing martyrs' palms; on either side are Palma Giovane's *Scenes from the Life of St Laurence*, on the right presenting the Roman authorities with the 'treasures of the church' that they had demanded (he brought them his poor and wretched); on the left Laurence is toasting on the grill for his brave gesture. If the sacristan is about, he'll open the **new sacristy**, with Veronese's *The Doctors of the Church* and *Faith*, and Francesco Bassano's *St John the Baptist*, who is preaching to the Bassano family and Titian (on the far left, in a red hat).

From S. Giacomo (begin from the plane tree behind the church), head north along Calle Larga; take the first left, Calle Spezier, then left again on narrow Calle del Capitello for Campo S. Zan Degolà. The Church of **San Zan Degolà** *(Venetian for 'Beheaded John') has been deconsecrated for over a 100 years, but if you get in for a concert, take a look at the 13th-century frescoes in the left apse. Calle dei Preti, on the left of S. Zan Degolà will take you to the Veneto-Byzantine Fondaco dei Turchi (see the Grand Canal section for the history of this venerable building) now home of Venice's* **Natural History Museum***.*

Open 9–1:30, closed Mon; adm L3000. Enormous and recently modernized, this is good fun, nature's quiet reminder in the world's most beautiful city that its creatures are all masterpieces in their own way—even the sponges, from the delicate little Basket of Venus to the mighty Elephant Ear Sponge. There's a Japanese crab, the *Macrocheira Kaempferi* that could play a villain's role in a James Bond film; incredible bugs, scorpions and centipedes (more in the Vincent Price vein); beautiful butterflies, beetles, and bees; and a collection of things you'd probably never pondered before like the embryos of the shark and ray, complete with photos of a shark giving birth on an Egyptian ship, or the 'Monstrous Chimera', a strange fish with peculiar sex organs. The Venetian natural habitat is explored in one section, with models of lagoon craft (including a pre-Roman boat found in the muck) and fishing nets, lagoon birds and 'Life on a *Briccole*' which shows all the tiny creatures and algae who have made those wooden posts their special home. The Museum is especially proud of its Dinosaur Room, with finds from the 1973 Ligabue Sahara expedition, starring a 37-foot long fossil, the largest ever discovered of the crocodile's ancestor, the *Sarcosuchus Imperator* and the complete skeleton of a never-before-seen reptilian bi-ped, the *Ouranosaurus Nigeriensis*, as well as a clutch of fossilized dinosaur droppings. These are followed by lovely shells, stones, minerals, and more fossils, and trophies and photos bagged on various safaris.

Backtrack down Calle Fondaco dei Turchi, Calle del Capitello and Calle Spezier; cross the bridge at the end of this last street for Ramo del Megio, turning right at Ramo del Tintor. Then turn left at Salizzada S. Stae for one of the landmarks of the Grand Canal, the church of **San Stae***.*

Non-Venetians call him S. Eustachio, or St Eustace, and his church was built in the 17th century, though the exuberant façade was added later in 1709, by Domenico Rossi, and decorated with saints who perform daredevil circus acts on the high trapeze of a bracket over the door. The interior, bright, bright white and grey after a recent restoration, is still used for mass in winter, though in summer it's given over to exhibitions. All the year round, however, you can see the slab in the floor marking the last resting place of Doge Alvise Mocenigo II (d. 1709) who paid for the façade, but chose the Latin epitaph, 'Name and ashes buried together with vanity'. The chancel resembles a gallery of small 18th-century paintings. Two of the best hang in the lower left row: the *Martyrdom of St James the Great* by Piazzetta; *St Peter Freed from Prison* by Sebastiano Ricci, and opposite, Giambattista Tiepolo's *Martyrdom of St Bartholomew*.

On the left side of the nave, you can see (if there's not an exhibit taking place) the **Monument of Antonio Foscarini**, with an inscription from the Republic noting that he was mistakenly executed for treason in 1621. Foscarini was a dashing patrician who served as ambassador to England, but got into trouble for being far too chummy with the English and was recalled, and imprisoned for three years under suspicion of treason. When he was finally cleared of the charge and released, Foscarini secretly paid frequent visits to the Palazzo Mocenigo-Nero, then the residence of Lady Arundel, wife of one of the most powerful nobles in King James' court. Renewed accusations of treason reached the Council of Ten, who acted swiftly; Foscarini was captured, questioned, and executed within 12 days. The first hint that justice had miscarried was when Lady Arundel immediately demanded an audience with the Doge (and became the first woman granted one), declaring that neither she nor her household were involved in any plot. Further investigations revealed that Foscarini's visits to the Palazzo Mocenigo-Nero were of an amorous nature, and that he had gallantly died with the secret; his real crime was having enemies in the stodgy Venetian bureaucracy. The Council of Ten executed his accusers, and tried to make posthumous amends with a state funeral and this inscription. Venice's critics sometimes accuse her of not doing enough for Foscarini's memory, but then again, how many governments, even these days, would have publicly admitted to a mistake in the first place?

Next to S. Stae is one of the most endearing (and smallest) buildings on the Grand Canal, the **Scuola dei Battiloro e Tiraoro** *(the Guild headquarters of the goldsmiths), built in 1711 and also used now for exhibits. Cross the bridge next to this and turn left on Calle Pesaro; this leads straight to the regal courtyard of one of Venice's grandest Renaissance palaces, Longhena's **Ca' Pésaro**.*

The palace is vast enough to be used for major exhibitions and to shelter two museums. The **Museum of Modern Art** (open 10–4, Sun 9:30–12:30, closed Mon; adm L3000, but closed for restoration at the time of writing) was founded to hold the works purchased by the city at the Biennale; it also contains a fair, if not wildly inspiring sample of contemporary Italian art—Giorgio Morandi, Filippo de Pisis, Manzù, and many lesser lights, interspersed by token foreigners. The most uncanny is Gustav Klimt's *Salomé*, a Madonna/sorceress dream girl for psychoanalysts, the embodiment of Freud's 'Eros and Thanatos'. The 19th-century Italian art, from artists little known outside Italy, usually comes as a pleasant surprise, especially the works of sculptor Medardo Rosso of Milan, and Venetian painters Giacomo Favretto, Guglielmo Ciardi, master of luminous lagoon-scapes, and Francesco Hayez. On the top floor, the **Museum of Oriental Art** (open 9–2, Sun 9–1, closed Mon; adm L2000) was founded after World War I, when Austria, in reparation for damage caused by its incendiary bombs in World War I, tried to make amends by giving the city a higgledy-piggledy collection of screens, lacquer boxes, weapons, kimonos, armour, etc. amassed by a 19th-century Marco Polo, Count Enrico di Bourbon-Parma.

*Fondamenta Pesaro leads into Calle Tiossi; turn left here, noting the 14th-century **Palazzo Agnusdio**, named for its Byzantine patera of the Lamb of God. Take the very next right, into Corte Tiossi, and continue straight, under the Sottoportico del Fenestrer. This will take you up to the Istrian stone façade of **Santa Maria Materdomini**. Open 10–12 and 3:30–5:30.*

An early 16th-century church of uncertain paternity (Mauro Codussi or Giovanni Buora) S. Maria Materdomini has a cool grey and white Renaissance interior with half-moon clerestory windows and its own Tintoretto, *The Invention of the Cross*, to the left of the main altar. Its subject is the medieval *Legend of the Holy Cross* (see S. Alvise, p. 256), only with an eccentric Tintorettonian twist—who the lady with the newly made cross in her lap might be (St. Helen?) is anyone's guess; the glaringly anachronistic bishop and Turk in the assemblage do their best to look nonchalant. On the first altar on the right are *Three Saints*, sculpted by Lorenzo Bregno in 1524, who is responsible for most of the carving in the church; Bonifazio's *Last Supper*, opposite the Tintoretto, also merits a look, as does the *Martyrdom of St Christina* by Vincenzo Catena, one of the favourite paintings of the Venetians, who love its sweet little angel holding the millstone.

> *Just opposite the church is the entrance to the charming Campo di S. Maria Materdomini, which, with its old well-head and houses, wears the Middle Ages like a worn, but very comfortable pair of shoes. Leave it by way of the bridge to Ramo della Regina, turning left in Calle della Regina, then right, under the Sottoportico de Siora Bettina, and over the bridge to Campo S. Cassiano, a dowdy old square that once held the first public opera house in the world, opened in 1637 while Monteverdi was maestro di cappello at St Mark's. Nowadays the focal point, such as it is, is the lacklustre façade-less* **San Cassiano**. *Open 7:45–11:30 and 4:30–7.*

Another old church reincarnated in the 17th century (except for its detached medieval campanile), it has more than a touch of Great Auntie, with its chandeliers and pillars wrapped in flocked fabric, but it also has a startling masterpiece by Tintoretto: a dynamic *Crucifixion*, composed as if the viewer were just under the cross, looking up as the Roman soldier climbs the ladder to nail on the sign reading INRI. Two other Tintorettos (*The Descent into Limbo* and *The Resurrection*) that keep it company have suffered from an unhappy restoration, although in the former the painter's usual flair for drama finds expression in the fury of Christ bursting out of the tomb (L100 for the lights). The chapel to the right of the altar contains a more typical *Crucifixion* by Palma Giovane, and Leandro Bassano's *Announcement of the Birth of St John the Baptist*, with quirky rows of Venetian heads underneath.

> *Leave Campo S. Cassiano by way of Calle di Cristo (behind the right side of the church), turning left in Calle dei Botteri, and then right in narrow Calle dei Beccarie ('Butchers'); beyond Campo Beccarie lies a maze of even narrower lanes where sugar was once sold for its weight in gold and pepper and spices for only slightly less: the* **Rialto markets**.

I will buy with you, sell with you, talk with you, walk with
you, and so following; but I will not eat with you, drink with
you, nor pray with you. What news on the Rialto?
—Shylock speaking to Bassanio, in *The Merchant of Venice*

The housewives and elderly gents who gravitate here for their daily
shopping are continuing one of Venice's oldest traditions. The Rialto
markets have been the city's centre of trade—and as such, the heart of
the Republic's mercantile empire—since the 11th century. When Venice's first bank, the Banca Giro, was opened in the 1100s others quickly
followed, making the Rialto the medieval equivalent of Wall Street,
Europe's most glittering and powerful exchange, controlling the commercial links between East and West; in its houses incredible fortunes
were gambled, won, or lost. 'All the gold of the Orient passes through the
hands of the Venetians, grumbled one commentator. And so it did until
1499, when news of Vasco da Gama's voyage around the Horn caused
several banks to instantly fail. Those that survived saw their establishments burn to the ground in the great fire of 1514.

*The northern edge of the markets are occupied by the lively neo-
Gothic halls of the fish market, or* **Pescheria**, *built in 1907 to
replace an iron shed. The porticoed* **Fabbriche Vecchie**, *built
after the fire by Scarpagnino, extend along the Grand Canal; they
are continued by Sansovino's curving* **Fabbriche Nuove di
Rialto (1554)**, *now the assize courts. Behind these, Campo Battisti
leads into Campo S. Giacomo Cesare; around the apse of its little
church,* **San Giacomo di Rialto** *the 12th-century legend reads:
'Around This Temple Let the Merchant's Law Be Just, His Weight
True, and His Covenants Faithful'.*

Fondly known as S. Giacometto, tradition has it that this was the first
church built in what is now Venice, perhaps as early as the 5th century. In
1097 it was rebuilt in conjunction with the markets, and then fiddled with
in 1531 and 1601, to make a stylistic collage that from the outside makes
the whole church look like an overgrown mantelpiece clock. Its 24-hour
face has shown the wrong time ever since its installation in the 14th
century; its hands get stuck in the same place for so long that art
historians have dated scenes of Venice by the time shown on it. The
five-columned porch, a type once common in Venetian churches, is the
only original one left in the city; the little bell tower over the clock is
Baroque. The Veneto-Byzantine interior is a miniature mixture of

basilica and a Greek cross, decorated with six ancient Greek columns, topped with foliage added in 1097; Alessandro Vittoria contributed the statue of *St James with Angels* for the main altar.

The *campo* in front of S. Giacomo, with Renaissance arcades to complement the church, makes an elegant ensemble—if it ever reappears from its eternal scaffolding. The shabby planks and pipes also conceal the 16th-century granite figure of the **Gobbo di Rialto**, the 'hunchback' upon whose shoulders the decrees of the Republic were read to the public; minor criminals were forced to run stark naked through a gauntlet of blows from Piazza S. Marco to safety at the Gobbo's feet.

> *The* **Erberia**, *the fruit and vegetable market that fills most of the space between Campo S. Giacomo and the Grand Canal, adjoins the white* **Palazzo dei Camerlenghi**, *(1528) next to the Rialto Bridge on the sharp curve of the Grand Canal. This was the treasury of the Republic, a well-proportioned building built by Guglielmo de Grigi of Bergamo, the only one in Venice where each façade is given equal attention. Cross* **Ruga degli Orefici**, *the raucous main drag of the Rialto bazaar, leading up to the Bridge; even though the golden treasures of the East have given way to tourist trinkets, the street and its rows of open-air stands cannot help keeping something of its old colour.*
>
> *On the other side of Ruga degli Orefici is Scarpagnino's* **Palazzo dei Dieci Savi**, *home of the* Serenissima's *financial ministers. From here, the Fondamenta del Vin—a good name for a street packed with restaurants and cafés—runs along the Grand Canal. Take the first right, at Calle del Gambero, leading back to* **San Giovanni Elemosinario**.

This, too, was rebuilt by Scarpagnino, but it preserves its Greek cross plan. If restoration work has been completed, go inside to see Titian's *Patron Saint Distributing Alms* (1545) on the high altar, and from the same year, in the chapel to the right, Pordenone's *SS. Catherine, Roch, and Sebastian*, a painting Venetian in its colouring but quirky Tuscan Mannerist in its composition. The recently discovered paintings in the cupola are also Pordenone's.

> *Retrace your steps to the Fondamenta del Vin and turn right; besides occasional views of the Grand Canal over the heads of the gawkers*

*and waiters and gondoliers there's little to see. Turning up
Sottoportico Traghetto, at the end of the Fondamenta, you pass the
indistinguished Neoclassical church of* **San Silvestro**, *most noted
for an unusual painting of* St Thomas à Becket Enthroned with
Angels *(1520, Gerolamo Santacroce). Facing the Church is the
Palazzo Valier (no. 1022) where Giorgione lived, and in 1510 died
of the plague contracted from his mistress. Calle del Luganegher (on
the end of the* campo *opposite the Church's campanile) leads from
here into a* campo *named after the deconsecrated brick Gothic
church of* **Sant'Aponal** *(Apollinare), with a tabernacle over the
portal bearing 1294 reliefs of the* Crucifixion; *the base of its
Romanesque campanile once had the oldest known relief of the* Lion
of St Mark *(since pensioned off to the Correr Museum). And don't
bother looking in; the interior is entirely filled with metal shelves,
containing all the city's marriage records.*

*One file a little thicker than the others (if the records go back that
far) would be that of Bianca Capello. Her house is just around the
corner; take Calle Ponte del Storto (left of the church façade) up to
another 'crooked' bridge, Ponte Storto; hers was the house overlooking it, the one with the Neoclassical busts at the head of narrow
Rio S. Aponal.*

An exceptional Venetian beauty, Bianca eloped to Florence in 1563 with
Pietro Bonaventura, a humble bankers' clerk, an impetuous act of love
that called down the full fury of the unsentimental Senate. The young
couple were sentenced to death *in absentia*, and forgotten until it was
discovered that Bianca had abandoned her clerk in favour of a much
more palatable catch: the Grand Duke of Tuscany, Francesco de'
Medici, who ignored his dumpy Habsburg duchess for her. Diplomacy
at this stage was a delicate affair, but as soon as his wife died and the
Grand Duke married Bianca, Venice promptly proclaimed 'the adopted
and beloved daughter of our Republic'. But the Republic fell discreetly
silent when the Francesco and Bianca suddenly died of poison—ironically, for the Grand Duke's hobby, as a weekend alchemist, was brewing
poisons from crates of scorpions.

*Cross the bridge here, and walk under the Sottoportico Banco
Salviati, turning right up Calle Stretta—*stretta *it certainly is, at
one point less than three feet wide. Squeeze through, and you'll end
up in* **Campiello Albrizzi**, *scarred by another Austrian shell and
a plaque bearing an anti-Austrian war cry from the jingoist poet*

Gabriele D'Annunzio: 'This fragment of barbarism, fixed in the noble stones as a denunciation of the eternal enemy...'.

*From here take Calle Albrizzi, then left on Calle Rio Terrà Ca' Rampani, and then right, for the **Ponte delle Tette**, a favourite of all who dally in Venetian street names; this one means 'Bridge of Nipples', apparently for the courtesans who used to display their ample charms in the windows to bring in custom, back in the 16th century when this was the red light district. These days there's nothing larger than geraniums in the windows, so continue straight ahead, along Calle d'Agnello, over the Rio delle Due Torri, turning left down Calle Lungo. Continue straight on Calle Cristo, and then right on Calle Bernardo, named for **Ca' Bernardo**, one of Venice's most beautiful Gothic palaces, overlooking the canal you're crossing.*

*The end of the lane opens up to vast and lively **Campo San Polo**, full of children playing and old men sunning themselves on the benches. Overlooking the action are several interesting palaces, which once faced a small curving canal since filled in: the **Palazzo Tiepolo** by Giorgio Massari, covered with masks, and its red neighbour, the **Palazzo Soranzo**, once the residence of the nobleman who adopted Casanova as his son, and now the Institute of Chinese Language and Literature. The exterior of the Church of **San Polo** (Paul), tucked in the corner of the campo, has a number of interesting details, from its great plaited Gothic doorway and rose window attributed to Bartolomeo Bon to the hungry Romanesque lions under the detached 14th-century campanile.*

Open 7:30–12 and 4–7, Sunday morning only. Founded in 837, S. Polo has been much altered throughout the centuries, especially in 1804, when it was given a set of Neoclassical columns to support its ship's keel roof. Inside is Tintoretto's darkest and most violent **Last Supper** (on the left), where Christ is shown literally leaping up from the table. Equally extraordinary in its own way is Giandomenico Tiepolo's *Via Crucis* series in the **Oratory of the Crucifix**, entered under the organ (but watch out for the imperious sacristan). Giandomenico got the commission in 1749, at the tender age of 20, and filled it with a certain amount of piety and an even greater amount of precocious pre-*paparazzi* interest in Venetian high society; the paintings look remarkably like snapshots.

From Campo S. Polo, walk west along Salizzada S. Polo, running along the side of S. Polo Church; follow it through the bridge over the

Rio di S. Polo, and down Calle dei Saoneri. Then take the first left, on Rio Terrà di Nomboli, and then the first right on Calle dei Nomboli. Here stands the **Casa Goldoni**, where Carlo Goldoni, the King of Venetian Comedy, was born in 1707, just in time to chronicle Venice's twilit play days. The Palace predates Goldoni by a good three centuries, and has one of the city's most delightful Gothic courtyards. Open 8:30–1:30, closed Sundays and holidays, free, and only worth a visit if you happen to be a student of Venetian theatre, an art descended directly from the Commedia dell'Arte. Goldoni's house is a goldmine of dusty lore, with first editions of plays by unknown Venetians, playbills, engravings of early sets, and more 18th-century genre scenes, including a rollicking kitchen scene.

> *Continue along Calle di Nomboli to the Campo di S. Tomà and the blank façade of* **San Tomà**, *a mystery inside as well as out because it's permanently closed. In its better days it was reputed to contain the biggest batch of relics in all Christiandom, including a record twelve intact bodies. Opposite the pathetic church is the School of the Shoemakers, or* **Scuola dei Calegheri**, *its façade bearing a charming but badly worn relief by Pietro Lombardo of St Mark Healing the Cobbler Ananias.*
>
> *From behind the Scuola dei Calegheri, turn left on Calle del Cristo, then right on the Fondamenta della Donna Onesta (the 'Honest Woman') and the bridge of the same name, which is the subject of a favourite Venetian anecdote: two men were walking this way, discussing the opposite sex and its virtue, when one pointed to a statue of a woman on this bridge: 'There, sir, is the only honest woman in Venice!' he declared. She isn't there any more. Walk up the Fondamenta and turn right at Calle Ca'Lipoli (Gallipoli), which will bring you into Campo dei Frari, a square encompassing the greatest concentration of Venetian art after the Accademia. The campo, of course, is named after the giant brick Gothic church of the* **Frari**.

Open 9–12:30 and 3–6 (sometimes a small fee is charged for lighting). S. Maria Gloriosa dei Frari, as its full name runs, was the chief Franciscan rival to the Domenican SS. Giovanni e Paolo, on the other side of town; from St Mark's campanile the two stand above the higgledy piggledy of Venice like a pair of brick bookends. The original Frari, founded in 1250 (just after St Francis' death) was no sooner completed in 1330 than the

the current Gothic pile started to rise right next to it. Based on a design by Friar Scipione Bon, it wasn't completed until 1469.

For Venice, the exterior is very severe, showing only a hint of the native delight for decoration. Venice's second tallest campanile is its most memorable feature, though there are some good carvings that liven up its stark exterior: a 15th-century Tuscan bas-relief of the *Madonna, Child, and Angels* on the north door, and another nearby with a statue of St Peter; on the west side the Gothic door has works by the school of Bartolomeo Bon and others by Alessandro Vittoria. A Gothic edging along the cornice, like dripped icing on the cake, unites the mass of bricks; the curved 'crowning', added afterwards to make the façade higher, was a bid to match rival SS. Giovanni e Paolo across the Grand Canal. Around the left side, near the door, you'll see some small plaques marking the level of the *acqua alta* of 20 August, 1902—that was a good one; the plaques are almost a metre high.

The long cruciform interior is pinned together by wooden tie beams, which visually not only unite the vast space, but add an interesting abstract quality to the run-of-the-mill Gothic aisle bays and ceiling. On ground level, the eye is drawn through the arch of the monks' choir in the nave to Titian's vividly coloured *Assumption* in the sanctuary. The plain brick walls are covered with works of art and monuments ranging from the sublime to the ridiculous, beginning (inside the front portal) with the very vertical **Tomb of Pietro Bernardo** (d. 1538) [1], believed to be one of Tullio Lombardo's last works, but lacking the 800 stanza heroic poem the deceased specified in his will. The other monument on this wall, the **Tomb of Procurator Alvise Pasqualino** (d. 1528) is by Lorenzo Bregno.

Both of these men ordered tombs long before they died; a sound policy, seeing the monument Titian got (the second altar on the right). It is a tradition in Italy to give the greatest artists the most unartistic memorials, and the **Tomb of Titian** [2] is even worse than Michelangelo's in Florence. Titian died at age 90 or more in the plague of 1576, and was the only casualty of that epidemic to get a church burial, owing to his fame; the massive inanity piled on top of his presumed burial place was added in the 19th century. The first altar, to the right, is dedicated to St Anthony of Padua; it has attracted some unusual ex-votos, including a pair of brass epaulets left by some grateful general or bandmaster. The third altar (to the left of Titian) is graced by Vittoria's statue of *St Jerome*, one of his finest works, and said to be a likeness of Titian at the age of 93.

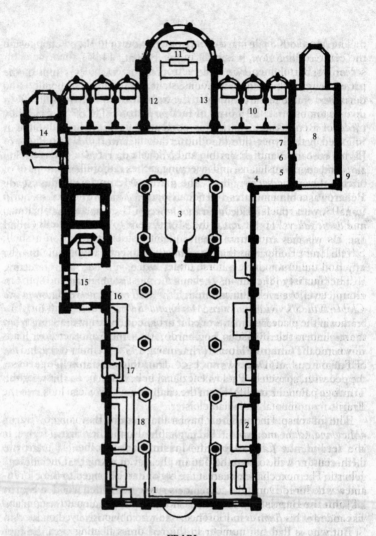

FRARI

1 Tomb of Pietro Bernardo
2 Tomb of Titian
3 Monks' Choir
4 Tomb of Iacopo Marcello
5 Tomb of Beato Pacifico
6 Memorial of Benedetto Pésaro
7 Monument of Paolo Savelli
8 Sacristy

9 Chapter House
10 Chapel of S Massimiliano Kolbe
11 Titian's *Assumption of the Virgin*
12 Tomb of Doge Nicolò Tron
13 Tomb of Doge Francesco Foscari

14 Cappella Corner
15 Capella Emiliani
16 Monument of Bishop Jacopo Pésaro
17 Tomb of Doge Giovanni Pésaro
18 Tomb of Canova

The **Monks' Choir** [3], the only one in Venice to survive in place in the centre of the nave, was built in the 1460s, and has a marble choir screen by Bartolomeo Bon and Pietro Lombardo, but even more impressive are its three tiers of monks' stalls, carved by Mauro Cozzi and decorated with intarsia designs. In the **right transept** are four markedly diverse tombs: first, the **Tomb of Iacopo Marcello** (d. 1484) [4], a fine piece of Renaissance quirkiness attributed to Giovanni Buora; it is followed by the hyper-florid Gothic terracotta **Tomb of Beato Pacifico** [5] by Tuscans Nanni di Bartolo and Michele da Firenze, with ranks of *putti* and angel musicians, and sweeping arches rather like the tops of S. Marco. Over the sacristy door, the marine **Memorial of Benedetto Pésaro** [6] commemorates a Venetian *capitano da mar* who died in Corfu in 1503, with reliefs of *Ionian island fortresses* (Levkas and Cephalonia) and *battle galleys*. To the left is the **Monument to Paolo Savelli** (1405) [7], his wooden equestrian statue quaintly stuck high up on a shelf; Savelli, from Rome, was the first *condottiere* to earn a monument in the city, and the first to have a horse under him.

The **Sacristy** [8] contains perhaps the most compelling and spiritual altarpiece Giovanni Bellini painted, his 1488 *Triptych of the Madonna and Child, with SS. Nicolas, Peter, Mark, and Benedict*, still in its original frame, in the place Bellini intended it to be seen. Sharing the sacristy is a marble tabernacle by Tullio Lombardo; if it's open, another door leads down into the **Chapter House** [9], housing a 17th-century clock and the **Sarcophagus of Doge Francesco Dandolo and his Dogaressa**, topped with a fresco by Paolo Veneziano, believed to be the first portrait of a doge painted from life. From the chapter house you can look into the Frari's monumental Palladian cloister.

The first chapel in the **Choir** has an altarpiece by Bartolomeo Vivarini (*Madonna, Child and Saints*, 1482), notable also for the original frame; in the second, the **Chapel of St Massimiliano Kolbe** [10], are two 14th-century wall tombs, the one on the left of a knight, Duccio degli Uberti. The next chapel, nearest the high altar, belonged to the Florentines, who hired Donatello to make its rustic but gilded wooden **Statue of John the Baptist** in 1438, his earliest work in the Veneto region, and like many of his *Baptists* in Florence, one who obviously lived on locusts.

But who is that hot number in the red dress floating over the high altar? Titian's enormous **Assumption of the Virgin** [11], painted in 1516–18, was the painter's first public commission in Venice. It caused a sensation for its extraordinary colour and revolutionary spiralling composition, of the Virgin ascending into Heaven, and did much to make

Titian's reputation, the way the *David* did Michelangelo's. For all that, the Frari monks didn't want it at first, graciously accepting the work only after they heard Emperor Charles V, Titian's great patron, wanted to buy it. Later Franciscans, sharing the taste of their 16th-century predecessors, shuffled the thing away into storage, where it remained until this century.

But this questionable *Assumption* has perhaps suffered more at the hands of its friends. 'The Most Beautiful Painting in the World' according to some critics of generations past—such a tribute itself betrays the essential kitsch sensibility lurking at the heart of the work and the age that created it, the dotage of the expiring Renaissance. After the Bellini in the sacristy its virtues seem mere virtuosity, and its big-eyed, heaven-gazing Virgin as spiritual and profound as a Sunday school holy card. Pious sentimentality, especially on such a grand scale, rarely appears elsewhere in Venetian art or even in Titian's own *oeuvre*. One wonders what the artist thought about it in his old age.

In the chancel, to the left of the *Assumption*, the Renaissance **Tomb of Doge Nicolò Tron** (d. 1473) [12] by Antonio Rizzo, a serene and lovely antidote with its Renaissance allegories. To the right is the **Tomb of Doge Francesco Foscari** (d. 1457) [13], who wore the ducal bonnet the longest, reigning 34 years before the Senate pressured him to retire; he died a week later of a broken heart. Among the chapels to the left of the sanctuary, the third contains the grave of Claudio Monteverdi (1567–1643), marked by a plain slab; the crowded scene that shares the chapel with him was begun by Alvise Vivarini and finished by Marco Basaiti. The fourth chapel, the **Cappella Corner** [14] in the left transept, is usually locked, but you can see through the grill Bartolomeo Vivarini's crystal clear painting of *St Mark Enthroned with Four Saints*, an early Renaissance Tuscan **tomb of Federico Corner**, and Sansovino's broken but beautiful marble *St John* on the font. Don't miss the carved wooden bench back in the transept, a masterpiece of Gothic tracery.

Continuing down the left aisle, a door leads into the **Cappella Emiliani** [15], with its numberous statues by the 15th-century school of Jacobello Dalle Masegne; next to it is the fine **Monument of Bishop Jacopo Pésaro** (d. 1547) [16], and Titian's *Madonna di Ca' Pésaro*, commissioned in 1519 by the same bishop. This painting, nearly as revolutionary in its time as the *Assumption*, had a more lasting influence on Venetian art, especially in its diagonal composition. Titian's wife Celia modelled for the Madonna, and paying her homage below are members of the Pésaro clan, including the Bishop (kneeling on the left); some Turks he captured in the Levant are dragged into the scene as well.

There's no known reason, though, for the ungainly, ragged Moors created to hold up the next monument, the godawful **Tomb of Doge Giovanni Pésaro** (d. 1659) [17], though the sculptor, a certain Melchiorre Barthel, at least carved pillows for them to make the load lighter. Of all the stupefying tombs in the Frari, this one takes the cake. It rises nearly to the church's roofline, with decomposing bodies on top to add an endearing Hallowe'en note, together with some funhouse dragons and skeletons. Next comes the **Tomb of Canova** [18], with a nearly full-sized pyramid, its door left ajar (a conceit taken from ancient Roman funeral steles); the ensemble, including sorrowful mourners and a sad, crouching winged lion, was designed by the sculptor as a tomb for Titian, but carved after his death as his own memorial, although only his heart is buried here.

The adjacent monastery and Palladian cloister have, since the early 1800s, housed the **State Archives of Venice**. The Republic left behind 70 km of files (about the distance from here to Vicenza) beginning in the 9th century, covering every aspect of Venetian life from important state secrets down to reports prepared by spies and busybodies on which patricians were gambling or whoring too much: a horde of paper occupying 300 rooms. Two or three times a year exhibitions are held here, based on archival material.

> *Behind the apse of the Frari is the Church of **San Rocco**, built by Bartolomeo Bon in 1489 but rebuilt in 1725, with an ornate façade (1771).*

On either side of the main door are refined Rococo statues that could audition for parts in a Christmas pantomime: *David with Goliath's Head* and *St Cecilia* (1743) by Giovanni Marchiori. If you're lucky enough to find it open, the first altar on the right has Sebastiano Ricci's *Miracle of S. Francesco di Paola*, and the first on the left Pordenone's *SS. Christopher and Martin*. Most mesmerizing, though, is Tintoretto's series on the life of St Roch (see 'Venetian Topics', p. 32), a preview or postscript to the masterpieces in the Scuola di S. Rocco: *St Roch Taken to Prison* and the recently restored *St Roch Cures Victims of the Plague* are the best.

> *Next to the Church is the climax of this walk, the celebrated **Scuola di S. Rocco**; its interior, called Venice's Sistine Chapel, was painted by Tintoretto over a 23 year period; like Michelangelo, he worked alone without assistants; like Michelangelo he created a visionary cycle of paintings from the depths of the imagination.*

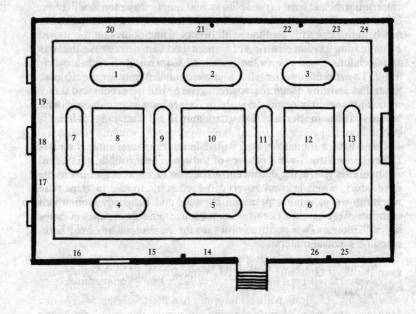

SCUOLA DI S. ROCCO
Tintoretto's Paintings in the Chapter House

Ceiling:
1 God Appearing to Moses
2 Vision of Ezekiel
3 Elisha Feeding the Multitude
4 Moses and the Pillar of Fire
5 Jacob's Ladder
6 Elisha fed by an Angel in the Desert
7 Adam and Eve
8 Moses Striking Water from the Rock
9 Jonah Emerging from the Whale

10 The Miracle of the Brazen Serpent
11 Sacrifice of Isaac
12 The Fall of Manna
13 The Passover

Walls:
14 Ascension
15 Christ at Bethesda
16 Temptation of Christ
17 S. Rocco

18 Vision of S. Rocco
19 S. Sebastiano
20 Adoration of the Shepherds
21 Baptism of Christ
22 Resurrection
23 Christ in the Garden of Gethsemane
24 Last Supper
25 Miracle of the Loaves and Fishes
26 Resurrection of Lazarus

Open 9–1 and 3:30–6:30, winter 10–1 (L5000). Founded in 1478, the Scuola di S. Rocco was dedicated to caring for the ill, especially those ill with plague. Bartolomeo Bon the Younger designed the new confraternity's headquarters, though it was hardly completed when the Venetians nabbed the relics of St Roch from Montpelier, even before he was canonized. With subsequent outbreaks of plague, donations poured in, hoping to secure Roch's aid, but also so enriching the Scuola that Bon's building was given a beautiful, lively façade by Scarpagnino in 1549. To embellish the interior, a competition was held for the Scuola's inaugural painting. Four artists were asked to bring a prepartory sketch to the judges on a certain day, but Tintoretto won the contest by a blatantly unfair trick: rather than make a mere sketch, he finished a painting, and rigged it up behind a curtain where the winning picture was destined to be hung, unveiling it with a flourish and offering it as a gift to the confraternity. To the outrage of the other competitors, the judges accepted this *fait accompli*, and commissioned more works from him up until 1585, when he had covered nearly every square inch with an awesome 54 paintings. A curious sidelight to the story is that one member of the scuola offered to contribute to the cost of the decoration only if Tintoretto was *not* the artist—one of the first recorded instances of stylistic distaste.

But controversy was Tintoretto's middle name. He strove to depict even the most conventional subjects from a fresh point of view; while other artists of the High Renaissance often composed with the epic vision of a Cecil B. de Mille, Tintoretto had the revolutionary eye of a 16th-century Orson Welles, creating audacious, dynamic 'sets', often working out his compositions in his little box-stages, with wax figures and unusual lighting effects. But unlike the virtuoso theatrics of the Baroque, Tintoretto's fireworks come entirely from within the subjects, and ignite their spiritual meanings more intensely than ever achieved by others before. Vertigo is not an uncommon response.

To follow Tintoretto's development, begin where he did, upstairs in the **Sala dell'Albergo**, just off the main hall. In the middle of the ceiling is his prize-winning panel, the *Glory of St Roch*, though it has since been completely overpowered by the vast *Crucifixion* (1565), the greatest and most engrossing work in the cycle, where the noble sacrifice is the central drama of a cosmically busy human world. When you can draw your eye away, there are more Tintorettos on the opposite wall: *The Way to Calvary*, *Christ Crowned with Thorns* and *Christ before Pilate*. The easel painting of *Christ Bearing the Cross* (1510), long attributed to Giorgione, is now generally thought to be a Titian, and was long venerated as a holy picture in the church of S. Rocco, while the *Pietà* is believed to be by a pupil of Giorgione.

Tintoretto frescoed the adjacent **Chapter House**, in an intense period between 1575–81, with a programme of Old Testament scenes on the ceiling. The three dominant panels are the stunning *Moses Striking Water from the Rock*, *The Miracle of the Brazen Serpent*, and *The Fall of Manna*. All the smaller paintings are just as remarkable (see plan); the only works not by Tintoretto are the *chiaroscuro* panels along the sides repainted for some reason in the 1770s. Lining the walls are New Testament scenes, if anything even more dizzyingly conceived. The satirical allegorical carvings on the benches and *trompe l'oeil* bookcases beneath them were added in the late 17th century by Francesco Pianta as an antidote to the mystically feverish paintings; Tintoretto himself, holding a bunch of brushes, represents Painting (near the high altar), while the comical figure of the cloak and dagger Spy (Curiosity) is perhaps the most endearing piece of sculpture in Venice. If you have the time, you can follow the other allegories conveniently listed by Pianta himself by the main entrance. Other works asking for your attention are the easel painting by the altar: Titian's *Annunication*, Tintoretto's *Visitation* and Giambattista Tiepolo's *Abraham and the Angels* and *Hagar and the Angels*, the last works acquired by the Confraternity in 1785.

The last set of paintings Tintoretto did for the Scuola are downstairs, but as you descend Scarpagnino's grand staircase, take a look at the two large canvases commemorating the end of the 1630 plague, by Antonio Zanchi and Pietro Negri, Tintorettoesque paintings that more than anything bring out the unique qualities of the real thing. The paintings devoted to the life of the *Virgin* in the **Ground Floor Hall** (1583–87) were executed in Tintoretto's last years, when (unlike Michelangelo) he mellowed enough to take in landscapes—and few by any artist can match the luscious charm of *The Flight into Egypt*, or the autumnal essences in the *Mary Magdalene* and *St Mary in Egypt*, both shown reading books. But he never compromised on the blasts when the subject was of blasting importance: *The Annunciation* startles the viewer as much as Mary, and the *Massacre of the Innocents* is aptly horrible and confusing.

Walk along the left side of S. Rocco on Calle Fianco della Scuola to the Rio della Frescada, where someone with a sense of fun and a home overlooking the canal has installed two floors of brightly coloured wind toys that clatter around madly in the slightest breeze.

Cross the bridge, and turn left on Calle dei Preti, only to make the next right for **San Pantalon**, *its unfinished façade a slightly outrageous gift that someone forgot to wrap.*

For inside (open 8–11:30 and 4:30–7) it contains *The Miracles and Apotheosis of S. Pantalon*, the most extraordinary *trompe l'oeil* ceiling in Italy, the life's work of Gian Antonio Fumiani—literally, since he died in 1704, falling off the scaffolding after 24 years on the job. Rather than paint in *fresco*, Fumiani used 60 panels, which all put together make not one of the world's greatest paintings, but certainly one of the largest. S. Pantalon, martyred under Diocletian, was a healer like St Roch, and as such was very popular in plague-torn Venice.

One of his miracles was the subject of Veronese's last paintings *St Pantalon Healing a Child* (1587), in the second chapel on the right; sombre, twilit, and melancholy in tone, you can sense Veronese's foreboding of his own death (and perhaps not a whole lot of confidence in Pantalon's ability to do anything about it). Another painting to look for is in the chapel to the left of the high altar: Antonio Vivarini and Giovanni d'Alemagna's glossy *Coronation of the Virgin*, in an elaborate tabernacle.

As you leave the church, turn left for Campiello da Ca'Angaran, which preserves something you'll probably never see in any other tiny square in Italy, or anywhere else: a rondel in bas-relief from the 12th century, portraying a Byzantine emperor, holding a sceptre and a symbol of the world he still pretended to rule.

To escape the labyrinth from here, take Calle S. Pantalon back along the side of the Church, and then a right in Calle Crosera. Then turn left in Calle Marconi, right down Fondamenta Frescada to Calle Campaniel; from here Calle del Traghetto leads down to the S. Tomà stage on the Grand Canal.

Walk VI
Cannaregio

Portal ⎯ *Gesuiti*

Rialto—S. Giovanni Cristosomo—S. Maria dei Miracoli—
SS. Apostoli—Gesuiti—Ca' d'Oro—S. Marziale—Madonna
dell'Orto—S. Alvise—Ghetto—S.Giobbe—Scalzi—
Palazzo Labia—S. Marcuolo

Originally a reedy cane (*canna*) swamp, the *sestiere* of Cannaregio is the
largest in Venice, encompassing moods ranging from the cool Renaissance perfection of S. Maria Miracoli to the cramped bittersweet con-
fines of the Ghetto to the tarnished tourist tinsel of the Lista di Spagna,
leading from the railway station. But best of all is the Cannaregio in
between, still wrapped in the silence that once enveloped the rest of
Venice. Crumbling and piquant, it offers your best chance to see the city
behind the glitz; here children play tag on the bridges on the broad
fondamente, without much fear of knocking a tourist into the drink; shirts,
sheets, and some amazing examples of the Italian underwear cult flutter
gaily overhead; old geezers and cats soak up the sun in front of no-name
bars. The cavernous, narrow lanes of Venice spread into broad parallel-
ograms in northern Cannaregio, where swampy islets were reclaimed on
the banks by the northern lagoon and made into long straight lanes and
canals, horizons and horizontals open to the setting sun.

To see everything on this little marathon requires some planning: a
phone call as far in advance as possible to the Palazzo Labia, with its
ballroom of ceiling frescoes by Giambattista Tiepolo (tel 781 111). The

appointments given are usually between 3 and 4 in the afternoon, which fit in conveniently enough after lunch. RAI uses the ballroom to record concerts once or twice a week; the tickets are free, but again you have to ring in advance to get one. On Saturday the Jewish Museum and synagogues are closed; on Monday it's the turn of the Ca' d'Oro. Also, if you want to see the newly restored cycle of Palma Giovanes at the Oratorio dei Crociferi, check the flighty opening hours (see below) and plan accordingly.

Walking Time: 4¹/₂ hours.

LUNCH/CAFÉS

Nane Mora, Primo Corte del Milion; Venetian cuisine, nice atmosphere and outdoor tables (L30 000, less for pizza).

Osteria al Milone, Corte del Milion, lively, fun atmosphere, where many Venetians meet for wine, snacks or a meal (L30 000).

Fiaschetteria Toscana, Saliz. S. Giovanni Cristosomo 5644, (Visa, EC, AE) Tuscan specialities, wines from all over Italy; outdoor tables in Campo S. Giovanni Cristosomo (L30 000).

Boldrin, Saliz. S. Canzian (S. Canciano) 5550, wine and snack bar, near S. Maria Miracoli.

Casa Mia, Calle dell'Oca 4430, off Campo SS. Apostoli; popular *pizzeria* (L8000).

A la Vecia Cavana, Rio Terrà dei Franceschi 4624, off Rio Terra SS. Apostoli, north of Campo SS. Apostoli (AE, DC, Visa) Cannaregio's poshest eatery; Venetian cuisine and lots of seafood; tourist menu (L20 000).

Hong Kong, Strada Nova 4392, good solid Chinese, some outdoor tables (L20 000).

Vini da Gigio, Fondamenta di S. Felice 3698a, wines, *tavola calda*, and restaurant; full sit down meals around L30 000.

Paradiso Perduto, Fondamenta della Misericordia 2540, a *trattoria* (good pasta and seafood, L20–30 000) and popular bar, especially in the evening.

Trattoria all'Aurelia, Saliz. dei Specchieri 1888, near the Gesuiti, just off the Fondamenta Nuova. Venetian cuisine (L20 000).

Trattoria al Antico Mola, Fondamenta degli Ormesini 2800; close to the above, but a bit fancier and nicer food, with grilled fish, risottos, *zuppa di pesce*, etc. (L25–30 000).

No-name Café, Fondamenta dei Ormesini 2859, has wooden tables out by the canal and a L10 000 *pranzo* few tourists ever eat.

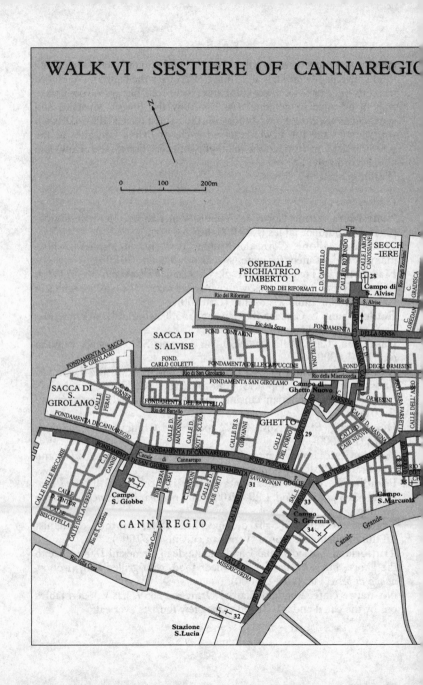

WALK VI - SESTIERE OF CANNAREGIO

N

0   100   200m

OSPEDALE
PSICHIATRICO
UMBERTO 1
FOND DEI RIFORMATI

SECCH
–IERE

C.D. CAPITELLO

CALLE D. RO ONDO

CALLE LARGO
CANOSSIANE

28

Campo di
S. Alvise

C.
GRADISCA

Rio degli Zecchini

Rio del Riformati

Rio di   S. Alvise

Rio della Sensa

FONDAMENTA   DELLA SENSA

C.
LOREDAN

SACCA DI
S. ALVISE

FOND CONTARINI

FOND.
CARLO COLETTI

FONDAMENTA DELLE CAPPUCCINE

C. TURLONA

C. CAPITELLO

C. SPEZIER

FOND   DEGLI ORMESINI

FONDAMENTA D. SACCA
S. GIROLAMO

Rio di San Girolamo

FONDAMENTA SAN GIROLAMO

Rio della Misericordia

Campo di
Ghetto Nuovo

ORMESINI

RIO TERRA FARSETTI

CALLE DEL ASEO

SACCA DI
S.
GIROLAMO

CALLE FERAU

FORNER

FONDAMENTA DEL BATTELLO

Rio del Battello

FARNESE

GHETTO VECCHIO

CALLE D. MASENA

FONDAMENTA DI CANNAREGIO

CALLE D.
MADONNA

SOTT. SCURO

CALLE DI S.
GIOVANNI

GHETTO

CALLE
DEL FORNO

GHETTO NUOVO

29

CASE NUOVE

CALLE DELLE BECCARIE

CALLE
D. LINTOR

CALLE
BISCOTELLA

C.D.
CANNE

FONDAMENTA DI SAN GIOBBE

Canale   di   Cannaregio

FONDAMENTA DI CANNAREGIO

FOND PESCARIA

RIO TERRA S. LEONARDO

CALLE D.
CRISTO

RIO TE
DI

RIO T

CALLE DELLA CERERIA

RIO TERRA
CREA

C. CENDON

CALLE 2 D.
DUE CORTI

FONDAMENTA
SAVORGNAN GUGLIE

P.
GUGLIE

CALLE D. PRETI

31

RIO TERRA S LEONARDO

SAL SEN

Campo.
S.Marcuola

35

CH

30

Campo
S. Giobbe

33

Campo
S. Geremia

34

CANNAREGIO

Rio di S. Giobbe

Rio della Crea

CALLE D.
MISERICORDIA

RIO TERRA DELLA MADDALENA

Canale   Grande

32

Stazione
S.Lucia

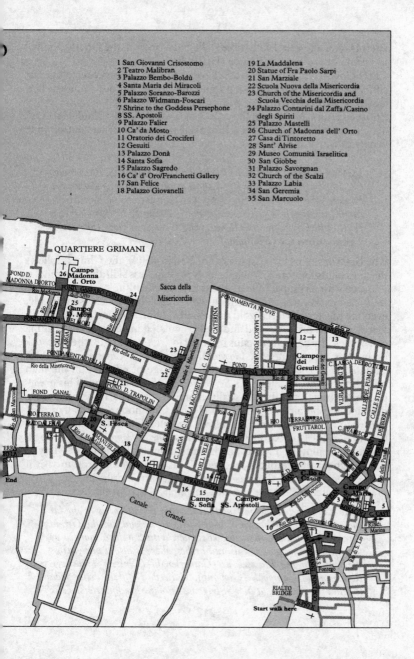

1 San Giovanni Crisostomo
2 Teatro Malibran
3 Palazzo Bembo-Boldù
4 Santa Maria dei Miracoli
5 Palazzo Soranzo-Barozzi
6 Palazzo Widmann-Foscari
7 Shrine to the Goddess Persephone
8 SS. Apostoli
9 Palazzo Falier
10 Ca' da Mosto
11 Oratorio dei Crociferi
12 Gesuiti
13 Palazzo Donà
14 Santa Sofia
15 Palazzo Sagredo
16 Ca' d' Oro/Franchetti Gallery
17 San Felice
18 Palazzo Giovanelli

19 La Maddalena
20 Statue of Fra Paolo Sarpi
21 San Marziale
22 Scuola Nuova della Misericordia
23 Church of the Misericordia and
   Scuola Vecchia della Misericordia
24 Palazzo Contarini dal Zaffa/Casino
   degli Spiriti
25 Palazzo Mastelli
26 Church of Madonna dell' Orto
27 Casa di Tintoretto
28 Sant' Alvise
29 Museo Comunità Israelitica
30 San Giobbe
31 Palazzo Savorgnan
32 Church of the Scalzi
33 Palazzo Labia
34 San Geremia
35 San Marcuolo

Bich Dao, Calleselle 1424, (take Calle Farnese from the Ghetto Nuovo) tastiest Chinese food in Venice (L20 000).

Caffè Costarica, Rio Terrà di S. Leonardo 1563, one of Venice's oldest coffeehouses, but no frills—it's stand up, drink, and out you go. Their iced coffee (*frappé*) can be a godsend on a hot day.

Enoteca Due Colonne, at the corner of Calle dell'Cristo and Rio Terrà del Cristo, by San Marcuolo, a fun, noisy place full of Venetians; a wide variety of wines and beers.

☆   ☆   ☆   ☆   ☆

Start on the right bank of the Rialto Bridge at Campo S. Bartolomeo (see Walk 2). From here it's a short walk north along Salizzada Fontego over the bridge that separates the sestiero *of San Marco from Cannaregio. The first square north of Campo S. Bartolomeo is nearly filled with the fine Renaissance Church of* **San Giovanni Crisostomo** *(or Grisostomo).*

The last work of Mauro Codussi (finished in 1504), the Church follows the lines of his famous S. Michele, only perhaps less skilfully. In form it is a square with a compact Greek cross inscribed within, perhaps as a nod to its namesake, the 'golden mouthed' Archbishop of Constantinople; even the plaster has a red gold tint, thanks to the addition of brick dust. Harmoniously proportioned and well articulated inside, with its vaulting and domes, the church contains its equal in art: on the right, the last work of another great Venetian, Giovanni Bellini's *SS. Christopher, Jerome, and Louis of Toulouse* (1513, painted at the age of 82) and on the high altar, Sebastiano del Piombo's *Seven Saints* (1508–11), one of his greatest works though too dirty to really appreciate; some art historians have detected the helping brush of the elusive Giorgione, especially in the figures of St John the Baptist and St Liberale. The marble altar on the left, by Tullio Lombardo (1502), shows *The Coronation of the Virgin* where the sculptor concentrated his attention on the figure of Mary to the detriment of the bland Apostles. This is a good church to visit if you've been misbehaving, as there's a plenary indulgence on offer; prayer instructions on the right, by the altar to the Virgin.

Take a brief detour down Calle della Stua, a small alley at the far end of Campo S. Giovanni, to the left; at the end, on the Grand Canal is the little Campiello del Remer, with a palace adorned by some fine Byzantine capitals and arches; there is also a view across the water to the Palazzo dei Camerlenghi (Venice's Treasury). Returning to Campo S. Giovanni, Calle de l'Uffizio della Seda (behind the Church, at No. 5864) was once the headquarters of silk *workers and merchants from the Tuscan city of Lucca. From here, Calle del Teatro leads around to the **Teatro Malibran**, built in the 17th century as the Teatro S. Giovanni Crisostomo, but renamed after a famous singer of the 1830s, then rebuilt in the 1920s. Its Veneto-Byzantian arches are believed to have belonged to the family home of **Marco Polo**.*

At the 1298 Battle of Curzola, Marco Polo was taken prisoner by the Genoese, and spent his time in the clink dictating the saga of his 17 years at the court of Kublai Khan to his cellmate, Rusticiano da Pisa. The resulting *Description of the World* was known, at least locally as *'Il Milion'*, for what everyone thought were Polo's million exaggerations and tall tales, though in truth Polo's book was for long Europe's most accurate account of the East. And so the pair of enclosed courts adjacent to the theatre were named: the **Corte Primo del Milion**, and beyond it, the picturesque **Corte Secondo del Milion**, with its collage of architectural fragments from the 11th–15th centuries, and a lovely Byzantine arch.

*Return to the the main Salizzada S. Giovanni Crisostomo, and turn right; cross a canal and take the first right, Salizzada S. Canzian. This leads to Campiello B. Crovato; turn right when you reach it, and right again into the adjacent Campiello S. Maria Nova. Note the hairy fellow holding a solar disc, a bit of 16th-century classicizing on the façade of the Gothic **Palazzo Bembo-Boldù** (he is said to be Saturn, but the odd faces and the duck underneath him resist explanation). Turn left under the duck, onto Calle dei Miracoli. Just down this street the chief jewel in Venice's Renaissance crown, **Santa Maria dei Miracoli** comes suddenly into sight, prettily rinsing its skirts in the canal.*

Open 10–12 and winter 3–5, summer 3–6. The miracle in its name comes from a popular wonder-working painting that once had a shrine in the neighbourhood. It received enough donations to afford a proper, if small church to shelter it, and one was designed by Pietro Lombardo and his sons, Tullio and Antonio in 1481–89. But the real miracle is the church itself—the perfect expression of Venice's half-archaic brand of Renaissance, bending the classical laws to its own decorative ends. With a façade topped by a Mauro Codussi-style half circle crowning, the church is covered inside and out with a pearly sheath of rich marbles like St Mark's—one tradition has it that it got all the leftovers. The Lombardos embellished it with their trademark discs and geometric designs in porphyry or green serpentine marble, not to mention some of the most masterful stonecutting in Venice, beginning with the angels on the façade, believed to be by Pietro Lombardo himself.

The glory of the luxuriant grey and pink interior is the exquisite carving on the pillars of the *barca*, or nuns' gallery, at the entrance, where the sculptors' fancy was given free reign to frolic among the delightful motifs of a Renaissance spring. These gallery carvings are attributed to the three Lombardos; the statues on the balustrade in front of the raised altar are by Tullio, and the reliefs of *children and mermaids* under the great arch are believed to be by Antonio. The miraculous painting (by Nicolò di Pietro) is still in place, and may have to be called upon to do its stuff to protect the church from damage inside the marble walls caused by a recent over-hasty restoration. The raised choir and altar, with stairs leading to a small crypt is an anachronistic feature, common in medieval churches throughout central Italy, but surprisingly rare in Venice, where it is the only way to have a crypt at all, or at least one above the water line. Have a look at the barrel-vaulted ceiling before you go, decorated with 50 fine Renaissance portraits of the prophets and other Old Testament figures by Pier Maria Pennacchi.

Before leaving S. Maria, duck down Calle Castelli (in front of the church) to see the **Palazzo Soranzo-Barozzi** *(1470s) the only one in Venice to have kept its original wooden door and fish-shaped knocker in place, on its stately Gothic entrance; on Mon, Wed and Fri from 11–1 you can get in to see its fine courtyard and stair.*

From behind S. Maria Miracoli, Fondamenta del Piovan crosses the forking Rio di Ca' Widman in a setting almost too bijou *to be real. The lanes lead straight on to SS. Giovanni e Paolo (see Walk 3); instead take the first left (under the arches, just after Ponte del Piovan) to the next bridge, the Ponte Widmann. From the bridge you can see the* **Palazzo Widmann-Foscari**, *with a façade by Long-hena, embedded with Byzantine paterae; this was the headquarters of one of Venice's later noble and wealthiest families, though the older patricians scorned them for having started out as street porters in Carinthia; the neighbouring Palazzo Loredan is noted for its 16th-century doorway. Over the bridge and you're back in Campo S. Maria Nova. Bear right into Campiello Crovato; on the northern end of the square is the sleepy Campo and Church of* **San Canciano**, *a yawner rebuilt in the 18th century. From here take Calle d. Malvasia (left of the façade) to the next bridge (Ponte*

*S. Canzian). Look at the palace on the other side, and you will see, of
all things, a **shrine to the goddess Persephone***.

The building was once known as the Ca' Strozzi, a possession of the
famous Florentine Renaissance family, powerful foes of the Medici.
Later it belonged to two antiquarians named Amadeo Svayer and David
Weber, who covered it inside and out with their collections. All that is left
are the fragments of ancient Greek reliefs on the side facing the bridge.
The first one, a battered figure and a wheel, would have been a scene of
the Lord of the Underworld carrying off Persephone in his chariot.
Around the corner are two reliefs from grave steles, stock scenes from
Greek funerary art; one showing the Goddess and Hades reclining on
couches, and another with a small figure, a newly arrived soul, making
supplication before her.

*Once over the bridge, continue straight, through Campiello della
Cason (once the home of Angelo Participazio, the first doge to move to
modern Venice from Malamocco, in the early 800s) and follow Calle
del Manganer to the Campo and Church of **SS. Apostoli**, with its
tall, landmark campanile (1672).*

This was one of the first of the Rialtine islets colonized in the Dark Ages,
and the church went up soon afterwards, though it has been rebuilt
several times since. The star attraction inside is on the right, the Renaissance **Cappella Corner** by Mauro Codussi, dedicated to the family of
Caterina, Queen of Cyprus, who was buried here before being trans-
ferred to S. Salvatore. Giambattista Tieopolo's 1748 *Communion of S.
Lucia*, on the chapel's altar, is rated among that artist's most spiritual
works; Tullio Lombardo is given credit for the tomb of Caterina's father
Marco (d. 1511), and for the marble relief of *St Sebastian's head* (located
among the detatched 14th-century frescoes in the chapel to the right of
the high altar). In the chapel to the left of the altar is Francesco Maffei's
brightly coloured *Guardian Angel*, a popular subject during the Counter-
Reformation, when amidst all its terrors people really needed one, and a
15th-century Tuscan relief of the *Madonna and Child*.

From the bridge spanning the Rio dei SS. Apostoli (to the right of the
façade) you have a good view of the Veneto-Byzantine **Palazzo Falier**
with its portico, begun in the 13th century; this was the family home of
the traitor Doge Marin Falier, deprived of his head in 1355. Its neighbour to the west, facing the Grand Canal, is the **Ca' da Mosto**, whose

most famous resident, Alvise da Mosto (d. 1483) enjoyed a happier fate as the discoverer of the Cape Verde islands, while in the employ of the Portuguese king Henry the Navigator. Ca' da Mosto later became the Leon Bianco Inn, the equivalent of the Ritz of Venice from the 16th to 18th century, with a guest list that stretched from Emperor Joseph II to J.M.W. Turner to James Fenimore Cooper.

> *Behind SS. Apostoli, backtrack a bit on Calle del Manganer and turn left at Calle Muazzo; carry straight ahead north from here until the string of lanes widens to form the Campo dei Gesuiti ('of the Jesuits'); just on the left is the little* **Oratorio dei Crociferi**, *once part of the Crociferi Church, demolished by the Jesuits; its paintings were restored in 1984.*

Open April, May, June and Oct, Fri, Sat and Sun 10–12, and July–Sept, Fri–Sun 4:30–6:30; free. Founded by Doge Ranier Zeno in the 13th century, the Oratory was devoted to charity, its chief moments illustrated in glowing colours by Palma Giovane between 1583–91. The events in themselves lack the drama of some of Venice's other altruistic organizations, but Palma, whose paintings elsewhere are often workmanlike rehashes of Tintoretto, manages to convert them into some of his most charming images.

> *The Campo is best known, however, for one of Venice's most out-landish churches, the* **Gesuiti**.

Open 10–12 and 5–7. The Jesuits, banned from the Republic in 1606 for supporting the Pope during the Great Interdict, were permitted to return to the Republic only in 1657—a permission subject to a review every three years. Because the city had forbidden the construction of new churches, the Order purchased the former church of the Crociferi and demolished it, hiring Domenico Rossi to design a new one in 1715–29. After the charms of S. Maria dei Miracoli, the Gesuiti has the sad air of a fat, overdone girl who can't get a date, no matter how much money her parents lavish on her appearance; the parents in this case were the Manin family (who also produced Venice's equally unloved last doge). They paid Giambattista Fattoretto for a façade larded with saints and angels, pinned to the wall with iron bars, wearing iron haloes that bleed rust over the white marble.

The Jesuits were convinced that the glory and richness of this world could bring the faithful closer to that of the next: Baroque architecture was a direct descendent of what used to be called the 'Jesuit style'. This style of ecclesiastical theatre, which delighted in *trompe l'oeil* (as in the remarkable ceiling of S. Pantalon) here reaches new heights of mouldering excess; what at first sight looks like green and white damask along the walls, curtains around the pulpit, and grandmotherly carpeting leading up to the high altar—is all really marble, carefully carved to resemble swags of fabric. Under the Jesuitical gold and cream stucco frosting , the eye is drawn to the unutterably grotesque *baldacchino* over the high altar, with fat twisted macaroni columns of *verde antico* and a huge dome and marble globe. The Manin family financed it as a tribute to themselves (something that, for a high altar, could happen only in Venice); many of them are buried underneath.

The only work of art that can top the interior decoration is one inherited from the previous church: Titian's restored *Martyrdom of St Lawrence* (1558, first altar on the left, lighting best around noon) one of his finest religious works, a revolutionary night scene of the Saint roasting on a Roman gridiron, lit and composed with a Tintoretto-esque touch. The Gesuiti's pavement is sagging perilously in a few spots; the entire church badly needs restoration, but it doesn't seem to be high on anyone's list of priorities.

The grid of lanes around the Campo—rational, broad streets laid out about the same time as the Church—sport a number of worn reliefs and plaques of the guilds who once had their headquarters in the area; the tailors' guild's relief includes a member holding a pair of scissors large enough to trim hedges. The northern end of the Campo *funnels onto the* **Fondamente Nuove**, *'new' in this case meaning 1589.*

Unfortunately the construction of this quay meant the demolition of a row of pleasure gardens, one of the most beautiful belonging to Titian, who lived and entertained his buddies Sansovino and Aretino and Europe's VIPs in this neighbourhood for half his lifetime (a plaque on the flats at Calle Larga dei Botteri 5179 marks the site of his small estate). He was living here when invited to Augsburg to paint Emperor Charles V, news that spread like fire through Venice and led to a siege of buyers outside his door, prepared to buy anything from the brush of the master—the 16th century saw the beginning of modern art marketing, as well as the beginning of modern artistic egos. But although the Venetians admired Titian, they thought he was untrustworthy for hanging around Aretino and mercenary because of his calculating interest in money—by far the main topic of his surviving correspondence.

Stripped of their lagoonside gardens, the *fondamente* have the dusty air of never have found their proper destiny; only one major palace was built, the austere **Palazzo Donà**, begun in 1610 by the intellectual Doge Leonardo Donà, at the corner of the Rio dei Gesuiti (no 5038). Just beyond are the landing stages for *vaporetti* sailing to S. Michele's cemeteries (the floating citadel of cypresses that lies straight ahead), Murano (just beyond) and Burano and the mainland port of Treporti (both hidden from sight). If it's a clear winter's day, you should be able to see the white outlines of the Dolomites, hovering like the mountains in a Chinese painting, sometimes made unnaturally sharp and clear by an optical illusion—a view that helped soothed Titian's longing for his native Cadore. On the *fondamente* themselves, there's little else to see, though if you continue east to the Rio dei Mendicanti, the border of Cannaregio, there's a *squero* (gondola building yard) which may be 300 years old.

From the southern end of Campo dei Gesuiti, follow the Fondamenta Zen (lined by the massive palace of the Zen, or Zeno, family, whose famous Carlo came to the rescue in the battle of Chioggia) to the Fondamenta S. Caterina, named for the little church that had its 14th-century ship's keel roof go up in flames in 1978. This has since been replaced, but the church is still closed for restoration, so cross the first bridge to the left, at Calle Zanardi, and continue straight along Ruga Due Pozzi.

At the end of this street, cross the iron bridge. Continue straight through Campiello Priuli and Calle del Cristo; this street circles around the back of **Santa Sofia**, a little church hidden by houses; inside (entrance on the Strada Nova), the four statues of saints, brought here from the former Church of the Servi, are generally attributed to the workshop of Antonio Rizzo. In Campo S. Sofia, overlooking the Grand Canal with a view of the Rialto markets, the **Palazzo Sagredo** is perhaps too embarassed to let visitors in to see the most ridiculous ceiling in Venice—a Fall of Giants (1734) by genre painter Pietro Longhi, who couldn't hold Dr Seuss's felt pen.

The **Strada Nova** is one of Venice's busiest shopping streets, bulldozed through the little alleyways in 1871 to provide a fast track from the Rialto Bridge to the railway station. Go right, towards the station, and take the next left: Calle di Ca' d'Oro takes you to another world altogether, that of the fairytale Gothic **Ca' d'Oro** and the collection of the Franchetti Gallery.

Open Tues–Sat 9–2, Sun 9–1; adm L2000. Marino Contarini, a procurator of S. Marco (the Venetian equivalent of a prince), purchased a
Veneto-Byzantine palace on this site to match his newly elected dignity,
and hired Marco d'Amadio to redesign it and Matteo Raverti to rebuild it
in Venice's unique brand of Gothic. Raverti used Lombard craftsmen,
but many of the finest touches of the Ca' d'Oro are by Giovanni and
Bartolomeo Bon. Finished in 1434, it was known as the 'Golden House'
because of the golden pinnacles along the roof, while its intricate floral
tracery on its main façade was dazzlingly illuminated with vermilion and
ultramarine. The original gold is now long gone, and subsequent owners
didn't always keep the old place up, most notoriously the 19th-century
ballerina Maria Taglioni. In this century Baron Giorgio Franchetti
bought the palace and filled it with his art collection, which he left to the
State in 1916. After a couple of rounds of restoration, the lovely courtyard was salvaged, with it fine open stair and well-head with *allegories of
virtues* by Bartolomeo Bon. Inside, however, the restorers were guilty of
overkill, blasting away all the old palatial clutter, making the walls plain
and white as any new art gallery.

Upstairs, the first exhibit, set in its own little marble shrine, is Andrea
Mantegna's grimacing, unfinished *St Sebastian*, one of the artist's last
paintings (1506). Sebastian here looks like a hedgehog, skewered by
enough arrows to trouble even a saint. Sculpture lines the walls of the
portego, or main hall, with its *loggia* overlooking the Grand Canal: a
charming double portrait bust called *The Young Couple* by Tullio Lombardo, bronze reliefs by Andrea Briosco, a lunette of the *Virgin and Child*
by Sansovino, and a 16th-century English alabaster relief of the *Life of St
Catherine*, one of many similar alabasters that made their way to Italy. In
the little rooms to the right of the *portego*, look for the fine collection of
Renaissance bronzes, statuettes and medals by Pisanello and the Man-
tuan Pier Alari Bonacolsi, known as '*L'Antico*' for his classical style. A
carved 16th-century ceiling survives in one room, overlooking two of
Carpaccio's paintings on the *Life of the Virgin* from the Scuola degli
Albanesi. On the left side of the *portego* are paintings by non-Venetians:
among them a miniscule *Flagellation* by Luca Signorelli and the *Coronation of the Virgin* by Andrea di Bartolo.

The beautiful 15th-century stairway in carved wood was brought here
from another palace; it leads up to a collection of minor works by major
artists, by Tintoretto, Titian, Van Dyck, Pordenone, and some good
sculptures by Vittoria. One room has a fine coffered ceiling from a palace
in Verona; another contains the ghosts of Giorgione and Titian's exterior

frescoes from the Fondaco dei Tedeschi, including a once-juicy pink nude by Giorgione bleached into a cartoon character. The two fine views of Venice in the same room are by one of the Guardi brothers, most likely Francesco.

> *Returning to Strada Nova, turn left; the next bridge crosses to* **San Felice***, a 1532 church of simple design, with Tintoretto's armed* St Demetrius *on the third altar on the right. But before continuing along Strada Nova, you may digress briefly up the porticoed Fondamenta di S. Felice to see one of the narrowest palaces in Venice and the last bridge in the city without parapets. Two hundred years ago, when street lighting was practically nonexistent, nearly all the bridges were as precarious, and though the natives could get around like cats, foreign visitors stuck to their gondolas or hired lantern-bearing guides to keep from tumbling in the canals. And as the law was that anyone could build a bridge, as long as it was high enough, many of them used to charge a toll.*
>
> *Continuing down Strada Nova, stop on the next bridge for the view of the lovely* **Palazzo Giovanelli** *(15th century), with its striking corner windows. Now an auction house, you may want to take advantage of any pre-sale viewings to see the well-preserved interior, with its delightful neo-Gothic stair. Soon after the bridge, turn left into the Campiello dei Fiori, and then right on Calle del Ogio (or dell'Olio). At the end of this street, follow the pretty, gently winding Rio Terrà della Maddalena, lined with old houses, some with exotic chimney pots; on its bank, set back in a little* campo, *is the peculiar small round church of* **La Maddalena**.

Usually open for weddings only, La Maddalena was built by Neoclassical architect Tommaso Temanza in 1760, round and domed like the Pantheon. Temanza was primarily a scholar (author of the *Lives of the Most Famous Venetian Architects and Sculptors*) and apparently a dabbler in the same undercurrent of esoteric Masonry as George Washington, Mozart and lots of other folks, judging by the 'eye of God' symbol over the main door (similar to the one on the back of the US dollar bill), the inscription over the door, and perhaps also by the dedication to Mary Magdalen. The original art was probably just as provocative, but has all but disappeared from the Church's hexagonal interior.

> *From the Maddalena, turn right, back into the bustling Strada Nova. Few in the thundering herd pause in front of the otherwise*

lacklustre church of **Santa Fosca** *(straight ahead) to ponder the* **statue of Fra Paolo Sarpi***, the only great intellectual Venice produced, a friend of Galileo, discoverer of the contraction of the iris, historian of the Council of Trent. Yet it is one of the things every visitor would have sought out 50 years ago, and its current neglect— covered with teenage grafitti, its pedestal a tumulus of street rub- bish—reflects not only a major change in tourist taste, but a global lack of interest in public statues.*

Although Paolo Sarpi (d. 1623) was a Servite priest at the Convent of S. Maria dei Servi (which stood near until it was demolished in 1812) he has always been a kind of honorary saint for Protestants—while he was alive there was even some fervent speculation that Venice would join in the Reformation. Sarpi, a close friend of Doge Leonardo Donà, was his chief advisor during the Great Interdict of 1606, arguing always for a strict separation of Church and State (Venice insisted on trying priests guilty of secular crimes in a secular court, and also limited the amount of money its religious houses could send to Rome). While the rest of Europe watched, Paul V excommunicated the whole Republic, but with the attitude that St Mark was just as good as St Peter, Venice didn't budge (when one priest declared that the Holy Spirit had moved him to obey the Interdict, the Council of Ten's answer was that the Holy Spirit had moved them as well—to hang any priest who refused to say mass). Thanks to the good offices of the French the Interdict was lifted, and although a face-saving gesture was made to Rome by handing over two convicted priests (not to the Pope, but to the French), Venice conceded nothing, and kept right on taxing monasteries and trying priests in courts.

Paul V could not forgive Sarpi for forever defusing the chief weapon of the papal arsenal, and six months after lifting the Interdict, sent three hired assassins to do him in. They ambushed him where his statue now stands, plunging a dagger into his cheek-bone. Sarpi could still make a pun: 'I recognize the *stylum* (style, or sharp instrument) of the Roman Curia' he said. After a miraculous recovery, the Senate gave him a pension, and he lived for 22 more years, advising the Republic on spiritual matters and providing a living symbol of religious freedom and tolerance in the darkest days of Italy's Counter-Reformation.

Cross the bridge behind Sarpi's statue into Calle Zancani; the next bridge leads to **San Marciliano** *(San Marziale), a medieval church rebuilt in the 17th century.*

251

Although most of the changes imposed on S. Marziale have not been to the Church's advantage (no other church in Venice has a basketball hoop fixed to it), it has held on to its ceiling frescoes by Sebastiano Ricci (1700–05), early works by this gallant and colourful if not very demanding knight of the brush; in the centre the subject is the *Glory of St Martial*, too grimy to really appreciate, while at the sides are paintings referring to the miraculous icon of the *Virgin* carved from a tree trunk in the 15th century, which still occupies the second altar on the left. Across the nave, there is a painting of *St Martial* by Tintoretto, of interest only as an example of botched restoration.

The chapel around it is florid Baroque to match the ceiling; even better is the high altar, with a unique sculptural frame designed by an unknown berserker of the 18th century. In it all pretence of architecture and structure disappears, giving way to a free-form composition of *angels, saints and clouds*, floating around a giant golden globe and crown.

> Cross the bridge in front of the Church, and turn right in Fonda-menta della Misericordia for Campo Misericordia, address of the **Scuola Nuova della Misericordia**, *a large building designed by Sansovino in 1534, its interior finished 50 years later, but the façade still lacking its costly marble sheathing. Its grand Renaissance salons are now home to an athletic association; not content with gobbling rebounds off the side of S. Marziale, the local sportsmen seem to be turning Sansovino's huge main hall into a basketball arena.*
>
> Turn left after the Scuola, and follow the Fondamenta della Misericordia over a wooden bridge to Campo d. Abbazia, with the Confraternity's church, the **Misericordia** (or Santa Maria di Valverde).

Campo dell'Abbazia is a slice of concentrated Cannaregio: open, un-cluttered, a hodgepodge of styles, a shadowy portico, a wide and straight canal, all a bit pungent and down at heel. But in its day the Misericordia was one of the six *scuole grandi*; its now deconsecrated church, founded in the 10th century, was rebuilt in the 13th, and given an inoffensive Baroque façade in 1651 by Clemente Moli, a follower of Bernini. It's the kind of bland façade that would help people forget the unholy murder that took place here in the 18th century, when a jealous priest slipped a poet a poisoned Host after he caught him dallying with his mistress. At a right angle to the church is the Gothic **Scuola Vecchia della Miseri-icordia**, built in 1308, with a pair of white rabbit-ear pinnacles and a curved crown roof. Most of its ornate, canopied doorway by Bartolomeo Bon is in the Victoria and Albert Museum, although two angels and an inscription survive in the architrave. When the Confraternity moved to its new quarters, this building was given to the guild of silk weavers. If it's open, you can see the old cloister between the Church and Scuola; the whole complex is now used as a restoration centre.

> Take the brick-paved Sottoportico dell' Abbazia under the Scuola Vecchia. The first bridge, **Ponte dei Muti**, is the site of another boatyard, or squero; but instead of crossing the bridge, turn right on Corte Vecchia to Fondamenta Gasparo Contarini. This overlooks a melancholy basin, the Sacca della Misericordia, with a view over the funeral island of S. Michele. Directly in front stands the 16th-century **Palazzo Contarini dal Zaffo**, a gloomy enough place, though the ghost legends are attached to the pleasure pavilion in its garden, the so-called **Casino degli Spiriti**.

A traditional rendezvous for the odd tryst or noisy orgy, the Casino is supposedly haunted by the screams and rattling chains of the damned souls of its old sinners. The most celebrated spirits belonged to a pair of lovers worthy of Boccaccio. The wife of a rich nobleman was having an affair with his best friend. The husband found out and raised the roof, and in grief and chagrin the best friend died. A few days later the sorrowing lady also determined to die, and asked to be brought to the Casino degli Spiriti; her last wish was that her wake be kept by only one of her serving maids. Yet as the little maid watched over the bier, in walked the 'ghost' of the lover, who picked up the 'corpse' and ordered the maid with her candle to lead them outside, whereupon the poor girl fainted in fright, and could recall nothing more. The Palace is now home to a charitable organization, and what the nuns do with the old casino is hard to tell.

> The Fondamenta continues past the **Palazzo Mastelli**, (across the canal) whose magpie builders adorned the long wall of its façade with everything from a Roman altar (on the corner column with the ox heads) to a marble relief of an Eastern merchant with a camel carrying a heavy load—which lends the Palace its more popular name, Palazzo Camello. Unlike its fellows in the neighbourhood, it faces north, and was the home of the three Mastelli brothers, 12th-century merchants from the Peloponnese. To the west, the Fondamenta opens up to the Church and Campo of the **Madonna**

*dell'Orto, where the local kids play Venetian court football; on the left they bounce the ball off the 16th-century **Scuola dei Mercanti** (Merchants' Guild), and hope the ball doesn't fall into the canal or one of the jet-black outboard hearses usually moored by the bridge.*

Open 9:30–12 and 4:30–7 (winter 3:30–5). The most beautiful Gothic church in Venice, Madonna dell'Orto was built by Fra Tiberio of Parma in the mid-14th century and originally dedicated to the giant Saint Christopher, the patron of the boatmen who used to sail from here to the north lagoon. Before long, though, Christopher was upstaged by the miracles performed by an equally large and rather ungainly statue of the *Madonna* by Giovanni de' Santi in a nearby vegetable garden. Eventually the *Madonna* came out from the cabbages and carrots for a place inside the church, which was altered in the early 1400s and officially re-dedicated. A 15th-century Istrian stone statue of *St Christopher carrying Baby Jesus*, by Tuscan sculptor Nicolò di Giovanni, still holds pride of place over the doorway (a late work of Bartolomeo Bon); he keeps company with two rows of *Apostles* (by the Dalle Masegne brothers) in niches along the cornice. The distinctive onion dome on the campanile was added in the Renaissance.

The Madonna del Orto was Tintoretto's parish church, and he and his talented children, Domenico and Marietta, are buried within. There's a rather dubious tradition that he was forced to take refuge in its sanctuary after adding cuckold's horns to a portrait he had made of a doge. The furious doge, the story goes, would only forgive the painter on the condition that he fill the church with art, which Tintoretto did with his usual demonic speed in only a few months, to the doge's chagrin (even Aretino once suggested that he ought to change his *prestezza del fatto* or 'quickness of the deed' into *pazienza del fare*, or the 'patience of the doing'. But if it was quick work, it was cheap; he only asked for his expenses). In the 1860s the Church suffered a misguided restoration that destroyed its once-celebrated organ. Some of the damage was corrected in the 1930s, and much of the rest tidied up after the 1966 flood, an early effort of the 'Venice in Peril' Fund.

The interior is fairly traditional Gothic, culminating in a vaulted apse. The first altar on the right glows with Cima da Conegliano's *St John the Baptist and Saints* (1493) standing in a ruined classical pavilion, with a brown city in the background, more Tuscan than Venetian in its austerity. After the fourth altar is a pair of organ doors where Tintoretto painted his delightful *The Presentation of the Virgin at the Temple* (1552), a compositional cousin to Titan's in the Accademia, though very different in light and colouring, with the child Mary lit in a kind of holy spotlight. Further up, the Cappella di S. Mauro contains the enormous stone statue of the *Madonna* that gave the Church its name. Tintoretto lies under a simple slab in the chapel to the right of the choir, the site of two of his more mastadonic works: *The Making of the Golden Calf* (with a self-portrait, fourth from left, holding up the calf) and a *Last Judgement* that gave Ruskin's wife Effie such a bad case of heebie-jeebies that she refused to ever return to the church. Back in the apse are Tintoretto's less harrowing *Vision of the Cross to St Paul* and *Beheading of St Paul*, flanking an *Annunciation* by Palma Giovane; Tintoretto also painted four of the five *Virtues* in the vault (the painter of the centre one is unknown). In the left aisle, the Contarini chapel has two busts of family members by Vittoria (in the centre) and another Tintoretto, *St Agnes raising Licinius*. At the end, in the elegant Cappella Valier (1526) is Giovanni Bellini's 1478 *Madonna* set in a sculpted tabernacle.

> Cross the canal in front of Madonna dell'Orto for **Campo dei Mori**, an elongated square that earned its name for its quaint statues of three 'Moors', popularly believed to be the Mastelli brothers, residents of the 'Camel' palace (see above).

Named Rioba, Sandi and Afani, they became 'Moors' perhaps for their Peloponnesian homeland (the Morea), or from their trade with the East. One of the brothers, in a turban and standing on a fragment of a Roman altar, is by himself on the *Fondamenta*, at No. 3399, decorating the façade of Tintoretto's house; the painter lived here from 1574 until his death in 1594. In the early years he was plagued by slanders written by Aretino, who often came to Cannaregio to visit Titian. Tintoretto took as much as he could bear before he invited the writer in for a free portrait. Aretino came eagerly enough, then sat perfectly still as the painter measured his features with a loaded pistol before sending him off. The warning was heeded, and Aretino changed the poison in his pen to honey.

A fourth 'Moor' embedded in the corner of the square, with a metal nose, is Sior Antonio Rioba, once the source of much malicious fun (being sent to visit him was an initiation ritual for any greenhorn in Venice). He was also, like the statue of Pasquino in Rome, made to sign any wicked or satrical verse that was likely to get the author in trouble; denunciations could be left at his feet. Besides the Moors, the *Campo* has another indignant plaque for the fourteen victims of an Austrian zeppelin attack in 1917.

From Campo dei Mori turn right down the Fondamenta della Sensa, a long straight walk (and one of the most serene places in Venice to watch a sunset). This outlying section of muddy swamps was drained in the 11th and 12th centuries, with three canals (Sensa, Misericordia, and Madonna dell'Orto) laid out in a regular plan. Equally straight lanes and canals were cut to the north, opening up views of the lagoon; turn right at one of these, Calle del Capitello, which leads back to **Sant'Alvise***, a prime candidate for the title of 'loneliest church in Venice'.*

When this island was reclaimed in the 14th century, a Doge's daughter named Antonia Vernier had a vision of St Louis of Toulouse and founded a monastery in his name (*Aloisius* in Latin, hence *Alvise* in Venetian). Its brick Gothic façade of 1388 is so severe it hurts; 'OW—!' says its peephole rose window and doorway; behind it stands an equally severe little campanile. The interior is hardly as stern: rearranged in the 17th century and recently restored, it features an early version of a *barca*, or 'nuns' choir', hanging over the door, with wrought iron grilles over the windows to preserve the nuns' anonymity. S. Alvise's weightiest art is by Giambattista Tiepolo: *The Crown of Thorns* and *Flagellation* (both 1738–40) on the right wall, and the enormous, scenographic *Road to Calvary* (1743) newly restored in the choir, a composition inspired by Tintoretto and glowing with freshly restored health. The *trompe l'oeil* ceiling, with a huge building rising up in crazy perspective, is a joint effort by two obscure 17th-century painters, Antonio Torri and Paolo Ricchi.

To the left of the entrance are eight charmingly naive panels of Old Testament scenes in tempera (currently under restoration) that are known as the 'baby Carpaccios' thanks to the overheated brain of Ruskin, who considered them precocious works by the Renaissance master (Carpaccio would have been about eight when they were painted). More solid art scholars assign the paintings to Carpaccio's master, Lazzaro Bastiani or more likely, to his workshop. Ruskin's favourite was the second panel, *Solomon and the Queen of Sheba* with its scene of the medieval *Golden Legend of the Holy Cross*—the bridge in the picture is made of a tree St Michael gave to Seth to plant over the tomb of Adam, and the Queen of Sheba is warning Solomon not to cross it, for she has had a prophetic dream that it would some day bring about the end of the Jews. Solomon goes on to bury the beam, but it is dug up and shaped into the Cross. Another of the panels is *Joshua at the Walls of Jericho*, a ripping subject but one that painters rarely cared to tackle.

*If your arches are going the way of Jericho, there's a possible escape: the S. Alvise vaporetto stop just to the north (No. 5 circolare). But if you're still game, retrace your steps 'Sempre diritto!', as the Venetians say, straight on down Calle del Capitello, Calle de la Malvasia, and Calle degli Ormesini ('of the dealers in ormesin', a delicate fabric made in the Persian city Ormuz). Turn right at Calle del Porton ('big door'), where in the bad old days two massive doors would seal in the residents of the world's first **ghetto**. To reach its evocative, if melancholy and claustrophic centre, Campo di Ghetto Nuovo, walk down Calle del Ghetto Nuovissimo and right on Calle Farnese, where the houses loom over the water like a wall.*

One of Venice's Jewish historians, Elia Capsali, wrote: 'Having heard that the Germans were approaching Padua, like thorns in our eyes and prickles in our hearts, the majority of Jews hurried to escape to Venice. They took their money and came, for they feared for their very lives'. The *campo*'s seven bas-reliefs by Arbit Blatas in memory of 202 Holocaust victims may suggest that this is recent history. But Capsali was writing in 1508 about the approach of Emperor Maximilian's troops, in the War of the Cambrai. So many refugees swelled Venice's Jewish population that in 1516 the Senate decreed they should be isolated in one place, on an island known as the Ghetto Nuovo.

The word 'ghetto' derives from the foundry (*geto*) that occupied the island until 1390, when it was moved to the Arsenale; and the word came to be pronounced with a hard G thanks to its first German residents. The name was quickly borrowed for similar segregated neighbourhoods all over Europe, perhaps because it's poignantly apt in Hebrew (where the root for 'cut off' sounds very similar). And cut off its residents were, from midnight to dawn, on an island surrounded by a moat-like canal, all its watergates locked and patrolled by a miniature Christian navy whose wages were levied from the Jews. And although there were no restrictions in the daytime, the Church insisted that the Jews wear distinctive badges.

As bad as it was, the Republic seemed like a bed of roses compared to many states, and was one of the few places in Counter-Reformation Italy where Jews could live in peace; Venetian law specifically protected them and forbade preachers from inciting mobs against them—a common enough practice during the Counter-Reformation. Unfortunately, this treatment had little to do with any precocious concept of human rights: Venice's Jews were blackmailed for their security. Like most governments, Venice's exploited the Jews mercilessly, while their legal activities were limited to the rag trade, medicine, and money lending. Stalls were set up in the *campo*, known by the colours of their receipts, and some of the fittings of the red **Banco Rosso** still survive under the brick portico at No. 2912.

But the Venetians were also receptive to the culture and learning in the Ghetto, and had plenty of empathy for the Jews, whose tradition-bound mercantile society, halfway between Western and Eastern cultures, was similar to their own. The Ghetto's salons were among the most fashionable in the city; in the autumn people would come to see it as white as snow with goose down, plucked from the main ingredient of the season's religious feasts. And there was enough money left after gouging by the Republic for each new wave of immigrants to build a sumptuous synagogue, locally known as *scuole*.

To cope with the influx of refugees, the Ghetto was expanded twice, in 1541 into the adjacent Ghetto Vecchio (the old foundry, around Campo delle Scole) and in 1633, into the Ghetto Nuovissimo (Calle Farnese). Even so, to squeeze in a population that once numbered 5000, the houses of the Ghetto are the tallest in Venice, some rising seven storeys, with cramped low ceilings, eerily presaging the ghetto tenements of centuries to come. When Napoleon threw open the gates in 1797, it is said the few impoverished residents who remained were too weak to leave (although they recharged quickly; 50 years after Napoleon, it was a Jew named Daniele Manin who led the revolt against Austria).

Today the Ghetto remains the centre of the Jewish community in Venice, even if its 600 members now live all over the city: a nursing home, nursery school, library, and kosher restaurant are here, as is the **Museo Comunità Israelitica**, *on the edge of the* campo.

Open 10:20–1 and 2:30–5, Sun 10:30–1, closed Sat and Jewish holidays (adm L2000; L6000 for the guided tour of the synagogues at 11, 12, 3 and 4). The Museum opened in 1953 to display 17th- and 18th-century ritual objects—exotic *Rimmonim* (Torah finials) made in Turkey and Venice, old marriage contracts painted on parchment, prayer shawls, etc. Upstairs you can visit the elegant **Scuola Grande Tedesca** (1528), the first one built in the Ghetto, by German Jews, while the optional tour also gets you into two synagogues in the Campiello delle Scuole: the lavish **Scuola Spagnola** (for the Spanish congregation, redesigned by Longhena) and the equally deluxe **Scuola Leventina** (1538, for Levantine Jews). Two others, the **Scuola Italiana** (1575) and **Scuola al Canton**

(1531; not Chinese Jews, but from Provence) have long been closed for restoration, but you can make out their wooden roof gables around the Campo di Ghetto Nuovo.

*Sottoportico di Ghetto Vecchio (left of the Museum) leads past a Jewish baker's (no. 1143) and a large stone plaque, on the right, warning converted Jews of punishments ranging from the lash to the gallows for returning to the Ghetto. Duck under a last arch, and suddenly you are out on the broad, sundrenched fondamenta of one of Venice's main arteries, the **Canale di Cannaregio**, the mainland entrance to the city before the construction of the rail bridge. Turning right up the fondamenta, you'll pass the former French Embassy (No. 967) where Jean-Jacques Rousseau lived and worked as a secretary to the ambassador between 1743 and 44. Despite its setting in Venice, Rousseau manages to make this chapter the dullest in his* Confessions, *whining that he did all the work, although the truth was he was sacked after ten months. His few sordid visits to the ladies were just as inept—and described down to the smallest painful detail.*

*At the far end of the Canal, cross over by way of Andrea Tirali's **Ponte dei Tre Archi**, the only bridge in Venice with more than one arch; continue straight ahead to the Campo and Church of **San Giobbe**.*

Open 8:30–12 and 3–6. Job, the man who bore all, was canonized in the Eastern Church and in Venice for his hoped-for efficacy against the plague. The Church, founded by Doge Cristoforo 'Othello' Moro for the Franciscan Observants, dates back to the 1450s, but was remodelled soon after by Pietro Lombardo, who added its fine doorway, with statues in the lunette of *SS. Job and Francis*, and above, *SS. Louis of Toulouse, Anthony, and Bernardino* (the patron saint of advertising, who preached here and is the co-dedicatee). Inside, over the second altar is a *Vision of Job* in the marble frame of Bellini's great *Madonna Enthroned*, unfortunately removed to the Accademia, for it depicts the Virgin seated in the sanctuary of this very church. The grandiose **Monument of the Ambassador Paulmy d'Arge** (d. 1651) though cut in half in 1935, retains a pair of the ugliest, baldest cauliflower-eared lions in all Italy. In contrast with these shabby cats, the **sanctuary** is a sublime grey and white Renaissance vision by Pietro Lombardo, decorated with elegant carvings and the tomb slab of *Cristoforo Moro* (d. 1471) and his *Dogaressa*. The first chapel on the left was designed by Lombardo's Tuscan contemporaries for homesick silk workers from Lucca, with majolica tiles and della Robbia rondels.

A door on the right leads into the sacristy, passing by way of a *Nativity* (c. 1530), the only painting left in Venice by Gian Girolamo Savoldo, an artist who spent most of his career in the city, pioneering *tenebroso* night scenes that anticipate the Bassanos and Caravaggio. The sacristy preserves a wooden ceiling of the 1500s, a portrait of *Cristoforo Moro*, and a triptych of the *Annunciation, St Michael and St Anthony* by Antonio Vivarini and Giovanni d'Alemagna.

> *From S. Giobbe, walk back to the Cannaregio Canal. You may digress to the left, where the* fondamenta *continues to the Macelli Pubblici, or 'slaughterhouse', a site for which Le Corbusier designed a hospital in 1964 (though it was rejected by an architectural review board and never built, and even Le Corbusier agreed they were right). Across the Canal from the slaughterhouse is the locked-up* **Ricovero Penitenti***, a convent where Venice's prostitutes once came for a five-year reform course, far from the bright lights of the Ponte delle Tette (see Walk V).*
>
> *Otherwise, turn right at the Canal; the* fondamenta *approaches the vast 17th-century* **Palazzo Savorgnan***, Venetian headquarters of a Friulian dynasty of great wealth and impeccable service to the Republic. Just before it, though, turn left on the anonymous Calle Riello, turning left again at the Calle di Misericordia, for the tawdry and unabashedly touristy* **Lista di Spagna***; in its more dignified heyday, this street led to the Spanish Embassy (no. 168, now the regional offices of the Veneto) instead of to a soggy slice of pizza. In 1618, when Venice was the European capital of intrigue and espionage, the Spanish Ambassador, the Marquis of Bedmar, masterminded a comic plot involving spies and a ruse to bring in a Spanish army, a few men at a time, in civilian clothes. Thanks to a patriotic prostitute, the Ten sniffed out the plot, resulting in the arrest and execution of 300 people, including many down and out patricians whose service were for sale.*
>
> *Turn right; the Lista di Spagna ends at the station. Right before it, eternally obscured by a wall of African pedlars, stands the Church of the* **Scalzi***. It was built in the 1670s by Geromalo Cavazza, a nouveau riche celebrating his recent admission to the Golden Book.*

The Carmelite Scalzi ('barefoot', though they wore sandals) were a prestigious religious order, and although Cavazza flamboyantly financed them (74,000 ducats, he boasted), the friars could have spent it better than on the petrified operetta stuck on Giuseppe Sardi's perilous façade—the figure of *Hope* has already fallen off and broken into bits. Letting Baldassare Longhena follow his fancy in the interior wasn't a good idea, either, resulting in gloomy, opulent, overpopulated Baroque encrustations from the dark side of his imagination (shadows he managed to keep out of his masterpiece, the Salute). In 1915 an Austrian bomb addressed to the train station fell through the Scalzi's roof, turning the Scalzi's prize work, Giambattista Tiepolo's celebrated buoyant ceiling of *The Miracle of the House of Loreto*, into a million-piece jigsaw puzzle. The largest fragments have been preserved in the Accademia, which also has a study of the work—a Baroque version of Dorothy's twister-blown house in the *Wizard of Oz*. The house was the Virgin Mary's, which miraculously picked itself up and flew to Dalmatia, and later took off again to settle at Loreto, near Ancona, where you can see it today. In its place is Ettore Tito's modern *Council of Ephesus*.

The second chapel on the right bears a stone marked: 'Manini Cineres', all that marks the passing of the last doge, the weak and melancholic Ludovico Manin (d. 1802). The chapel's ceiling, *S. Teresa in Glory*, is one of Tiepolo's less exalted works. Altogether this is the spookiest church in Venice, with an ambience that can only be matched by the major basilicas of Rome and Naples. The filthy Baroque ensemble entertains a chorus of odd women whenever the church is open, chanting prayers in loud metallic voices, often with an audience of snoring railroad workers who have ducked out of the station for a quick snooze.

> *There are plenty of bars around the station to stop for an* ombretta *before stumping through the last leg of Cannaregio, back down the dire Lista di Spagna to* **Campo San Geremia**, *once a favourite venue for bullfights; on one memorable occasion, the mighty patrician Girolamo Savorgnan joined the toreadors and neatly decapitated two sharp horned bulls with single strokes of his sword to the admiring cheers of the Spanish ambassador. The far side of the square has the* **Palazzo Labia** *(1750, with its main façade on the Canale di Cannaregio).*

By appointment only (see above). Now owned by the RAI, Italy's state radio and television, something about this Palace has always made its residents go over the top (perhaps because it was designed in part by Alessandro Tremignon, the architect of S. Moisè). It was built for a fabulously wealthy and slightly dotty Spanish family who paid their way into the Golden Book and then paid Giambattista Tiepolo to fresco their ballroom with *The Life of Cleopatra* (1745–50), obviously a family role model in extravagance. Recently restored, along with Gerolamo Mengozzi-Colonna's fine *trompe l'oeil* architectural frescoes, they are a sheer delight, sensuous and lavish in their illusionist perspectives; on one wall, a very 18th-century Venetian Antony and Cleopatra seem to step down the painted stair to join the guests in the ballroom.

The very thin line in Venice between the real and illusionary inspired one of the Labias, at a legendary party, to toss the family's gold dinner service out the window into the canal, a memorable occasion for his pun: '*L'abia or non l'abia, sarò sempre Labia*' ('Have it or not, I'll always be a Labia'). Nets hidden in the canal, however, made sure that the Labias kept it.

The Labia's Palace shares the campo *with the 18th-century Church of* **San Geremia** *and its hoary 11th-century campanile.*

Though not much of a looker from the outside, S. Geremia improves within. Unlike most churches, however, the focal point is not the high altar but the **Cappella S. Lucia**, where St Lucy's mummy was moved in 1863, after her church was demolished to make way for the train station. It was only one of Lucy's many moves, as the recent paintings around her altar attest. Lucia was a maiden of Syracuse, in Sicily, who was martyred in 304 or 310, during Diocletian's persecutions, and buried in Syracuse's catacombs. In 1038 the Byzantines took her to Constantinople; in 1204, the Venetians, who simply couldn't pass up a good saint, brought her to Venice. She was stolen again from this church in 1981 by an unknown party, but miraculously was rediscovered on her feast day.

The association of Lucia with *lux* or *luce* (light) went naturally with her appointed Feast Day, 13 December, close enough to the winter solstice to latch several old pagan holidays onto her name, especially in Scandanavia. From light, Lucia became associated with eyesight, and she has been portrayed in much religious art holding a pair of eyes on a tray like two sunnyside-up eggs (as in the little shop next to the mummy, where you can buy cards of the saint and her eye dish in a choice of 80 languages). And as many myths are believed to have been derived from misinterpreting drawings, so a whole legend has grown up that she was martyred by having her eyes pulled out, or that she pulled them out herself to keep from marrying a pagan cad.

From the campo, *Salizzada S. Geremia leads to the* **Ponte delle Guglie** *(1580, named after the four obelisks, or 'needles' on its parapets). Follow the throngs down Rio Terrà S. Leonardo, often crowded with market stalls, and turn right where it widens at Campiello dell'Anconetta, down Rio Terrà del Cristo. This winds around to* **San Marcuolo**, *whose unfinished corrugated grey façade is one the Grand Canal's sore thumbs.*

Although Marcuolo sounds like an affectionate diminuative of S. Marco, it is actually Venetian for Santi Ermagora e Fortunato, a remarkable transformation that even the Venetians themselves can't account for. Every Venetian church has its quirk: in S. Marcuolo it's two pulpits, facing each other across the nave as if set up for theological debate. A wildly Rococo canopy hangs over the altar. To the right there's a copy of Tintoretto's *Washing of the Feet*; the original is now in Newcastle.

Ponte Storto ('crooked bridge') leads from behind the Church to the land entrance of the **Palazzo Vendramin-Calergi**, *with a plaque recording the death here of Richard Wagner in 1883. If the ghost of the great Teutonic bandleader should ever choose to return, it would probably be frightened away by the vulgar clicking of chips and roulette balls, for this Palace is now the winter home of Venice's Casino, open from October to March. If you're not in the mood for giving the Venetians even more of your money, pass it by for* vaporetto *Nos. 1 or 2 and a chug down the Grand Canal.*

The Lagoon

S. Maria Assunta, Torcello.

S. Giorgio Maggiore—Giudecca—The Lido—Chioggia—Smaller Islands—S. Michele—Murano—Burano—S. Francesco del Deserto—Torcello—Cavallino and Jesolo—Villas along the Brenta

Venice's Lagoon is one of its wonders, a desolate, often melancholy and strange, often beautiful and seductive 'landscape' with a hundred personalities. It is 56 km long and averages about 8 km across, adding up to some 448 square km; half of it, the *Laguna Morta* ('Dead Lagoon'), where the tides never reach, consists of mud flats except in the spring, while the shallows of the *Laguna Viva* are always submerged, and cleansed by tides twice a day. To navigate this treacherous sea, the Venetians have developed highways of channels, marked by *bricole*— wooden posts topped by orange lamps—that keep their craft from running aground. When threatened, the Venetians only had to pull out the *bricole* to confound their enemies; and as such the Lagoon was always known as 'the sacred walls of the nation.'

> The city of the Venetians, by divine providence founded in the waters and protected by their environment, is defended by a wall of water. Therefore should anybody in any manner dare to infer damage to the public waters he shall be considered as an enemy of our country and shall be punished by no less pain than that committed to whomever violates the sacred border of the country. This act will be enforced forever.
>
> —*16th-century edict of the* Magistrato alle Acque

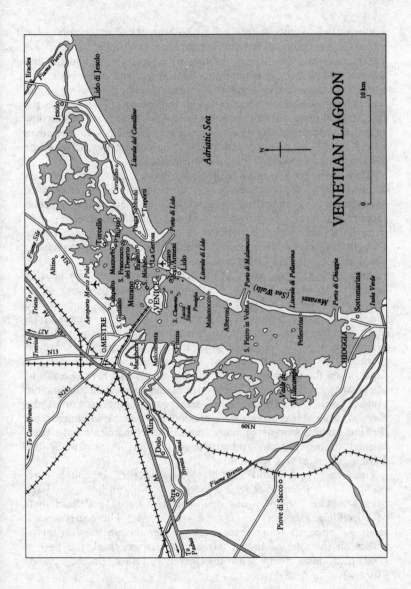

VENETIAN LAGOON

Adriatic Sea

10 km

0

N

Eraclea
Fiume Piave
Lido di Jesolo
Jesolo
Cavallino
Fiume Sile
Litorale del Cavallino
Punta Sabbioni
Treporti
Altino
To Trieste
To Treviso
A27
N13
Aeroporto Marco Polo
S. Giuliano
Campalto
MESTRE
N245
To Castelfranco
N4
To Padua
Stra
Dolo
Mira
Brenta Canal
Fiume Brenta
Piove di Sacco
N309
Valle de Millecampi
Torcello
Mazzorbo
Burano
S. Francesco del Deserto
S. Michele
Erasmo
Murano
Porto di Lido
Porto di Lido
La Certosa
S. Lazzaro degli Armeni
VENICE
Lido
Litorale di Lido
S. Clemente
Sacca Sessola
Poveglia
Malamocco
Alberoni
S. Pietro in Volta
Porto di Malamocco
(Sea Walls)
Litorale di Pellestrina
Pellestrina
Marghera
Malcontenta
Fusina
Porto di Chioggia
CHIOGGIA
Murazzi
Sottomarina
Isola Verde

265

Unfortunately Venice's 'forever' ended with the 20th century. New islands were made of landfill dredged up to deepen the shipping canals, upsetting the delicate balance of Lagoon life; outboards and *vaporetti* churn up the gook from the Lagoon and canal beds, and send corroding waves against Venice's buildings. Purists fight, without any notable success, to ban all motor boats. These effect the tide, and increase both the number of *aquae alte* and unnaturally low tides, that embarassingly expose Venice's underthings—and let air in where it was never supposed to go, accelerating the rot and the subsidence of its wooden piles and substructures.

Then there are the ingredients in the water itself. The Lagoon is a messy stew of 50 years' worth of organic waste, phosphates, agricultural and industrial by-products and sediments—a lethal mixture that local ecologists warn will take a hundred years to purify, even if by some miracle polution is stopped now. It's a sobering thought, especially when many Venetians in their 40s remember when even the Grand Canal was clean enough to swim in.

And more recently, the Lagoon has been sprouting the kind of blooms that break a girl's heart—algae, 'green pastures' of it, choking its fish and stinking out many tourists in the summer. No one is sure if the algae epidemic isn't just part of a natural cycle; after all, there's an ancient church on one Lagoon island called S. Giorgio in Alga (St George in Algae). Crops of algae are on record in the 1700s and 1800s and at the beginning of this century, at times when the water temperatures were abnormally high because of warm weather. But other statistics are harder to reconcile to climatic cycles: since 1932, 78 species of algae have disappeared from the Lagoon, while 24 new ones have blossomed, these mostly microalgae thriving off the surplus of phosphates. These chemicals have been banned in the Lagoon communities—and just coincidentally the 1990 algae count was way down.

Once the major islands (39 in all) were densely inhabited, each occupied by a town or at least a monastery. Now all but a few have been abandoned; many a tiny one, with its forlorn, vandalized shell of a building, has been overgrown with weeds. There are a wide range of plans to bring them back to life, though most seem to wither on the vine of Italian bureaucracy. If you think you have a good idea, take it up with the Revenue Office (Intendenza di Finanza).

Islands in the South Lagoon

San Giorgio Maggiore

The islet of S. Giorgio Maggiore (*vaporetto* No. 5) the most prominent landmark across the Bacino S. Marco from the Piazza, has been home to a Benedictine monastery since 982. A major restoration project in the 16th and 17th centuries endowed it with its present buildings by Palladio and Longhena, creating a major Late Reniassance and Baroque architectural showcase. All fell into decline in the 19th century, when Napoleon suppressed the monastery and confiscated its property and artworks; in compensation, with a keen sense of the absurd, he made the itty bitty island a free port (you can still see its twin Lilliputian lighthouses designed by a professor of architecture for the occasion). And although only a handful of monks still linger on to maintain the Church, most of the complex has been beautifully restored as part of the Giorgio Cini Foundation, established by Count Vittorio Cini as a memorial to his son, who died in a plane crash in 1949. The Foundation is dedicated to the arts and the sciences of the sea (it's the Foundation's ship you may see occupying most of the harbour of the old free port) and holds frequent conferences and special exhibits. Ring ahead (tel 528 9900) to make an appointment to visit the monastic buildings, as they aren't always open.

Palladio's **Church of S. Giorgio Maggiore** (open 9–12:30 and 2–6:30) like St Mark's Campanile, is such an integral part of Venice that many visitors, having seen it painted on a hundred pizza parlour walls, look at it without really seeing it. Its importance in the history of architecture is in Palladio's solution to the Renaissance problem of sticking a classical temple façade on a church with naves and side chapels. The dissenting opinion, as usual most thunderously expressed by Ruskin, is that the problem was ridiculous to begin with and the result couldn't be 'more childish in conception, more servile in plagiarism' etc. But if like Ruskin you find the façade ridiculous, a white mask of recycled classicism stuck on good red brick, it's hard to deny that its colour and clean lines are immensely effective where they are, hanging between the water and sky, bathed by a diaphanous, ever-changing light as magical as the variations caught in Monet's series on the *Cathedral of Rouen*.

The **interior** is equally white and clear of cluttering detail, but as theatrical as the façade in its play of light and shadow. To compensate for the exceptional length of the nave and aisle, Palladio subtly raised the height of the floor near the high altar. On the entrance wall is the **Tomb of Doge Leonardo Donà** (d. 1612), the great humanist and friend of Galileo and Sarpi, who calmly snapped his fingers at the Great Interdict of 1606. Above the first altar on the right, Jacopo Bassano's dark *Adoration of the Shepherds* is illuminated entirely (and rather alarmingly) by the Child; the 15th-century wooden *Crucifix* on the next altar is equally unnerving in its vivid agony. The painting over the third altar, with its striking diagonals, is from the workshop of Tintoretto. The **high altar**, black in contrast with the snowy whiteness, is topped by a statue of *Christ* with a triangular halo standing on a globe. On either side of the chancel hang the two masterpieces of Tintoretto's old age, *The Fall of Manna* and an extraordinary and dynamic *Last Supper* (1594).

In the choir behind the altar, *Scenes from the Life of St Benedict* (1590s) are told with Counter-Reformation fervour in the carvings on the wooden stalls and lectern. On the balustrade are two bronze saints, *George* and *Stephen*, by Niccolò Roccatagliata (1593); the latter's body was brought to this church from Constantinople in 1100, and on Christmas Eve, all Venice would sail over in fairy-lit boats to pay homage to his relics. From the choir a door on the right leads into a corridor containing the *Monument to Doge Domenico Michiel* (d. 1130), proudly described as the 'Terror of the Greeks' and the 'Lament of Hungary'; at the end is the **Cappella dei Morti**, or 'Chapel of the Dead', containing Tintoretto's last painting, rather appropriately a *Deposition*, completed by his son Domenico. The photo here of Carpaccio's *St George Slaying the Dragon*—a later variation on the canvas in S. Giorgio degli Schiavoni, more autumnal in tone, though the dragon's appetite, judging from the leftovers, is as fierce as ever. The original is housed in a locked room where the Conclave of 1799–1800 (on the run from Napoleon) met to elect Pius VII.

Left of the choir you'll find the lift up to S. Giorgio's **Campanile** (same opening hours as Church; L2000). Although its forerunner collapsed in 1791, as all Venice's bell towers seem cursed to do sooner or later, the replacement offers a view rivalled only by the one from St Mark's, and includes a bird's eye view into the cloisters of the **Monastery**.

Always the most important of several Benedictine houses in the Lagoon, S. Giorgio was noted for its scholarship, thanks to Cosimo de' Medici, who in 1433 spent his brief exile from Florence here in the company of his favourite architect, Michelozzo. The two busied themselves building and endowing the Monastery's first library, later demolished in the 16th-century rebuilding plan. The first, or **Cloister of the Cypresses** was designed by Palladio, which as has been noted, looks more like a palace courtyard than aa religious cloister. The **Library**, by Longhena, with elegant 17th-century wood shelving by Francesco Pauc, separates it from the second, or **Cloister of the Laurels**, by Andrea Buora. Adjacent to the latter is Palladio's first work for the Monastery, the magnificent **Refectory** (1559–63, now a conference hall); it was from here that Napoleon pinched Veronese's *Marriage at Cana*, now in the Louvre. Don't miss the **Grand Staircase** (1643) that Longhena built off Palladio's cloister, a theatrical masterpiece in a limited space that was very avant-garde in its day, and inspired many a northern Italian architect.

Giudecca

The beautiful painting of Venice in the Bodleian Library's *Codex of Marco Polo* shows a Lagoon full of swans and the Giudecca like a rocky desert, populated only by lions. No one is even sure if this long, tilde-shaped series of suburban islets was named for Venice's Jews, forced to live here before being removed to the Ghetto, or for its more rumbustious nobles, exiled here in the 9th century, far from the action on the Rialto. For many centuries it was a little garden oasis, until the 1800s, when it became a little Industrial Revolution oasis. Although many of its factories are now abandoned (especially the vast Mulino Stucky, the massive Neo-Gothic flour mill on the Giudecca's west end), some are still in business, making watches and Fortuny silks. A few trendy touches have accompanied the Cipriani Hotel, Venice's most expensive, but for the most part, the Giudecca is a place where the Venetians go about their daily business with a little more room than the centre affords; some even have flower gardens, an extraordinary luxury in Venice.

The Hotel is near the Church of **Le Zitelle** ('the old maids', 1582), built on Palladio's design after his death; the old maids in question lived in a benevolent hostel for the poor (on either side of the Church) and helped support themselves by making Venice's most rarefied, delicate lace, *punto in aria*. Inside, the Zitelle is built on a square plan with rounded corners for better accoustics; the girls from La Pietà used to perform here (only open Sunday mornings for mass). The Neo-Venetian Gothic house, with the large arched windows that you can't help but notice to the right of the Zitelle, was built in 1910 as a studio by a painter named Mario de Maria. Another artist named Michelangelo spent a few months in a nearby villa, sulking during his exile from Medici-ruled Florence in 1529. Calle di Michelangelo is the only street that crosses the width of the Giudecca; from its far end you can see the Lido. To the left are the Cipriani Gardens. The even larger 'Garden of Eden' (named after the Englishman who planted it) is to the west, down the picturesque Ramo della Croce and over an iron bridge, but there's no public access.

A short walk down the *fondamenta* stands the Giudecca's chief attraction, the Church of the **Redentore** (open 7:30–12 and 3:30–7), built in thanksgiving after the end of the savage plague of 1575–76 that killed 46,000 Venetians. Palladio was chosen to design a votive church by the Doge and *Signoria*, who vowed to pay an annual pilgrimage on the third Sunday in July for the *Festa del Redentore*—still a red letter day on the Venetian calendar. Of all Palladio's churches, the Redentore, concecrated in 1592, is the most successful and harmonious, the simple geometric triangles and rectangles of its façade composed in fine-tuned proportions; like Palladio's Venetian villas it is set atop a wide flight of stairs. The interior at first glance a simple rectangular nave leading back to an apse, actually opens up into curves on three sides crowned by a beautiful dome, the whole effect 'like a bubble structure softly blown from a tube,' as Michael Levey put it. This is where the *Signoria* gathered for the service. Unfortunately it's all become a bit dingy, and the dome area is apt to be roped off. On request, the sacristan will open the sacristy, where Alvise Vivarini's *Madonna with Child* holds pride of place among dusty paintings and some eyeball-rolling wax effigies from the 1700s.

Continuing west along the *fondamenta* and over the long iron Ponte Longo. the last church on the Giudecca is the oldest, **Sant' Eufemia**, founded in the 9th century on a basilican plan like Torcello's, and rebuilt in the same form in the 11th century (open 9–12 and 6–7). Like all the churches facing Venice, it has a classically-inspired façade, Doric this time, pasted on in the 1500s, while inside some of its Veneto-Byzantine capitals keep company with Rococo glitz and plush fittings added 700 years later. The first chapel on the right contains the Church's one notable painting, the 1480 *S. Rocco and the Angel* by Bartolomeo Vivarini. Weedy, seedy **Campo S. Cosmo** just inland from the S. Eufemia landing, is one of the most remote corners in Venice, and the last square to keep its 19th-century earth paving. There isn't much use continuing west of the Mulino Stucky to **Sacca Fisola**, a landfill island covered with modern flats, unless you're in a mood for a swim at the municipal pool.

The Lido

> ... the poetic desert of former days may only be regretted by
> self-centred and melancholy snobs.
>
> —*Pompeo Molmenti*

The Lido—*the* Lido that give its name to countless bathing establishments, bars, arcades and cinemas all over the world—is one of the long spits of land or *lidi* that form the protective outer barrier of the Lagoon. For most of its history it was a wild sandy place, a place to go riding, as Byron did daily to cure his urban claustrophobia, and a place to store the French Crusaders in 1202, until they agreed to Doge Dandolo's terms of paying for their transport by doing a favour or two for Venice *en route*.

In the 18th century, the only people who swam off the Lido were courtesans, whose lascivious beach parties were one of Venice's tourist attractions. In 1857, the first reputable bathing establishment was opened, and by the turn of the century seaside holidays on the Lido were the rage. On its 12 km of beach, the world's poets, potentates and plutocrats spent the halcyon days before World War I in palatial hotels and villas, making the Lido the pinnacle of Belle Epoque fashion, so brilliantly evoked in Thomas Mann's novel and Visconti's film version of *Death in Venice*. And even though families with their trunks and maids no longer descend on the Lido for the entire summer, it's still a popular enough place, the playground of the Venetians and their visitors, where they can drive their cars, go riding, play tennis or golf or parachute out of aeroplanes. It is also expensive, overcrowded, and annoying, with its sticky hierarchy of private bathing establishments and Italians showing off their fancy swimming togs, parked like tidy sardines under their parasols. The free beach, the **Spiaggia Comunale**, is on the north part of the island, a 15-minute walk from the *vaporetto* stop at S. Nicolò (go down the Gran Viale and turn left on the Lungomare d'Annunzio), where you can hire a changing hut and frolic in the fine sand and not-so-fine sea.

If, upon landing at the S. Nicolò stop, you walk north instead of east, you will soon pass the little church of **San Nicolò**, where the doge, in his role as bridegroom of the sea, would meet the patriarch for some mumbo-jumbo over the fake relics of Santa Claus, or St Nicholas of Myra. Though founded in 1044, there's nothing very compelling about it, if there ever was; if the body snatchers had grabbed the real bones it would have been far more grand. But near here, looking north towards

271

the **Porto di Lido** (the most important of the three *porti*, or sea entrances to the Lagoon, where the doge tossed his gold ring to the waves) is the mighty octagonal **Fortezza di Sant'Andrea** on the island of Le Vignole, built in 1543 by Venice's fortifications' genius Sammicheli. In times of danger, a great chain was extended from the fort across the channel. The Lido was also the site of Venice's first Jewish cemetery, founded in 1386 (from the S. Nicolò stop, follow Via Cipro. This first passes a small Catholic cemetery, where Protestant headstones from a graveyard, now under the airport runway, have been deposited).

Buses from the *vaporetto* stop will take you down Lungomare Marconi to the centre of Lido swish. *Death in Venice* was set and filmed in the **Grand Hotel des Bains**, just north of the Mussolini-style **Municipal Casino** and the **Palazzo de Cinema**, where Venice hosts its International Film Festival.

From the Lido to Chioggia

Buses/ferries (Line 11) from the Lido's *vaporetto* landing run all the way south to the fishing port of Chioggia, following the line between the sea and Lagoon. Schedules change, but the bus usually leaves once an hour; count on half a day to get to Chioggia, walk around (and perhaps have lunch) and return to Venice. It's a fine excursion when you need a rest for aching feet or a brain too saturated by art and churches, and if you go in the morning (except on Mondays) you can visit Chioggia's famous fish market.

After the Lido, the bus passes through **Malamocco**, a tranquil fishing village named after the first capital of the Lagoon townships, a nearby islet that lost its status after Pepin and the Franks nabbed it in 810. The capital moved to the Rialto, leaving the original Malamocco to poetically sink into the sea during a mighty storm in 1106. Next is the small resort of **Alberoni**, home of the Lido Golf Course and the ferry to cross over the Porto di Malamocca for the island of Pellestrina, an island reef even thinner than the Lido. It has two sleepy villages, S. **Pietro in Volta** and **Pellestrina**, where the **Murazzi**, or sea walls, begin, the last great public works project of the Republic's *Magistrato alle Acque*. Built in response to increased flooding in the 18th century, the 4-km long Murazzi are constructed of huge, white Istrian blocks and built, as their plaque proudly states: '*Ausu Romano—Aere Veneto*' ('With Roman audacity and Venetian money'). From 1782 until 4 November 1966 they succeeded in holding back the flood.

Chioggia, the dusty, southernmost town on the Lagoon, is one of the most important fishing ports on the Adriatic, a kind of working-class Venice where the canals and streets are arrow straight; where the sails of the fishing fleet are painted with brightly coloured pictures and symbols. The morning **fish market**, brimming with some of Neptune's most exotic and tastiest fry, is one of the wonders of Italy.

The Chioggians have a not entirely undeserved reputation for grumpiness, a temperament that is hardly improved when the uppity Venetians call their little lion up on its column in the Piazzetta Vigo (where the ferry deposits you) the 'Cat of St Mark'. Goldoni was amused enough by it all to make the town the setting of one of his comedies, the *Baruffe Chizzotte*.

Almost nothing remains of medieval Chioggia, thanks to the blockade and siege of Genoa's fleet in the 1380 War of Chioggia. But if you take the first bridge left from the port and continue straight, you will eventually reach the church of **San Domenico**, which boasts Carpaccio's last painting, *St Paul*. The town's other churches are strung out along the main street, the Corso del Popolo—the fish market is just beyond a large 14th-century grain warehouse, the **Granaio**, with a relief of the *Madonna* on the façade by Sansovino. Further up the Corso, past a couple of low-key churches, is the **Duomo**, or cathedral, built by Longhena after the 14th-century orginal, except for the campanile, burned in 1623. In the chapel to the left of the altar are some murky, unpleasant 18th-century paintings of martyrdoms, one attributed to Tiepolo though it's hard to believe.

And when you've had your fill of fish and the locals, you can stroll along the long bridge (or catch the bus at the Duomo) for a swim among the vivacious Italian families at Chioggia's Lido, **Sottomarina**. You can return to Venice by the same route or take the dismal shorter bus ride to Piazzale Roma.

Smaller Islands

One of the smaller islands just west of the Lido, with its landmark onion-domed campanile, is **San Lazzaro degli Armeni** (*vaporetto* No. 10 from Riva degli Schiavone, open to visitors Thurs and Sun 2:45). S. Lazzaro was Venice's leper colony in the Middle Ages, and was long deserted when in 1715 it was given to the Armenian noble and monk, Manug di Pietro, expelled from the Morea by the Turks. The Armenian colony in Venice already dated back to the 13th century (their church,

273

S. Croce degli Armeni, is right around the corner from St Mark's) and their presence has been maintained on a high level by these islanders, the Mechitarist Fathers of the Armenian Catholic Church; S. Lazzaro is one of the major centres of Armenian culture. Its monks are noted linguists and its famous polyglot press is able to print in 32 languages—one of the last presses to remain in a city celebrated for its publishing. It was the only island-monastery to survive Napoleon—apparently thanks to an Armenian in the French bureaucracy.

The fathers will take you on a guided tour of S. Lazzaro and its amazing library, with books dating back to the 5th century (the Armenians, after all, were the first nation to convert to Christianity, around the year 300). Elsewhere are oddities like a statue of *Napoleon's son*, the King of Rome, and a room of Byron memorabilia (Byron spent a winter visiting the fathers and bruising his brain with Armenian). The fathers offer inexpensive prints of Venice for sale; or else they would appreciate a donation.

Another islet just west of the Lido, **San Servolo**, was originally a Benedictine monastery, and from 1725–1978 an insane asylum. Now it is an International Centre of Oncology (the study of tumours), and there are projects to make it a European University of the Environment. The smaller islet of **La Grazia**, in the 13th century a stopover for pilgrims travelling to the East, is now a hospital for infectious diseases and rehabilitative medicine. To the south, **San Clemente**, long a monastery, has another hospital, for chronic mental diseases; planners think it would serve better as a tourist resort.

Further south is the **Lazzaretto Vecchio**, dedicated to St Mary Nazaretum (Nazareth), a 13th-century asylum for poor and sick pilgrims. In 1423 it became Europe's first public hospital for contagious diseases, its principal task to isolate plague victims. In time Nazaretum was corrupted to 'Lazzaretto'—the name given to all such hospitals and quarantine islands in Europe. In the 20th century the island became a military garrison, and now the huts are used as a home for stray dogs. There are some plans to make the island a centre of ancient Venetian crafts and trades.

Among the islands currently in a state of limbo are **Sant'Angelo delle Polveri**, first a women's convent and then a gunpowder factory that blew up in 1689 when struck by lightning; its last residents, the military, abandoned it in 1946. Then there's **Sacca Sessola**, an artificial island made of material dredged to make a commercial port for Venice in 1870. It was a tuberculosis hospital until 1980, and may someday be used as another youth hostel or a university of the environment. Between Sacca Sessola and S. Giorgio Maggiore flow the deep currents of a canal, making it the ideal place to execute death sentences by drowning, especially discreet ones ordered by the Ten; hence its sinister name, Orfano Canal, or 'orphans' canal'. **Santo Spirito**, a monastery since the 12th century, was given a major boost in the 16th century when Sansovino designed its church and Titian punted out to paint some of its ceiling frescoes. The Order was suppressed in 1656, and in 1965 the city council purchased it; badly vandalized, it waits, 'in a dramatic condition of decay' with only a few flakes of colour left from Titian's brush.

Further south lies the island of **Poveglia** (a corruption of *popilia*, or poplars) once boasting a thriving salt and wine economy. From the 9th century, it was inhabited by retired servants of the doge, who had their own government, run by a ducal chamberlain; according to legend, the residents of Poveglia led the fight against Pepin when he tried to approach the Rialto. In the War of Chioggia it wasn't so lucky, and was converted to a fortress, suffering such damage that it never regained its population. The hospital on it closed in the 1960s, and there are plans to convert it into an Italian Touring Club resort. One last little island, **San Giorgio in Alga** ('St George in Algae') was a monastery until Napoleon; it suffered further indignities under the Austrians, and has been abandoned ever since.

Islands in the North Lagoon

San Michele: the Island of the Dead

To get there take *vaporetto* No. 5 which runs from Venice to Murano.

All Venetians eventually take that last gondola ride to S. Michele, Venice's walled cemetery island, where the massive cypresses shoot up like the pinnacles of a secret evergreen metropolis. The first church was built on the island in the 10th century, and from 1212–1810 it belonged to a Camaldolesian monastery that produced many scholars, most notably the cosmographer Fra Mauro (d. 1459), of such international renown that King Alfonso V of Portugal commissioned a world map of him. All of his works have been lost, sadly, save his celebrated map in the Biblioteca Nazionale Marciana—the most accurate in showing the dimensions of the world of 1459. It is said that when Fra Mauro presented this map to a senator, the Senator's first question was: 'Well, so where's

Venice?' When Mauro pointed out the tiny dot, the Senator was enraged to find that the cosmographer had made the city so small. Mauro tried to explain: compared to the vast extent of the world, Venice was indeed quite tiny. The Senator listened to his reasoning impatiently, then ordered him as a patriotic son of the Republic: *'Strenze el mondo, e fé Venezia più grande!'* ('Make the world smaller and Venice bigger!').

Next to S. Michele's *vaporetto* stop is Mauro Codussi's first work in Venice, the church of **S. Michele** (1469), revolutionary not only in its style (an adaptation of the local Gothic tri-lobed church) but in its use of white Istrian stone in its façade, which soon became the rage in Venice. (If the front door isn't open, go under the gateway to the right, under the carving of *St George and the Dragon*, and cross the pretty cloister to the church's second entrance). Another famous Venetian friar, Fra Paolo Sarpi is buried under the lozenge by the front door (d. 1623; see p. 251); his remains were relocated here when his monastery S. Servolo was demolished in 1828. S. Michele's interior, with its muddly proportions, lacks the conviction of the façade, and is shown up by the domed, hexagonal **Cappella Emiliana** off to the left of the nave, a pale marbled Renaissance gem, designed in 1530 by Guglielmo dei Grigi.

The cemetery, joined from the cloister, is open daily from 7:30–4. Like any Italian *campo santo*, the deceased, depending on the station they attained in life, are installed in detached houses, villas, or council flats; here though, after ten years, the lease is up (unless you pay extra) and the bones are shipped out to an ossuary to make room for a new tenant. Signs indicate the way to the *'Acattolica'* section to the left of the first hemicycle, where Time and Neglect have staged a trial run for the Judgement Day. But here lie the cemetery's foreign celebrities: Serge Diaghilev (1872–1929), whose burial was marked by a devotee leaping into the open tomb, and Diaghilev's favourite composer, Igor Stravinsky (1882–1971), who died in New York but requested to be buried here, in the Russian Orthodox section; the Venetians were so pleased that they gave him a doge-like funeral in SS. Giovanni e Paolo. In the Protestant section you can find the quiet, rather neglected tombs of two writers who were certainly cranky and unpleasant enough in life, Baron Corvo and Ezra Pound. To get to these you must pass through a section of children's tombs. Venice traditionally had one of the highest birthrates in Italy, perhaps because the mortality rate historically has been high; when a child died, parents comforted themselves with the thought that they would serve as advocates for the family in Heaven.

Murano

In 1291 all of Venice's glass furnaces were moved to the ancient island city of Murano, the better to control the risk of fire and industrial espionage. For Venice made the finest glass in Europe—transparent crystal, spectacles, blown glass mirrors and coloured glass and beads (see Venetian Topics, 'Heart of Glass', pp. 29–31)—and it held on to its secrets until the early 17th century. To meet the demand for *cristallo di Venezia* the kilns burned day and night, where the glass workers laboured in shifts in the searing heat, except in August and September; in those months they relaxed at bullfights and 'other rowdy sports'.

But the glassmakers had other compensations as well. Even more than the pampered *arsenalotti* they were treated with kid gloves, the aristocrats of Venetian artisans, ennobled, they claimed, by the French King Henri III on his way from Poland to France. Murano was permitted to govern itself as a kind of autonomous republic of glass, with a population of 30,000, minting its own coins, policing itself, even developing its own 'Golden Book', whose enlistees built solid palaces along Murano's own Grand Canal. Patricians and humanist scholars from Venice retreated here to summer villas with luxurious summer gardens, where they strolled under the trees like the ancient Greeks discussing art and philosophy in their academies. In 1376 a law was passed declaring that any male child of a patrician and a glassblower's daughter could sit in the Maggior Consiglio; other laws were passed to discourage glassmakers from being tempted abroad and divulging their secrets (their families would be imprisoned, and assassins employed by the Ten would be set on their trail—though as before, these stories were mostly psychological bluster, for there are historical references to Murano glassblowers living quite well and openly in other cities).

The biggest diaspora of glassblowers occurred in the 1600s; the Republic didn't pay them well enough, compared to the offers of others. An even worse blow was the advent and immediate popularity of Bohemian cut crystal in the 1670s. The ensuing glass crisis was only resolved when Murano learned to make cut glass as well. The death of the Republic set off another decline, and only towards the end of the 19th century were the forges stoked up again on Murano. Nowadays visitors are more than welcome (it's traditional—even medieval pilgrims sailing out of Venice for the Holy Land wrote about glass tours in their chronicles) but in exchange you have to take the solemnly excruciating tour through the carpeted showroom, where you may feel like you've gone through the Looking Glass the wrong way, with the Mad Hatter in charge of colour.

Murano has three *vaporetti* landings: Colonna, Faro, and Museo. The Colonna and Faro stops are near Murano's main glass bazaar, the **Fondamenta dei Vetrai**. At the end of the Fondamenta is Gothic **S. Pietro Martire**, one of Murano's three surviving churches (open 9:30–12 and 2:30–7:30), and well worth a visit, especially for Giovanni Bellini's recently restored 1488 *Madonna with St Mark, St Augustine, and Doge Barbarigo*, a beautiful, serene painting, complete with angel musicians playing some celestial soul music that perhaps only the Bellinis of this world can hear (at the time of writing the Church's other Bellini is being restored). Veronese's *St Jerome* may be seen over the sacristy door; the sacristy itself has a collection of 17th-wood panels carved with a rather unexpected crowd of Roman and Greek emperors, gods, philosophers and villains. But most winsome of all are the local touches—the Murano chandeliers, the 15th-century frescoes of Dominican saints in the nave, the glass-doll *Madonna and Child*, covered with the candles and flowers of the devout, and on the first altar to the right, another *Madonna*, very much like a primitive idol.

Across the Fondamenta stands an isolated medieval **campanile**; its church, like 15 others on Murano, was demolished after 1797. Murano's palaces suffered the same fate, but around the corner from S.Pietro Martire and beyond the Ponte Vivarini, there's an exception, the **Palazzo da Mula**, a 14th-century palace altered in the 16th century to make a pleasure villa.

The Ponte Vivarini crosses Murano's own Grand Canal, where Fondamenta Cavour leads around 17th-century Palazzo Giustinian, built for the bishops of Torcello, and for over a hundred years the seat of the **Museo Vetrario**, or Glass Museum (open 9–6, Sun and holidays 9–12:30, closed Wed; L3000), where you can learn something of Murano's livelihood. The first floor contains ancient Roman glass; examples range from the 1st–3rd centuries AD including many cinerary urns found in Yugoslavia. Upstairs, beyond the 19th-century mosaics of *Garibaldi* and *Vittorio Emanuele II*, the multi-lingual description of ancient and modern glassmaking and its styles is a good background to the glass displayed: of medieval, utilitarian pre-1400s fragments, and some of the earliest surviving Murano glass, including the famous blue **Barovier nuptial cup** (1480), with its scene of merry frolicking in a basin, some of the earliest 'Murano crystal', and an example of the lamps that were painted by *quattrocento* artists. Simplicity and elegance went by the board in the

1500s, as the glassmakers indulged, and probably helped create, a taste for the extravagant and bizarre, reaching a kind of kitsch epiphany in a model of a garden made entirely of glass.

Just beyond the Glass Museum is one of the finest Veneto-Byzantine monuments in Venice, **SS. Maria e Donato** (open 8–12 and 4–7) a contemporary of St Mark's Basilica, with a beautiful arcaded apse reflected in the canal—altogether far too over-restored by the Austrians, according to many critics. Over the door, there's a good lunette of the *Virgin*, and inside, a beautiful 12th-century mosaic pavement, incorporating pieces of ancient Murano glass, with geometric figures encircling scenes straight from the Middle Ages, of two roosters bearing a fox on a pole, an eagle capturing a lamb, griffins, and other less explicable symbols. On the wall there's a fine 12th-century Byzantine mosaic of the *Virgin*, and some of the capitals are from the same period. To the left there's a large painted relief of *S. Donato of Euboea*, the Church's other titular saint, with a flock of midget donors gathered below. His relics were part of an 1125 Venetian relic raid, led by Doge Domenico Michiel, but in this case the holy raiders outdid themselves, bringing home not only S. Donato's bones but those of the dragon the good bishop slew with a gob of righteous spit; you can see four of them hanging behind the altar. In an old wall by the campanile, are the bas-reliefs of a war memorial.

Burano

Burano (Line 12 from the Fondamente Nuove) is the Lego-Land of the Lagoon, where everything is in brightly coloured miniature—the canals, the bridges, the leaning tower, and the houses, painted with a Fauvist sensibility in the deepest of colours. Traditionally on Burano the men fish (and there's a fair collection of *trattorie* where you can sample the catch, at prices that would be a bargain in Venice) and the women make Venetian point, 'the most Italian of all lace work', beautiful, intricate and murder on the eyesight. Burano is literally draped with the stuff, although beware! Among the real articles there's a lot that's machine made or imported. You can watch the women make it at the **Scuola dei Merletti** in Piazza Galuppi (open 9–6, closed Tues; adm L2000); though '*scuola*' is misleading—no young girl in Burano wants to learn such an excruciating art, and their mothers may well be the last generation to make lace. But you never know; the school was originally founded in 1872, when lacemaking had declined so drastically that only one woman remembered the stitches. Across from the school, in the sacristy of the church of **San Martino** (of the tipsily leaning campanile) a look for Giambattista Tiepolo's *Crucifixion*, which Mary McCarthy aptly describes as 'a ghastly masquerade ball'.

From Burano you can cross the bridge to the island of **Mazzorbo** (ancient *Majourbium*) another island once famous for its gardens and villas, one that even in the 18th century could still boast a dozen churches. Now it has mostly empty space to offer between its scattered cottages, though students of residential architecture may be interested in the island's new communal houses designed by Giancarlo De Carlo, inspired by the traditional houses of Burano (and painted bright blue too, to make the *Buranelli* feel at home. On Mazzorbo's southern end is its one surviving church, **Santa Caterina**, a medieval effort rebuilt in the 15th century.

San Francesco del Deserto

From Burano you can hire a *sandola* (small gondola) to **S. Francesco del Deserto**, some 20 minutes to the south. On this islet St Francis is said to have founded a chapel in 1220, when his boat ran aground on his return from the East. Not long after the island was given to Francis' followers, who founded a monastery. The friars were forced out to make room for a military depot in 1806, but were welcomed back in 1856. You can visit them from 9–11 and 3–5:30, but in true Franciscan fashion, it's not the buildings you'll remember (though there's a lovely 14th-century cloister) but the love of nature evident in the beautiful gardens. Leave a donation if you can.

Torcello

Of all the possible destinations hidden among the shadows and shallows of the Lagoon, this one is the real treasure; get there on the same No. 12 Murano/Mazzorbo/Burano line from the Fondamente Nuove. At first the Torcello stop looks unpromising, a concrete pier and a wilderness beyond. But take the only path, down a jungly canal that was once a busy urban *fondamenta*, pass the solitary old 'Devil's bridge', and you'll finally arrive at a piazza that contains two of the most remarkable churches in all Italy, and very little else.

Torcello was the heir of *Altinum*, and may have settled some refugees from it as early as the 5th century. The big exodus, however, came in 639, when the Altinese finally found life with the Lombards too expensive and too dangerous. According to the legend their bishop, Paolo, was commanded in a vision to ascend the city's tower and look. He saw certain stars rising over this lonely island, and led the people of *Altinum* there to their new home. The town developed quickly, and for the first few centuries it seems to have been the real metropolis of the Lagoon. Its cathedral, founded in 639 and rebuilt about 1008, is the oldest building in the Lagoon and still one of the most impressive. At its height, Torcello was said (probably with a modicum of medieval exaggeration) to have 20,000 inhabitants, and even long after the refounding on the Rialto, Torcello continued as the commercial centre of Venice.

It was no war or other disaster, but only the fickle Lagoon itself that ruined Torcello. The gradual silting up of the island's approaches doomed its trade, and also created malarial marshes. The population gradually drifted off to Venice proper. As they had done in *Altinum* a thousand years before, they came back for the building stone; after a few centuries service as a quarry, Torcello today is nearly picked clean, and but for the piazza in the centre it would be impossible to guess that this was ever anything more than overgrown farmland.

On Torcello's piazza, the most imposing building is the **Cathedral**. More than St Mark's, or any other Venetian building, this one shows the difficult balance between Byzantine and Italian styles that occupied local architecture on the threshhold of the Middle Ages. In form it is much more Italian, a typical Latin three-aisled basilica; such details as the blind arcading on the façade and apses and the massive, square campanile, a prototype for many later ones in Venice, suggest that it is the work of Lombard masons. There are some unusual features: stone shutters on stone hinges, over the side windows, and a baptistry set squarely in front of the main portal—only the foundations survive today.

Torcello has less than a hundred people, and you'll need to pay a small admission fee to see their deconsecrated cathedral. Inside, the mood shifts abruptly towards the east, and the eye is drawn to the apse, with an exquisite 13th-century **mosaic of the Madonna and Child**, a severe but compelling figure with the deepest Byzantine eyes, alone on a broad gold ground. Beneath, there is a mosaic row of the *twelve apostles*, and below that a marble veneer facing in symmetrical patterns. The Roman sarcophagus near the high altar was recycled for the remains of St Heliodorus, first bishop of *Altinum*; to the left, the foundation stone of the original cathedral bears an inscription from 639, the oldest in Venice.

There is more fine work in every corner of the Cathedral: an intricate coloured marble pavement, and beautiful capitals on the nave columns that seem to have come from ancient *Altinum*, but are really originals from the 11th century. Another series of mosaics, in the right transept, shows *four angels* supporting a crown and the lamb, representing Christ; below, *Christ* appears with the Archangels *Michael and Gabriel*. Some of the best work is around the iconostasis (altar screen) and pulpit: early bits taken from the original cathedral, like the relief of the *two peacocks* sipping from the fountain of life (an allegory of the Eucharist, and a common early Christian subject). Look carefully and you will find some genuine oddities—on the left side, *Ixion*, grandfather of the centaurs from Greek mythology, stretched on his wheel. More wheels appear on the opposite side of the screen, winged wheels said to represent *Occasion*, the counterpart to Fortune, the chance that can be seized.

Best of all is the spectacular **Apotheosis of Christ and Last Judgement** covering the entire west wall, the largest and most memorable mosaic in Venice. Begun probably in the 12th century, the work was heavily restored in the 19th. Few mosaics reveal with such candour the Byzantine mixture of intellectuality and imagination, an ensemble of taut precision and obsessive organization, with hosts of angels and devils in tidy symmetry. Whether you find it spiritually uplifting or not, it states its case with an overpowering air of authority—as if you were getting a lesson in religion from a Byzantine emperor himself, with an archangel's hand on your shoulder. It is divided into six levels:

1 On top, the *Crucifixion*, with the Virgin and St John.
2 *The descent into Hell*, with Jesus flanked by Michael and Gabriel (like all Byzantine archangels, they wear the dress of high officials at the court in Constantinople). Jesus treads under blue demons, and welcomes Adam from the tomb. The shower of broken locks and keys is another common Byzantine image, for the Last Day, when all earthly bonds are loosed.
3 *Christ in Glory*, in His mandorla, with Virgin, Baptist, Apostles and Saints.
4 The *beasts and fishes give up their human prey* to the call of angelic music; also the mystic *etoimasia*, the *Preparation of the Throne*. Ancient Greek art sometimes portrayed the same empty throne as a symbol of Zeus, only with a pair of thunderbolts on it instead of the Gospels.
5 *Michael Weighs the Souls in a Scale* (more ancient symbolism; this was the job of Minos and Rhadamanthys in antiquity, and traceable to Egypt). The virtuous elect look up with expectant faces, while angels

cast down the damned (many princes and clerics among them, along with Muslims in turbans) to the blue demons. The devil himself appears.

6 On the left, *Mary Comforts the Children* while St Peter (with banner) guards the *Gates of Paradise*; right, the interesting *Tortures of the Damned*: fire, dismemberment, water and hunger, with serpents floating through the eye-sockets of floating skulls.

Next to the cathedral stands the 11th-century **Santa Fosca**. This church was never really completed, and whatever internal decoration it ever had is gone. Nevertheless, the plain shell of it is the most elaborate work of late Byzantine architecture in existence, a lovely and unique conception. As in so many other churches, beginning with the Hagia Sophia itself, it takes a central Greek plan and elongates one side to form a nave with three apses; the front and sides are graced by an arcaded porch, and surmounted by a low cylindrical dome. Like all the best medieval buildings, this one was built by constructive geometry. It isn't accidental that everything in it seems somehow just right; both in the plan and the elevation its architects employed the proportions of the 'Golden Section' of the ancient Greeks.

S. Fosca was intended as a *martyrion*, a small church in honour of the saint, whose remains were buried here. Taken together, the ensemble of the lost baptistry, cathedral and martyrion were symbolically meant to recall the circle of birth, life and death, as pretty a conceit for a monumental centre as any town ever had.

After that, you may snap your sweetie's picture in **Attila's Seat**, in the centre of the piazza, just as Venice tourists have been doing for generations. The connection of this rugged old throne with the Hunnish supremo sounds suspiciously as if it were dreamed up by someone sprung from generations of tour guides. Some scholars believe that the throne, if it has any history at all, was used by Torcello's consuls in open-air assemblies. Behind it stand the two important secular buildings to survive, the Palazzo del Consiglio and the Palazzo dell'Archivio; together they now serve as the **Torcello Museum** (daily exc. Mon, summer 10–12:30 and 2–5:30; Sun 10:30–12:30 and 2–4. Oct to Mar: 10:30–12:30 and 2–4, including Sun; adm L2000).

In this pleasant grab-bag, you'll find architectural fragments from the 6th–12th centuries, a pair of *bocche di leone* (the long arm of the Ten reached even here), a lovely 6th-century marble holy water stoup from Murano, and a few gilded silver reliefs from the cathedral altarpiece—

Napoleon stole the rest of them. Upstairs, among big soppy canvases from followers of Veronese, there's the cathedral's original door key, Byzantine ceramics and coins, ivories and jewellery, Byzantine and Cretan-Venetian icons from the 1400s, and a big jolly *cinquecento St. Christopher* with fishes swimming around his toes.

Cavallino and Jesolo

The Litorale del Cavallino, the 10 km peninsula that protects the northern part of the Lagoon, was long known as a semi-wild place of beach, sand dunes and pine forests. There's still some of that left, among the 28 camping grounds, hotels and restaurants. There are two ports on the *litorale*: **Punta Sabbioni** (Line 14 to the Lido and the Riva degli Schiavoni) and **Treporti** (the last call on Line 12, connecting Torcello, Burano, Murano to Venice). **Lido di Jesolo** is a far more developed and densely packed resort, seeing some six million tourists a year, though the number has fallen off because of the dirty sea—a disaster the hoteliers have tried to stave off by adding pools. Buses connect the Jesolo with Punta Sabbioni to coincide with the ferries.

More Islands

These have played a much smaller role than the islets to the south. **Sant'Erasmo** is Venice's kitchen garden island, the source of some of the produce in the Rialto markets. **San Giacomo in Paluda** (St James in the Bog), now a ruined ghost island, was originally a rest stop for pilgrims, a monastery until the 1400s, then a leper colony, and a Franciscan monastery until 1810. **Campalto** was an anti-aircraft base and is now abandoned.

Villas along the Brenta

In *The Merchant of Venice*, Portia, disguised as a young male lawyer, left her villa of Belmonte on the Brenta Canal and proceeded down to Fusina to preserve Antonio's pound of flesh. For about the same price you can trace her route on the stately villa-lined Brenta in the modern version of the patricians' canal boat, the *Burchiello*, which makes the day-long excursion from the end of March to the end of Oct, Tues, Thurs, and Sat from Venice, and Wed, Fri, and Sun from Padua. The journey may be booked through any travel agent or CIT office abroad; the considerable price (L110 000) includes admission into the three villas open to the public, lunch, guide, and coach back to the city of origin (try to go from Venice rather than Padua, so that after lunch you can drink too much wine and snooze through the last, much less scenic part of the excursion). You can also follow the Brenta on your own, less romantically and far less expensively, along the road that follows the canal, by car or by way of the public bus to Padua, departing from Piazzale Roma. For Malcontenta, however, you have to take a different bus from Piazzale Roma, one that departs only once an hour.

Often called an extension of the Grand Canal, the Brenta Canal was one of the choice locations among the Venetian patricians to go a-squiring in the country and still be within easy communication with the city; over 70 villas and palaces lie on or just off the waterway. Originally the Brenta was hardly so tame, making itself universally unpopular by flooding the surrounding farms and clogging up the Lagoon with silt. In the 14th century the Venetians decided to control its antics once and for all, building artificial canals to divert its waters and raising its banks. And when that was sufficiently completed in the 16th century, Venice's patricians found it the perfect place for their summer *villeggiatura*. But for all the fuss, it's obvious that the Venetians, like most Italians, were city slickers at heart, and not the least interested in what we would call 'getting back to nature'; although no longer kept up as immaculately as before, you can see how their villas, lawns and gardens tried to exert as tight a control on the environment as if they were in the centre of the city.

The classical proportions and stately symmetry that are the hallmarks of Palladio were especially suited to the land and the Venetians' conceit, and his celebrated, temple-fronted 1560 Villa Foscari, better known as **La Malcontenta** was a major influence on all subsequent 17th- and 18th-century villa architecture. Viewed from the canal, the Villa is a vision begging for a Scarlet O'Hara to sweep down the steps—not all that surprising, for Palladio's *Quattro Libri dell'Architettura* were Bibles for the 18th-century builders of America's old plantation homes, as well as for the Palladian movement in Britain, led by Inigo Jones. (Located between Fusina and Oriago, La Malcontenta is open May–Oct on Tues, Sat, and the first Sun of each month from 9–12; adm L5000, which is really too much.)

Further up the canal lies the town of Mira Ponte, the site of the 18th-century **Villa Widmann-Foscari** (open 9–12 and 2–6, closed Mon; guided tours; adm L5000. If you only have time for one villa, don't make it this one—redone soon after its construction in the French

Baroque style, the villa contains some sticks of its original furniture and bright, gaudy murals by two of Tiepolo's pupils. Mira's post office occupies the **Palazzo Foscarini**, Byron's address while working on sections of *Childe Harold* in 1817–19.

'If you've got it, flaunt it,' was the rule in Venice even into the 18th century, when one of the grandest villas in the entire Veneto region went up at **Stra**: the **Villa Nazionale (or Pisani)**, built by the fabulously wealthy Pisani banking family to celebrate the election of one of their own, Alvise Pisani, as doge. More of a royal palace than a country manor, it was completed in 1760, in time to be purchased by Napoleon for his viceroy Eugène Beauharnais; in 1934 it was chosen by Mussolini as a suitable stage for his historic first meeting with Hitler. Although most of the Villa has been stripped of its decoration, and most of the 18th-century frescoes are either ludicrous or annoying, the ballroom absolves most of the boredom with one of Giambattista Tiepolo's most shimmering frescoes, depicting (what else?) the *Apotheosis of the Pisani Family*; son Giandomenico painted the *chiaroscuro* Roman scenes along the gallery (open Tues–Sun 9–1; group tours, L3000); its vast park (open till 6 pm) contains the monumental stables and one of Italy's finest mazes.

Food and Drink

Rialto fish market.

Of the panoply of pleasures celebrated in Venice, food and drink were naturally an important part, so much so as to encourage gastronomic voyeurism; there are paintings of lavish feasts in theatres, with a full audience on tap to watch the nobility dine in style. There are tales of the legendary Doge, Andrea Gritti, of Henry VIII-ish appetites, eating himself to death, and others of entire table settings, including the napkins, sculpted of sugar. Quantity and style were more important than quality, which is rarely mentioned: the wine, especially the swill in the cheap inns or *Malavasie*, is condemned outright, even by English visitors for its 'pall'd disgustful Taste'; of the bread, 'Even when fresh it could be so dry and solid that you had to take a hammer to it' and most damning of all, is the shocking fact that Venetian housewives not only did not make their own pasta (either they were too lazy or were simply having too much fun to bother) but they purchased it *already boiled* from the shop. Heresy comes in many forms, but in a land governed by the *al dente* convention, that takes the cake.

Unfortunately, the taint of heresy lingers in many of Venice's 320 restaurants. If the pasta isn't already boiled, it might have been improved if it had. Nowhere on the entire Italian peninsula can you, without any luck, dine so poorly so often; even paying more offers no protection from the heavy handed Venetian cook. Use the listings below as a guide through the labyrinth of indigestion; most of the restaurants included

287

have a history of being decent to good, so chances are they still will be when you plump for a meal.

As breakfast coffee in the hotels is overpriced and, in some establishments, tastes as if it were brewed with *eau de Lagoon*, you may want to do as the Venetians do and grab a quick stand-up breakfast in a bar or *pasticceria* of coffee (usually a *cappuccino* or *caffè latte*) and a warm *cornetto* ('horn', like a croissant, filled or empty) or a *brioche* (a flaky 'pastry' with chocolate inside). You can stop for refills as often as necessary, though around noon it's time to move on to an *aperitivo*: a Campari, some kind of vermouth (Italians prefer something bitter, to whet the appetite) or perhaps a fruit juice.

Between 1 and 2 is time for lunch (*pranzo*; most restaurants open at 12 and stop serving at around 2:30 or 3). This is traditionally the biggest meal of the day for Italians though in practice often less than that, as many people prefer to grab a quick meal in a cafeteria-buffet or *tavola calda* (a selection of hot, prepared foods) rather than commute home to Mestre. But most will have some form of pasta (rather than in the evening, when it tends to sit on the all-important stomach), a salad or vegetable, wine or water, and fruit, followed by a coffee (perhaps 'corrected' with brandy or grappa) in a nearby bar (the stomach bunch will have a *digestivo* to aid gastric action, perhaps an Amaretto, a Strega (made from saffron), a Fernet-Branca (made from mysterious herbs), or a Scotch.

Venetians eat dinner (*cena*) fairly early by Italian standards, as well they'd better, as the restaurants begin opening to accommodate German tourists at 5 or 6 pm and close at 10 or 11 pm (though see 'Entertainment and Nightlife', pp. 312–15, for some exceptions). A plate of *antipasti* or a salad and a pizza, is a popular (and economical) supper, or you can order the works. Flasks of the house wine, usually from Verona or Friuli, help fill out the evening. Last stop: another bar, another coffee (to help you sleep!).

Venetian cuisine is based on fish, shellfish, and rice, often mixed together in a succulent seafood risotto. Popular *antipasti* include *sard in saor*, or marinated sardines, *prosciutto San Daniele*, a delicious raw ham cured in Friuli, oysters from Chioggia, or any possible hot or cold seafood delicacy. *Risi i bisi* (rice and peas, cooked with ham and Parmesan) is perhaps the best known Venetian first course, while the local pasta dish of choice is *bigoli in salsa*, a kind of spaghetti topped with butter, onions, and anchovies or sardines. There are various very palatable *risotti*: *di mare*, with seafood, or *in nero*, with cuttlefish cooked in its own ink, or *alla sbirraglia* (with vegetables, chicken, and ham). Venetian fish soup, *brodetto*, is usually prepared with tomatoes and garlic. For *secondo*, liver (*fegato alla veneziana*) with cornmeal *polenta* (or *tecia*, but a lead weight on the stomach by whatever name) shares top billing with grilled scampi, *baccalà mantecato* (salt cod), Sile eel, cuttlefish in its own ink (*seppie alla veneziana*), *fritto misto* (Adriatic mixed fry) and for a big splurge, lobster (*aragosta*). Bitter red *radicchio* (chicory) from Treviso is a favourite side-dish, often in salads. Top it all off with a *tiramisù*, a traditional Veneto chilled dessert of layered chocolate, coffee, and cream (or *mascarpone*). For more menu items, see the glossary on pp. 387–93.

The wines, at least, will almost always compensate for the cuisine. Most of what you'll see in Venetian restaurants comes from the surrounding three regions of Venetia: the Veneto, Friuli-Venezia Giulia and Trentino-Alto Adige, which together produce nearly half Italy's wines, and many of her best. Most Italian wines are named after the grape and the district they come from. If the label says DOC (*Denominazione di Origine Controllata*) it means that the wine comes from a specially defined area and was produced according to a certain traditional method. Some of the Veneto's wines may already be familiar, especially Verona's red *Bardolino* and *Valpolicella* and white *Soave* and *Bianco di Custoza*. Others, like the dry or sweet bubbling white or rosé *Prosecco* of Conegliano, or the splendid array of wines from Friuli (whites *Tokai*, *Pinot Bianco* and *Pinot Grigio*, and reds *Refosco* and *Cabernet*) and Trentino-Alto Adige (*Riesling, Silvaner Chardonnay, Pinot Grigio* and *Gewurztraminer*) still seem to be Italian secrets. The province of Venice produces three DOC wines, centred around the village of Pramaggiore: the refined white *Tocai di Lison*, with an almond and peach bouquet, and two reds: hardy *Cabernet di Pramaggiore*, a fine companion to *polenta* and other strong dishes and the softer, smoother *Merlot di Pramaggiore*, so light that the locals even serve it with fish.

Restaurants

Venice's restaurants tend to be more expensive than the mainland norm; the few approaching great status tend to be very much more (not altogether because they batten off tourists—transport and handling charges add 30% to the cost of food). Even the moderate ones are liable to give you a nasty surprise at *conto* time with their excessive service and cover charges. If you're watching expenses, pizza is the most reliable standby, and not bad if it's freshly made.

Unfortunately the old habit of posting prices in the window has fallen out of fashion, so it's difficult to judge prices, though generally the fancier the fittings, the fancier the *conto* at the end, though neither price nor decor have anything to do with the quality of the food. When you eat out, mentally add to the bill the bread and cover charge (*pane e coperto*, between L1500–3000) and a 15% service charge. This is usually included in the bill (*servicio compreso*); if it says *servicio non compreso* you'll have to do your own arithmetic. An additional small tip is expected for good service.

Finally, note that when a restaurant advertizes a fixed-price menu (*menu turistico*), you won't see a trace of it inside—memorize what you want before you go in. Secondly, many of the places that take food seriously offer a *menu degustazione*—a set-price gourmet meal that allows you to taste whatever seasonal delicacies the chef has whipped up. Both are cheaper than if you had ordered *à la carte*. When you leave a restaurant you are given a receipt, which by law you must hold on to until you're 60 m from the door or risk an ambush from the not-very vigilant tax police.

The prices listed below are for an average meal (*antipasto*, first and second courses, dessert, and wine) per person. If you order seafood or truffles, the price will be considerably higher; with some discretion (and drinking the house wine only) it could be considerably less. In the summer, you would do well to book in the better restaurants to avoid disappointment.

Luxury:	L100–150 000
Expensive:	L60–100 000
Moderate:	L40–60 000
Inexpensive:	L25–40 000
Cheap:	L15–25 000

Credit Cards
AE=American Express, DC=Diner's Club

Cannaregio

MODERATE
A La Vecia Cavana, Rio Terrà dei SS. Apostoli 4624, tel 523 8644 (AE), is Cannaregio's smartest restaurant, where you can dine on Adriatic specialities (closed Tues).

INEXPENSIVE
Al Milion, behind S. Giovanni Cristosomo at No. 5841, tel 522 9302, a comfortable old *bacaro* with wine and food; a popular Venetian meeting place (closed Wed).

Antico Molo, Fondamenta degli Ormesini (by the Ghetto; no tel) long run by the same family, with some of Cannaregio's best food (closed Wed).

Malibran, Corte del Milion 5864 (near the above), tel 522 8028, a *trattoria/pizzeria* with a touch of class, by the òld theatre of the same name (closed Wed).

Tre Spiedi, Salizzada S. Canciano 5906 (near the Campiello F. Corner and the central post office), tel 528 0035 (BA), has a cosy atmosphere to go with its local specialities like *spaghetti alla veneziana* and *bracciola Bruno*; closed Sun eve and Mon.

CHEAP

Bich Dao, Calle Selle 1424, (take Calle Farnese from the Ghetto Nuovo) tel 716 269, is run by a genial family from Hong Kong, who make the most authentic Chinese food in Venice. Try the Chinese liqueurs (with a surprise on the bottom of the glass).

Casa Mia, Calle dell'Oca 4430 near Campo, SS. Apostoli, tel 528 5590, is lively, full of locals, and pizza pies (closed Tues).

Hong Kong, Strada Nova 4386, near the Ca' d'Oro, tel 523 6040 another very good Chinese, with tables outside on the Strada Nova.

Paradiso Perduto, Fondamenta della Misericordia 2540, tel 720 581, a favourite of the young and young at heart; the food varies in quality, but it stays open late and often has jazz concerts at weekends (closed Mon).

Vesuvio, Rio Terrà Farsetti 1837, south of Rio della Misericordia, tel 718 968, for pizzas cooked in a wood oven and grilled meats.

Castello

LUXURY

Danieli Terrace, in the Danieli Hotel, Riva degli Schiavoni 4196, tel 522 6480 (AE, DC, Visa), for classic cuisine (try the *spaghetti alla Danieli*, prepared at your table) and perfect service in an incomparable setting, overlooking St Mark's basin.

Les Deux Lions, Riva degli Schiavoni 4171, in the Londra Palace, tel 520 0533 (AE, DC, Visa) combines elegance with Venice's finest French cuisine; piano bar until 1 am.

MODERATE

Corte Sconta, Calle del Pestrin 3886, tel 522 7024 (AE, DC, Visa), off the beaten track, the Corte's considerable reputation rests solidly on its exquisite molluscs and crustaceans, served in a setting that's a breath of fresh air after the exposed beams and copper pots that dominate the typical Venetian restaurant decor. The Venetians claim the Corte Sconta is even better in the off-season; be sure to order the house wine (closed Sun, Mon, and much of July and Aug).

Hostaria da Franz, just north of the Giardini Pubblici at Fondamenta S. Isepo (or Giuseppe) 754, tel 522 7505 (AE). Well worth the trouble of getting lost several times en route, Franz's is one of Venice's finest restaurants: great oysters, *gnocchi*, seafood cooked the way it should be if all Venetians tried harder. The house wine, a delicate Tocai, is lovely, but there's a long list of other vintages, too (closed Mon and Jan).

INEXPENSIVE

Da Remigio, Salizzada dei Greci 3416, tel 523 0089, a neighbourhood favourite, with solid if basic Venetian cooking (closed Mon eve and Tues).

CHEAP

Aciugheta da Fabiano, Campo SS. Filippo e Giacomo, tel 522 4292, the 'Anchovy' is one of the best cheap restaurants and bars near the Piazza; good pizzas and atmosphere to boot (closed Wed).

Al Mascaron, Calle Lunga S. Maria Formosa 5225, tel 522 5995, a favourite neighbourhood bar and greasy spoon; good bar snacks.

La Grand Muraglia, Calle del Forno 3958, tel 523 2382, for average Chinese; can be rated moderate if you order the works (closed Mon).

Dorsoduro

MODERATE

Locanda Montin, Fondamenta di Borgo or Eremite 1147 (near S. Trovaso), tel 522 7151; reservations suggested (AE, DC, Visa) is Venice's most celebrated artists' tratt, where the food can range from the first to third division, but the garden setting is guaranteed to enchant (closed Tues eve, Wed, and half of Aug).

INEXPENSIVE

Isola Misteriosa, Rio Terrà Scoazzera 2894, by Campo S. Margherita, tel 523 8366, self-consciously trendy, but the food is better than the odds.

La Furatola, Calle Lunga S. Barnaba 2870, tel 520 8594. For a regal affordable seafood feast, hunt up this small but dedicated *trattoria* where the fish are jumping (or almost) as you select one that strikes your fancy (closed July and Aug).

Taverna San Trovaso, Fondamenta Priuli 1016, tel 520 3703, with Venetian home cooking and fish (closed Mon).

CHEAP

Trattoria della Donna Onesta, near the Frari in Calle della Madonna 3922, tel 522 9586; Venetian specialities with an extra friendly touch; closed Sun.

San Marco

LUXURY

Antico Martini, near La Fenice in Campo S. Fantin 1983, tel 522 4121 (AE, DC, Visa). One of Venice's best, all romance and elegance, it started out as a Turkish coffeehouse in the early 18th century but nowadays is better known for its excellent seafood and *pennette al pomodoro*. Excellent wine list; its intimate piano-bar restaurant stays open until 2 am (closed Tues, Wed noon, Dec, and Feb).

Tiepolo, in the Europa & Regina Hotel, Calle Larga XXII Marzo, tel 520 0477 (AE, DC, Visa), is named for the grand Venetian family that produced both doges and painters, who once lived in this palace on the Grand Canal, overlooking the Salute. Delicious house and Venetian specialities, like *sampietro alla gondola*—John Dory with *polenta*, prawns, and artichokes.

EXPENSIVE

Da Ivo, Ramo dei Fuseri 1809, tel 528 5004 (AE, DC, Visa), is Venice's best-known Tuscan restaurant, where you can sink your molars into a *bistecca fiorentina* while you grind them on the Florentine attitudes of the help (closed Sun and Jan).

Do Forni, Calle dei Specchieri 468, tel 523 2148 (AE, DC, Visa). For many Italians as well as foreigners, this is *the* bodacious place to eat in Venice. Two dining rooms, one 'Orient Express'-style and the other rustic, serving seafood *antipasti*, *polenta*, and well-prepared fish (closed Thurs in winter).

Harry's Bar, Calle Vallaresso 1323, tel 523 6797 (AE, DC, Visa). In a class by itself, as much a Venetian institution as the Doges' Palace, though food has become secondary to its celebrity atmosphere. The sandwiches and house cocktail (a Bellini, Tiziano, or Tiepolo—delectable fruit juices mixed with Prosecco) are justly famous. The tables downstairs near the bar are good for a hobnob—upstairs is the more formal restaurant (closed Mon).

La Caravella, Calle Larga XXII Marzo 2397, an annex to the Saturnia Hotel, tel 520 8901 (AE, DC, Visa). For sheer variety of local and exotic dishes, prepared by a master chef, few restaurants in Italy can top this merrily corny repro of a dining hall in a 16th-century Venetian galley. Try *bouillabaisse*, Turkish stuffed *calamari*, French onion soup, *gazpacho*, or the house's famous *bigoli*, followed by scampi in champagne or the delicious chicken in a paper bag (*en papillote*); closed Wed in the winter only. A second restaurant, **Il Cortile**, tel 520 8938 is in the charming courtyard of the same hotel.

MODERATE

Al Colombo, by the Goldoni Theatre at S. Luca 4620, tel 522 2627 (AE, DC, Visa) a famous tourist enclave, hung with contemporary art, but the homemade pasta and seafood have yet to fall victim to its popularity; try the salmon in champagne. If you aren't careful when ordering the prices can soar into the expensive range.

Al Conte Pescaor, Piscina S. Zulian 544, tel 522 1483, a small, traditional fish restaurant that makes few concessions to international tourism (closed Sun, Mon lunch, and half of Aug).

Da Raffaele, Fondamenta delle Ostreghe 2347, tel 523 2317 (AE, DC, Visa) has a mock knights-in-shining-armour atmosphere to go along with a collection of geninue medieval relics, but the food is much better than typical castle swill. The menu follows the market, with game dishes in the autumn, and the day's catch at other times (the sea bass and *filetto al gorgonzola* are especially good. If it's nice out, you can skip the Middle Ages altogether and dine on the canal-side terrace (closed Thurs and Jan).

Trattoria Vini da Arturo, on the infamous Calle degli Assassini 3656 near La Fenice, tel 528 6974. A former *bacaro* that marches to a different drummer, with not a speck of seafood on the menu. Instead, try the *tagliatelle al radicchio* and *stinco* (shin) *all'Amarone*, or Venice's best steaks; its *tiramisù* is famous; (closed half of Aug and Sun).

INEXPENSIVE

Al Bacareto, Calle Crosera 3347, near S. Stefano, tel 528 9336, for filling *bigoli in salsa* and *baccalà*; can be cheap if you eat standing downstairs (closed Sun).

Al Teatro, Campo S. Fantin 1916, tel 522 1052 (AE, DC, Visa) a combination bar/restaurant/*pizzeria* that stays open after La Fenice closes (closed Mon).

CHEAP

Rosticceria San Bartolomeo, Calle della Bissa 5423, tel 522 3569 (AE, Visa, DC), good honest cooking and a variety of dishes featuring codfish. For a really cheap meal, fill up in the snack bar downstairs.

Vino Vino, Campo S. Fantin 1983, tel 522 4121 (AE, DC, Visa) is an offspring of the hoity toity Antico Martino, where you can eat a well-cooked filling main dish with a glass of good wine at prices even students can afford (closed Tues, Wed noon, Dec and Feb).

San Polo/Santa Croce

EXPENSIVE

La Regina, Calle della Regina 2331, S. Croce, tel 524 1402 (AE, Visa) this queen of a restaurant may be small but is big on innovation in the kitchen, offering a fine synthesis of Italian and French recipes, as well as wines; price in the moderate range if you order the *menu degustazione* (closed Mon and Aug).

Poste Vecie, across its own wooden bridge from the Rialto fish markets at Pescheria 1608, tel 721 822 (AE, DC, Visa) a charming seafood eatery in a former posthouse; same owner as La Regina (closed Tues, except in the summer).

MODERATE

Antica Besseta, Calle Savio, S. Croce 1395, tel 721 687, is a family-run citadel of Venetian homecooking, where you can experience an authentic *risi e bisi*, or *bigoli in salsa*, scampi, and the family's own wine (closed Tues, Wed, and some of July and Aug).

Da Fiore, Calle del Scaleter 2202, near Campo S. Polo, tel 731 308 (reservations suggested; AE, DC, Visa) an intimate place, with superb *antipasti*, and exquisite *fritto misto*, fish and shellfish; even the bread is fresh and homemade; closed Sun and Mon, and half of Aug).

INEXPENSIVE

Alla Madonna, Calle della Madonna 594, S. Polo (near Rialto), tel 523 3824 a large, popular, and very Venetian fish restaurant; closed Wed and Jan.

Antico Giardinetto da Erasmo, behind the Church of S. Cassiano at S. Croce 2315 (tel 721 301). Rather hard to find, the Giardinetto features delicious fresh seafood, in the form of *antipasto* or as a main course, cooked in a variety of styles. In good weather you can eat out in the little garden (closed Sat, Sun and Aug).

Da Ignazio, near S. Polo at Calle dei Saoneri 2749, tel 523 4852 (AE, DC, Visa) an old fashioned seafood restaurant with a garden (closed Sat).

CHEAP

Al Bacareto del Nono Ristorto, Campo S. Cassiano, S. Polo, tel 524 1169, a popular resort of the young, where the food ranges from nibblers like *cichetti* and Spanish *tapas* to pizza and unusual salads; closed Tues, except in the summer.

Alle Oche, Calle Tintor 1459, south of San Giacomo dell'Orio, S. Croce, tel 524 1496, in a quiet little square by a canal, with outdoor tables. Good pasta dishes, like *tagliatelle al gorgonzola* and less expensive, 50 different kinds of pizza, including one topped with cream and shrimps; get there early in the summer; closed Mon.

San Tomà, Campo S. Tomà 2864/a, S. Polo, tel 523 8819, a *trattoria/pizzeria* with convivial outdoor tables and some of Venice's best pizzas.

Elsewhere

Dall'Amelia, Via Miranese 113, in **Mestre**, tel 913 951. For exceptional food and wine, Italian gourmets cross the big bridge to dine here at least once, on delicious oysters and a divine *tortelli di branzino* (bass), but offers a choice of wine from one of Italy's most renowned cellars. Depending on what you order and drink, L60 000.

Dell'Hotel Excelsior, Lungomare Marconi 40, **Lido**, tel 526 0201, for the classic Venetian turn-of-the-century experience, with nearly anything you could possibly desire—even a traditional Venetian meal (L110 000 and up).

Altanella, Rio del Ponte Longo 268, **Giudecca**, tel 522 7780 (reservations suggested) a delightful old seafood restaurant with canal-side tables near the Redentore, where the *risotto di pesce* and *fritto* are worth the trip (L25–30 000; closed Mon eve, Tues, and half of Aug).

Dell'Hotel Cipriani, **Giudecca** 10, tel 520 7744 (AE, DC, Visa) where the movers and shakers in Venice retreat from the maddening crowd; perfect service to complement the perfect food, and the exclusive bill— L120 000 and up.

Do Mori, Fondamenta S. Eufemia 588, **Giudecca**, tel 522 5452, is a delightful, unpretentious place owned by two former waiters at Harry's, where for a change the best dishes are the cheapest—homemade pasta and pizza (L25–35 000); closed Sun.

Ai Pescatori, Via Galuppi 371, **Burano**, tel 730 650, is the most popular restaurant on the island, where you can try the old standby, *risotto di fagioli* (rice and beans) or *anguilla in brodo di branzino* (eel in sea bass sauce)—the latter must be ordered in advance (L50 000).

Locanda Cipriani, **Torcello**, tel 730 757 (AE) a consciously rustic descendant of Harry's Bar. A private motor boat picks up diners at 12:20 by the Danieli Hotel and returns them at 3:20; the food is good but not great, as it should be at the price: L90–100 000 (closed Mon, Tues and Oct–Mar).

Villa 600, **Torcello**, tel 730 999, is less pretentious in the kitchen, but has the charms of a late Renaissance villa, with outdoor dining on the terrace in the summer (L40 000; closed Wed and Jan).

Trattoria Buon Pesce, Stradale Ponte Caneva 625, **Chioggia**, tel 400 861 where you can start with *gnocchetti alla marinara* and follow it with oysters, crab or whatever the waiter suggests. The atmosphere is traditional; full meals begin at L30 000.

Nalin, Via Nuovissimo 29, **Mira**, tel 420 083, has a lovely poplar shaded veranda that offers one of the traditional ways to round off an excursion along the Brenta Canal. The emphasis is on Venetian seafood, finely grilled; good Veneto wines as well (L40–60 000; closed Mon and Aug).

In Between: Bars and Cafés

What skill the Venetians may lack in the kitchen, they have made up for by introducing the perky joys of caffeine to the West back in 1640. Like Coca-Cola, *kahvé* was initially regarded as medicine and sold only in pharmacies, until 1720, when Europe's first 'boutique of coffee' was opened in Piazza S. Marco, with the proud name of *Venice Triumphant*, modelled by its founder, Floriano Francesconi, on the houses in Istanbul. Like many innovations, coffeehouses were once very *risqué*; Bach's lighthearted *Kaffee Kantata* is a dialogue between a young lady who wants to go to a café and her father who forbids it. And if he were Venetian, he would have had good cause, for they were the favourite rendezvous for extra-marital shenanigans. Perhaps this is why, to this day, you always pay double the price for sitting down.

Nowadays the steam-hissing espresso machine dragons provide most of the thrills. You can still get a good, if outrageously costly, thimbleful of espresso at **Florian's** or **Quadri**, the Piazza's historic rivals; Florian's has a charming and cosy 18th-century decor of mirrors and frescoes put up in a nostalgic mood in the 1850s, and every Venetian must learn in school to have coffee here rather than at Quadri, patronized by the hated Austrian occupation forces in the days of their great great grandparents. You're never too far from a bar for a quick or leisurely coffee perk-up; two places that take special pride in their brews are **Rosa Salva** (branches throughout Sestiere S. Marco), where the atmosphere still reflects the view that coffee is pharmaceutical, and the much grittier **Caffè Costarica**, in Cannaregio's Rio Terrà di S. Leonardo, where you can have an especially good iced coffee (*frappé*) while the bean grinder growls away in the back.

Other bars are combined with *pasticcerie*, though caution is recommended (see 'Cake Crumbs', p. 25). The best and most high priced cakes in Venice come from the delicate-fingered pastry-chefs at **Marchini**, by Ponte S. Maurizio in S. Marco, though the 'Glutton', **Il Golosone**, in Castello's Salizzada S. Lio comes in a close second, and has decent slices of pizza as well. **Harry's Dolci**, Fondamenta S. Biagio 773 on the Giudecca is a popular Sunday destination for smart Venetians, for its elegant teas, ice creams, and cakes.Other bars combined with *gelaterie* include the popular **Paolin**, with tables out in Campo S. Stefano, in S. Marco, scooping out a pistachio ice cream acclaimed the best in the land (closed Fri). **Nico**, on the Zattere ai Gesuati, Dorsoduro, is another must on anyone's ice cream tour, specializing in luscious combinations (closed Thurs); other good places that make their own *gelato* are **Il Doge**, in Campo S. Margherita, Dorsoduro, and **Zorzi**, Calle dei Fuseri, S. Marco, for ice cream and fruit concoctions.

Many Venetians forgo the sweets altogether, and even begin the day with a glass of white wine and a savoury snack, a ritual to be repeated as often as possible during the day (they even swallow the wine in one go, the way most Italians drink their coffee). If a Venetian invites you to duck in the shade *'andemo al ombra'*, it means a wine stop, especially nice in a *bacaro* (old fashioned wine bar) or *osteria*, or *enoteca*, which stocks a wide variety of vintages. These usually offer snacks, or *cichetti*—mussels, pickled onions, artichoke hearts, vegetables cooked in oil, or a bit of cuttle-fish. These titbits are also popular late night fare for a *giro de ombra* (a Venetian pub crawl), especially if you want bizarre dreams.

For the greatest variety of wines, try Venice's oldest wine bar, **Al Volta**, Calle Cavalli di S. Marco 4081, with over 2000 Italian and foreign labels to chose from as well as a sumptuous array of *cichetti* (open 9–1 and 4:30–9, closed Sun). For the best atmosphere and delicious snacks and sandwiches, seek out **Do Mori**, a characteristic Rialto market bar, just off Ruga Vecchia S. Giovanni (no tables, 9–1 and 5–8, closed Wed afternoon and Sun). **Due Colonne**, at the corner of Calle dell' Cristo and Rio Terrà del Cristo, by S. Marcuolo is a fun, noisy place full of Venetians; nearby, **Alla Maddalena**, by the winter Casino at Rio Terrà della Maddalena, is known for its good snacks. **Cantinone già Schiavi**, Fondamenta Meravegie 992, by S. Trovaso, Dorsoduro, has a friendly bar along with its comprehensive wine shop, where you can try the wares before buying a bottle (9–1:30 and 3:15–8:30). Another wine bar, a pretty old place popular with locals, is **Al Bottegon**, on Fondamenta Toffetti, on the Rio S. Trovaso near the Zattere. The aforementioned **Harry's Bar** and **Vino Vino** (listed under S. Marco), **Al Milion** (Cannaregio). and **Al Mascaron** are also potential stops, as is **Da Codroma**, Fondamenta Briati in Dorsoduro, which often has snacks out of the ordinary.

Venetians feeling peckish between 5 and dinner time indulge in a beer and *tramezzini*, finger sandwiches that come in a hundred varieties (prawns, spinach and cheese, asparagus tips, etc.); some of the best, and more susbstantial lunch-size sandwiches, may be found at the **Osteria alle Botteghe**, Calle delle Botteghe, by S. Stefano in S. Marco. Takeaway slices of pizza are popular and good everywhere else in Italy except Venice, though you won't go wrong at **Cip Ciap** in Calle Mondo Novo, over the bridge from Campo S. Maria Formosa in Castello, where you can get a measure big enough for a hearty lunch. For those Teutonic urges, there's a stand selling *bratwurst* sandwiches on the S. Polo side of the Rialto Bridge. And finally, tourism has spawned only one big-name American hamburger stand, just off the Mercerie near S. Marco; unlike its originals in the States, this one is unspeakably bad.

Where to Stay

For hundreds of years it was the Senate's policy to lodge guests free of charge in the best palaces in the city, and if they insisted on staying in an inn, the Senate made sure the grub was as lousy as the bed. This magnanimity probably had as much to do with the desire to spy on the guest as the fact that hosts were exempt from the restrictions of the sumptuary laws; a guest meant they could dress up in forbidden jewels and serve extra courses at dinner.

Well, in this city where change is slow, you can still stay in a palace and flaunt every sumptuary law left on the books—for a pound of flesh (blood included this time). Even the cheap hotels go for more than the odds—about 30% more than you'd pay on the mainland—and if you're really counting the kopecks you can stay in Padua's municipal hostel or in Mestre and commute to Venice. But it isn't as much fun as trying to find your hotel in the labyrinth after dark, especially after knocking back a couple of bottles of *Soave* at dinner.

Not surprisingly, the most charming hotels in such a popular destination are no secret, and to get a room in any of them, book several months in advance or even earlier if possible, to give the snails at the Posta Italiana a fair chance to deliver your letter (and remember to request a room with a view). Also make sure to use the full address; the *sestieri* (Cannaregio, S. Marco, etc.) are used as Venice's postal codes, and your letter may not be delivered without one. Better yet, ring the hotel (the prefix for Venice 041) and make arrangements to pay a deposit directly, which insures your booking, though if you cancel your reservation, the hotel will keep the deposit unless another agreement has been reached. If you're coming in the summer without reservations, take pot luck with the tourist office's free hotel-finding service in the train station or Piazzale Roma.

Prices for rooms in a hotel can also vary, depending on quality, views, size of room, etc. Rates are often lower, as much as a third less, in the off season (6 January–1 April and 4 November–21 December). Many hotels close at other times. All five and four star hotels include air conditioning in the price; others that have it charge a daily fee (L8–15 000) for their coolness. New pricing regulations make it possible to avoid the hotel breakfast and the absurd charges the management has cooked up for mere coffee and rolls—take a look at the prices posted by the reception desk if you think we're kidding. **All the prices in this book are for a double room**. As a general rule, expect to pay (in lire) in 1991:

Category	Double with bath
Luxury (*****)	L280–800 000
Class I (****)	L140–500 000
Class II (***)	L150–250 000
Class III (**)	L100–150 000
Class IV (*)	L60–80 000

For rooms without private baths, subtract 20–30%. For a single, count on paying 70% of a double; to add an extra bed in a double will add 33% to the bill. Taxes and service charges are included in the given rate. Many resort hotels in particular offer discounts for children. Prices are by law listed on the door of each room; any discrepancies could be reported to the local tourist office.

Cannaregio

***Giorgione**, SS. Apostoli 4587, tel 522 5810, combines traditional Venetian with modern comforts to create one of the most classy hotels of its category (L105–160 000, off season L75–120 000).
***Malibran**, S. Giovanni Crisostomo 5864, tel 522 4626, located in the Corte Milion, next to, or perhaps even incorporating Marco Polo's house. 29 rooms, all with bath, L80–158 000.

**Guerrini, Lista di Spagna 265, tel 715 333, is one of the quieter hotels near the station, off the garish Lista in a cul-de-sac, overlooking a shady courtyard (L50–58 000 without bath, L70–85 000 with).

**Mignon, SS. Apostoli 4535, tel 523 7388, is in a fairly quiet area, not far from the Ca' d'Oro, and boasts a little garden for leisurely breakfasts, though rooms are rather plain (L55–58 000 without bath, L75–85 000 with).

*Casa Carettoni, Lista di Spagna 130, tel 716 231, is the most pleasant and comfortable cheap hotel near the station, and doesn't force its breakfast on guests, because it doesn't serve any—head for a nearby bar instead (L45 000).

*Eden, della Rio Terrà della Maddalena 2357, tel 720 228, not far from the Grand Canal and the winter Casino; 8 adequate rooms (L35–48 000 without bath, L50–75 000 with).

Castello

*****Danieli, Riva degli Schiavoni 4196, tel 522 6480, the largest and most famous hotel in Venice, in the Gothic palace of the ducal Dandolo family transformed into a hotel in 1822 and now owned by the Ciga chain. Nearly every room has some story to tell, and you can add your own in a beautiful setting of silken walls, Gothic stairs, gilt mirrors, Oriental rugs. The dull new wing, much vilified ever since it was built in the 1940s, is comfortable but lacks the charm and stories. Rates range from L420–600 000.

****Gabrielli Sandwirth, Riva degli Schiavoni 4110, tel 5231580, a Venetian Gothic style hotel, built around a large garden and courtyard (complete with hammocks and lounge chairs). Large well-furnished rooms and famous views of the Lagoon (L95–125 000 without bath, L170–320 000 with).

****Londra Palace, Riva degli Schiavoni 4171, tel 520 0533 was made by linking two palaces together. It has been a favourite of Russian composers, especially Tchaikovsky, who composed his Fourth Symphony in room 108, to Igor Stravinsky. It has one of the cosiest lobbies in Venice, and a good restaurant to boot (see 'Eating Out', p. 291) L200–400 000.

****Metropole, Riva degli Schiavoni 4149, tel 520 5044, was built at the beginning of the 19th century and used by the military before its incarnation as a hotel, with a picturesque gondola landing on a side canal. Completely renovated and finely furnished, many rooms have views over the Lagoon (L190–325 000, in low season L110–215 000).

***Bisanzio**, Calle della Pietà 3651, tel 520 3100, is housed in the former home of sculptor Alessandro Vittoria, a bit back from the Riva degli Schiavoni, near *vaporetto* stop S. Zaccaria and Vivaldi's Church of La Pietà. The decor of wood and stone is fairly conservative by Venetian standards, and the rooms are much quieter than other hotels nearby. Air conditioning available (L110–165 000, all with bath).

***Savoia & Jolanda**, Riva degli Schiavoni 4187, tel 520 6664, is another fine hotel near the centre of action, though not too noisy. The nicest rooms are on the top floor, but there's no air conditioning (L80–160 000).

***Scandinavia**, S. Maria Formosa 5240, tel 522 3507, offers 27 comfortable rooms and a touch of class on one of Venice's prettiest *campi*. Air conditioning extra (L158 000 with bath).

Da Bruno, Salizzada S. Lio 5726/a, tel 523 0452, not far from the Rialto Bridge, enjoys a central location and very pleasant, if smallish, rooms for the category (L45–58 000 without bath, L63–88 000 with).

La Residenza, Campo Bandiera e Moro 3608, tel 528 5315, located in a lovely 14th-century palace in a quiet square between S. Marco and the Arsenale. The public rooms are flamboyantly decorated with 18th-century frescoes, antique furniture and paintings, but the bedrooms tend to be far more spartan (L58 000 without bath, L88 000 with).

Paganelli, Riva degli Schiavoni 4182, tel 522 4324, is a charming 15-room hotel overlooking the Lagoon, attractively furnished. Try to get a room here rather than in the annex (*dipendenza*) located back in S. Zaccaria (L86 000, L57 000 without bath).

*Caneva**, Ramo della Fava 5515, tel 522 8118, stands between the Rialto and S. Marco on a quiet canal. Simple rooms simply furnished, but well kept (L33–48 000 without bath, L50–75 000 with).

*Casa Verardo**, Ruga Giuffa 4765, tel 528 6127, a classy, 9-room *locanda* with friendly owners (L60–70 000, with bath).

*Doni**, S. Zaccaria 4656, tel 522 4267, a cosy 11-room *pensione*, isolated from the madding crowd but only a few minutes from S. Marco. Ask for a room overlooking the Rio del Vin (L46 000, no private bath).

*Sant'Anna**, S. Anna 269, tel 528 6466, a fine little hotel popular with those who want to escape tourist Venice, located just north of the Giardini Pubblici. Only 8 rooms, including some triples (L48 000 without bath, L75 000 with).

*Silva**, Fondamenta Rimedio 4423, tel 522 7643, is a bit hard to find—on one of the most photographed little canals in Venice between the S. Zaccaria *vaporetto* stop and S. Maria Formosa. Though the rooms are basic, there's a friendly owner, and Venice's most arrogant black cat (L48 000 without bath, L60–74 000 with).

*Toscana-Tofanelli, at the foot of Via Garibaldi No. 1650, tel 523 5722, has 9 no-frills rooms on the grand boulevard of Castello, near the Riva; undignified by a sign and run by a band of grandmas (L38–44 000).

Dorsoduro

Perhaps the most relaxed and serependitious *sestiere* for sleeping, containing by Venetian standards, many of the most pleasant 'economy' hotels.

***Accademia-Villa Maravegie, Fondamenta Bollani 1058, tel 521 0188, offers a generous dollop of slightly faded charm in a 17th-century villa with a garden, just off the Grand Canal. The 26 rooms are furnished with a menagerie of antiques, some of which look as if they were left behind by the villa's previous occupant—the Russian Embassy. The Accademia is a favourite of many, so book well in advance (L64–82 000 without bath, L105–135 000 with. off season discounts).

***American, S. Vio 628, tel 520 4733, is near the Accademia *vaporetto* stop but far enough from the crowds to be an oasis on a little canal. Each of the 29 rooms has TV, bath, and optional air conditioning (L80–155 000).

***Pausania, S. Barnaba 2824, tel 522 2083, is in an old palace near the Rio Gerardini, in a serene corner of Venice that few tourists ever visit. The 24 rooms are comfortable, and air conditioning is included in the rates (L80–158 000, all with bath).

**Agli Alboretti, Rio Terrà S. Agnese 882/4, tel 523 0058 is a charming little hotel on a rare tree-lined lane, near the Accademia; 19 rooms, all with private bath, L77–86 000.

**Alla Salute Da Cici, Fondamenta Ca' Balà 222, tel 523 5404, a well-scrubbed, recently renovated 50 room hotel in an old *palazzo*, prettily located in a quiet corner of the city (L51 000 without bath, L83 000 with).

**La Calcina, Zattere ai Gesuati 780, tel 520 6466, was Ruskin's *pensione* in 1877, near the Gesuati Church and overlooking the busy Giudecca Canal. Simply furnished but comfortable, rooms are L48–58 000 without bath, and L76–86 000 with; off season discounts.

**Messner, Salute 216, tel 522 7443, is a recently modernized hotel only a couple of minutes from the Salute, very suitable for families. Great showers but awful coffee (L56 000 without bath, L85 000 with).

**Seguso, Zattere ai Gesuati 779, tel 522 2340, is in a 15th-century house next to La Calcina. Rooms in the front overlook the Giudecca Canal, while side rooms have views on one of its finest 'tributaries'. The Seguso has plenty of character, antiques, and outdoor tables for a sunny breakfast (L54–60 000 without bath, L82–87 000 with).

*Antico Capon, Campo S. Margherita 3004/b, tel 528 5292, owes most of its charm to its sociable *Campo*; 7 simple rooms, and, Halleluia! no breakfast (L50 000 without bath, L74 000 with).

*Ca' Foscari, Calle della Frescada 3888, tel 522 5817, is hidden in a wee lane near San Tomà; 10 nice, quiet, bathless rooms (L48 000).

*Casa di Stefani, Calle del Traghetto S. Barnaba 2786, tel 522 3337, an 11-room hotel in a Gothic palace near the S. Barnaba *vaporetto* stop. Good rooms for L48 000 without bath, L58 000 with.

*Montin, Fondamenta di Borgo 1147, tel 522 7151, is one of the last old-fashioned Venetian hosteleries, with 7 character-filled rooms, and an excellent (but expensive) restaurant to boot. Book early, as it is very popular (L44–48 000, all rooms without bath).

San Marco

*****Bauer Grünwald & Grand Hotel, Campo S. Moisè 1459, tel 520 7022, has two faces—a beautiful 13th-century palace facing the Grand Canal and a 1960s concrete addition facing the *campo*. The large rooms vary widely in decor and price, but all are elegant and comfortable (L245–480 000, off season L150–290 000).

*****Europa e Regina, Calle Larga XXII Marzo 2159, tel 520 0477. Across the Grand Canal from the Salute, old, nicely renovated by the Ciga people. Large rooms, many with view of Grand Canal, others on a quiet garden courtyard. Pretty, high-ceilinged rooms and a majestic Venetian drawing room, furnished with every amenity (L275–525 000).

*****Gritti Palace, S. Maria del Giglio 2467, tel 794 611. The 15th-century Grand Canal palace that belonged to the dashing glutton and womanizer Doge Andrea Gritti has been preserved as a true Venetian fantasy and an elegant retreat. For a real splurge do as Somerset Maugham did and stay in the Ducal Suite (L380–680 000).

****Cavalletto & Doge Orseolo, Calle Cavalletto 1107, tel 520 0955, overlooks the basin where most of the gondoliers moor their vessels, in a building that in the 10th century was a hostel for pilgrims waiting to embark for the Holy Land. A hotel since the 18th century, it offers far more luxury than the pilgrims ever enjoyed—complete with air conditioning, window boxes, mini bar, and colour TV (L140–275 000; off season discounts).

****Concordia**, Calle Larga S. Marco 367, tel 520 6866, is the only hotel overlooking Piazza S. Marco. Recently rennovated with a touch of Hollywood in some of the furnishings, the central air conditioning keeps you fresh and cool when the rest of Venice swelters (L145–295 000; off season discounts).

****Luna Hotel Baglioni**, Calle dell'Ascensione 1243, tel 528 9840, claims to be Venice's oldest hotel, founded in 1474 as a hospice for pilgrims, who were favoured with a fine marble stair and airy rooms, now renovated and air conditioned. Some have views over the Grand Canal (L195–375 000).

****Monaco & Grand Canal**, Calle Vallaresso 1325, tel 520 0211, a medium sized hotel in an 18th-century palace, overlooking the mouth of the Grand Canal, near Piazza S. Marco, rooms have view of the canal or garden at the back; garden terrace another plus (L185–360; off season discounts).

****Saturnia & International**, Via XXII Marzo 2398, tel 520 8377, is a lovely hotel in a romantic *quattrocento palazzo*, that has preserved centuries of accumulated decoration. Very near S. Marco, it has a garden court, faced by the nicest, and quietest rooms, many furnished with Venetian antiques (L245–360 000; off season discounts).

***Bel Sito & Berlino**, S. Maria del Giglio 2517, tel 522 3365, is a charming and comfortable 34 room hotel that looks over the ornate façade of S. Maria del Giglio. Its only demerit is the lack of a lift, especially if your room is on the top floor. All have private bath and air conditioning (L97–150 000).

***Bonvecchiati**, Calle Goldoni 4488, tel 528 5017, is a midpoint between S. Marco and the Rialto Bridge, set back in a small square flanking a canal. Rooms are furnished with antiques or repros; modern art hangs everywhere else, and you can dine on the canal terrace (L100–110 000 without bath, L140–160 000 with; off season discounts).

***Boston**, Calle dei Fabbri 848, tel 528 7665, is a tasteful hotel with 42 rooms, the best furnished with antiques and little balconies overhanging the canals (L120–155 000; off season discounts).

***Casanova**, Frezzeria 1284, tel 520 6855, is very near Piazza S. Marco. Public rooms are furnished with monastic furniture and art, while the bedrooms are considerably more in the vein of Casanova with their worldly comforts (L160 000; all with bath and optional air conditioning).

***Do Pozzi**, Corte do Pozzi 2373, tel 520 7855, has 29 serene rooms on a charming little square, only a few minutes from S. Marco. Friendly and well run; L110–153 000; all with bath and optional air conditioning.

***Flora**, Calle Bergamaschi 2283/a, tel 520 5844, a small hotel on a small street near the Piazza, with a charming garden and patio, spilling flowers. Very quiet; air conditioning available; ask for a large room (84–110 000 without bath, L120–160 000 with; off season discounts).

***Kette**, Piscina S. Moisè 2053, tel 522 2730, a short walk from the Piazza, has small but cosy rooms, each equipped with frigo bar, private bath and air conditioning (included in the price of the room). Triples available (L95–160 000).

***La Fenice et des Artistes**, Campiello Fenice 1936, tel 523 2333, is a favourite of opera buffs in Venice, next to the theatre, where you can sit out on a terrace at breakfast and hear the evening's soprano doing her scales. Lots of mirrors, antiques and chandeliers to make artistes feel at home. Air conditioning available (L160 000).

***Panada**, Calle Specchieri 646, tel 520 9088, is in an old building on a narrow street very near Piazza S. Marco, but has been charmingly renovated, with pleasant Venetian style rooms. All have bath and air conditioning as an extra (L120–160 000; off season discounts).

***Rialto**, Riva del Ferro 5149, tel 520 9166, stands at the foot of the Rialto Bridge near the centre of day to day Venice. Many of the rooms have Venetian furnishings, and all have bath (L90–160 000).

***San Moisè**, Piscina S. Moisè 2058, tel 520 3755, is both very quiet, on its dead end canal, and very close to the bustle of S. Marco. Rooms, furnished with antiques and Venetian bric-à-brac, vary widely in quality. Air conditioning is optional (L96–160 000).

*Centauro, Campo Manin 4297/a, tel 522 5832, is one of the older inns in Venice; 31 rooms, L44–60 000 without bath, L65–90 000 with).

*San Fantin, Campiello Fenice 1930/a, tel 523 1401, a simple little hotel, conveniently located near the opera, with 14 rooms and modernized décor (L58 000 without bath, L90 000 with).

*San Gallo, Campo S. Galloe 1093/a, tel 522 7311, is a family run 12-room hotel with the plus of a rooftop terrace near Piazza S. Marco. The rooms are bright and cheerful, though noise may be a problem if you go to bed early (L38–60 000 without bath, L55–88 000 with).

*Casa Petrarca**, Calle delle Colonne 4386, tel 520 0430. Petrarch didn't really sleep in one of these six friendly rooms by the Piazza, but who cares? (L50 000 without bath, L60–75000 with).

307

*San Samuele, Piscina di S. Samuele 3358, tel 522 8045, nice rooms between S. Marco and the Accademia Bridge (L48 000 without bath, L70 000 with).

San Polo

***Carpaccio, Calle Corner 2765, tel 523 5946, lies in a casbah of winding alleys, though the elegant lobby overlooks the Grand Canal near the San Tomà *vaporetto* stop. The 17 rooms aren't as ripping, but nice enough (L100 000 without bath, L155 000 with; off season discounts).

**Marconi & Milano, Riva del Vin 729, tel 522 2068, is only a hop and a skip from the Rialto Bridge in a 16th-century palace. The sumptuousness of the salons dissipates in the bedrooms, but all is kept in tiptop shape by the German-Italian management. Outdoor tables overlooking the Grand Canal are an added bonus (L52–60 000 without bath, L80–90 000 with).

*Alex, Rio Terrà Frari 2606, tel 523 1341, near the Frari, its 11 rooms on the mod side; could be jarring if you belong to the Venice cult (L50 000 without bath, 62 000 with; off season discounts).

*Sturion, Calle del Sturion 679, tel 523 6243, is a popular choice—the only cheap hotel on the Grand Canal—so book ahead for one of its 8 fine large rooms (L33–50 000, without bath).

Santa Croce

***Al Sole Palace, Fondamenta Minotto 136, tel 523 2144, a large hotel by Venetian standards with 62 rooms, is located in a beautiful Venetian Gothic palace on a peaceful canal (L158 000, all rooms with bath).

***San Cassiano—Ca' Favretto, Calle della Rosa 2232, tel 524 1760, is located in a converted 14th-century palace, with fine views across the Grand Canal to the Ca' d'Oro (the closest *vaporetto* stop is S. Stae). The rooms have an old-fashioned elegance, and half look out over the Grand Canal or the little canal nearby. TV, frigo bar and reasonably priced air conditioning are added features (L92–160 000, all with bath).

**Ai Due Fanali, S. Simone Grande 946, tel 718 344, is a quiet hotel on a square overlooking the Grand Canal, a few steps from the station bridge. Although a bit shabby on the outside, it is comfortable enough inside, and has tables in front for drinks or loitering (L57 000 without bath, L86 000 with; off season discounts).

**Falier, Salizzada S. Pantalon 130, tel 522 8882, a small hotel near Campo S. Rocco, is elegantly furnished, and has two flower-filled terraces to lounge around when your feet rebel (L54–58 000 without bath, L75–86 000 with).

Giudecca

*****Cipriani, Giudecca 10, tel 520 7744, has been since 1963 one of Italy's most luxurious hotels, a villa isolated in a lush garden on one end of the Giudecca, but linked day and night by private motor launch to Piazza San Marco. No place will pamper you more, anywhere. Olympic pool, sauna, jacuzzis in the bathrooms, tennis, live music in the evening are some of the treats; as each room has a different view and facilities, prices vary from L410–810 000.

**Casa Frollo, Giudecca 50, tel 522 2723, is the funky/trendy Giudecca's *other* hotel; a homey place with a garden—for a tenth the price of the Cipriani (L58 000 without bath, L80–86 000 with).

Lido

*****Excelsior Palace, Lungomare Marconi 41, tel 526 0201, an immense fantasy confection, built in 1907 as the largest and most luxurious resort hotel in the world. Part Hollywood and part Alhambra-Neo-Gothic, the interior is designed with a solemn flamboyance to match the outrageous exterior. Forget all the puffy clouds and cherubs in those Baroque heavens—to the average upwardly mobile Italian of today, this is Paradise. Try and get a room during the film festival to ogle the stars. Private beach, swimming pool, *cabanas* that are more comfortable than some bedrooms on the Grand Canal, tennis courts, golf, nightclub with a retractable roof, and a private launch service to Venice are some of its amenities. Closed Nov–March (L340–570 000).

****Des Bains, Lungomare Marconi 17, tel 526 5921, is a grand old luxury hotel, in large park designed for dalliance. Thomas Mann stayed here on several occasions, and had Aschenbach sigh his life away on the private beach. There's also a salt water swimming pool, tennis courts, a private pier and motor boat service into Venice. 233 large rooms, perfect service, magnificent Liberty style salon and breeze-filled veranda dining room. Closed Nov–March (L240–450 000).

****Quattro Fontane, Via delle Quattro Fontane 16, tel 526 0227, the best of the smaller hotels, Quattro Fontane is the former seaside villa of a

Venetian family. Its white stucco exterior and green shutters and its cool walled-in courtyard are inviting and tranquil; the public and private rooms are sophisticated and decorated with antiques. Near the beach and casino, it has its own tennis courts as well. Book as early as possible. Closed Nov–March (L170–190 000 without bath, L200–310 000 with). ***Villa Parco**, Via Rodi 1, tel 526 0015, is a renovated villa a block from the sea and has a fine little garden for a bit of privacy—and children are welcome (L85–125 000 with bath).

Elsewhere

***Locanda Cipriani**, Piazza S. Fosca 29, Isola di **Torcello**, tel 730 150. Only 5 rooms in the quietest, most haunted spot in the *comune* of Venice, at least once the day trippers melt back into the Lagoon; perhaps you can even stay in the room where Hemingway wrote his awful Venice novel, *Across the River and Into the Trees*—standing up because of haemorrhoids (L335 000 a person, full pension).
***Villa Margherita**, Via Nazionale 312, **Mira**, tel 420 879, offers the chance to live the life of a Venetian patrician (who wouldn't be caught dead in the city, in the summer anyway); the hotel restaurant, specializing in seafood is one of the best in the area (L90–150 000).
*Raspo de Ua**, Via Galuppi 560, Isola di **Burano**, tel 730 095, is a simple 6-room *locanda*, offering visitors a chance to know Burano after the tourists have gone for the day (L50 000, all without bath).

Hostels and Camping

The tourist office at S. Marco has a current list of all inexpensive hostel accomodation in Venice; as the city nowadays discourages sleeping out in the streets, schools have been pressed into use to take the summer overflow, charging minimal rates to spread out a sleeping bag or for a camp bed.
Ostello Venezia, Fondamenta delle Zitelle 86, **Giudecca**, tel 523 8211, enjoys one of the most striking locations of any youth hostel in Italy, right on the Giudecca Canal, with views of S. Marco. In the winter you can book by phone, but from June–Sept you have to book in person (office opens at 6 pm, but doors open at noon for waiting). To be assured of a place in July or Aug it's best to book by spring. Members only, but cards at the door, and 11:30 pm curfew; 12 000 a head, including breakfast; good value meals for L8000.

Foresteria Valdese, Calle della Madonnetta 5170, **Castello** (near the end of Calle Lunga S. Maria Formosa), tel 528 6797, an old *palazzo* converted into a dormitory/*pensione* by the Waldensians; one room is an inexpensive self-catering flat for up to 6 people. Check in between 11–1 and 6–8:30; L16 000 for the dorm, including bath and breakfast, L20 000 per person for a room.

Domus Cavanis, Rio Terrà Foscarini 912, **Dorsoduro**, tel 528 7374, a proper Catholic-run institution that mother would approve of; open June–Sept only, single sex single, double, and triple rooms for L27 000 a head; meals L8000.

Camping in the northeast corner of the Lagoon, in the seaside sprawl of Cavallino, Jésolo, and Punta Sabbioni is big business, with plush sites, swimming pools, etc. in their tens of thousands. A complete list is available from the tourist office.

S. Nicolò, Riviera S. Nicolò 65, **Lido**, tel 767 415, the closest campsite to Venice; International Camping Card required.

Fusina, Via Moranzani, **Malcontenta**, by Fusina, tel 969 064, has 1000 places open year round, but the *vaporetto* No. 16 to S. Marco exists only in the summer, though the Padua–Venice bus runs nearby every half hour.

Serenissima, Via Padana 338, Oriago, **Mira**, tel 920 286, has 300 camping places and 4 bungalows just off the Brenta Canal; the same Padua-Venice bus passes nearby (April–Sept).

Miramare, Lungomare Alighieri 19, **Punta Sabbioni**, tel 966 150; a 40 minute ride on *vaporetto* No. 14; one of the nearest campsites to the stop (540 places, open April–Sept).

Self-Catering Flats

If you mean to spend a week or more in Venice, consider renting a self-catering flat. Firms that offer them include:

CHAPTER TRAVEL, 126 St John's Wood High Street, London NW8, tel (071) 586 9451

CITALIA, Marco Polo House 3–5, Lansdowne Road, Croydon CR9 9EQ, tel (081) 686 5336

INTERHOME 383 Richmond Road, Twickenham, tel 081–891 1294

VENETIAN APARTMENTS, 1a Warrington Rd, Richmond, Surrey, tel (081) 948 6950

VILLAS ITALIA , 227 Shepherds Bush Road, London W6, tel (081) 748 8668.

Entertainment and Nightlife

'Here they are getting dressed while the rest of world is going to bed' it was said—and if all were right with the world, Venice would still be a real blowout after dark, the one city in the world where you could dress up outrageously, catch a gondola with your sweetheart and dance under the fairy lights in the company of a *Casablanca* mix of people from all over the world, gathered in the eternal capital of romance and pleasure. The sad truth, however, is that the Venetians and most of their visitors tuck themselves in early like old biddies. The locals are content with a twilight *passegiata* to Campo S. Bartolomeo, Riva degli Schiavone, Piazza S. Marco, or to their neighbourhood *campo*, for a chat with friends and an *aperitivo* before heading home to dinner and the dubious delights of Italian TV, while the more hotblooded amphibians may go to the clubs, discos, or bars in Mestre or Marghera.

Visitors who aren't ready for bed at 10 pm are left to become even poorer at the **Municipal Casino**, out on the Lido from April–Oct (*vaporetto* every half hour from S. Marco), and other times at Palazzo Vendramin on the Grand Canal (hours are 3 pm–2 am, dress up and take your passport). You may spend less more memorably on a moon-lit gondola ride (L65 000 an hour) or you can do as most night owls do—wander about. Venice is a different city at night, when the *bricole* lights in the Lagoon are a fitting backdrop for a mer-king's birthday pageant. For all that, there are things to do after hours on the magic Lagoon.

Opera, Classical Music and Theatre

Although no longer bubbling over with effervescent homegrown talent on the level of Goldoni or Vivaldi, Venice at least holds its own in the highbrow league. Pick up a copy of the tourist office's free Italian/ English booklet, *Un Ospite di Venezia*, published weekly in the summer and monthly in the off season, with its calendar of what's on, or try the Department of Culture, in the Ala Napoleonica, Piazza S. Marco 52, tel 520 9288. For listings in the entire Veneto region (Verona's Arena, most notably, has summer opera, major rock and jazz concerts, and other block busters) check the newspapers or the monthly *Marco Polo* maga- zine. Concerts nearly always mean classical music: opera, ballet, recitals, and symphonies are the main fare at Venice's opera house, **La Fenice** and its smaller chamber, Sala Apollinee (Campo S. Fantin, S. Marco, tel 521 0161 between 9:30–12:30 and 4–6; closed Aug). The other main theatre, **Teatro Goldoni** (Calle Goldoni 4650/b, S. Marco, tel 520 5422) has mostly plays, mostly by—surprise—Goldoni, but music of all varieties crops up often, too; in the summer performances are often moved to Campo S. Polo.

Two concert venues are worth visiting, as much for the decor as the music. The state radio admits the public free of charge to the concerts it records among Giambattista Tiepolo's Cleopatra frescoes in the **Palazzo Labia**, in Campo S. Geremia, Cannaregio, as long as you ring ahead for tickets (tel 716 666). For the second, Vivaldi's lovely Rococo church of **La Pietà**, you have to pay for your music, usually above the odds, and usually for less than riveting performances, though the acoustics are well-nigh perfect (info and tickets, tel 520 8722 or 520 8711). Other currently active theatres in Venice are **L'Avogaria**, with a bill of Goldoni, Gozzi, and even some non-Venetians (Calle de l'Avogaria 1617, Dorsoduro, tel 520 6130); **Del Ridotto**, with classic and contemporary plays (Calle Vallaresso, S. Marco, tel 522 2939; and Mestre's **Teatro Toniolo**, Piazzetta Battisti, tel 505 7217, that special- izes in 20th-century Italian theatre. In the summer there are perform- ances in the garden of **Ca' Rezzonico**. Other concerts take place at the **Frari, Ca' Giustinian, S. Stefano**, the **Scuola Grande di S. Giovanni Evangelista**, the court of the Doge's Palace, the **Palasport dell' Arsenale**, and the **Palazzo Prigione Vecchie**.

Art Exhibitions and Cinema

Venice is one of Europe's top cities for exhibitions: major international shows have become the norm at the Palazzo Ducale and Palazzo Grassi, and high calibre art and photographic exhibitions frequently appear at the Palazzo Querini-Stampalia, Ca' Pésaro, Correr Museum, Museo Fortuny, Peggy Guggenheim Collection, and in the smaller galleries occupying a host of churches; *Un Ospite di Venezia* has all the listings.

Outside the week of the Film Festival, Venice's cinemas rarely show anything you can't see back home in English rather than dubbed in Italiano. The exceptions, mostly under the auspices of the Cinema Club (tel 524 1320) are listed in *Un Ospite* under 'Cinema d'Essai' and occur at the **Cinema Accademia,** by the Accademia Gallery, Dorsoduro 1019, tel 528 7706; **Olimpia,** Campo S. Gallo 1094 (just north of Piazza S. Marco, tel 520 5439) and **Ritz,** Calle dei Segretaria 617 (by S. Giuliano), S. Marco, tel 520 4429.

Jazz, Dancing, and Nightspots

There are a few oases in the desert. On a good night, any can be fun; on a bad night, they'll be almost empty or dominated by posing androids squeezed into £400 designer pants. We refuse to be responsible for what you find (try ringing ahead) but the following is a fairly comprehensive list of what's happening after the typical Venetian turns into a pumpkin:

Paradiso Perduto, Fondamenta Misericordia, Cannaregio (tel 720 581) Venice's best known late night restaurant and bar, has inexpensive and sometimes good food, and often live jazz at weekends; members of Venice's non-assertive gay community occasionally check in (open 6 pm–midnight; closed Wed). The relaxed and informal **Osteria Da Codroma,** Fondamenta Briati 2540, Dorsoduro (tel 520 4161) is the seat of Venice's backgammon club, but has other games going, shows by local artists, a wine bar, and occasional live jazz (open 7 pm–2 am; closed Thurs). Another restaurant/bar with music and periodic live rock or jazz (and dancing) is **Ai Canottieri,** Ponte Tre Archi 690, Cannaregio (tel 715 408); open 7 pm–2 am (closed Sun).

Fancier joints at fancier prices include **Harry's Dolci** on the Giudecca (tel 522 4844) which has dining *al fresco* and, rather surprisingly for Venice, Dixieland concerts from 8–11 pm on Fridays during the season. Dorsoduro's **Linea d'Ombra** on the Zattere near the Salute (tel 528 5259) has a tinkling piano bar and occasional concerts from

8 pm–1 am (closed Wed). Another, swankier piano bar/night club, **Antico Martini**, by the Fenice in Campo S. Fantin 1980. S. Marco (tel 522 4121) has food until 2 am and stays open until 3 am (closed Tues). **El Souk**, Calle Corfu 1056/a, by the Accademia (tel 520 0371) is Venice's only disco, complete with a bouncer ready to give you the bum's rush if your togs don't appeal (10 pm–4 am; closed Sun). In July and August there's a more convivial disco on the Lido: **Club 22**, Lungomare Marconi 22, tel 526 0466. The Lido is also the place to hie for a late night game of billiards, either *chez* **Al Delfino**, an 'American Bar' with music and snacks at Lungomare Marconi 96, tel 526 8309 (open until 2 am) or **Villa Eva**, Gran Viale 49, tel 526 1884, with music and snacks from midnight until 4 am (closed Thurs except in the summer). Or try a favourite Venetian haunt, **Al Vapore**, Via Fratelli Bandiera 8, in Marghera, tel 930 796, for live jazz and concerts.

Main late night refueling points are **Harry's Bar**, Calle Vallaresso, S. Marco (open till 1 am; an especially good bet if someone else is paying); **Osteria ai Assassini**, Calle degli Assassini, S. Marco (open til midnight except Sun, with wines, beers, and *cichetti veneti* (Venetian snacks). **Haig's**, Campo S. Maria del Giglio, S. Marco, tel 528 9456, has snacks and a gay/straight clientele (until 2 am, closed Wed); another late-night rendezvous **Sottosopra**, Dorsoduro 3740, tel 528 5320, has cocktails, music and snacks until 1 am. For more filling victuals, try **Vino Vino** (the down-scale section of Antico Martini; open until 2 am); If you need a pancake after dark, try the **Creperia Poggi**, Cannaregio 2103 (tel 715 971) which has music and stays open until 2 am, flipping crêpes until midnight (closed Sun), or **Osteria al Postali da Lilli**, Rio Marin 821, S. Croce (tel 715 156) open 8:30 pm–2 am, with music, visual projections, and crêpes until 1 am (closed Tues). Venice's last ice cream cones are served up at 3 am on the Lido at the **Gelateria Bar Maleti**, Gran Viale 47 (closed Wed).

Shopping

glass figures from Murano

Since the Middle Ages Venice has been one of Italy's top cities for shopping, and the vast influx of monied visitors insures it will remain so in the future, whether you're looking for tacky bric-à-brac to brighten up the den (just walk down the Lista di Spagna or through the Rialto) or the latest in hand-crafted Venetian design. Most of the big name designer boutiques are clustered to the west of Piazza S. Marco, with the same clothes you can get anywhere else, though we've made a special note of what's unique to Venice. Most Venetians, however, buy their clothes at the **COIN** department store, a national chain based in the city (Rioterrà S. Leonardo 5788, Cannaregio), or in the long daily outdoor market spread along the middle of the street. Jewellers are clustered in Piazza S. Marco and on the Rialto Bridge. Murano still has the best selection of glass, Burano the best selection of lace.

Many Venetian shops neither have nor display a name, and not a few below will be mere addresses. But they are no less interesting for that. A flea market appears periodically in Campo S. Maurizio, the principle antiques area. The main public auction house is **Franco Semezato**, Palazzo Giovannelli, Cannaregio 2292, tel 721 811.

Size Chart
Italian clothes are lovely, but if you have a large-boned Anglo-American build, you may find it hard to get a good fit, especially on trousers or skirts

316

(Italians are a long-waisted, slim-hipped bunch). Men's shirts are sold by collar size only, and shoes are often narrower than the sizes at home. Feel fortunate, at least, that Venice no longer uses its own weights and measures, where a pound of coffee was lighter than a pound of butter, and five feet made a *passa* and six a *perch*, and a square perch was a *tarola* and there were ten *ingiustare* of wine in a *staie* and fourteen *staie* in a *bigoncio*, and you even had to weigh the coins because they weren't always the same.

Women's Shirts/Dresses

UK	10	12	14	16	18
US	8	10	12	14	16
Italy	40	42	44	46	48

Sweaters

UK	10	12	14	16
US	8	10	12	14
Italy	46	48	50	52

Women's Shoes

UK	3	4	5	6	7	8
US	4	5	6	7	8	9
Italy	36	37	38	39	40	41

Men's Shirts

UK/US	14	14½	15	15½	16	16½	17	17½
Italy	36	37	38	39	40	41	42	43

Men's Suits

UK/US	36	38	40	42	44	46
Italy	46	48	50	52	54	56

Men's Shoes

UK	2	3	4	5	6	7	8	9	10	11	12
US	5	6	7	7½	8	9	10	10½	11	12	13
Italy	34	36	37	38	39	40	41	42	43	44	45

Weights and Measures

1 kilogramme (1000 g)—2.2 lb	1 lb—0.45 kg
1 etto (100 g)—¼lb (approx)	
1 litre—1.76 pints	1 pint—0.568 litres
1 quart—1.136 litres	1 Imperial gallon—4.546 litres
	1 US gallon—3.785 litres
1 metre—39.37 inches	1 foot—0.3048 metres
1 kilometre—0.621 miles	1 mile—1.161 kilometres

Antiques

Antonietta Santomanco della Toffola, Frezzeria 1504, S. Marco, for Russian and English silver, prints, antique jewellery and glass.

Bastianello Arte, Campo S. Bartolomeo 5042, S. Marco, specialize in western and oriental antiques, as well as Art Nouveau and jewellery.

Fondamenta del Soccorso 2609, a real 'Old Curiosity Shop', everything from Baroque clocks to bills printed by the 1848 revolutionary government.

Giancarlo Ballarini, Calle delle Botteghe 3174, restoration/antique shop, has a good eye for the more florid styles.

Pietro Scarpa, whose shops are as much museums, Campo S. Moisè 1464 and Calle XXII Marzo 2089, S. Marco (old drawings).

Xanthippe, Dorsoduro 2773 (by Ca' Rezzonico), a new, cosy and highly eclectic shop specializing in the 19th century, with unusual styles like Piedmontese Biedermeier.

Salizzada S. Lio 5672, Castello, an ecletic antique shop with prints of Venice, old clock, and other curious odds and ends.

Art Supplies

Cartoleria Accademia, Accademia 1052, on the Rio Terrà della Carità, Dorsoduro, is jampacked with paints, paper, easels, etc. for those who want to make their own souvenir of Venice.

Books

Alla Toletta, Sacca della Toletta 1214, Dorsoduro, in spite of its name ('at the toilet') sells perfectly decent new books at half price, some in English.

Calle Crosera 3951, near the Frari, good selection on art, crafts and music.

Fantoni, Salizzada di S. Luca 4121, S. Marco, has a monumental display of monumental art books.

Filippi, Calle del Paradiso 5763, Castello, has the city's best selection of Italian books about Venice—covering Venetian folktales, dialect, theatre, costumes, navy, etc., including many facsimiles of antique books from the days when Venice was one of Europe's centres for printing.

Il Libraio a San Barnaba, Fondamenta Gerardini 2835/a, Dorsoduro, for Venice's best general selection of novels and other books in English.

Libreria Cassini, Calle Larga XXII Marzo 2424, S. Marco, for old prints, antique books, and rare editions.

Nuova Cluva, 197 S. Croce (by the School of Architecture), has an excellent selection of books on architecture.

Punto Libri, Salizzada di S. Pantalon, for art and architecture books.

Sangiorgio, Calle Larga XXII Marzo 2087, S. Marco, for books in English, especially about Venice; also some hefty art tomes.

Sansovino, Bacino Orseolo 84 (just outside the Procuratie Vecchie), S. Marco, has a large collection of art and coffee table books, and hundreds of postcards.

Serenissima, Merceria dell'Orologio 739, S. Marco has a good selection of books about Venice, in English.

Clothes and Accessories

Betta Scarpa, Frezzeria 1797, S. Marco, a boutique with handmade cashmere knits.

Camiceria San Marco, Calle Vallaresso 1340, S. Marco, for men's shirts and ladies' dresses made to order in 24 hours.

La Coupole, Via XXII Marzo or Frezzeria 1674, for fashions by maverick Italian and French designers.

Delphos, S. Marco 2403, for pleated silk Fortuny scarves, dresses, and bags.

Elisabetta alla Fenice, Campo S. Fantin, S. Marco, where the female descendents of the doges disperse their patrimony on some of Venice's most exclusive fashions.

Emilio Ceccato, Sottoportico di Rialto, S. Polo, the place to buy gondolier's shirts, jackets, and tight trousers.

Emporio Armani, Calle dei Fabbri 989, S. Marco, for relatively affordable big name designs.

Giorgio Armani da Elysée, Frezzeria 1693, S. Marco, where Armani sells at the prices you'd expect.

Krizia, Calle delle Ostreghe and Via XXII Marzo, S. Marco, for colourful, imaginative knits.

Laura Biagiotti, Via XXII Marzo 2400a, for designer clothes that most people feel safe wearing.

M. Antichità, S. Marco 1691, for velour dresses of Renaissance richness and jewels to match

Missoni, Calle Vallaresso 1312, S. Marco, for some of Italy's most beautiful knitwear (open Sun 10–7).

Roberta di Camerino, Lungomare Marconi 32, Lido. One of Venice's homegrown designers.

Aldo Strausse, Campo S. Giustina, in Castello, for fashionable second-hand clothes.

Valentino, Salizzada S. Moisè 1473, S. Marco, for that designer's distinctive wear (open Sun 10–7).

Fabrics

Trois, S. Marco 2666, a Venetian institution, with Fortuny silks made to traditional specifications on the Giudecca.

Valli, Merceria S. Zulian 783, S. Marco, designer silks and fabrics.

Food

Colussi, Rugheta S. Apollonia 4325, near Campo SS. Filippo e Giacomo, with unusual pastries including Sicilian *martorana* fruits (marzipan in the form of strawberries, oysters and sardines).

Il Pastaio, Calle del Varoteri 219, in the Rialto markets, offers pasta in a score of different colours and shapes, including *tagliatelle* made with cuttlefish ink or curry.

Pastificio Artigiano, Strada Nuova 4292, Cannaregio. Paolo Pavon's 48 years of experience has gone into creating Venice's tastiest and most exotic pastas; for kicks, take home a bag of *pasta al cacao* (chocolate pasta), or *pasta al limone* (lemon), or beetroot, garlic, mushroom . . .

Rizzo, Calle delle Botteghe, S. Marco, just off Campo F. Morosini, has absolutely everything you could want for a picnic.

1563 Rio Terrà S. Leonardo, a wonderful, brightly coloured sweet shop crammed full of pure tooth decay.

Glass

Arte Veneto, Campo S. Zanipolo 6335, one of the few places where glass and ceramic trinkets escape being merely ridiculous.

Guido Farinati, Campo S. Giacomo dell'Orio 1658, S. Croce,for fine leaded glass.

Industrie Veneziane for your souvenir Harry's Bar carafes.

Paolo Rossi, Campo S. Zaccaria 4685, very nice reproductions of ancient decorative glass at very reasonable prices.

Pauly, at the end of Calle Larga, by Ponte Consorzi, S. Marco.

Salizzada San Moisè 1470, S. Marco, a glass spectacular; Murano's most ambitious creations, including life-size toucans, abstract pieces and lots of chandeliers, all at astronomical prices.

Ta'Kala', Strada Nuova 4391, near Campo SS. Apostoli, artisan ceramic figurines, puppets, glass jewelery and trinkets, some quite original.

Household

Domus, Calle dei Fabbri 4746, for name-brand porcelains.

Rubelli, in Palazzo Corner Spinelli, S. Angelo 3877, S. Marco, where the damasks, velours, and brocades are produced in the rich colours of the *Cinquecento*, many with an Imperial Russian and Byzantine touch.

Jewellery

Codognato, S. Marco 1295, one of the oldest jeweller's in Venice, with rare pieces by Tiffany and Cartier, and Art Deco baubles.

Junior, Piazza S. Marco 135, on the Quadri side of the square, has one of the widest selections of cameos in the city.

Missiaglia, Piazza S. Marco 125, near Quadri's, for some of the most elegant work by Venetian gold and silversmiths, as well as necklaces, etc.

Nardi, Piazza S. Marco 69-71, adjacent to Florian's, one of Venice's luxury establishment jewellers, celebrated for its series of 'Othellos', a series of elaborate jewelled pieces of carved ebony, each unique; also clocks, frames, and other glittering dust magnets.

Kosher Food and Souvenirs

Art Shops: There are two in Calle Baracchi, near the Ponte Vecchio, with jewellery, souvenirs, and religious articles. A third, more

idiocyncratic shop is in Campo Ghetto Vecchio, Cannaregio, with elaborate but playful figurines amd other handicrafts.
Food shop, Ramo Ghetto Vecchio 1143, Cannaregio, specializes in Venetian-Jewish pastries and snacks and kosher wines.

Lace and Lingerie

This is fiendishly hard to avoid on Burano, though beware because the bargains you find are probably neither handmade nor Buranese. Pick up a lace connoisseur's eye at the Lace School (which also has samples on sale) or try:

Jesurum, Ponte Canonica 4310, just behind St Mark's Basilica, which not only has a vast quantity of lace (tableclothes, lingerie, etc.) on display in a former 12th-century church, but also includes an array of swimming costumes and summery togs.
Mazzaron, Castello 4970, traditional homemade Venetian point.
Jade Martine, Frezzeria 1762, for expensive designer underthings.

Leather

La Bauta, Mercerie S. Zulian 729, for designs by Ferragamo and Prada.
Vogini, Via XXII Marzo 1300, the greatest name in Venetian leather, with designs by Venetian designer Roberta di Camerino.

Masks and Costumes

Even if you miss Carnival a mask makes a good souvenir, either in inexpensive papier mâché (*carta pesta*) or in leather. Mask shops are hard to avoid, but for the real traditionally crafted item, try **Giorgio Clanetti (Laboratorio Artigiano Maschere)**, on Barbaria delle Tole 6657, near SS. Giovanni e Paolo, Castello, or the master of them all **Emilio Massaro**, Calle Vetturi, by Campo Morosini, S. Marco, where you may watch them being made.
Balocoloc, Calle del Scaleter 2235, S. Polo, specializes in theatrical capes and the black mantels and tricorns you need to spook someone à la *Amadeus*.
Mezà, Calle del Cappeller 3215, Dorsoduro, makes theatre and carnival costumes.
Mondo Novo, Rio Terra Canal 3063, near Campo S. Margherita, Dorsoduro, some of the best masks in town: camels, sphinxes, moonfaces and everything else.

Mosaics

An even older Venetian craft, but a bit hard to carry home. If you've been smitten by the wonders in St Marks, you can buy some glass or gold *tessere* to try making your own mosaics. Find out more from:

Arte del Mosaico, Calle Erizzo 4002, Castello
Angelo Orsoni, Campiello del Battello 1045, Cannaregio
Donà Ugo & Figlio, Fodamenta d. Vetrai 61, Murano.

Paper/Stationary

A Calle della Mandorla (S. Angelo) that's all the sign says anymore; Florentine paper at lower prices than elsewhere.
Legatoria Piazzesi, S. Maria del Giglio 2511 (Calle del Piovan), S. Marco, for beautiful hand printed paper, traditional *carta varese*, and marble paper, block prints etc., and other beautiful and useful things for your desk and study, nearly all of which are locally made; one of Stravinsky's favourite shops.
Il Pavone, Calle Larga S. Maria Formosa 6133, for marbled paper and marbled animals.

Perfume

L'Artisan Parfumeur, Campo S. Maria Formosa 5183, the Venetian branch of a Parisian shop specializing in very exotic scents brewed by alchemists.

Shoes

La Fenice, Via XXII Marzo 2255, S. Marco, has posh shoes by French and Italian designers.
Giorgio Moretto, S. Marco 1820, for new designs.
Mario Valentino, Ascensione 1255, S. Marco, with that Neapolitan designer's shoes.
No Name cobbler, Calle delle Bande 5268, for atmospheric old fashioned shoe repairs.

Stamps

Degani, Procuratie Nuove 79, Piazza S. Marco, is the place to buy a souvenir for your favourite philatelist.

Toys

Città del Sole, Via Palazzo 50, in Mestre. If you're serious about toys, you have to go to the mainland. Città del Sole is a national chain specializing in quality kids' stuff from many countries.

Doll Hospital, Campiello di S. Giustina, Castello, a small shop that will do its best to heal a wounded toy.

Pettenello, Campo S. Margherita 2977, Dorsoduro, brightly coloured gimcracks from around the world.

Signor Blum, Calle Lunga S. Barnaba 2864, Dorsoduro, jigsaw puzzles and brightly painted wooden toys.

Venetian Blinds

Almet, Via Giustizia 11, Mestre, has the widest selection of blinds in the *comune* of Venice, if you want to take home the real thing.

Wine and Booze

5595 Calle de la Fava, just off Campo S. Lio, S. Marco, a serious, no frills wine and liquor shop.

Cantinone già Schiavi, Fondamenta S. Trovaso 992, Dorsoduro, a fine old wine shop with plenty to choose from.

Unusual

Consorzio Artiginato Artistico Veneziano, Calle Larga S. Marco 412, has a fair selection of local, handmade Venetian crafts.

Caffè Costarica, Rio Terrà di S. Leonardo, three generations in the same family; *espresso* subscriptions or gift packs available for your favourite Java junkies.

Calle Lunga 2137, in Dorsoduro, a workshop specializing in decorative wrought iron.

Colori da Campioni, Calle Lunga 2729, sells paint for walls, but has a fascinating window display of coloured powder in every conceivable hue that comes as a revelation on this rusty, dusty street.

Fondamenta Minotto 154 near S. Nicola Tolentino, gold and brass items including that really Venetian doorknocker you've always wanted.

Il Liuto, Fondamenta Rossa 2519, Dorsoduro, for handmade stringed instruments.

La Scialuppa, Calle Seconda dei Saoneri 2695, S. Polo, a little shop run by woodworker Gilberto Penzo, who carves beautiful *forcole*, walnut gondola oar locks; or you can pick up make-your-own little gondola kits, replicas of Venetian guild signs or a marine ex-voto, painted on wood.

Rialto Markets. You never know what you may find here, among the acres of tourist detritus; one stand, near the S. Polo side of the bridge, sells lovely inlaid wood *intarsia* from Sorrento; trays, boxes and such from L30 000 upwards, and some of the prettiest things you'll find in Venice.

Sports

a relaxed sport on the Lido

Until the refined and dandified 18th century, sport in Venice long had a rough and tumble character—bullfights, cudgel and fist fights, *calcio* (a nearly free-for-all kind of football) and fencing were favourites, although duels went out of fashion when the first to draw faced the death penalty. In the 60s people still swam in the Lagoon and Grand Canal. Nowadays most Venetians are content with the considerable exercise they get by just walking.

But **boating and regattas** (from *riga*, or starting line), understandably remain Venetian passions. There are traditional regattas for gondolas and rowing crews (see 'Calendar of Events', p. 16), and at the other extreme, the *Serenissima* Offshore Gran Prix for European formula one motor boats in the first week of June; contestants begin at Jesolo and zip along the sea coast off the Lido.

Bicycling

You can rent a bike, or a wonderfully touristy tricycle with a canopy on it, to explore the length of the Lido at **Giorgio Barbieri**, Via Zara 5. Another favourite place to bike is along the Brenta Canal; you can hire wheels near the first bus stop after Marghera, at Oriago.

Flying and Parachuting

The Lido's **Nicelli Airport** (tel 526 0823) is a favourite for parachuting, and often holds international team competitions.
The **Aeroclub G. Ancillotto**, tel 526 0808, has a flying school and short excursion flights over Venice.

Football

Venice's C1 division football team, VeneziaMestre, strives to reach the B division on Sundays in Mestre.

Golf

Alberoni Golf Course, an attractive 18-hole course on the Lido, sees a few minor competitions throughout the year (tel 831 015).

Riding

Like Byron and Shelley, you can ride on the Lido, though it's no longer the wild, romantic, hooves-in-the-dunes-and-surf affair. The main address is the Circolo Ippico Veneziano, Ca' Bianco, Lido, tel 526 1820.

Rowing

Foreigners can try their luck in Venice's many regattas, especially the Vogalonga Marathon on Ascension Day. Finding a boat to hire for a holiday row is much harder, though you may try one of the rowing clubs, or join one if you plan to spend some time in the city: Canottieri Bucintoro, Punta Dogana, Dorsoduro, tel 520 5630; or Canottieri Francesco Querini, Fondamente Nuove 6576, Cannaregio, tel 522 2039; or Canottieri Diadora, Ca' Bianco, Lido, tel 526 5742.

Sailing

The **Compagnia della Vela**, or sailing club can give you precise information, tel 522 2593.

Swimming

Despite dire reports about toxic bi-products in the Adriatic, people still swim off the Lido without turning into mutants. The other alternative is the swimming pool on Sacca Fisola, tel 528 5430.

Tennis

Venice's tennis courts are concentrated on the Lido, in the hotels and at two clubs—ring ahead to see if there are any available courts:
Tennis Club Venezia, Lungomare Marconi 41/d, tel 526 0335.
Campi Comunali Tennis, Lido, tel 526 5689.

Children's Venice

Like all Italians, Venetians are very fond of children, sometimes poignantly so, because there are so few around in the old city. There is little for kids to do in Venice, and few open places to play; families who can, usually move to Mestre. On the whole, most crumbsnatchers enjoy visiting Venice—all those boat rides and bridges (and no cars to watch out for!). At some point, give your map to the children and see where they lead you in the labyrinth. All the walking, however, tires young children easily, and adults, too, as the steps on the bridges render prams and pushchairs more of a nuisance than a help. If your tot is too big to fit comfortably into a back carrier, think again about your mother's offer to babysit.

Besides boat rides (especially a gondola ride, if you can afford it), Italian ice cream and feeding the vultures in St Mark's Square, most kids in Venice like to climb the Clock Tower and watch the mechanical giants, or take in the views from the Campanile or from the campanile of S. Giorgio Maggiore, or to spend an hour in the little aquarium behind St Mark's. The museums kids usually like best are the Naval Museum by the Arsenal, with its ships' models and cannons, the Natural History Museum in the Fondaco dei Turchi and the Peggy Guggenheim Collection. Most kids can even take small doses of the Accademia. Older children often like the Doge's Palace and the Secret Itinerary, the odds and ends in the Museo Correr, and the Carpaccios in the Scuola di S. Giorgio degli Schiavoni.

Most offspring under 10 will give their parents a decent interval in St Mark's, but for good behaviour in other churches and museums, you may have to barter away an afternoon on the Lido, to swim or just run in the sand and build castles. There's a small playground in the Giardini Pubblici, which is also good for a picnic. Watching a crew dredge a canal is almost as good as watching the Murano glassblowers.

Check the 'Calendar Of Events', pp. 14–17, for other ideas. At Carnival they can dress up in costumes like the Italian kids and get sick on fritters and other sticky sweets. The regattas are usually fun, as is the fireworks show for the *Redentore*. There's a fun fair along the Riva degli Schiavoni in January, and travelling circuses appear two or three times a year, though usually at Mestre. For toys see 'Shopping', p. 324.

Living and Working in Venice

Living in Venice has been compared to life in a convent or a desert; a convent in that life without cars is slow and leisurely enough to invite the contemplation of the cloister, and a desert in its lack of growing things, in its emptiness after dark, in the low-wattage of its social life, in the silence so deep that church bells seem to blast; you'll note that Venetians, once famous for singing in the streets, now almost never raise their voices. Even mainland Italians who move to the city complain that the Venetians are reserved and hard to make friends with. The Venetians counter by saying that outsiders are more interested in a romantic idea of Venetians, not in the people themselves; Venice in winter, they claim, is a city of broken hearts, and the Venetians' reluctance to meet outsiders is partly from a reluctance to be hurt again. Even on a more every day level, so many people come and go in Venice that it takes much longer to establish onesself as one who means to stay. Having kids helps to break the ice—you can also meet people in places like rowing clubs and political or cultural institutions. Most newcomers end up spending most of their time with their fellow foreigners, or with their colleagues at work or school, though even then it usually takes a long time before one's invited in to a Venetian's home.

Whether you're coming to Venice to work, study, retire, or just live for more than three months, you will save yourself a lot of trouble by getting the appropriate visa before you arrive. If you're an EC citizen, this may not even be necessary but do check. Students will require a declaration from an Italian consulate certifying that they have been accepted to study in Italy, and will have to prove that they've taken out health insurance. (British nationals need only the E111 form that entitles them to medical coverage in Italy). If you intend to study in Venice, especially to do post-graduate work, ask your Italian Embassy about scholarships offered by the Italian Ministry of Foreign Affairs (many are never used through lack of requests); or write directly to the Italian Ministry of Foreign Affairs, Direzione Generale per la Cooperazione Culturale Scientifica e Tecnica, Piazzale della Farnesina 1, Rome.

Upon arrival in Venice, anyone who plans to live in the city or stay for more than three months should go to the Questura (police station, at Fondamenta di S. Lorenzo, Castello, tel 520 3222) and get a *Permesso di Soggiorno* or a *Permesso di Soggiorno a scopa residenza* if you mean to reside in Italy. Once you have your *Permesso* you can go the *Ufficio Anagrafe* or Municipal Registry Office at Ca' Farsetti (you can imagine the jokes the Venetians make with Farsetti and farce) tel 781 111, to get your residence certificate. This document entitles you to move household goods and motor vehicles into Italy within six months without paying duty or taxes. If you are coming to Venice to work, your employer may well require you to take up residency to keep things nice and legal. The problem comes if you're looking for a flat to rent. Because of rent control (*Equo Canone*) many landlords will only let to foreign non-resident tenants. Many people are partly legal or lie a bit to get by.

One unavoidable fact is that Venice is expensive, in Italy second only to Milan. The two main reasons are the costs of transporting goods from the mainland by boat and porter; the second reason is the insatiable demand for a Venetian palace, flat or *pied-à-terre* by outsiders, Italian or foreign, who purchase *half* of the properties that come on the market. At the turn of the century, a palace on the Grand Canal went for the same price as a London garret; in the 1990s you'd best bring pots of money if you're looking for a place to rent or buy—at the time of writing a three-bedroom flat that needs restoration, in the historic centre, goes for L345 000 000 (about £172,000, or $300,000); rent for a one-bedroom flat in the historic centre start around L700 000 a month. Nearly all business is done through estate agents, though check the papers and ask around in neighbourhood bars. Estate agents who deal in rentals as well as sales are:

Cannavò: Via S. Gallo 5/a, Lido, tel 526 0071
Ferro: Via Cerigo 7, Lido, tel 526 0006 (also does seasonal lets)
Giaretta: Calle degli Orbi 5212, Castello, tel 520 9747
Narduzzi Immobiliare: Fondamenta Nani 330, near the Zattere, in Dorsoduro, tel 523 0486
S. Marco: Campo S. Lio 5620, tel 523 5935
S. Angelo: Campo S. Angelo 3818, S. Marco, tel 522 1505
Serena: Ponte Bareteri 4931, S. Marco, tel 522 4622
Venezia: S.Leonardo 1413/a, Cannaregio, tel 720 401.

If you're renting, most landlords insist on a deposit of two, and sometimes three months, in advance, and it can be the devil to get it all back when you leave, even if you give the required three months' notice (note: Contessa-landladies are especially bad about it). If you find your flat through an estate agent, their commission is usually 10% of the first year's rent. Rental leases are signed through a *Commercilista* who represents both you and the landlord and is paid to know all the complicated legal niceties (landlords often have their lawyers along, so you may want to have one too). The lease (usually for one year) may very well specify that you are **not** to become a resident.

That, of course, isn't a problem if you're buying your own place. Chances are what you find is going to need some major restoration (for instance, nearly half the houses lack decent bathrooms, and many have subsided to some degree) and it doesn't come cheaply, especially if you want to have it done properly, by Venetians who have a feel for the unique quirks and materials of their watery hometown. Before buying, have an independent estimate done on how much the repairs will cost. Then, if you still want to buy, make an offer, and if the seller accepts it, you'll be expected to pay 10–15% on signing an agreement called the *compromesso*, which penalizes either you or the seller if either party backs out. The paperwork is handled by a *notaio*, who works for you and the seller, though many people also hire a *commercialista* to look after their affairs. A payment schedule is worked out; Italian mortgages are usually for 50% of the selling price, payable over a 10 year period. Foreigners pay 10% more than Italians, but never have to pay rates. Always transfer payment from home through a bank, taking care to save certificates of the transactions so you can take the money out of Italy when you leave. *Living in Italy*, published by Robert Hale, London 1987, and your Italian consulate are good sources for all the details.

Finding a job in Venice is probably harder than in any city in Italy. EC residents may register at the *Ufficio di Collocamento* (employment office) at Calle del Megio, S. Stae; it occasionally publishes a list of available jobs in *Il Gazzettino* (look under the heading *Taccuino*, which lists events, night pharmacies, etc.). Both *Il Gazzettino* and *La Nuova Venezia* carry a few want ads. English teaching jobs, the usual standby, are harder to find in Venice than anywhere else in Italy—too many people want to teach English, and too many Venetians have already learned it. English speaking au pair, catering or secretarial jobs sometimes come up, though for the latter you won't get far without some Italian. In short, you'll need to have been born under a lucky star to find work by just showing up.

It's easier if you hone your Italian and take a course: literature, economics, philosophy and languages are the main curricula at the Università degli Studi di Venezia, Ca' Foscari, Dorsoduro 3246; architecture and urban design courses and workshops at the excellent Istituto Universitario di Architettura, S. Croce 191, tel 529 7711; art at the Accademia di Belli Arti, Dorsoduro 1090, tel 522 5396 (though the Accademia is not exactly known for its innovations) or at the Università Internazionale dell'Arte di Venezia, at the Palazzo Fortuny, S. Marco 3780, tel 528 7542, with courses especially designed for foreigners. Your school may be able to help you with lodgings, or you can ask try for one of a handful of **furnished rooms** in the city (Alloggi Biasin, Cannaregio 1252, tel 717 231; Casa Linger Dora, Castello 3541, tel 528 5920; Ottolenghi, Cannaregio 180, tel 715 206); during the school year the Lido and resort areas are good places to look for a temporary apartment.

Finding the right school for your children is a bit harder. The only English school in Venice is the British Centre, Campo S. Luca 4267/a, tel 528 6612, which offers a full-time course for children from the age five and up. The state schools in Italy are a viable alternative, offering a good, rounded education, free to all children living in Italy (after you get all the proper documents translated into Italian and stamped, that is). Sending a young child to a *scuola elementare* or *asilo* (nursery school/kindergarten, run by the *comune* or nuns) will have him or her fluent in Italian in a matter of months. Foreign children adapt amazingly fast because the teachers and their peers are irresistably *simpatico* and helpful.

A good source of useful information and phone numbers in Venice is the annual *Tutto Città* booklet distributed with the yellow pages; it has a section covering every possible emergency, including an *acqua alta*, with a useful map of the lowest and most vulnerable sections of the city, or what number to call if a buildings starts dropping bits of statue or masonry on the heads of passers-by (tel 788 644). Other titbits that you may need to know as a resident of Venice:

Acupuncture: Not big in Italy, but try the Centro Biodinamico ARU, 2260 Dorsoduro, tel 520 4645.

Alcoholics Anonymous: Drink in Italy is so cheap that not a few foreigners go over the edge. AA's branches at Fondamenta d. Tana 1924, Castello, tel 520 9933, and at the Frari 2986, S. Polo, tel 522 4333, hold meetings on alternate evenings.

Baby Sitters: Qualified baby sitters may be had from Fersel, Corso Popolo 94, Mestre, tel 531 4534.

Cars: You have to be a resident to buy one second-hand; non-residents are only allowed to purchase a new car on condition it leaves the country in five days. The law says residents have to change their driving licences and number plates over to Italian ones within a year. Non-residents are only allowed to keep a foreign car in Italy for six months.

Chinese Meals can be delivered to your home by China Cena, tel 522 3090.

Environmental Venice: This is a hot issue in Venice, as groups argue to and fro about the best way to keep the city afloat. Italia Nostra (similar to National Trust), S. Marco 1260, tel 520 4822, concerns itself not only with buildings but the problems of the Lagoon. The local branch of the World Wildlife Fund is at Via Salomone 2/b, Mestre, tel 950 800; the Lega Italiana Protezione Uccelli (for the protection of birds and their nesting places) is at Via Caneve 3, tel 989 772, Mestre.

Laundry: Some of Europe's cleanest and most scenic laundry waves over the back streets of Venice. There are many laundries to keep yours up to snuff, but few launderettes: try S. Leonardo, by Rio Terrà S. Leonardo 1414, and coin-operated A Gettone S. Marco, near S. Luca at S. Marco 3801, and La Moderna, Via Loredan 4, on the Lido.

Mango Chutney and Peanut Butter: When you feel homesick for the things that make life worth living, try Colussi, Rugheta S. Apollonia 4325, near Campo SS. Filippo e Giacomo, which stocks peanut butter, lemon curd, maple syrup, and mincemeat, while the shop in Salizzada S. Giovanni Crisostomo 5778 is a good source for Mexican beer, French mustard, mango chutney and brownie mixes.

Movers: Moving household furnishings in and out of Venice usually means a ride on a boat. Several long established Venetian furniture movers and storers are Gondrand, Piazzale Roma 487, S. Croce, tel 521 0045; Nicolè, S. Marco 4176, tel 520 3028, Traslochi La Veneta, Via Torino 15, Mestre, tel 531 0856; or Cooperativa Brentella, Via Paruta 38/a, Mestre, tel 951 243.

Music: Venice's Conservatorio di Musica B. Marcello is the Pisani palace in Campo S. Stefano 2810, S. Marco, tel 522 5604. For instruments, recordings, sheet music, and information on lessons try Ricordi, Calle dello Spezier 2765, tel 520 3329. You can rent pianos at Regazzo, Campo S. Provolo 4700a, tel 528 7350.

Natural and Macrobiotic Foods: even if you don't believe you are what you eat, you may crave some fibre after a spell of soggy Venetian pasta. You can get information from the natural foods cooperative in Mestre: Cooperative di Consumo Natura Vera, Via Querini 25, tel 958 801 or pick up organically grown produce etc. at the Cooperative Prasadam, also in Mestre at Via Verdi 75, tel 970 393. In historic Venice there are two shops: Dietaverde, Fondamenta delle Romite 1358, tel 523 1077, and El Quetzal, Campo S. Margherita 2932, Dorsoduro, tel 523 7444.

Natural Medicines in Italy are available at an *Erboristeria*. Try Melograno, Campo S. Margherita 2999, Dorsoduro, or Vepharma, Via Ospedale 38, in Mestre.

Radio: You can get the BBC's schedule of broadcasts to Italy by writing to Auntie at Casella Postale 203, Roma 00100 (though you can nearly always find the BBC if you fiddle with the dial long enough). Vatican Radio broadcasts news in English on the hour. The US Armed Forces radio comes in after sunset at 1107 AM, with major league baseball games nightly during the season beginning around 2 am local time (but that's about all it's good for).

Renting Formal Wear: Nicolao Atelier, Cannaregio 5565, tel 520 7051, is the only place in Venice that rents evening clothes for men and women.

Sailing Lessons might come in handy. Europa, S. Samuele 3421/a, tel 523 7022, and Base Mare 21, Punta S. Giuliano, Mestre, tel 531 1523, offer sailing courses and lessons leading to a motor boat pilot's licence. The latter is also offered by Il Sesante, Via Felisati 71, Mestre, tel 940 287. Marina 2, Corso del Popolo 247, in Mestre, tel 930 124, has a sailing school. La Compagnia della Vela, by the Giardinetti in S. Marco, tel 522 593, offer sailings lessons for adults and children as young as seven, as long as they know how to swim.

Television: Italian TV, especially the cabaret-variety dross featuring endless telephone chats with celebrities or viewers, are so godawful bad they can become habit forming. If you somehow resist and yearn for more substantial fare, satellite antennaes may be installed by Erreci, Via Castellana 61/Q, tel 988 122, or Videoservice Mestrina, Via Molmenti 54, tel 970 535; Videosette, Pescheria Rialto 374; S. Polo, tel 520 7955, has VCR and video rentals.

Translations: You never know when the Italian bureaucracy is going to demand an official translation of some fiddly bit of paper. Try TER Centro Traduzioni, Castello 3640/a, tel 528 9879; Benedict School, Frezzeria 1688, tel 522 4034; Fersel, Corso del Popolo 94, Mestre, tel 531 4534.

UNICEF's office in Venice is at Calle Carbon 4179, S.Marco, tel 528 5838.

Day Trips from Venice

Gattamelata

Padua—The Euganean Hills, Monsélice and Este—Vicenza—
Treviso—The Marca Trevigiana: Conegliano and Vittorio Veneto—
Bosco del Cansiglio and the Alpago—Cittadella and Castelfranco—
Villas around Castelfranco—Ásolo and Villa Masèr—Bassano del Grappa
and Maróstica

When the water and stone of the city begin to take their toll on your
equilibrium, do as the Venetians do and take a break on the *terra firma* of
the Veneto. Nearly every town bears some reminder of Venetian rule, but
Venice never suffocated its possessions, nor sucked up all their art and
talent, like Rome, Paris, London and other bossy parasites; its system of
regional government could serve as a model today.

The Veneto is now one of the richest regions in Italy, and much of it
has been cluttered with by-products of progress. But take heart: the
centres of Padua, Vicenza, and Treviso have kept intact their special
character, and nearly all the villas of Venice's patricians remain in
settings their owners would recognize. Although the Veneto proper
extends from the heart of the Dolomites to the bogs of the Po Delta,
below are listed destinations that are feasible as day trips—within two
hours of Venice by public transport, though some of the bus connections
can be tenuous.

338

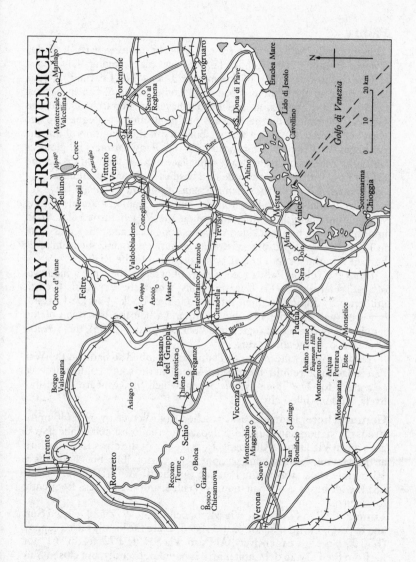

DAY TRIPS FROM VENICE

Padua

Although only half an hour from Venice by motorway (A4), Padua (*Padova* in Italian) can rightly claim its own place among Italy's most artistic and historic cities. Nicknamed *La Dotta* ('The Learned'), Padua is the brain of the Veneto, since 1222 home to one of Europe's most celebrated universities, an intellectual haven to Petrarch, Dante and Galileo. Decorated by the brushes of Giotto and Mantegna and the chisel of Donatello, Padua was a laboratory in the evolution of art, the paradigm for Venetian artists who followed. Padua attracts religious as well as art pilgrims; it is the last resting place of St Anthony of Padua and his exotic seven-domed mosque of a basilica is the city's landmark.

Although Livy, the most famous son of ancient *Patavium*, gave his town credentials as good as Rome's, Padua remained a simple fishing village until the 4th century BC, when the Veneti turned it into an important town, one that sided with the Romans against the Gauls and, in 45 BC, became a prosperous Roman *municipium*. In 602 the Lombards burned it to the ground and all who could fled to the Rialto.

From the rubble Padua rose, a slow phoenix, to become a medieval *comune*, ruled by the Da Carrara family, whom the Venetians tried to influence by admitting them into the Golden Book. The Da Carrara, however, had ambitions of their own, and when the last scion of the family was discretely strangled in a Venetian prison (1405), the *Serenissima* took over the direct rule.

Though the northern half of Padua was bombed so badly in the War that it had to be rebuilt, the arcaded streets in the south could still serve as a stage for *The Taming of the Shrew*, which Shakespeare set in this lively, student-filled city.

Getting There: Padua is easily reached from Venice by train (30 min). From the station, city bus No. 3 departs for the Prato della Valle; No. 6 goes down Via Dante. Alternatively, make use of the city's free bike hire at the station, leaving your passport as security. The bus station is a 10-minute walk away in the Piazzale Boschetti, Via Trieste 40, tel 820 6811, with buses every half-hour to Venice, and slightly less frequently to Vicenza.

Lunch: Try **Da Giovanni**, Via Maroncelli 22, tel 772 620 (closed Sun and in Aug); the homemade pasta is good, as are the locally raised capons (L30 000) or, less expensively, **Al Pero**, Via S. Lucia 72, tel 36 561, not far from the Palazzo del Capitanio; it is popular, friendly, but closed Sun (L17 000).

Cappella degli Scrovegni and the Eremitani

Padua's attractions merit at least a day, but if you only have a couple of hours it's a 5-minute walk from the railway station to the city's most celebrated sight, Giotto's Cappella degli Scrovegni, entered with same ticket as the adjacent **Nuovo Museo Civico** (open daily, 9–5, April–Sept 9–7, closed Mon in the winter, adm). The Museum's chief treasures are its 14 *stele patavine*, rectangular funerary monuments from the 6th–1st centuries BC, inscribed in bastard Etruscan. Padua is the only place in the north where such stele have been found; apparently the local aristocracy, like Livy, wanted to put on Greek airs. Upstairs, glass cases hold some of the small *bronzetti* that made Padua's reputation in the Renaissance, by Il Riccio, Girolamo Campagna, Niccolò Roccatagliata, and a certain 'Il Moderno', whose agent must have thought up his name. Paintings include Giotto's *Crucifixion*, originally designed for the Cappella degli Scrovegni, and the small *Leda and the Swan* by Giorgione.

Next to the Museum, the crusty shell of *Patavium*'s Roman amphitheatre shelters a lovely pearl, the **Cappella degli Scrovegni**, or Madonna dell'Arena. In Canto XVII of the Divine Comedy, Dante condemned the miser and usurer Scrovegni to the Inferno (apparently Scrovegni had it coming—even the Church denied him Christian burial for his pathological greed). In 1303, in expiation for his father's sins, his son Enrico built this chapel, and commissioned Dante's favourite artist, Giotto, to fresco the interior with scenes from the New Testament (1304–13). Giotto was then at the height of his power and this magical blue temple is his masterpiece.

One day, the story goes, Dante came to watch Giotto at work, assisted by his sons, who like their father were remarkably ugly. 'How is it,' the poet had to ask the artist, 'that you make painted figures so well and real ones so badly?' 'Because I do the former by day and the latter by night,' Giotto replied. This is the best place to understand how well indeed he worked by day, and what made his art so revolutionary at the turn of the 14th century—his innovative response to the problems of three-dimensional space and volume, and his skill at creating 'natural' narrative compositions.

Until an air raid in 1944, another wonder of Early Renaissance art stood on the other side of the Museo Civico: the Augustan church of the **Eremitani** (1306) with its magnificent Ovetari chapel, frescoed in 1454–57 by an Andrea Mantegna in his early 20s. Although the church was shattered—the greatest loss to Italian art in the war, along with Pisa's Campo Santo—what could be salvaged of Mantegna's precise master-

341

piece was carefully pieced together like a jigsaw: *The Martyrdom of St Christopher and St James* is remarkable for Mantegna's use of scientific perspective in its masterful foreshortening from below. (Open 8–12 and 3:30–6:30, till 5:30 in the winter).

Central Padua: the University and Palazzo della Ragione

Piazza Cavour, the historic heart of Padua, is the site of one of Italy's most renowned coffeehouses, the **Caffè Pedrocchi**, built in 1831 by Giuseppe Jappelli in a kind of mausoleum-Neoclassical-Egyptian-Revival style, with columned stone porches at either end; originally open 24 hours a day, it was famous for having no doors—and for its intellectual customers who came to debate the revolutionary politics of Mazzini. You can still have a coffee at the Pedrocchi before taking in Jappelli's adjacent Neo-Gothic, bullet-scarred **Pedrocchino**, where the students turned words into deeds in 1848, clashing with the Austrian police.

Diagonally opposite the café on Via VIII Febbraio, is the central seat of the University, Andrea Moroni's 16th-century **Palazzo del Bo'** ('of the ox'), a nickname derived from the sign of a tavern on the site when the University was founded in 1222 (open 9–12 and 3–6, guided tours on the hour; closed Sat afternoon and Sun and all afternoons in Aug). The tour includes the old wooden pulpit from which Galileo lectured, the golden Great Hall with walls covered with the armorial devices of its illustrious *alumni*, and the steep, uncomfortable **Anatomical Theatre** (1594), believed to be the first permanent one anywhere, designed by Fabricius, tutor of William Harvey, discoverer of the circulation of blood. Other famous lecturers were Vesalius, author of the first original work on anatomy (1555) since Galen, and Gabriello Fallopio (1523–62), discoverer of the Fallopian tubes.

Across Via VIII Febbraio, hiding behind the 16th-century **Municipio**, not improved by a bland fascist façade, is Padua's lively market piazza, split into the Piazza delle Frutta and the Piazza delle Erbe by the massive, arcaded **Palazzo della Ragione** (open 9:30–12:30, and 2:30–5:30, closed Sun pm and Mon; adm). Built in 1218 as Padua's law courts, in 1306 Fra Giovanni (the architect of the Eremitani) enlaced it with loggias and topped it with an upstairs hall, Il Salone, one of the largest medieval halls in existence, measuring 79 m by 27 m, with a ceiling 26 m high—like 'vaulting over a market square', as Goethe described it. Its great keel-shaped roof was rebuilt after a fire in 1756—an earlier blaze, in 1420, destroyed most of the original frescoes, some by Giotto. They were replaced by 300 scenes of often mysterious import by Nicolò Miretto. The Salone still has its *pietra del vituperio*, a stone block where repentant debtors were made to sit, bare-bottomed, and a giant **wooden horse**, built for a joust in 1466; its rather fierce glance is complemented by testicles as big as bowling balls.

Just to the west, the stately **Piazza dei Signori** saw many a joust in its day, and today can boast of Italy's oldest astronomical clock, built by Giovanni Dondi in 1344 (and rebuilt in 1427). On the left is the fine Lombard Renaissance-style **Loggia della Gran Guardia**, finished in 1523. Behind Dondi's clock, Padua University's Arts Faculty, the **Liviano**, was built in 1939 by Gio Ponti, incorporating the upper floor of the old Carrara palace, the **Sala dei Giganti**—a name derived from its huge 14th-century frescoes of ancient Romans, repainted by Domenico Campagnola in the 1530s. It also has a more intimate 14th-century portrait of Petrarch sitting at his desk, attributed to Altichiero (to visit, ring ahead, tel 875 0644).

Around the corner from Piazza dei Signori stands the **Cathedral**, a blank-faced concoction begun in the 12th century. Its Romanesque **Baptistry**, built by the Carrara family, is far more rewarding, for its colourful, recently restored frescoes by Giotto's follower, Giusto de' Menabuoi in the 1370s; the dome, with its *multitude of saints* seated in a circular paradise is awesome but chilling (open 9:30–12:30 and 3–7 summer, 2:30–5:30 winter, closed Mon and Sun afternoons, adm).

Piazza del Santo: Basilica di Sant' Antonio

Below the commercial heart of Padua rise the exotic domes of its most famous monument, the Basilica di S. Antonio. St Anthony of Padua was a Portuguese missionary who was shipwrecked in Italy, fell under the influence of St Francis, worked a number of miracles, and was canonized the year after his death, in 1232. This Basilica was begun in the same year over his tomb and finished in the following century. For pure fantasy it is comparable only to St Mark's in Venice, and though it lacks the Venetian basilica's colourful decoration, its cluster of seven round domes around a lofty, conical cupola, two octagonal *campanili* and two smaller minarets make it a delightful experiment in medieval fantasy.

Sharing the large piazza before the Basilica, with the pigeons and exuberantly garish souvenir stands, is one of the most important works of the Renaissance, Donatello's great equestrian **Statue of Gattamelata**, the cool *condottiere* who served Venice so well and honestly that it paid for this monument. *Gattamelata* owes its importance not only to its excellence and serene Renaissance spirit, completely devoid of the arrogance of Verrocchio's *Colleoni* statue in Venice, but for technical reasons as well: it was the first large equestrian bronze cast since antiquity.

More by Donatello awaits in the Basilica's Byzantine-inspired **interior**—probably not what a monk vowed to poverty would have ordered, but certainly a sign of the esteem in which his devotees held and continue to hold him—they throng his sumptuous chapel on the left, patiently waiting to touch or kiss his sarcophagus. A motley array of homemade votive offerings credit the Saint with the usual miraculous cures and interventions, while others thank him for finding things—Anthony apparently runs Heaven's Lost Property Office. The series of 16th-century marble reliefs lining the chapel are among the highpoints of the Venetian Renaissance: the fourth and fifth are by Sansovino, the sixth and seventh by Tullio Lombardo, and the last, by Antonio Lombardo. Just outside the chapel is a fine work by their father, Pietro: the **Tomb of Antonio Roselli** (1467).

The **high altar**, much re-arranged over the centuries, is the work of Donatello and his helpers (1445–50), crowned by the famous *Crucifixion*, with bronze statues of the *Madonna* and *six patron saints of Padua* and reliefs of the *miracles of St Anthony* below. The great Paschal Candelabrum is the masterpiece of Il Riccio, who also, with his master Belluno, cast the 12 bronze reliefs of *Old Testament scenes* on the choir walls. Behind the high altar, in the ambulatory, don't miss the **Treasury** where a hundred glittering gold reliquaries contain most preciously the tongue and larynx of Il Santo, whose humble Franciscan cassock is spread out in a glass case below. In the right transept, the **Cappella di S. Felice** contains beautiful frescoes, and a remarkable *Crucifixion*, painted in the 1380s by Altichiero, the leading Giottoesque artist of the day. And if you've been wondering about the quaint blue stylized decoration of the apse and dome, it dates from 1903–1940s.

Flanking the piazza opposite Donatello's *Gattamelata*, the **Oratorio di San Giorgio** was built in 1377 and beautifully frescoed by two heirs of Giotto, Altichiero and Jacopo Avanzi; open 9:30–12:30 and 2:30–6:30 only in Jan and Dec; adm. The same jovial custodian will also unlock the adjacent **Scuola del Santo**, a confraternity that keeps some paintings on the *Life of St Anthony* in a panelled room upstairs, some of which are winningly absurd; four of them, and not the best, are attributed to a teenage Titian.

Prato della Valle

Just south of the Basilica grows Padua's **Orto Botanico**, one of Europe's oldest botanical gardens, laid out in 1545 with a variety of unusual and ancient specimens (open 9–1 and 3–6, Sun 9:30–1; closed Sun and afternoons in the winter; adm).

Beyond 'Italy's largest piazza', the **Prato della Valle** (1775) does service as municipal parking lot, flea market, amusement park and pantheon of 87 illustrious men associated with Padua, whose statues surround the moat. On one side towers the 396-ft **Basilica of Santa Giustina** (7:30–12 and 3:30–7:30), designed by Il Riccio in 1502, its cluster of eight domes is similar to St Anthony's but its façade is unfinished and its interior still-born Baroque. The large apse painting of *The Martyrdom of S. Giustina* is by Veronese (1575), and the stalls of the choir are finely carved. But S. Giustina's best bits are outside Il Riccio's Basilica; pass through the venerable arch in the right transept to visit the ancient Hall of Martyrs, where their bones were once kept, and the 5th-century **Sacellum di S. Prosdocimo**, the burial place of Padua's first bishop.

South of Padua: the Euganean Hills, Monsélice and Este

Within sight of Padua, the conical Euganean Hills, or *Colli Euganei*, are a pleasant geological oddity plopped in the middle of the Veneto plain. They were volcanic islands when the surrounding land was still covered by the sea, and very early on attracted the region's first prehistoric settlers, whose centre was *Ateste* (Este). Later the Imperial Romans discovered the two secrets of the Euganean hills: hot mud and good wine, both results of the hills' volcanic origins. Livy, Suetonius and Martial all recommended the virtues of these hot mineral springs (they rise out of the ground at 87°C and are the most radioactive in Italy) and today some 130 hotels/thermal establishments cater to those seeking health or beauty cures.

Getting Around: The spas and towns in the Euganean Hills are easily reached from Padua by car on the SS 250 or by AMTAT bus from Padua's train station. Fewer buses make it directly from Padua to the lovely village, Arquà Petrarca; you may have to change in Monsélice. Monsélice is on the main railway line from either Padua (20 min) or Venice (50 min); Este is only a few minutes further down the track, though it requires a change of trains in Monsélice.
Lunch: The health-filled environment of the spas is not the place to look for a good meal, though the local wines may tempt you to misuse your

liver: there are seven white and red DOC *Colli Euganei* wines, all bearing the symbol of 'Gattamelata' on the label. Save your appetite for Arquà Petrarca and the lovely **La Montanella**, Via Costa 33, tel (0429) 718 200, where you can enjoy not only the garden and view over the village itself, but an exquisite *risotto* and well prepared game dishes (L40 000; closed Thurs eve and Wed).

The oldest of the principal spas, **Abano Terme** is only 9 km from Padua and has some 100 thermal swimming pools and the most celebrated mud therapy; its name derives from the Roman's favourite pool *Aponeus*, named after a god of healing.

Because of their unique conditions, the Euganean Hills are home to some interesting flora, highlighted in the natural park-botanical garden, **Lieta Papafava da Carraresi**, located around **Teolo** (Livy's birthplace), on the jagged, western flank of the hills. To the south on the N16 lies the prettiest village in the Euganean Hills, **Arquà Petrarca**. The world-weary Petrarch, accompanied by his daughter Francesca and his stuffed cat, named Laura II, chose Arquà as his last home; his villa, the charming **Casa del Petrarca**, given to him by the Carraresi, still preserves much of its 14th-century structure and furnishings. Later admirers added the frescoes illustrating his works, and you can browse over the autographs of some of the house's famous visitors. Even the delightful view has changed little since the days of the great poet (open 9:30–12:30 and 3:30–7:30 in the summer; 9:30–12:30 and 1:30–4:30 in the winter; closed Mon; adm). Petrarch died here in 1374 and is entombed in a simple marble sarcophagus near the church.

Monsélice

On the southern slopes of the Euganean Hills the natural volcanic citadel of **Monsélice** was first fortified by the Romans who gave it its name, *Mons silicis*. In its heyday it bristled with five concentric rings of walls and 30 towers, built by Frederick II's henchman, Ezzelino da Romano, to control the road linking Padua to Este; most fell victim to medieval Italy's greatest enemy—19th-century town planners. Still, the citadel that remains is one of the finest and best restored in the northeast.

From the station, an iron bridge crosses the canal to the centre of town; just here you can see part of the outer ring of walls and the one surviving tower, the **Torre Civica** (1244). On the other side of this is Monsélice's arcaded **Piazza Mazzini**. From here, Via del Santuario leads up to the **Castello di Ezzelino/Ca' Marcello** (open for guided tours, April–Sept, Tues, Thurs, Sat at 9, 10:30, 3:30 and 5, Sun morning only; Oct–Nov same days, 9, 10:30, 2:30, and 4; adm). First built in the 11th century, it was expanded into a castle-residence by Ezzelino, and re-decorated by the Carraresi in the 14th century; in this century, when it was on its last legs, it came into the hands of industrialist and art patron Count Vittorio Cini, who restored it according to his charmingly romantic view of the Middle Ages. Furnishings were brought in to match the period and frescoes—medieval and Renaissance arms, antiques, tapestries, kitchen utensils.

Further up Via del Santuario passes the Baroque **Palazzo Nani-Mocenigo**, with its monumental pseudo-Roman stair, and the 13th-century **Duomo Vecchio**. This is next to the **Lion Gate**, the entrance to Vicenzo Scamozzi's unusual **Via Sacra delle Sette Chiese**, a private road leading up to his elegant **Villa Duodo** (grounds open mornings until noon, and Nov–Feb 1:30–7; Mar–May and Sept–Oct 1:30–7, summer 3:30–8). A condensed version of the seven churches of Rome, Scamozzi's six chapels and Church of San Giorgio also offer a proportionately smaller indulgence. The Villa itself is now a study centre in hydrology, while Ezzelino's **Rocca**, at Monsélice's highest point, has become a nesting area for endangered birds and is strictly off limits to featherless bipeds.

Este

Monsélice's old rival, **Este**, is only 9 km to the west; its name, from the ancient *Ateste*, was adapted by a noble 11th-century Lombard family who conquered and ruled it before moving on to greater glory in Ferrara. Like Monsélice it was a hotly contested piece of real estate, as evidenced by the ruined walls and towers of the **Castello dei Carraresi** (1339), now the public garden. Within this, and made of material cannibalized from its walls, is the 16th-century Palazzo Mocenigo, home of the **Museo Nazionale Atestino** (open 9–1 and 3–6, Sun 9–2, closed Mon; adm), with one of northern Italy's finest pre-Roman collections: outstanding 5th–6th century BC bronze statuettes and a charming 8th-century BC vase in the shape of a pig. Among the paintings, the star is Cima da Conegliano's *Madonna and Child*.

Behind the castle, **Villa De Kunkler** was Byron's residence in 1817–18; here Shelley, his guest, penned 'Lines Written Among the Euganean Hills', after his little daughter Clara died. Some 15 km west of

Este lies **Montagnana**, famous for some of the best-preserved medieval fortifications in Italy, built by Ezzelino da Romano after devastating the town in 1242. The walls extend for two km, and are defended by 24 towers and battlemented gates—impressive but not very effective, as Venice lost and regained the town some 13 times during the War of the Cambrai.

Vicenza

'The city of Palladio', prettily situated below the Monti Bérici, is an architectural pilgrimage shrine and knows it; where other Italians grouse about being a nation of museum curators, the prim and often grim Vicentini glory in it. Perhaps classical, monumental High Renaissance cities are better to visit than live in; there's little room for chance or fancy in their planned, symmetrical perfection, the intellectual product of a gentry immersed in humanistic and classical thought.

Although Vicenza was heavily damaged during World War II, restorers have tidied up most of the scars for these days the rouble rolls in Vicenza; the city promotes itself as the *Città d'Oro*, 'the City of Gold', for its huge goldworking industry that counts some 700 producers. The birthplace of the inventor of the silicon chip, Federico Faggin, it has developed electronic industries that allow it to call itself the 'Silicon Valley' of Italy; add machine tools, textiles, and shoes to this list, and you have the Veneto's wealthiest city.

Getting There: Vicenza is on the main railway line to Verona, an hour from Venice or 35 min from Padua. The station is south of the centre, at the end of Viale Roma (tel 324 396). From here FTV buses (tel 544 333) depart for Bassano and Maróstica (see below) as well as Treviso, Padua, etc. If you drive to Vicenza, parking is most convenient in the two large guarded lots, one at the west end of town by the Mercato Ortofrutticolo, and the other to the east, by the stadium, both linked to the centre by special bus service every 5 minutes. As in Venice, the street names are in dialect—instead of '*via*' look for '*contrà*'.

Lunch: Vicenza is *polenta* and *baccalà* (salt codfish) country, which is about as close to 'Made in Italy' soul food as you can get. At the popular **Vecchia Guarda**, Contrà Pescherie Vecchie 11, tel 321 231, near the Piazza delle Erbe, pizzas are about L5000, and the *polenta* and cod works will cost around L15 000; the even more popular and lively **Antica Casa della Malvasia**, Contrà delle Morette 5, near Piazza dei Signori, has the kind of basic meals a Vicentine *nonna* serves (L15 000).

Porta Castello to the Piazza Signori

From the station, Viale Roma enters the city proper through the **Porta Castello**, marked by a powerful 11th-century tower. This dominates one end of Vicenza's long pedestrians-only **Corso Palladio**, a showcase of palaces of various eras; one of the first, Piazza Castello's **Palazzo da Porto Breganze** of the enormous columns, was designed by Palladio and partly built by his pupil Vincenzo Scamozzi before the very monumentality of the design defeated him.

From the Piazza Castello, Contrà Vescovado leads to the **Duomo**, a Gothic temple with a diamond pattern façade, carefully pieced together after being flattened in the War. Inside a polyptych by Lorenzo Veneziano survives in the 5th chapel on the right. Excavations in the cathedral crypt have reached the level of Roman Vicenza and revealed parts of the original 8th-century church, while in the square you can visit the **Cryptoporticus** (underground passageway) of a 1st-century palace (Piazza Duomo 2, open Thurs and Sat 10–11:30).

Piazza dei Signori

This large and kingly square is the heart and soul of Vicenza, its public forum in Roman times and today. In the 1540s, the Vicentines decided the piazza's crumbling old medieval Palazzo della Ragione no longer matched their new, Renaissance-humanist aspirations. They hired a young unknown freshly dubbed Palladio to give it a facelift. In 1549 he began his work on the building now called the **Basilica** and kept at it on and off until his death. The result perfectly fulfills its aims with two tiers of rounded arches interspersed with Doric and Ionic columns, apparently all with Roman regularity, though in truth Palladio had to vary the sizes of the arches to compensate for the irregularities of the Gothic structure. The roof hides behind a pediment lined with life-size statues in the Roman mould, a hallmark of Palladio's later work; stare at them long enough and the urge to shoot them off like ducks in a penny arcade becomes almost irresistible. The great Gothic hall of the Basilica is open 9:30–12 and 2:30–5, Sun 9–12, closed Mon. To see what Palladio was disguising, go behind the Basilica to the 16th-century **Piazza delle Erbe**, guarded by the pleasantly-named **Torre del Tormento**, the medieval prison.

The Basilica shares the Piazza dei Signori with the needle-like **Torre di Piazza** (1100s); in the 14th century the civic authorities tamed it with a mechanical clock and in 1444 added its headdress. Across the square Palladio's **Loggia del Capitaniato**, decorated in 1571, celebrates the victory at Lepanto. The neighbouring 16th-century **Monte di Pietà**, built in two sections, was frescoed in the 1900s with amazing Liberty-style pin-up girls, some still faintly surviving moral outrage, war damage, and Father Time.

From the piazza's obligatory Lion of St Mark column, a right turn down Via S. Michele leads to the pretty **Ponte S. Michele** (1620). Just across this bridge, the **Oratorio di S. Nicola** is remarkable for the creepiest altarpiece in Italy, *La Trinità* by Vicenza's own 16th-century artist Francesco Maffei, whose tumultuously feverish brush infected some of the Oratorio's walls as well (July–Sept 9–12 and 3–6, though for digestion's sake, see it before rather than after lunch).

Contrà Porti and Around

A left turn at the Piazza dei Signori's columns will return you to Corso Palladio and the city's prettiest Gothic palace, the 15th-century **Palazzo da Schio**, also known as the 'Ca' d'Oro' for its long-gone gilt decoration. It's enough to make the Palladian palaces, concentrated in the quarter just north of the Corso, seem as exciting as bank branches—the best are along the **Contrà Porti**, Vicenza's most dignified street.

Just west, near the corner of Contrà Riale and Contrà Zanella stands Vicenza's mighty Gothic palace, **Casa Fontana**; across the street, the church of **Santo Stefano** contains one of Palma Vecchio's most beautiful paintings *Madonna with SS. George and Lucy*. More of Vicenza's finest art is just around the corner on the Contrà S. Corona, in the chapels of the early Gothic church of **Santa Corona** (9:30–12:15 and 3:30–6): Veronese's *Adoration of the Magi* (1573) and Giovanni Bellini's *Baptism of Christ*, a late painting set in a rugged, very un-Venetian landscape. Under the *Madonna* hanging nearby is an accurate portrayal of *Vicenza* just before Palladio came on the scene.

More art is on display at the end of the Corso in Palladio's classic Palazzo Chiericati (1550–1650) now home of the **Museo Civico** (open 9:30–12:20 and 2:30–5, 10–12 on Sun, closed Mon; adm; your *biglietto cumulativo* includes the Teatro Olimpico). On the ground floor are some of the original frescoes, with an hilarious ceiling by a certain Busascorci, portraying the naked *Sun God and His Steeds* at noon. Upstairs the best works are by Paolo Veneziano, the Vicentine Bartolomeo Montagna (a follower of Mantegna), Cima da Conegliano, Sansovino, Tintoretto, Veronese, the irrepresible Francesco Maffei and his wild and woolly sidekick, Giulio Carpioni.

Teatro Olimpico

Across the street, the Teatro Olimpico was Palladio's swansong and one of his most original and fascinating works, a unique masterpiece of the Italian Renaissance, said to be the oldest indoor theatre in Europe. For the stage, Palladio as always went back to the ancient buildings he had seen during his sojourns in Rome and created an amphitheatre of wood and stucco, while his pupil Scamozzi added the amazing piazza and streets radiating out in the then popular Piazza del Popolo style in flawless, fake perspective—designed especially for the theatre's first production, Sophocles' *Oedipus Rex*, and meant to represent the city of Thebes. But here Thebes has become a pure ideal, a Renaissance dream city, so perfect that no one ever thought to change the set. If you come between April and October, you may be able to see a performance in this most historical of theatres: otherwise, it's open from 15 March–15 Oct 9:30–12:20 and 3–5:30, in winter 9:30–12:20 and 2–4:30, Sun 9:30–12:20; same ticket as Museo Civico (sometimes it may be closed for rehearsals).

Monte Bèrico and Villa Valmarana

Vicenza's holy hill, Monte Bèrico, rises just to the south of the city. Buses make the ascent approximately every half hour from the coach station, or you can walk up in half an hour from the centre (this area is not well signposted, so be sure to pick up the tourist office's map), through the 150-arch covered walkway, or **portici**, built in the 18th century to shelter pilgrims climbing to the Baroque **Basilica di Monte Bèrico** that crowns the hill. The Basilica commemorates two apparitions of the Virgin in the 1420s, announcing the end of a plague that devastated Vicenza. It still does a busy pilgrim trade, and its well-polished, candle-flickering interior contains two fine paintings: *La Pietà* by Montagna, hanging near the altar, and the *Supper of St Gregory the Great* by Veronese, appropriately hung in the refectory in the cloister (down the steps to the left), and carefully pieced together after Austrian soldiers sliced it to shreds in 1848. The Basilica is open from 7–6, till 7 in the summer.

From the Basilica, it's only a 10-minute walk to **Villa Valmarana** (take Via M. D'Azeglio where the Portici bends, to Via S. Bastiano and continue straight). The Villa is also called 'dei Nani' after the statues of dwarfs in the garden, but the main reason to visit is its sumptuous frescoes by Giambattista and Giandomenico Tiepolo. Giandomenico's intimate, ironical country scenes in the *Foresteria* (guest house) mark his

351

(and his generation's) divergence from his father's grand manner, though one wonders if Giambattista realized Baroque was dying right under his nose (open every afternoon except Sun from the 15 March–15 Nov, 2:30–5:30; May–Sept from 3–6; also 10–12 Thurs, Sat, and Sun; adm.

Villa Rotonda

Palladio designed his celebrated Villa Capra-Valmarana, better known as the **Villa Rotonda** for Cardinal Capra in 1551, but it wasn't completed until after his death by the faithful Scamozzi. Unlike the master's other villas, which, under their stuccoed, classical surfaces were really functional farmhouses, the Villa Rotonda was built for sheer delight, the occasional garden party, and though no one knew it at the time, as the perfect setting for Joseph Losey's film version of *Don Giovanni*. The Villa is an exercise in geometrical form—a circle (expressed by the dome) in a cube, complemented by four symmetrical porches, and it inspired a number of celebrated buildings in England and America, including Thomas Jefferson's Monticello and Chiswick House in London. Come on a Wednesday, 15 March–15 Oct, when you can tour the interior (10–12 and 3–6; adm exp.), otherwise the best you can do is walk around the exterior (Tues, Wed, and Thurs 10–12 and 3–6; adm).

Treviso

Treviso is one of the pleasant surprises of the Veneto. Famous in Italy for its cherries and Benettons, it is laced with little canals (or *canagi*) diverted from the river Sile, langorous with willow trees, and humming with more than a little discreet prosperity. It formed its character in the century preceding its domination by Venice (1389–1796), when it was ruled by the Da Camino family and when its churches were embellished by one of Giotto's greatest pupils, Tommaso da Modena, who did little outside of Treviso. Another charming feature is the frescoed façades of its houses and palaces; attractive building stone was scarce, so it became the custom to cover the humble bricks with plaster and painted decoration—in the 1300s, with simple colours and patterns, and by the 1500s, with heroic mythologies and allegories. Although faded and fragmented since then—on Good Friday 1944 an air raid destroyed half of Treviso in five minutes—you can still pick out frescoes under the eaves, or hidden in the shadows of an arcade. The tourist office, Via Toniolo 41, can give you a map and an itinerary for them.

Getting There: Treviso's station is just south of the city walls, at the end of Via Roma, and the coach station is on the same street, only just within the walls. There are frequent buses and trains ($^1/_2$ hourly) from Venice or Mestre to Treviso.

Lunch: **Le Beccherie**, at Via Ancilotto 11 (tel 540 871) is one of Treviso's bastions of local atmosphere and cooking—a great place to try *pasta e fagioli* with red *radicchio* (a local speciality); complete meals L35 000; closed Thurs eve, Fri and July.

Piazza dei Signori and Duomo

From the bus or train station, it's a 10-minute walk over the Sile along the Corso del Popolo and Via Venti Settembre to the **Piazza dei Signori**, the heart of Treviso dominated by the large brick **Palazzo dei Trecento**. Tucked behind this and an iron door you can visit the recently restored **Sala dei Reggitori**, part of the municipal pawn shop, or **Monte di Pietà** (weekdays, 10–12). The Sala is a rare survivor of 16th-century interior design, with walls of gilt leather, frescoed panels in their original place, and a lovely, painted, beamed ceiling. The other two rooms have paintings by Sebastiano Ricci and the Neapolitan Luca Giordano, works with the air of having been pawned long ago and never reclaimed.

In the same irregular little square the Romanesque **Santa Lucia** has a chapel frescoed by Tommaso da Modena.

Treviso's arcaded main street, **Calmaggiore**, leads from Piazza dei Signori to the **Duomo**, an oft-rebuilt church topped by a cluster of domes, founded in the 12th century. Its **Cappella Malchiostro** was frescoed by Pordenone and his arch-enemy Titian; Vasari tells how Pordenone always painted with a sword at his hip in case Titian showed up (Titian is responsible for the *Annunciation*, and Pordeonone the rest).

Museo Civico

From the Piazza Duomo, Via Riccati meets the Borgo Cavour near the **Museo Civico** (9–12 and 2–5, closed Mon and Sun afternoons; adm). Its archaeological collection on the ground floor includes unusual 5th-century BC bronze discs from Montebelluno, a bronze winged *penis*, a favourite Etruscan motif, some Etruscan *sarcophagi*, and *Gaulish swords*, bent and buried with their warriors. Upstairs, the best paintings are all conveniently hung in the same room: Jacopo Bassano's *Crucifixion*, Titian's *Sperone Speroni*, a lush coloured portrait, and best of all, Lorenzo Lotto's reflective *Portrait of the Guardian of S. Zanipolo*, a Dominican looking up from his writing.

Borgo Cavour exits the city through the great Venetian gate, the **Porta dei Santi Quaranta** (1517), encompassed by an impressive stretch of the ramparts. From here you can stroll along the top of the walls north towards the city's other great gate, Guglielmo Bergamasco's exotic white Istrian stone **Porta San Tommaso**, guarded by the Lion of St Mark.

Back towards the centre on the Via Canova, the frescoed **Casa Trevigiana** is a reliquary of the city's architecture and decorative arts, containing bits and pieces salvaged from her ruins. Especially notable are the fire screens and other furnishings in wrought iron, a local craft since Renaissance times (but closed because of an endemic lack of funds).

San Francesco and Santa Caterina

The northeast quarter of Treviso is at times the smelliest, thanks to the lively and colourful **fish market** (*pescheria*), built over a canal for hygienic reasons. From here, Via S. Parisio leads north to the tall, brick Romanesque-Gothic **S. Francesco**, a 13th-century church with a ship's keel roof, two frescoes by Tommaso da Modena—a giant *St Christopher* and a *Madonna and Saints* to the left of the altar—as well as the tombs of Francesca Petrarch and Pietro Alighieri, the children of Italy's two greatest poets, whose final meeting-place here in Treviso is only a coincidence. There are several frescoed houses between here and Piazza Matteotti. Around the corner from the piazza is **Santa Caterina**, a deconsecrated church where the powers that be have squirreled Tommaso da Modena's masterful *St Ursula* cycle of frescoes, which, though worn, show some of the same charm that Venice's Carpaccio would later bestow on the subject. Unfortunately you need to book at least a day ahead to see them: tel (0422) 51 337, or ask at the Museo Civico.

San Nicolò

Treviso's best church, the Dominican S. Nicolò is located southwest of the Piazza dei Signori; take Via A. Diaz from the Corso del Popolo. S. Nicolò is the finer twin of S. Francesco, with an interior of lovely frescoes—from a huge *St Christopher* on the south wall to the charming pages by Lorenzo Lotto on the *Tomb of Agostino d'Onigo* sculpted in 1500 by Antonio Rizzo. Tommaso da Modena and his school painted the Saints on the columns, a medieval conceit that symbolically made the Saints part of the congregation. Even better are his candid frescoes of *40 famous Dominicans* in the chapter house of the adjacent **Seminario**; painted in 1352, the artist leapt ahead a century in the spontaneity and individuality of his figures—one is wearing what is believed to be the first portrayal of spectacles in art (ring the bell; open Mon–Fri 9–12 and 3:30–7).

The Marca Trevigiana: Conegliano and Vittorio Veneto

North and west of Treviso is the Marca Trevigiana, the medieval territory ruled by the lords of the city, and in the 14th century, one of the first *terra firma* properties annexed by Venice. This trip takes in the towns of Conegliano and Vittorio Veneto—territory synonymous with Prosecco, the seductive local version of champagne that constantly tempts the Venetians from their appointed tasks for a little nip 'in the shade'.

Getting There: To get to Conegliano from Venice, hop on any train running to Udine (50 min); from there you can make the 15-minute connection to Vittorio Veneto, by train or bus. The pretty country around Vittorio Veneto, including the Bosco del Cansiglio and the Alpago, is served by bus—the station is just across from the train station, in Piazza del Popolo.

Lunch: As big an attraction as the sites is lunch at Conegliano's **Tre Panoce** restaurant, at Via Vecchia Trevigiana, tel 60 071, located just outside town in an old farmhouse crowning a hill of vineyards, with outdoor dining available in the summer. The food matches the lovely surroundings, prepared with fresh ingredients from the country; the menu changes daily, but game specialities and mushroom dishes appear frequently (closed Mon and all of Aug; L45 000).

The old castled town of **Conegliano**, north of Treviso on the N13, is the capital of Prosecco, home of Italy's first wine school, founded in 1876, and the birthplace of Giambattista Cima (1460–1518)—'the sweet shepherd among Venetian painters', as Mary McCarthy called him, the son of a seller of hides, who used his native countryside as a background in many of his works. Reproductions are displayed at his birthplace, the **Casa di Cima** (Via Cima 24, behind the Cathedral; open Sat and Sun 4–6, Dec–Feb 3–5; adm). An original and beautiful Cima, *Madonna with Child, Saints and Angels* (1493) forms the altarpiece of the 14th-century **Duomo**, its façade frescoed by Ludovico Pozzoserrato. Pozzoserrato also had a hand in the adjacent **Scuola di Santa Maria dei Battuti** (the confraternity of flagellants); open 9–12 except Wed.

The Duomo is on Conegliano's finest street, **Via Venti Settembre**, lined with old palaces. The **castle** on the hill, though founded in the 10th century, has mostly been reconstructed to house the **Museo Civico** (9–12 and 3:30–7, winter 9–12 and 2–5:30, closed Mon; adm), with its permanent exhibit on a local obsession—grapes—this time in art instead of in the bottle. The views over the rolling Prosecco countryside make the walk up worthwhile; to see and taste it at its best on ground level, take the 42-km **Strada del Vino Bianco**—the white-wine route between Conegliano and **Valdobbiàdene** to the west. On the way, be sure to visit the parish church **San Pietro di Feletto**, founded around the year 1000 and frescoed in the 15th-century by an unknown itinerant painter. His 'Poor Man's Bible' is a jewel of popular religious art; his *Nativity*, especially, is more moving than many from more famous brushes.

The Venetian Pre-Alps saw a heavy share of battles in both World Wars, and the hills around Asiagio, Monte Grappa and the Piave, are often crowned with war cemeteries. **Vittorio Veneto** north of Conegliano, saw Italy's final battle in World War I (October 1918). The Vittorio in its name, however, comes not from the victory but from Italy's first king, Vittorio Emanuele II; in 1866, to celebrate the birth of Italy, two rival towns were united—Cèneda down below, and the upper, walled town of Serravalle.

Cèneda, which has developed into the commercial half of Vittorio, is mostly to be visited for its 16th-century **Loggia** attributed to Sansovino and now home of the Museo della Battaglia, devoted to the long, final engagement (open 10–2 and 4–6:30, from Oct–April, 10–12 and 2–5, closed Mon, same ticket for S. Lorenzo and museum in Serravalle). Also worth seeking out is the Church of **Santa Maria del Meschio**, where a lovely *Annunciazione* by Andrea Previtali (early 16th-century), where the Virgin has a view of a delightful early spring landscape through her window.

Serravalle, promoted as the 'little Florence of the north' has retained most of its austere Renaissance character, its old palaces, squares, ancient tower and gates. Like Cèneda, it has a museum in its shield-encrusted **Loggia Serravallese** (1460s), this sheltering a lovely terra-cotta *Madonna and Child* by Sansovino, belonging to the **Museo del Cenedese** (open 10–12 and 4:30–6:30, Oct–April 10–12 and 3–5, closed Tues). The same ticket (see above) will get you into see the fine mid-15th-century fresco cycle in **San Lorenzo dei Battuti** (another flagellants' church) by the south gate (open 3:30–4:30, closed Tues; arrange visits through the Museo del Cenedese). On the far side of Piazza M. Flaminio, the 18th-century **Duomo** has an 1545 altarpiece by Titian of the *Madonna and Saints*.

Bosco del Cansiglio and the Alpago

Vittorio is the base for visiting the enchanting **Bosco del Cansiglio**, a forest of beech and red pine interspersed with flowery meadows on a lofty karstic plateau. Known as the Republic of Venice's *Bosco da reme*, the 'wood of oars', it was administered by a special *counsilium*, who saw that the trees were planted to grow straight and suitable for galley duty. The penalty for cutting one down was death. **Fregona**, linked by bus with Vittorio Veneto, is a small town noted for its production of a heady dessert wine called Vin Santo and a good base for walks in the woods, and the **Grotte del Calieròn**, a series of caves driven through the karst by a torrent. Monte Cansiglio itself offers the closest downhill skiing to Venice.

The slopes may also be reached from the beautiful **Alpago** valley on the northern side. The Alpago, the Veneto's 'balcony of flowers' has a picture postcard lake, **Lago di Santa Croce**, where the boating, fishing, and watersports have yet to become trendy and expensive. The lake is the focal point for the Alpago's little villages, celebrated for their kitchens more than anything, and **Valdenogher**, site of the pretty 15th-century Palazzo d'Alessandria, with mullioned windows and a portico. Art historians have identified the lovely natural amphitheatre of the **Val Belluna**, leading north from the Alpago into the Dolomites, as the background in Titian's *Sacred and Profane Love* (in the Borghese Gallery, Rome).

Cittadella and Castelfranco

West of Treviso, the Marca Trevigiana holds more surprises: Castelfranco, birthplace of Giorgione and the well-walled town of Cittadella, a stronghold of Ezzelino da Romano, and a trio of Renaissance villas to boot.

Getting There: Castelfranco and Cittadella are on the main rail line between Treviso and Vicenza. From Castelfranco there are buses to Piombino Dese, and less frequent ones to Fanzolo.

Lunch: in Castelfranco, a delight at **Barbesin**, just above town on the Circonvallazione Est, tel (0423) 490 446; its setting is as idyllic as the products of its kitchen, based entirely on fresh, seasonal ingredients; the veal with apples melts in your mouth (L35 000; closed Thurs and Aug).

Most people who come to **Castelfranco Veneto**, 9 km further north, come to pay homage to an earlier and more important genius. Giorgione was born here in 1478 and left behind one of the very few paintings undisputedly from his brush, the *Castelfranco Madonna* (1504), now hanging in the 18th-century **Duomo**. Although squirreled away in a chapel behind a grille, the painting casts the same dream-like spell as the painter's *Tempest* in the Accademia. Fragments of allegorical frescoes by Veronese, from another demolished building, are in the sacristy.

Near the Cathedral, the **Casa del Giorgione** (open 9–12:30, 3–6, closed winter mornings; free) is notable for a curious *chiaroscuro* frieze attributed to Giorgione, of musical, scientific, and draughtsman's instruments, books, and portraits of philosophers; and a few elusive items vaguely related to this most elusive of painters.

Castelfranco itself is a fine, old brick-walled city built by the Trevisans in 1199 to counter the ambitions of the neighbouring Paduans; the Paduans, tit for tat, founded an egg-shaped frontier fortress 15 km to the west, **Cittadella**. Cittadella's most remarkable features are its fine, 13th-century walls and 16 towers, still in excellent condition. Near the south gate, or Porta Padova, stands the ominous **Torre di Malta**, where Ezzelino da Romano had his prison and torture chamber (cf. *Paradiso*, IX, 54), where he was accused of mutilating children and other atrocities. The **Duomo** has Cittadella's finest painting: Jacopo Bassano's *Supper at Emmaus*, austerely coloured and austerely rustic in a way more Tuscan than Venetian.

Villas around Castelfranco

Piombino Dese, just off the Padua-Castelfranco road, is a must-detour for Palladio-philes, for its **Villa Cornaro** (1554). One of Palladio's more monumental structures, it is fronted by a two-storey portico that was to prove irresistible to his imitators; the interior is frescoed with sleepy 18th-century *Biblical scenes* (open May–15 Sept, Sat only 3:30–6; adm).

There are two other impressive (and visitable) villas in the area. South of Cittadella, on the banks of the Brenta river in **Piazzola sul Brenta**, sprawls the **Villa Contarini**, with a 1500s core, and considerable later Baroque-ing: one of its most impressive features is its long waterfront balustrade, so quintessentially Italian in its subtle, abstract, artificial effect. Inside, the frescoed rooms usually hold an exhibition of some kind (open summer 9–12 and 2–7:30, winter 9–12 and 2–6, closed Mon; adm). The second villa is at **Fanzolo**, five km to the northeast of Castelfranco: Palladio's lavish **Villa Emo**, decoratively frescoed with mythological subjects by Giambattista Zelotti (open Sat, Sun, and holidays, May–Sept 3–6, Oct–Apr 2–5; adm exp.).

Ásolo and Villa Masèr

This trip contains a heady dose of Venetian magic: Ásolo, where the Queen of Cyprus held her fabled Renaissance court and noblemen discoursed on love, and Masèr, where Palladio and Veronese collaborated to create perhaps the most amazing villa of them all.

Getting there: From Venice, go to Treviso and catch the Bassano del Grappa bus, which stops in Masèr and Ásolo; there are less frequent buses from Padua. Neither, however, go all the way into Ásolo, but drop passengers by the main road, where a minibus sooner or later collects them for a ride up the hill. For Masèr, do note the opening times below before setting out.

Lunch: Some of the best food in Ásolo is served at **Charly's One**, Via Roma 55, tel 52 201, offering excellent versions of local and international specialities, and in the autumn, mushroom dishes. Delicious fish, English pub atmosphere and fair prices (L35 000; closed Fri). After visiting Palladio's villa at Masèr, you can dine in similarly enchanting surroundings at **Da Bastian** (Via Cornuda, tel 565 400); great paté, *risotto*, Venetian-style snails, and desserts (L30 000 and up; closed Wed eve, Thurs, and Aug).

In the cypress-clad hills above the Veneto flatlands rises the old walled town of **Ásolo**, the consolation prize given by Venice to Queen Caterina Cornaro after demanding her abdication from the throne of Cyprus. With its arcaded streets and little palaces, its piazzas and gardens, Ásolo prettily fits the elegant legend of Caterina's Renaissance court, famous for its cultivation of the arts and music. Pietro Bembo used it as a setting for his dialogues on love, *Gli Asolani*. Giorgione is said to have strolled through its rose-gardens strumming his lute. In the last century, Ásolo was also a beloved retreat of Robert Browning (his last volume of poems was entitled *Asolando*), and of Eleonora Duse, who is buried in the local cemetery.

Asolo's **Rocca**, a citadel built over Roman foundations, has superb views to reward anyone who makes it all the way up. Caterina Cornaro's **Castello** and remains of the garden where she lived in 'lace and poetry' is at the time of writing undergoing restoration. The **Duomo** on the main square boasts two paintings of the *Assumption*, one by Lorenzo

Lotto and one by Jacopo Bassano; the 15th-century **Loggia del Capitano**, also in Piazza Maggiore, contains a museum of local works of art and memorabilia dedicated to Queen Caterina, La Duse and Browning (open 8–12 and 4–8, closed Mon; adm).

Ásolo is a good base for visiting the **Villa Bàrbaro** at **Masèr**, 7 km to the east (open Sat, Sun and Mon 3–6, June–Sept, and 2–5, Oct–May; adm). Built in 1568 for Daniele Bàrbaro, one of Venice's true 'Renaissance' men, a botanist, humanist scholar, Venice's diplomat in London, its official historian, and Patriarch of Aquileia, the Villa is a unique synthesis of two great talents—Palladio and Veronese, whose interior frescoes are one of the masterworks of his career. Bàrbaro and Palladio had worked together on an edition of Vitruvius and collaborated on the design of the Villa: functional on the ground floor, and serenely classical upstairs in the living quarters.

Palladio, it is said, taught Veronese about space and volume, and nowhere is this so evident as in these ravishing architectonic, *trompe l'oeil* frescoes, where the figures literally seem to inhabit the villa. While Bàrbaro suggested the scheme for the *Olympian allegory* in the main hall, it would seem that Veronese was left to follow his fancy elsewhere; there are portraits of the original owners, gazing from painted balconies; a very convincing dog sits beneath a ceiling of allegorical figures, dwarfs open the doors, painted windows offer views of totally convincing landscapes. The famous huntsman entering the imaginary door in the bedroom is Veronese's self-portrait, while the woman he gazes at on the other side of the house is believed to be his mistress. The elegant carvings inside the villa and the nymphaeum are by Alessandro Vittoria, who also did the sumptious stuccoes in the serene circular **Tempietto**, a miniature Pantheon that Palladio added to the grounds in 1580, the year of his death.

Bassano del Grappa and Maróstica

Lying in the foothills of the Dolomites, where the Brenta river widens its flow down the plain, Bassano del Grappa is charming, picturesque and relatively unspoilt; its landmark is a Palladian covered bridge. Nearby, in medieval Maróstica, it's a chessboard, where the citizens dress up and re-enact a famous Renaissance match.

Getting There: There is a regular train connection from Venice to Bassano (1 hour). Bassano's bus station is in the Piazzale Trento, near the tourist office, tel 30 850, while the train station is at the top of Via Chilesotti (tel 25 034). Buses from Bassano head west for Maróstica;

there are regular bus connections from Bassano to Ásolo, Masèr, Possagno, and Treviso.

Lunch: Bassano attracts gourmets in the spring when asparagus is in season, or in the autumn when it's the turn of *porcini* mushrooms. Try them at the very elegant **Ristorante Belvedere**, Viale delle Fosse 1, tel 26 602, where you can enjoy other specialities such as *risotto* with shrimp and spinach, fish flavoured with fennel, and Venetian *tiramisù* for dessert (L40 000; closed Sun and last two weeks of Aug). In Maróstica, your best bet is near the chessboard at **Pizzeria-Trattoria all'Alfiere**, Piazza Castello 16, tel (0424) 72 165 (L8000 for a pizza, L20 000 for a meal).

The 'Grappa' in Bassano's name comes from lofty Monte Grappa to the north, scene of terrible fighting in World War I; it is also synonymous with grappa, the firewater Italians use to spark up their post-prandial coffee. From the station, it's a short walk to the centre of town, Piazza Garibaldi, dominated by the square, medieval **Torre Civica** and the old Gothic church of **San Francesco**. The cloister behind the Church leads to the **Museo Civico** (open 10:30–12:30 and 3–6:30, closed Mon; adm), with paintings by the da Ponte (alias Bassano) family, this town's contribution to the Renaissance; the best of them was Jacopo (his masterpiece is here, the Titianesque twilit *Baptism of St Lucy*). The strangest work here is Alessandro Magnasco's *The Refectory*, depicting a crowd of wraith-like friars in a hall as big as Victoria Station, racing back into a twilit vanishing point. The Museum also has drawings by another local boy who made good, the Neoclassical sculptor Antonio Canova (born in nearby Possagno, where he left a huge monument to himself called the 'Tempio').

But it was Palladio who designed Bassano's landmark, the **Ponte degli Alpini** (1568), the unique covered wooden bridge that spans the Brenta. At the end of the bridge is Italy's oldest grappa distillery, Nardini, founded in 1779, and on the other side, the **Museo degli Alpini** at Taverna al Ponte, the sacred shrine of grappa (8–8, closed Mon).

A GRAPPA DIGRESSION

Although a lot of grappa comes from Bassano del Grappa, its name doesn't derive from the town or its mountain, but from *graspa*, or the residues left at the bottom of the wine vat after the must is removed; it can be drunk unaged and white, or aged in oak barrels, where it takes on a rich, amber shade. First mentioned in a 12th-century chronicle, grappa, or *aqua vitae* 'the water of life' was chugged down as a miracle-working concoction of earth and fire to dispel ill humours. In 1601 the doge created a University Confraternity of Aqua Vitae to control quality; during World War I, Italy's Alpine soldiers adopted Bassano's enduring bridge as their symbol and grappa as their drink. One of their captains described it perfectly:

> Grappa is like a mule; it has no ancestors and no hope of
> descendants; it zigzags through you like a mule zigzags
> through the mountains; if you're tired you can hang on to it;
> if they shoot you can use it as a shield; if it's too sunny
> you can sleep under it; you can speak to it and it'll answer,
> cry and be consoled. And if you really have decided to die,
> it'll take you off happily.

These days the rough, trench quality of grappa appeals to few Italians; from 70 million litres guzzled in 1970, only 25 million were drunk in 1989. The Veneto with its 20 distilleries is a leading producer, and Bassano's a good place to seek out some of the better, harder-to-find labels that might make a grappa convert out of you: besides Nardini, look for names like Da Ponte, Folco Portinari, Jacopo de Poli, Maschio, Rino Dal Toso, or Carpenè Malvolti.

Maróstica, 7 km west of Bassano, is a storybook medieval town, with chivalric 13th-century walls, an upper **Castello Superiore** built by Ezzelino da Romano sprawled over the hill and a lower castle in the piazza, the **Castello Inferiore**, built by Cangrande della Scala. This Castle, long time residence of the Venetian governor and now the Town Hall, is the perfect setting for the event that put Maróstica on the map: the *Partita a Scacchi*, or the human chess match, which takes place in September in even-numbered years, on a 22-square-metre board painted in the Piazza del Castello. Townsfolk in 15th-century costume make the moves announced in Venetian dialect, re-enacting the 1454 contest for the hand of Linora Parisio; her father, the *podestà*, had refused to let her two suitors fight the traditional duel for humanitarian reasons and suggested the chess match, even offering the loser the hand of his younger daughter. If you can't make the match, go on a Sunday afternoon to see the elaborate costumes on display in the Town Hall. The other outstanding sight in town is the view from the Castello Superiore, but before starting the long walk up, make sure the Castle bar is open.

Chronology

Date	Events	Doge
401	Alaric the Goth's sack of Aquileia	
425	Venice founded, according to tradition, on 25 March; first settlement on the Rivoalto (Rialto); S. Giacomo built	
452	Attila the Hun destroys the great city of Aquileia and plunders Venetia; people seek safety in the Lagoon	
466	The 12 Lagoon communities elect their own tribunes	
539–66	Greek-Gothic Wars in Italy	
560	Venetians assist Narses the Eunuch and are rewarded with Church of S. Teodoro on the Rivoalto	
568	Lombards invade; inhabitants of *Altinum* flee to Torcello	
639	Altino's bishop founds cathedral on Torcello	
697	Traditional date for the election of the first doge	Paoluccio Anafesta
717		Marcello Tegalliano
726	Iconoclast struggles in Byzantium: First documented use of the title of *Dux* or Doge, in a show of independence from Byzantium	Orso Ipato
737	Rule of the Six Maestri de Militi	
742	Capital established at Malamocco	Orso Deodato
755		Galla Gaulo
756		Domenico Monegario
764		Maurizio Galbaio
774	Pepin, claiming the kingdom of Italy, leads his Franks against the Venetians gathered on the Rialto but is defeated by the Lagoon	
787		Giovanni Galbaio
804		Obelario de'Antenori
810	Pepin (Charlemagne's son) unsuccessfully besieges the Lagoon. Charlemagne and Byzantine Emperor Nicephorus sign a treaty recognizing Venice as subject to Constantinople but enjoying special trading concessions in Italy	
811		Angelo Participazio
827		Giustiniano Participazio
828–9	St Mark's body stolen by Venetian merchants and welcomed with tremendous pomp in Venice; building of the original St Mark's to house it	Giovanni Participazio I
836	Arab raiders in the Adriatic	Pietro Tradonico
864		Orso Participazio I

363

866	Venice sacks salt rival Comacchio	
881		Giovanni Participazio II
887	Pietro Candiano I dies in battle with Narentine pirates	Pietro Candiano I
888		Pietro Tribuno
912		Orso Participazio II
932	Venice sacks Comacchio again and removes its population to create a salt monopoly in the Adriatic	Pietro Candiano II
939		Pietro Participazio
942		Pietro Candiano III
959		Pietro Candiano IV
960	Dalmatians raid Venice	
976	Doge Pietro Candiano IV slain in revolt by populace; Basilica of S. Marco destroyed by fire	Pietro Orseolo I
977		Vitali Candiano
978		Tribuno Memmo
991		Pietro Orseolo II
998	Emperor Otto III visits Venice	
1000	The Doge leads Venice's fleet in crushing the pirates of Dalmatia, beginning conquest of the Adriatic	
1008		Otto Orseolo
1026		Pietro Centranico
1032	Ostracism of the Orseolo family to prevent the founding of a dynasty; doges forbidden to nominate their own successors	Domenico Flabanico
1043		Domenico Contarini
1071		Domenico Selvo
1082	In gratitude for Venice's aid against the Normans, Emperor Flexius Comnenus signs the *Crisbolo*, absolving the merchants of Venice of all taxes and tolls in the Byzantine Empire	
1085		Vitale Falier
1095	First Crusade preached	
1096		Vitale Michiel I
1098	Crusade expedition; first naval battles with Pisa	
1102	Venice establishes trading quarter in Sidon	Ordelafo Falier
1104	Founding of the Arsenal	
1106	Great flood destroys Malamocco	
1109	Commercial rivalry with Genoa intensifies in the east	
1117		Domenico Michiel
1123	Siege of Tyre leaves Venice with a new trading base	
1128	First street lighting in the city	
1130		Pietro Polani
1148		Domenico Morosini
1156		Vitale Michiel II
1166	Zara and Dalmatia rebel against the 'Big Cat'	
1171	Venice's trading colony in Constantinople, 200,000 strong, is arrested and its goods confiscated by the Emperor, on the instigation of the Genoese. Doge	

	declares war on Empire, and leads Venice into one of its most humiliating setbacks. The six sestieri are established to facilitate tax collections	
1172	Doge Vitale Michiel II killed, after returning home, defeated by plague; the establishment of self-electing Great Council limits the doge's power	Sebastiano Ziani
1173	First bridge at the Rialto	
1177	Barbarossa apologizes to Pope Alexander III in Venice, earning the city a rare papal brownie point	
1178		Orio Malipiero
1193		Enrico Dandolo
1204	Taking charge of the Fourth Crusade, 90 year-old Doge Dandolo subdues Dalmatia, Zara, and captures Constantinople. Venice now controls the Adriatic, the Aegean, the Sea of Marmora, the Black Sea, and seaports of Syria and the major East-West trade routes	
1205		Pietro Ziani
1229		Giacomo Tiepolo
1249		Marin Morosini
1253	First war with Genoa	Ranier Zeno
1261	Greeks retake Constantinople; Merchants Nicolò and Matteo Polo make first visit to Kublai Khan, who sends message to pope, expressing interest in Mongol-Christian alliance against Muslims	
1268		Lorenzo Tiepolo
1271	Polos return to Mongolia, with Nicolò's son Marco	
1275		Jacopo Contarini
1280		Giovanni Dandolo
1284	First minting of the golden ducat	
1289		Pietro Gradenigo
1291	Glass furnaces moved to Murano; Muslims retake Tyre	
1297	Venice becomes an oligarchy with the *Serrata*, or closing, of the *Maggior Consiglio*, limiting membership to patricians	
1298	Genoa defeats Venice at Curzola, sinking 65 out of the total fleet of 95 ships; Marco Polo's *Description of the World* written	
1300	The disenfranchised people of Venice rebel; ringleaders are beheaded to discourage others. Around this time, spectacles *(rodoli da ogli)* are first mentioned, in the regulations of a Venetian guild	
1308	First papal interdict against Venice	
1310	Nobles led by Tiepolo conspire to seize power; Council of Ten established to arrest rebels. Constitution takes form that will endure until 1796	
1311		Giorgio Marin
1312		Giovanni Soranzo

365

1325	Names of patricians inscribed in the Golden Book	
1329		Francesco Dandolo
1335	Council of Ten becomes a permanent institution	
1338	Church of the Frari begun	
1339	Annexation of Treviso	Bartolomeo Gradenigo
1343		Andrea Dandolo
1346	San Giovanni e Paolo begun	
1348	The Black Death cuts the city's population by half	
1353	Venice soundly defeats Genoa at Alghero	
1354		Marin Falier
1355	Falier plots to take real power and is beheaded	Giovanni Gradenigo
1356		Giovanni Dolfin
1358	Revolt in Dalmatia	
1361		Lorenzo Celsi
1363	Revolt in Crete	
1365		Marco Corner
1368		Andrea Contarini
1373	Arrival of Jews in Venice	
1380	Arch-rival Genoa defeated once and for all at Chioggia	
1382		Michele Morosini/ Antonio Venier
1400	Birth of Jacopo Bellini	Michele Steno
1402	Death of Milan boss Gian Galeazzo Visconti leaves most of northern Italy up for grabs	
1405	Venice eliminates the Carrara lordlings of Padua and picks up its first mainland possessions: Padua, Verona, Bassano and Belluno	
1406	Angelo Correr, Patriarch of Venice, becomes Pope Gregory XII	
1414		Tommaso Mocenigo
1416	Venice victorious in its first battle against the Turks, at Negroponte (Euboea)	
1420	Venice weasels Udine and the Fruili from the King of Hungary	
1423		Francesco Foscari
1429	Birth of Gentile Bellini	
1431	Birth of Giovanni Bellini Ca'd'Oro begun	
1432	Execution of the *condottiere* Carmagnola for losing a battle; he is replaced by the luckier captain, Gattamelata	
1450	Birth of Carpaccio	
1453	Mehmet II captures Constantinople; Venice quickly signs trade agreement with Sultan and sends Gentile Bellini to paint his portrait	
1454	Expansion on the mainland includes Treviso, Bergamo, Friuli, and Ravenna; Venice signs a peace treaty with Milan	

1456	Venetian Alvise da Mosto discovers Cape Verde islands	
1457	Foscari sent packing	Pasquale Malipiero
1462		Cristoforo Moro
1464	First Turkish war; Venice loses Negroponte and part of the Morea (Peloponnese) but in 1479 signs peace treaty, saving Fruili and her trading rights in exchange for the payment of tribute; Patriarch Pietro Barbo elected Pope Paul II	
1469	First books printed in Venice, soon to become the printing capital of Europe	
1471		Nicolò Tron
1473		Nicolò Marcello
1474		Pietro Mocenigo
1476	Giovanni Caboto (John Cabot) granted Venetian citizenship	Andrea Vendramin
1478	Birth of Giorgione	Giovanni Mocenigo
1481	S. Maria dei Miracoli begun	
1484	Venice wins Rovigo and the Polesine from Ferrara, completing a *terra firma* empire that was to last until Napoleon	
1485	Titian born (sometime between 1480 and 1490)	Marco Barbarigo
1486		Agostino Barbarigo
1488	Caterina Cornaro 'cedes' Cyprus to Venice	
1493	Aldus Manutius prints his first book	
1494	Italy invaded by Charles VIII of France; Venice allies with other states to fight the French and pick up a few gains	
1498	Vasco da Gama's voyage around the Horn to India spells the end of Venice's old trade monopolies with the East	
1499	Turkish victory at Zonchio, a port in the western Morea, leaves the Adriatic vulnerable	
1501	Ottaviano Petrucci, the first commercial music printer, sets up shop in Venice	Leonardo Loredan
1508	Birth of Palladio. League of Cambrai formed against Venice by jealous rivals Emperor Maximilian, Pope Julius II, Louis XIII, and Ferdinand of Aragon	
1510	League of Cambrai defeats Venice at Agnadello but mutual jealousies prevent members from holding her mainland possessions Population of Venice around 115,000	
1512	Birth of Tintoretto	
1516	Jews confined to the Ghetto	
1521		Antonio Grimani
1523		Andrea Gritti
1527	With the Sack of Rome artists, architects, and scholars flee to Venice, bringing the High Renaissance in tow New arrivals include Sansovino and Aretino	

1528	Birth of Veronese	
1536	Sansovino's Library of S. Marco begun	
1537	Turkish wars, territorial losses in Greece	
1539	Council of Three established	Pietro Lando
1545		Francesco Donà
1553		Marc'Antonio Trevisano
1554		Francesco Venier
1556		Lorenzo Priuli
1559	Pope Paul IV's Index is the beginning of the end for Italy's dominance of European printing	Girolamo Priuli
1564	Arsenal enlarged, for the fourth and last time	
1567	Population of Venice rises to 169,000	Pietro Loredan
1569	300 Arsenal workers burst into the Ducal palace with axes to personally tell Doge of their grievences	
1570	Turks take Cyprus and skin Bragadin alive	Alvise Mocenigo
1571	Battle of Lepanto, great naval victory over the Turks in the Gulf of Patras, won by the Holy League led by Venice	
1573	Henry III of France visits Venice and is overwhelmed with hospitality	
1576	A vicious outbreak of plague carries off 60,000, including Titian	
1577	Fire in Doge's palace	Sebastiano Venier
1578		Nicolò da Ponte
1580	Birth of Longhena	
1581	Francesco Sansovino publishes the first guide to Venice	
1585		Pasquale Cicogna
1592	Giordano Bruno, hiding in Venice, is betrayed to the Inquisition by his host and later burned at the stake in Rome	
1595		Marino Grimani
1606	The Great Interdict: Pope Paul V excommunicates Venice, but thanks to Paolo Sarpi the Republic stands strong	Leonardo Donà
1607	Papal spies try to knife Sarpi	
1612		Marc' Antonio Memmo
1615		Giovanni Bembo
1618	The 'Spanish Conspiracy', a crazy plot hatched by the Spanish ambassador to overthrow the Republic	Nicolo Donà/ Antonio Priuli
1621	Antonio Foscarini executed for Treason	
1623		Francesco Contarini
1624		Giovanni Corner I
1630	Venice decimated by the most deadly plague of its history	Nicolò Contarini

1631	S. Maria della Salute begun	Francesco Erizzo
1640	The Republic introduces coffee (as a medicine) to Europe	
1646		Francesco Molin
1655		Carlo Contarini
1656		Francesco Corner/ Bertuccio Valier
1658		Giovanni Pésaro
1659		Domenico Contarini
1669	After holding out against a siege of 21 years, the Venetians surrender Candia (Herakleon), Crete, to the Turks	
1674		Nicolo Sagredo
1676		Alvise Contarini
1678	Venetian Elena Lucrezia Corner Piscopia becomes the first woman to receive a university degree (in philosophy)	
1683		Marc'Antonio Giustinian
1685	Francesco Morosini reconquers the Morea for Venice, but blows the roof off the Parthenon in the process	
1688		Francesco Morosini
1693	Birth of Tiepolo	
1694		Silvestro Valier
1697	Birth of Canaletto	
1700		Alvise Mocenigo II
1709	Lagoon frozen solid in worst winter ever; people walk to Mestre	Giovanni Corner II
1712	Birth of Guardi	
1718	With the Congress of Passarowitz, Venice loses the Morea, its last possession in the eastern Mediterranean, to the Turks	
1720	Florian's opens its doors 'that never close'	
1722		Alvise Mocenigo III
1732		Carlo Ruzzini
1735		Alvise Pisani
1741		Pietro Grimani
1752	Completion of the Murazzi, the great sea walls	Francesco Loredano
1762		Marco Foscarini
1763		Alvise Mocenigo IV
1779		Paolo Renier
1789		Ludovico Manin (d. 1802)
1790	Construction of La Fenice	
1797	Napoleon abolishes Venetian Republic: Venetian apathy is replaced by anger when he sells it to the Austrians S. Marco is made Venice's cathedral	
1800	Papal conclave held in Venice	

1805	Veneto annexed to Napoleon's Cisalpine kingdom, with its capital in Milan; the French steal as much art as they can
1806	Napoleon actually visits Venice for the first time; St Mark's Square illuminated on the occasion with 4094 torches
1814	Thrown back into the detested Austro-Hungarian empire
1816	Byron swims up the Grand Canal
1820	25% of the population lives by begging
1836	Cholera plague strikes the city
1840	More than a thousand patricians on state dole
1846	Railway bridge forever ends Venice's isolation
1848	Daniele Manin's heroic uprising against the Austrians, foiled in part by another cholera epidemic; Nicolotti and Castellani, ancient rivals, make peace in a secret ceremony, united against the Austrians
1853	Ruskin's *Stones of Venice*
1866	Venice is joined to the new Kingdom of Italy; becomes provincial capital
1902	Collapse of S. Marco Campanile on 14 July
1903	Patriarch of Venice elected Pius X, the last pope to be canonized
1912	Publication of Mann's *Death in Venice*
1913	'Baron Corvo' croaks
1928	Massive celebration in honour of the 1100th anniversary of the 'pious' theft of St Mark's body; new port of Maghera completed; Harry's Bar the place to be seen
1931	Mussolini builds road causeway
1938	Venice's population 280,000; Mestre 44,530; and Marghera 6510; birthrate at 33 per 1000 is double that in the rest of Italy
1959	Patriarch Roncalli elected Pope John XXIII
1960	Venice gets an airport
1966	On 4 November, the worst flood in modern times sets off international alarms for the city's safety
1973	Italian government constructs aqueducts to the city and Marghera to stop subsidence caused by drawing water from the Lagoon
1978	Patriarch Albino Luciani elected as the 'smiling pope' John Paul I
1988	First section of the Lagoon tidal barrier towed into place
1990	Italian government cancels bid for Expo 2000 in Venice; Venice's population sinks to 79,518, while that of Mestre rises to 190,000, and Marghera 30,115

Further Reading

Andrieux, Maurice, *Daily Life in Venice in the Time of Casanova* (Allen and Unwin, 1972). A thorough account of that lively period, seen through French eyes.

Crawford, Francis Marion, *Gleanings from Venetian History* (Macmillan, 1907). A 19th-century point of view, but not as purply as his classic on Rome.

Hemingway, Ernest, *Across the River and Into the Trees* (Panther, 1977). Even his greatest fans wonder about Papa in this macho saga of duck hunting in the Lagoon.

Howard, Deborah, *The Architectural History of Venice* (Batsford, 1980) has lots of helpful photos to bring out the fine points of the subject.

Lane, Frederic C., *Venice, A Maritime Republic* (John Hopkins, 1973). The most thorough history in English.

Honour, Hugh, *Companion Guide to Venice* (Collins, 1965). The classic guide in English, especially to Venice's art.

Lauritzen, Peter, *Palaces of Venice* and *Villas of the Veneto* (Pavilion, 1988). Lush pictures and light descriptions.

Links, J. G., *Venice for Pleasure* (Bodley Head, 4th edition, 1984) a slightly precious but still very readable guide to strolling from café to café, with plenty of musings on what things were like in Canaletto's day.

Lorenzetti, Giulio, *Venice and its Lagoon* (first English edition, 1961, Edizioni Lint Trieste) since 1926 must be the fattest guide ever published on any city; Lorenzetti can even tell you what's inside palaces closed fast to the public.

Mann, Thomas, *Death in Venice* (Penguin, 1971). Anthony Burgess wrote that the people in the Venetian tourist office must hate this book, but when asked, they only smile.

McCarthy, Mary, *The Stones of Florence and Venice Observed* (Penguin 1986). Brilliant evocations of Italy's two art cities, with an understanding that makes other works on the subject seem sluggish and pedantic.

Morris, James/Jan, *Venice* (Faber, 1960, revised 1983). Another very knowledgeable classic, full of anecdote; by the same author, *The Venetian Empire* (Faber, 1980) and *A Venetian Bestiary* (Thames and Hudson, 1982).

Norwich, John Julius, *A History of Venice* (Penguin 1983). An excellent, encyclopaedic and witty chronicle of the *Serenissima*.

Okey, Thomas, *The Story of Venice* (J.M. Dent, 1907). Another in the fine series on 'Medieval Cities.'

Rolfe, Frederick (Baron Corvo), *The Desire and Pursuit of the Whole*, Oxford 1986, a bizarre mix of gorgeous descriptions of Venice and wicked (but funny) descriptions of the English community at the turn of the century.

Ruskin, John, *The Stones of Venice*. For many of our grandparents, the essential work. First printed in 1853, the only copy you're likely to find is J. G. Links' abridgement (Da Capo, 1960).

Steer, John, *A Concise History of Venetian Painting* (Thames and Hudson, 1984). A good, well-illustrated introduction.

Zorzi, Alvise, *Venice: City-Republic-Empire* (Sidgwick & Jackson, 1980). Beautifully illustrated account, with large sections devoted to Venice's dealings on the mainland and eastern Mediterranean.

Historical, Artistic
and Architectural Terms

Altana: roof terrace of a Venetian house, where the ladies would repose and bleach their hair blond in the sun.

Atrium: entrance court of an ancient Roman house or early church.

Baldacchino: baldachin, a columned stone canopy over an altar.

Basilica: a rectangular building, usually divided into three aisles by rows of columns. In ancient Rome, this was the common form for law courts and other public buildings, and Roman Christians adopted it for their early churches.

Bocca di Leone: literally 'lion's mouth'; boxes for anonymous denunciations of traitors and criminals.

Cà: *casa*, a word the Venetians preferred to *palazzo* for even the grandest mansions.

Campanile: a bell tower.

Chiaroscuro: monochrome painting using only light and shade; always more popular in Venice than elsewhere in Italy.

Ciborium: a tabernacle; a construction on or behind an altar containing the sacramental host.

Confraternity: a religious lay brotherhood, often serving some specific charitable work; in Venice they are called *scuole*.

Contrapposto: the dramatic, but rather unnatural twist in a statue, especially in a Baroque work.

Cornu: the peculiar 'horned' cap worn by doges.

Cupola: a dome.

Etoimasia: in Byzantine symbolism, the 'preparation of the Throne' for Christ at the Last Judgement.

Exedra: (It. *esedra*) a semicircular recess.

Ex-voto: an offering (a terracotta figurine, painting, medallion, silver bauble or whatever) made in thanksgiving to a god or Christian saint; the practice has always been present in Italy.

Graffito: originally, incised decoration on a building façade; only lately has the word come to mean casually scribbled messages in public places.

Greek cross: in the floor plans of churches, a cross with equal arms. The more familiar plan, with a long nave and shorter transepts, is called a *Latin cross*.

Grotesque: decoration with carved or painted faces, used by the Etruscans and Romans, and back in fashion during the Renaissance.

Iconostasis: a transenna (see below) in a Byzantine church, often more elaborate and decorated.

Intarsia: inlay work in wood or stone.

Loggia: an open-sided gallery or arcade.

Lunette: semicircular space on a wall, above a door or under vaulting.

Matroneum: the elevated women's gallery around the nave of a church. Segregating women at mass was a Byzantine practice that spread to Italy in the 6th–7th centuries.

Narthex: the enclosed porch of a church.

Orders: architectural systems of proportion, based on the widths of a building's columns, ranging from the squat, plain Doric to the slender Ionic and the Romans' favourite, the even more delicate Corinthian. Codified by the classical writer Vitruvius, and rediscovered in the Renaissance.

Palazzo: not just a palace, but any large, important building (the word comes from Rome's *Palatium*.

Paterae: exterior plaque or rondo often carved with reliefs.

Pendentives: four curved, triangular pieces, springing from four piers, that help support a dome.

Portego: the main hall of a Venetian house.

Piscina: a swimming pool, tank, or reservoir.

Predella: smaller paintings on the panel below the main subject of a painted alterpiece.

Putti: (or *Amoretti*) flocks of painted or plaster cherubs with rosy cheeks and bums, derived from ancient decoration, that infested much of Italy in the Baroque era.

Quadriga: chariot pulled by four horses.

Quattrocento: the 1400s, in the Italian way of referring to centuries (*trecento, quattrocento, cinquecento, seicento, settecento*, etc.).

Rio Terra: a Venetian street replacing a filled-in canal.

Salizzada: a paved street in Venice.

Scuola: Venetian word for a confraternity or its headquarters (see above).

Tenebroso: the contrast of darkness and illuminated subjects used with such effect by Caravaggio and his followers.

Tessera: one of the stone or glass cubes, or enamelled chips, used in mosaics (pl. *tesserae*).

Transenna: marble screen separating the altar from the rest of an early church.

Trompe l'oeil: art that uses perspective effects to deceive the eye—for example, to create the illusion of depth on a flat surface, or to make columns and arches painted on a wall seem real.

Language

The fathers of modern Italian were Dante, Manzoni and television. Each did its part in creating a national language from an infinity of regional and local dialects; the Florentine Dante, the first to write in the vernacular, did much to put the Tuscan dialect into the foreground of Italian literature. Manzoni's revolutionary novel, *I promessi sposi*, heightened national consciousness by using an everyday language all could understand in the 19th century. Television in the last few decades is performing an even more spectacular linguistic unification; although the majority of Italians still speak a dialect at home, school and work, their TV idols insist on proper Italian.

Perhaps because they are so busy learning their own beautiful but grammatically complex language, Italians are not especially apt at learning others. English lessons, however, have been the rage for years, and at most hotels and restaurants there will be someone who speaks some English. In small towns and out-of-the-way places, finding an Anglophone may prove more difficult. The words and phrases below should help you out in most situations, but the ideal way to come to Italy is with some Italian under your belt; your visit will be richer, and you're much more likely to make some Italian friends.

Italian words are pronounced phonetically. Every vowel and consonant is sounded. Consonants are the same as in English, except the *c* which, when followed by an 'e' or 'i', is pronounced like the English 'ch' (*cinque* thus becomes cheenquay). Italian *g* is also soft before 'i' or 'e' as in *gira*, or jee-ra. *H* is never sounded; *z* is pronounced like 'ts'. The consonants *sc* before the vowels 'i' or 'e' become like the English 'sh' as in *sci*, pronounced shee; *ch* is pronouced like a 'k' as in *Chianti*, kee-an-tee; *gn* as 'ny' in English (*bagno*, pronounced ban-yo); while *gli* is pronounced like the middle of the word million (*Castiglione*, pronounced Ca-stee-lyon-ay).

Vowel pronunciation is: *a* as in English father; *e* when unstressed is pronounced like 'a' in fate as in *mele*, when stressed can be the same or like the 'e' in pet (*bello*); *i* is like the 'i' in machine; *o* like 'e', has two sounds, 'o' as in hope when unstressed (*tacchino*), and usually 'o' as in rock when stressed (*morte*); *u* is pronounced like the 'u' in June. But beware of the Venetian accent where vowels and consonants are often slurred into a porridge of 'u's, 'v's, 'x's (pronounced 'sh') and 'z's.

The stress usually (but not always!) falls on the penultimate syllable.

Useful words and phrases

yes/no/maybe	*si/no/forse*
I don't know	*Non lo so*
I don't understand (Italian).	*Non capisco (italiano).*
Does someone here	*C'è qualcuno qui*
speak English?	*chi parla inglese?*
Speak slowly	*Parla lentamente*
Could you assist me?	*Potrebbe mi aiutare?*
Help!	*Aiuto!*
Please	*Per favore*
Thank you (very much)	*(Molto) grazie*
You're welcome	*Prego*
It doesn't matter	*Non importa*
All right	*Va bene*
Excuse me	*Scusi*
Be careful!	*Attenzione!*
Nothing	*Niente*
It is urgent!	*E urgente!*
How are you?	*Come sta?*
Well, and you?	*Bene, e lei?*
What is your name?	*Come si chiama?*
Hello	*Salve or* ciao (both informal)
Good morning	*Buongiorno (formal hello)*
Good afternoon, evening	*Buona sera (also formal hello)*
Good night	*Buona notte*
Goodbye	*Arrivederla (formal), arrivederci, ciao (informal)*
What do you call this in Italian?	*Come si chiama questo in italiano?*
What?	*Che*
Who?	*Chi*
Where?	*Dove*
When?	*Quando*
Why?	*Perché*
How?	*Come*
How much?	*Quanto*
I am lost	*Mi sono smarrito*
I am hungry	*Ho fame*
I am thirsty	*Ho sete*
I am sorry	*Mi dispiace*
I am tired	*Sono stanco*
I am sleepy	*Ho sonno*
I am ill	*Mi sento male*
Leave me alone	*Lasciami in pace*
good	*buono/bravo*
bad	*male/cattivo*
It's all the same	*Fa lo stesso*
slow	*piano*
fast	*rapido*
big	*grande*
small	*piccolo*
hot	*caldo*
cold	*freddo*
up	*su*
down	*giù*
here	*qui*
there	*lì*

Shopping, Service, Sightseeing

I would like...	*Vorrei...*
Where is/are...	*Dov'è/Dove sono...*
How much is it?	*Quanto viene questo?*
open	*aperto*
closed	*chiuso*
cheap/expensive	*a buon prezzo/caro*
bank	*banco*
beach	*spiaggia*
bed	*letto*
church	*chiesa*
entrance	*entrata*
exit	*uscita*
hospital	*ospedale*
money	*soldi*
museum	*museo*
newspaper (foreign)	*giornale (straniero)*
pharmacy	*farmacia*
police station	*commissariato*
policeman	*poliziotto*
post office	*ufficio postale*
sea	*mare*
shop	*negozio*
telephone	*telefono*
tobacco shop	*tabaccaio*
WC	*toilette/bagno*
men	*Signori/Uomini*
women	*Signore/Donne*

TIME

What time is it?	*Che ora sono?*
month	*mese*
week	*settimana*
day	*giorno*
morning	*mattina*
afternoon	*pomeriggio*
evening	*sera*
today	*oggi*
yesterday	*ieri*
tomorrow	*domani*
soon	*presto*
later	*dopo, più tarde*
It is too early	*E troppo presto*
It is too late	*E troppo tarde*

DAYS

Monday	*lunedì*
Tuesday	*martedì*
Wednesday	*mercoledì*
Thursday	*giovedì*
Friday	*venerdì*
Saturday	*sabato*
Sunday	*domenica*

LANGUAGE

NUMBERS

one	*uno/una*	seventy	*settanta*
two	*due*	eighty	*ottanta*
three	*tre*	ninety	*novanta*
four	*quattro*	hundred	*cento*
five	*cinque*	one hundred and	*cento uno*
six	*sei*	one	
seven	*sette*	two hundred	*duecento*
eight	*otto*	thousand	*mille*
nine	*nove*	two thousand	*duemila*
ten	*dieci*	million	*milione*
eleven	*undici*	billion	*miliardo*
twelve	*dodici*		
thirteen	*tredici*		
fourteen	*quattordici*	**TRANSPORT**	
fifteen	*quindici*	airport	*aeroporto*
sixteen	*sedici*	bus stop	*fermata*
seventeen	*diciassette*	bus/coach	*auto/pulmino*
eighteen	*diciotto*	railway station	*stazione ferroviaria*
nineteen	*diciannove*	train	*treno*
twenty	*venti*	track/platform	*binario*
twenty-one	*ventuno*	port	*porto*
twenty-two	*ventidue*	port station	*stazione marittima*
thirty	*trenta*	ship	*nave*
thirty-one	*trentuno*	automobile	*macchina*
forty	*quaranta*	taxi	*tassi*
fifty	*cinquanta*	ticket	*biglietto*
sixty	*sessanta*	customs	*dogana*
		seat (reserved)	*posto (prenotato)*

TRAVEL DIRECTIONS

I want to go to ...	*Desidero andare a ...*
How can I get to ...?	*Come posso andare a ...?*
Do you stop at ...?	*Ferma a ...?*
Where is ...?	*Dov'è ...?*
How far is it to ...?	*Quanto siamo lontani da ...?*
When does the ... leave?	*A che ora parte ...?*
What is the name of this station?	*Come si chiama questa stazione?*
When does the next ... leave?	*Quando parte il prossimo ...?*
From where does it leave?	*Da dove parte?*
How long does the trip take ...?	*Quanto tempo dura il viaggio?*
How much is the fare?	*Quant'è il biglietto?*
Good trip!	*Buon viaggio!*
near	*vicino*
far	*lontano*
left	*sinistra*
right	*destra*
straight ahead	*sempre diritto*
forward	*avanti*
backward	*in dietro*
north	*nord/settentrionale*
south	*sud/mezzogiorno*
east	*est/oriente*
west	*ovest/occidente*
around the corner	*dietro l'angolo*
crossroads	*bivio*
street/road	*strada*
square	*piazza*

DRIVING

car hire	*noleggio macchina*
motorbike/scooter	*motocicletta/Vespa*
bicycle	*bicicletta*
petrol/diesel	*benzina/gasolio*
garage	*garage*
This doesn't work	*Questo non funziona*
mechanic	*meccanico*
map/town plan	*carta/pianta*
Where is the road to...?	*Dov'è la strada per...?*
breakdown	*guasto* or *panne*
driver's licence	*patente di guida*
driver	*guidatore*
speed	*velocità*
danger	*pericolo*
parking	*parcheggio*
no parking	*sosta vietato*
narrow	*stretto*
bridge	*ponte*
toll	*pedaggio*
slow down	*rallentare*

Italian Menu Vocabulary

Antipasti

These before-meal treats can include almost anything; among the most common are:

Antipasto misto	mixed antipasto
Bruschetto	toast with garlic or tomatoes
Carciofi (sott'olio)	artichokes (in oil)
Crostini	liver pâté on toast
Frutta di mare	seafood
Funghi (trifolati)	mushrooms (with anchovies, garlic, and lemon)
Gamberi ai fagioli	prawns with white beans
Mozzarella (in carrozza)	buffalo cheese (fried with bread in batter)
Olive	olives
Prosciutto (con melone)	raw ham (with melon)
Salame	cured pork
Salsicce	dry sausage

Minestre e Pasta

These dishes are the principal typical, first courses (*primo*) served throughout Italy.

Agnolotti	meat-filled pasta half circles
Cacciucco	spiced fish soup
Cannelloni	meat and cheese rolled in pasta tubes
Cappelletti	small ravioli, often in broth
Crespelle	crepes
Fettuccine	long strips of pasta
Frittata	omelette
Gnocchi	potato dumplings
Lasagne	sheets of pasta baked with meat and cheese sauce
Minestra di verdura	thick vegetable soup
Minestrone	soup with meat, vegetables, and pasta
Orecchiette	ear-shaped pasta, usually served with turnip greens
Panzerotti	ravioli filled with mozzarella, anchovies and egg
Pappardelle alla lepre	pasta with hare sauce
Pasta e fagioli	soup with beans, bacon, and tomatoes
Pastina in brodo	tiny pasta in broth
Penne all'arrabbiata	quill-shaped pasta in hot spicy sauce
Polenta	cake or pudding of corn semolina, prepared with meat or tomato sauce

Risotto (alla Milanese)	Italian rice (with saffron and wine)
Spaghetti all'Amatriciana	with spicy sauce of salt pork, tomatoes, onions and hot pepper
Spaghetti alla Bolognese	with ground meat, ham, mushrooms, etc.
Spaghetti alla carbonara	with bacon, eggs, and black pepper
Spaghetti al pomodoro	with tomato sauce
Spaghetti al sugo/ragu	with meat sauce
Spaghetti alle vongole	with clam sauce
Stracciatella	broth with eggs and cheese
Tagliatelle	flat egg noodles
Tortellini al pomodoro/panna/in brodo	pasta caps filled with meat and cheese, served with tomato sauce, cream, or in broth
Vermicelli	very thin spaghetti

Second Courses–Carne (Meat)

Abbacchio	milk-fed lamb
Agnello	lamb
Anatra	duck
Animelle	sweetbreads
Arista	pork loin
Arrosto misto	mixed roast meats
Bistecca alla fiorentina	Florentine beef steak
Bocconcini	veal mixed with ham and cheese and fried
Bollito misto	stew of boiled meats
Braciola	pork chop
Brasato di manzo	braised meat with vegetables
Bresaola	dried raw meat similar to ham
Capretto	kid
Capriolo	roe deer
Carne di castrato/suino	mutton/pork
Carpaccio	thin slices of raw beef in piquant sauce
Casoeula	winter stew with pork and cabbage
Cervello (al burro nero)	brains (in black butter sauce)
Cervo	venison
Cinghiale	boar
Coniglio	rabbit
Cotoletta (alla Milanese/alla Bolognese)	veal cutlet (fried in breadcrumbs/with ham and cheese)
Fagiano	pheasant
Faraono (alla creta)	guinea fowl (in earthenware pot)
Fegato alla veneziana	liver and onions
Involtini	rolled slices of veal with filling
Lepre (in salmi)	hare (marinated in wine)
Lombo di maiale	pork loin
Lumache	snails
Maiale (al latte)	pork (cooked in milk)
Manzo	beef
Osso buco	braised veal knuckle with herbs
Pancetta	bacon
Pernice	partridge
Petto di pollo (alla Fiorentina/Bolognese/Sorpresa)	boned chicken breast (fried in butter/with ham and cheese/stuffed and deep fried)
Piccione	pigeon
Pizzaiola	beef steak with tomato and oregano sauce
Pollo (alla cacciatora/alla diavola/alla Marengo)	chicken (with tomatoes and mushrooms cooked in wine/grilled/ fried with tomatoes, garlic and wine)
Polpette	meatballs
Quaglie	quails
Rane	frogs
Rognoni	kidneys

Saltimbocca	veal scallop with *prosciutto* and sage, cooked in wine and butter
Scaloppine	thin slices of veal sautéed in butter
Spezzatino	pieces of beef or veal, usually stewed
Spiedino	meat on a skewer or stick
Stufato	beef braised in white wine with vegetables
Tacchino	turkey
Trippa	tripe
Uccelletti	small birds on a skewer
Vitello	veal

Pesce (Fish)

Acciughe or Alici	anchovies
Anguilla	eel
Aragosta	lobster
Aringa	herring
Baccalà	dried cod
Bonito	small tuna
Branzino	sea bass
Calamari	squid
Cappe sante	scallops
Cefalo	grey mullet
Coda di rospo	angler fish
Cozze	mussels
Datteri di mare	razor (or date) mussels
Dentice	dentex (perch-like fish)
Dorato	gilt head
Fritto misto	mixed fish fry, with squid and shrimp
Gamberetto	shrimp
Gamberi (di fiume)	prawns (crayfish)
Granchio	crab
Insalata di mare	seafood salad
Lampreda	lamprey
Merluzzo	cod
Nasello	hake
Orata	bream
Ostrice	oysters
Pesce azzuro	various types of small fish
Pesce S. Pietro	John Dory
Pesce spada	swordfish
Polipi	octopus
Rombo	turbot
Sarde	sardines
Seppie	cuttlefish
Sgombro	mackerel
Sogliola	sole
Squadro	monkfish
Tonno	tuna
Triglia	red mullet (rouget)
Trota	trout
Trota salmonata	salmon trout
Vongole	small clams
Zuppa di pesce	mixed fish in sauce or stew

Contorni (Side Dishes, Vegetables)

Asparagi (alla fiorentina)	asparagus (with fried eggs)
Broccoli (calabrese, romana)	broccoli (green, spiral)
Carciofi (alla giudia)	artichokes (deep fried)
Cardi	cardoons, thistles
Carote	carrots

Cavolfiore	cauliflower
Cavolo	cabbage
Ceci	chickpeas
Cetriolo	cucumber
Cipolla	onion
Fagioli	white beans
Fagiolini	French (green) beans
Fave	fava beans
Finocchio	fennel
Funghi (porcini)	mushroom (boletus)
Insalata (mista, verde)	salad (mixed, green)
Lattuga	lettuce
Lenticchie	lentils
Melanzana (al forno)	aubergine/eggplant (filled and baked)
Mirtilli	bilberries
Patate (fritte)	potatoes (fried)
Peperonata	stewed peppers, onions, etc. similar to ratatouille
Peperoni	sweet peppers
Piselli (al prosciutto)	peas (with ham)
Pomodoro	tomato(es)
Porri	leeks
Radicchio	red chicory
Radice	radishes
Rapa	turnip
Sedano	celery
Spinaci	spinach
Verdure	greens
Zucca	pumpkin
Zucchini	courgettes (zucchini)

Formaggio (Cheese)

Bel Paese	a soft white cow's cheese
Cascio/Casciocavallo	pale yellow, often sharp cheese
Fontina	rich cow's milk cheese
Groviera	mild cheese
Gorgonzola	soft blue cheese
Parmigiano	Parmesan cheese
Pecorino	sharp sheep's cheese
Provalone	sharp, tangy cheese; *dolce* is more mild
Stracchino	soft white cheese

Frutta (Fruit, Nuts)

Albicocche	apricots
Ananas	pineapple
Arance	oranges
Banane	bananas
Cachi	persimmon
Ciliegie	cherries
Cocomero	watermelon
Composta di frutta	stewed fruit
Dattero	date
Fichi	figs
Fragole (con panna)	strawberries (with cream)
Frutta di stagione	fruit in season
Lamponi	raspberries
Macedonia di frutta	fruit salad
Mandarino	tangerine
Melagrana	pomegranite
Mele	apples

Melone	melon
More	blackberries
Nespola	medlar fruit
Pera	pear
Pesca	peach
Pesca noce	tangerine
Pompelmo	grapefruit
Prugna/susina	plum
Uve	grapes

Dolci (Desserts)

Amaretti	macaroons
Cannoli	crisp pastry tube filled with *ricotta*, cream, chocolate or fruit
Coppa gelato	assorted ice cream
Crema caramella	caramel topped custard
Crostata	fruit flan
Gelato (produzione propria)	ice cream (homemade)
Granita	flavoured ice, usually lemon or coffee
Monte Bianco	chestnut pudding with whipped cream
Panettone	sponge cake with candied fruit and raisins
Panforte	dense cake of chocolate, almonds and preserved fruit
Saint Honoré	meringue cake
Semifreddo	refrigerated cake
Sorbetto	sherbet
Spumone	a soft ice cream
Tiramisù	cream, coffee, and chocolate dessert
Torrone	nougat
Torta	tart
Torta millefoglie	layered custard tart
Zabaglione	whipped eggs and Marsala wine, served hot
Zuppa inglese	trifle

Bevande/Beverages

Acqua minerale con/senza gas	mineral water with/without fizz
Aranciata	orange soda
Birra (alla spina)	beer (draught)
Caffè (freddo)	coffee (iced)
Cioccolata (con panna)	chocolate (with cream)
Gassosa	lemon-flavoured soda
Latte	milk
Limonata	lemon soda
Sugo di frutta	fruit juice
Tè	tea
Vino (rosso, bianco, rosato)	wine (red, white, rosé)

Cooking Terms, Miscellaneous

Aceto (balsamico)	vinegar (balsam)
Affumicato	smoked
Aglio	garlic
Alla brace	braised
Bicchiere	glass
Burro	butter
Caccia	game
Conto	bill
Costoletta/Cotoletta	chop
Coltello	knife
Cotto adagio	braised
Cucchiaio	spoon
Filetto	fillet

382

Forchetta	fork
Forno	oven
Fritto	fried
Ghiaccio	ice
Griglia	grill
Limone	lemon
Magro	lean meat/or pasta without meat
Mandorle	almonds
Marmellata	jam
Menta	mint
Miele	honey
Mostarda	candied mustard sauce
Nocciole	hazelnut
Noce	walnut
Olio	oil
Pane (tostato)	bread (toasted)
Panini	sandwiches
Panna	fresh cream
Pepe	pepper
Peperoncini	hot chilli peppers
Piatto	plate
Pignoli	pine nuts
Prezzemolo	parsley
Ripieno	stuffed
Rosmarino	rosemary
Sale	salt
Salmi	wine marinade
Salsa	sauce
Salvia	sage
Senape	mustard
Tartufi	truffles
Tazza	cup
Tavola	table
Tovagliolo	napkin
Tramezzini	finger sandwiches
Umido	cooked in sauce
Uovo	egg
Zucchero	sugar

Index

Notes: Important entries and references are indicated by **bold** type.
Churches in Venice are grouped together under 'churches'.